The
Water-Wise
Home

THE WATER-WISE HOME

How to Conserve, Capture, and Reuse Water in Your Home and Landscape

LAURA ALLEN

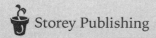
Storey Publishing

*The mission of Storey Publishing is to serve our customers by
publishing practical information that encourages
personal independence in harmony with the environment.*

Edited by Deborah Burns and Philip Schmidt
Art direction and book design by Mary Winkelman Velgos
Text production by Jennifer Jepson Smith
Indexed by Samantha Miller

Front cover and interior decorative illustrations © Michael Austin/Jing and Mike Company
Back cover and interior illustrations © Steve Sanford
Author's photograph © Rebecca Louisell
Interior technical illustrations © James Provost, 8714789 CANADA, Inc.
Showerhead icon used throughout © Mallinka1/Shutterstock.com

Storey Publishing
210 MASS MoCA Way
North Adams, MA 01247
www.storey.com

Printed in the United States by McNaughton & Gunn, Inc.
10 9 8 7 6 5 4 3 2 1

LIBRARY OF CONGRESS CATALOGING-IN-PUBLICATION DATA
Allen, Laura, 1976–
    The water-wise home : how to conserve, capture, and reuse water in your home and landscape /
    by Laura Allen.
        pages cm
    Includes index.
    ISBN 978-1-61212-169-7 (pbk. : alk. paper)
    ISBN 978-1-60342-920-7 (ebook) 1. Water reuse. 2. Water conservation. 3. Water-supply.
    4. Gardens—Irrigation. I. Title.
TD429.A424 2015
628.1'62—dc23
                                                2014033674

For Arlo, and the fishies

Contents

Preface 8

PART 1 WATER-WISE BASICS

Preface

DO YOU WANT TO USE LESS WATER? Capture rainwater falling from the sky? Redirect water from your shower to irrigate the landscape? Improve the health of rivers and creeks in your community? If so, this book is for you.

You may be interested in water conservation because your well is running dry, or maybe you work with a watershed restoration group. Perhaps you want to promote and protect clean rivers and oceans because you love to fish or swim, or you're a parent, grandparent, or aunt or uncle and want to create a healthy world for future generations. If you're a landscaper, plumber, or building contractor, offering sustainable services to clients makes good business sense. And if you don't have access to a municipal water supply, conserving and reusing water may be far preferable (and much more affordable) than acquiring a new water supply. Regardless of your motivation, you've already taken the first step.

Nearly 15 years ago, while I was living with six friends in a rented house in Oakland, California, I had my first water shock. A water bill arrived in the mail — first time I'd ever seen one. I can't remember exactly how many gallons we had used, or how much we had to pay, but I clearly remember my shock at seeing it. The first two questions in my mind were "How can we possibly be using this much water?!" and "Where does this water come from, anyway?" My search for answers to these questions sparked the beginning of my water education. As I learned more about this water system I depended on — and how damaging it was — I began to look for alternatives.

The first change I made was to redirect the bathroom sink drain to dump into a bucket. We used this greywater to "bucket-flush" the toilet. It was so simple we couldn't stop there. My housemate Cleo and I tackled the shower next; we reconfigured the pipes and built our first greywater system. How satisfying it was when the shower water finally flowed into the garden.

This book shares the knowledge I've gained over the past 15 years and shows you how my friends and I transformed our own home to conserve and protect Earth's precious freshwater. In these pages I will show you how to improve the efficiency of your fixtures, reuse household greywater, collect rainwater, and install waterless toilets.

Writing a how-to book is an exciting opportunity to share these concrete skills with more people. Besides the *how*, there is the *why*: in Part I, I talk about why our current water system is unsustainable and what simple, small-scale changes can help fix it. Part II covers the principles of simple greywater, rainwater catchment, and composting toilet systems, providing step-by-step instructions that anyone can implement with a few tools and basic construction skills. These simple, low-cost systems can cut your home's water consumption in half, or better. Because the book is intended for ordinary DIYers, I don't focus on complex systems requiring specialized tools and training, but have included profiles of people living with advanced systems, as well as resources for learning more about them.

I've also included tips for working with (and improving) state and local regulations, as well as interviews with progressive regulators and examples of what worked for us in California. Policy change isn't a standard feature for how-to books, but when it comes to water-wise systems, codes and local agencies can be a major barrier.

I hope this book helps you transform your home to save water and create productive, ecological landscapes.

PART 1
WATER-WISE BASICS

What's Wrong with Our Water Systems and How You Can Change It

"WATER, SAVE IT FOR what you love," is one of my favorite water utility slogans, designed to teach people the importance of conservation. Others, such as "Every drop counts" and "Got water? Do your part, be water smart," remind us of the small steps we can take to reduce overall consumption. While fixing a leaking toilet and installing a water-efficient showerhead may not be as exciting as building a greywater system, these simple actions can save as much, or even more, water.

The discussion in Part I of this book sets the stage for the how-to projects of Part II. Before crawling under the house to check out your plumbing, or researching local rainwater data to plan a rainwater catchment system, it's important to understand where your water comes from, where it goes, and what is impacted along the way. Chapters 1 and 2 help you understand the problems and challenges of municipal water systems, while chapter 3 presents a range of practical options for reducing water consumption at home: finding and fixing leaks, choosing efficient irrigation systems, and designing beautiful, productive and water-efficient landscapes. You'll also learn the basics of greywater, rainwater, and composting toilet systems so you can determine which are a good fit for your home (maybe all of them!).

Why Conserve Water?

WE NEED WATER FOR ALMOST EVERYTHING we have and do: our food, clothing, electricity, and almost every item in our homes, not to mention drinking, cooking, and cleaning. In the past, water shaped civilizations, determining the size and locations of population centers as well as travel routes and what food was available. Today, natural water systems have been re-engineered for human use: instead of flowing to the sea, most water flows toward cities, large agriculture, and industry.

When we turn on the kitchen faucet, out flows water — like magic. Only it's not magic. That water came from somewhere. If it hadn't been diverted by people, it would have flowed in a river, creek, spring, or underground aquifer. Where did that water come from? Which river? What creek? How deep an aquifer? Is it being recharged as fast as it's being pumped out?

Answers to these questions may not be obvious. The infrastructure connecting our taps to the water source has become practically invisible, and most people don't think about what river flushes down the toilet or how many salmon died when the dam was built to supply their town. But we should. And when we do examine our water system, it becomes apparent what needs to change.

Reasons to Conserve Water

WHEN WE SAVE A GALLON of freshwater, it's a gallon our water company won't look for in a new dam, a water transfer, or a desalination plant to provide more supply. It's a gallon that could keep a river deeper and cooler, oxygenating a salmon as it swims to its spawning grounds and preventing the growth of toxic algae. It's a gallon that emerges from a desert spring, providing lifesaving drinking water for animals. It's a gallon that can grow local food in a sustainable way without the waste and pollution of industrial agriculture.

Save Water, Save Energy, Spare the Air

Hidden behind each drop of water is a spark of energy. It takes energy to transport water from the

IN THIS CHAPTER:

source to our homes. It takes energy to clean the water to drinking quality and more energy to heat it. Just warming the water for one shower takes as much energy as it does to power a light bulb for more than 200 hours (25 gallons takes 17,000 Btus or 5 kilowatt-hours). This close relationship between water and energy, referred to as *watergy*, or the water-energy nexus, connects our water-conserving practices to climate change and air pollution. At the household level about 20 percent of our total energy use goes toward heating our water. At the sewer plant even more energy is used to clean the water for disposal. In California nearly 20 percent of the electricity and 32 percent of the natural gas used in the entire state is for water.

All this energy makes a lot of pollution! According to the National Resources Defense Council (NRDC), the energy to treat and distribute all this water releases approximately 116 billion pounds of carbon dioxide (CO_2) per year, causing as much global-warming pollution each year as ten million cars.

By redirecting water and nutrients that typically flow away from our homes into the yard, we can save water and enhance the ecological benefit of our landscapes. Rainwater and greywater can grow trees to shade the house, reducing cooling needs. Fruit trees and other edibles provide truly local food, reducing food miles and their associated carbon footprint.

Save Water, Save Money

Anyone who pays a water truck to haul in water knows how much that water costs. Anyone who pays a water bill knows water pricing involves more than just buying water. The costs reflected in the bill cover maintaining the delivery infrastructure and operating the sewer plant, while the water itself may be virtually free. Simple efficiency upgrades, like installing a low-flow showerhead, quickly pay for themselves, while payback for other systems, such as rainwater and greywater, take much longer under current water rates (although the savings do add up over time, and water rates are increasing). For water districts, monetary savings can be significant: Residents of San Antonio, Texas, once used 225 gallons per day. The city, faced with costs on new water rights to their aquifer of $5,000 per acre-foot and a new

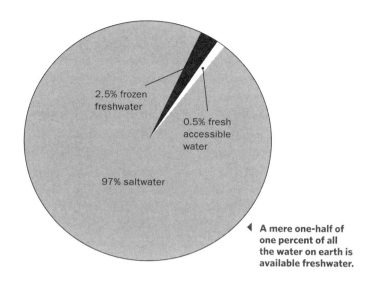

2.5% frozen freshwater

0.5% fresh accessible water

97% saltwater

◀ **A mere one-half of one percent of all the water on earth is available freshwater.**

dam-pipeline project priced at around $1,000 an acre-foot, opted to spend just $300 per acre-foot by investing in conservation. Between the beginning of the program in 1993 and the year 2008, San Antonio residents lowered their per-capita usage to 140 gallons a day, and the city saved nearly $550 million.

Drought-Proof Your Home

The most basic definition of drought is a lack of precipitation over an extended time. California and the other Southwestern states are considered "drought states" because they experience dry periods on a regular basis. But droughts occur in any climate when current precipitation is lower than historic averages. A drought in Florida looks different from a drought in Texas or Australia but can be just as devastating to the local environment. With climate change, even areas once considered water-rich, such as the Southeast, have recently experienced droughts.

Droughts also occur when the supply of water doesn't meet the demand of people, animals, and plants. Humans can create drought conditions by using more than their fair share. An increase in water use upstream can cause shortages for those living downstream, even if precipitation doesn't change.

What can we do to prepare for droughts? Our municipal water systems are large, inflexible, and unable to cope with changing precipitation patterns. A dam is impossible to move. Acquiring new water rights to an over-allocated river is not feasible. Agencies are slow to act until there is an acute crisis. Fortunately, there is much we can do to prepare our own homes, independent of centralized systems.

Each water-efficient fixture, greywater and rainwater harvesting system, or waterless toilet is a step to drought-proof our homes and landscapes. As we live more in tune with our local climate, we'll discover that you can't experience a shortage if you don't need additional water.

Reduce Everyday Waste

There's plenty wrong with our existing home water systems, ranging from basic logistical issues to cultural behaviors. Yet most of these problems are easily solved.

Problems with Conventional Home Water Systems

- Our homes are inefficient. Unnecessarily large amounts of water are used in toilets, sinks, showers, and washing machines.

- Water is used needlessly — for example, in spraying down driveways and over-irrigating plants.

- Water quality doesn't match the need. Potable water is used for everything, including flushing toilets and irrigating landscapes.

- All "wastewater" is sent to the sewage treatment plant or septic system. Water from the bath is treated the same as water leaving the toilet.

- Yards are designed so rainwater runs off the land, creating flooding and pollution problems and preventing rainwater from being used as a resource.

Where Does Your Water Come From?

I GREW UP with a neighborhood water supply in Northern California. An artesian spring filled a storage tank that fed a dozen houses on our country road. If a neighbor left the hose on all night, or if a pipe broke, the tank would run dry and we'd have to wait for it to refill. I knew where the water came from, and where it went — into the septic tank and leach line under the front lawn.

When I left home to go to college, it took four years for me to wonder where my new water supply came from. Thinking back, I find it ironic that I graduated with a degree in Environmental Science from UC Berkeley but had no idea where my drinking water came from. I'm thankful for that first water bill and the effect it had on me and my household.

It didn't take long for us to learn where Oakland water originates: 93 miles away from the Bay Area is the Mokelumne River, the source of our drinking water. Snow melting in the Sierra Nevada mountains forms rushing creeks that cascade into the river. The first time I went to see my drinking river, I savored the beauty of the clear, cold water, shaded by bay and maple trees as it flowed quickly by.

A few miles downstream the river stops, blocked by the Pardee Dam. The river that resumes on the other side of the dam bears little resemblance to the one upstream. The water district has rights to divert 325 million gallons per day. From that day on, I saw the flowing Mokelumne River in my mind's eye every time I turned on the tap.

So, where does *your* water come from — what river, creek, or aquifer? Many people are as ignorant of their water supply as I was. A recent Nature Conservancy poll found that 77 percent of Americans (excluding people using a private well) don't know the source for the water they drink, cook with, and shower in.

Getting to Know Your Watershed

We all know our street address, county, and state, but few of us know what watershed we live in. A watershed encompasses all the land that collects and drains water to a single outlet, such as a creek or river. Our drinking water may come from within a local watershed or be piped from a distant one. Our homes can be part of both a local watershed and a larger regional watershed.

Rainwater flows off our roof and into the street, where it mixes with rainwater flowing from all our neighbors' homes and enters the nearest storm drain, creek, or river. Everyday pollutants impact the health of our local waterways: oil and brake-pad dust on the streets, fertilizers and pesticides from our landscapes, all of these are washed into the creek after a rain.

Our local watershed may be connected to a larger watershed; the creek flows into a river, and into the ocean. In Oakland I lived in the Temescal Creek watershed, a culverted creek that flowed to San Francisco Bay. We were also part of the giant

San Francisco Bay Delta watershed, which receives water from the Sacramento and San Joaquin rivers, encompassing 75,000 square miles. Nearly half the surface water that falls as rain or snow in the entire state flows through this watershed, with every home along the way impacting the health of the bay.

There are many ways to get involved with your local watershed. Watershed groups, beach clean-ups, restoration projects, and creek groups are found all across the country. Creek hikes, sunsets at the beach, and strolls along the river are great ways to get to know the land and water. Websites of national organizations, such as The Nature Conservancy and the U.S. Environmental Protection Agency (see Resources), will help you discover the source of your drinking water and connect with local watershed organizations. Also check out your own water district's website to learn about the local supply and history of your water source.

What's a Water-Wise Home?

A WATER-WISE HOME conserves and reuses water to create ecological and efficient water systems. It can even be water-neutral, meaning that no more water is consumed in the home than is collected from the rain, and it can be disconnected from the sewer, treating and reusing all water on-site. No matter what steps you take to make your home more water-wise, it will most certainly use less water. A recent study (see Resources) found that an ordinary household saves nearly 15,000 gallons a year after installing a simple greywater system.

Features of a Water-Wise Home

- Fixtures and appliances are efficient.

- Water is reused. **Greywater** — water coming from sinks, showers, and washing machines — is used for irrigation or toilet flushing.

- Potable water is used only for potable needs: drinking, cooking, and showering.

- Rainwater is collected and infiltrated into the landscape.

- Products used in the water are nontoxic and compatible for irrigation.

- Systems foster awareness and stewardship of natural water systems.

Learning how to use water more intelligently is fun and empowering. Some of these changes are as simple as switching out a showerhead, while others, like installing a greywater system, require more effort.

At the simplest level, saving water and reusing what we already have is a commonsense way to save money and resources. Simple efficiency upgrades, such as fixing leaks and installing lower-flow showerheads, can reduce our household use dramatically. Nationally, if everyone upgraded their homes we'd save around 5.4 billion gallons per day!

Watershed Success

||||||||||||||||||||||||||||||||||||||||||||||||||||||||

PROBLEM: On the Mattole River, in Northern California, a combination of rural homes pumping water from the creeks for household use and the legacy of logging and watershed degradation culminated in creeks running dry just as salmon needed the water to spawn. Residents had to shift their water-use practices to coexist with salmon.

Solution: Sanctuary Forest, a local nonprofit, worked with residents and scientists to create an alternative system. By filling large water storage tanks during the wet season, residents didn't need to pump out of the creek in the dry season. Their success was immediate. For the first time since monitoring started, with 65 percent of pumps turned "off" during the dry season, the stream flow was the same downstream of houses as it was upstream of them. The community also created infiltration ponds to recharge the groundwater to feed streams during dry weather.

2

What's Wrong with Our Water Systems?

THERE ARE A LOT OF THINGS WRONG with our water systems. From where we get water to how much we use, and from what we put into it to where it goes. If you have this book in your hands, you probably already know there are other options: we can conserve and reuse water instead of wasting and polluting it.

Deepening our understanding of the problems with our current system can strengthen our conviction to change it. This chapter offers an overview of some environmental and social challenges we face today, and what people are doing to solve them. Through our collective actions we can redesign our water systems — from the home scale to the community scale — for a secure and sustainable water future.

IN THIS CHAPTER:

The Good News and Bad News

BEFORE DIVING INTO THE PROBLEMS, let's consider the benefits of the current system. Most people in the United States and Canada (as well as in Europe, Australia, and really any "developed" country) have access to an affordable, clean, reliable water supply delivered right to their homes. Considering the 780 million people in the world who don't have clean water to drink, and the 1.8 billion who have to walk to collect water and carry it home, our water system is doing pretty well.

Did you use an indoor toilet today, or did you rise before dawn to go outside, fearful for your personal safety? Open defecation, performed each day by more than a billion people around the world, is degrading to human dignity as well as hazardous for public health. Most of us have no problem finding a safe, sanitary toilet to use or a sink to wash our hands. Building codes require these in every habitable dwelling, and most establishments offer them to their customers free of charge.

Looking Back

Not so long ago, in the 1800s, cholera and dysentery outbreaks were commonplace in every major city. From Paris to New York, London to Montreal, cholera outbreaks killed people by the thousands. Neither sewage nor drinking water was treated, as it wasn't understood how contaminated water caused illness. In the late 1800s, with the acceptance of the germ theory of disease transmission, municipal water suppliers began treating drinking water before distributing it to the populace. Later, the Clean Water Act of 1972 in the U.S. required sewage to be treated, and the Safe Drinking Water Act of 1974 set national standards for water quality. Our modern plumbing system, with a drinking water treatment plant on one end and wastewater treatment plant on the other, has, without a doubt, greatly improved public health. As the plumbers say, "The plumber protects the health of the nation."

Hidden Costs

The problem with these advances in health and sanitation is that we have ignored their hidden costs. What was lost to achieve these gains? And, importantly, are there alternatives to the current system? Can we have clean water to meet our human needs while protecting natural water systems? Can we work with Nature instead of against her?

Yes, we can. Solutions are plentiful, and many can be found in this book.

The Bad News: Our Water System Is Destructive and Unsustainable

Here is a laundry list of problems with our current water delivery system. With our collective efforts, each problem has an attainable solution.

We consider local rainwater a problem and attempt to get rid of it as quickly as possible, instead of using it to supply our water needs and recharge local water tables.

We rely heavily on dams for water storage, which can destroy river ecosystems.

We withdraw too much from rivers, altering the ecosystem and damaging aquatic life.

We pump groundwater at a rate faster than it can be replenished. This water will eventually run out.

We store water in reservoirs and transport it in open canals, losing massive quantities to evaporation.

We rely on centralized water systems (large dams and reservoirs), which are vulnerable to climate change and cannot be easily altered.

Our water systems take as much water as possible for municipal or water company use, disregarding the negative effects on those downstream: wildlife, fish, fishing and rafting industries, and native communities whose culture, sustenance, and religious practices are rooted in their local waters.

There is little connection between the water user and the water supply. People don't see the impact their water consumption has on natural systems. This fosters a sense of entitlement and ownership over the water, rather than a sense of stewardship and respect for the water.

We try to overcome nature instead of working within natural limitations of a region. A simple example: green lawns in the desert.

Sources of Water

BEFORE CONTINUING, let's refresh our memories about the water cycle. The Earth's water is always on the move. Powered by the sun, the hydrologic (water) cycle is the massive movement of water between land, sea, and sky. Water evaporates from the oceans and travels up into the atmosphere, where it comes down to the earth as rain and snow. This precipitation may soak into the ground and be taken up by a plant, or soak down past the plant roots deeper into the soil, later to emerge from a spring or creek. Or, it may run off to flow in a creek or river back to the sea. Molecules of water cycle endlessly this way for billions of years.

The water cycle is simple yet complex, particularly the relationship between water flowing above and below the ground. Surface water flows are closely connected to local groundwater; hydrologists estimate that nearly half of stream flow comes from groundwater. It's important to understand that water flows through this cycle at very different rates. Some water molecules cycle rather quickly, moving from the ocean to the sky to the land in a few days or weeks. Water in a shallow groundwater table may return to the ocean in a few months, or years or even decades. But the deeper groundwater aquifers don't operate on a human timescale. It may take a water molecule centuries or millennia to emerge naturally.

Life on Earth depends on having water on the surface, with our rivers and lakes, as well as in the ground. As cities, industry, and agriculture pump water out from deep within the Earth, we are living out of balance with the renewable supply of water. We'll talk more about groundwater on page 18.

Rivers: The Circulatory System

Rivers are the Earth's circulatory system. Water flows through the rivers to the ocean to the clouds and back again. The hundreds of trillions of gallons flowing in rivers make up just a fraction of a percent of all the freshwater on Earth, yet they sustain so much terrestrial life. Salmon bring ocean nutrients upstream, fertilizing forests and feeding a web of aquatic life.

We know what happens when our arteries get clogged: a heart attack. What happens when a river is clogged — when the water flow is stopped by an immense concrete dam? In the U.S. alone, rivers are plugged by around 75,000 dams. Along with the water, these dams trap silt and nutrients. Instead of flowing downstream and being deposited in river deltas to sustain fertile floodplains and vital habitat, sediments clog the spawning area above the dam — that is, if the fish can even get past the dam (see Dams Kill Salmon on next page).

A dammed river is ecologically different from a free-flowing one. The artificial lake behind the dam stores massive amounts of water to be piped away for human use. Dams alter the amount of water flowing through the river, the temperature and oxygen levels of the water, and the speed with which it flows to the sea.

While dams provide millions of people with drinking water, irrigate our crops, electrify our cities, and control floods, they destroy our river ecosystems. We may be dependent on dams today, but that doesn't

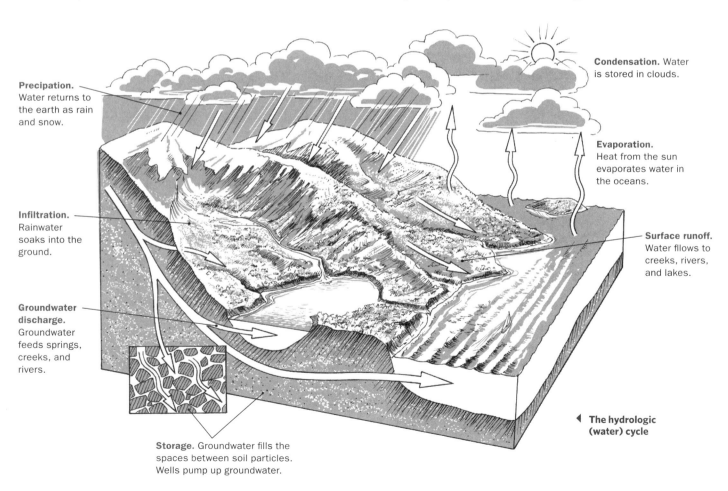

Precipitation. Water returns to the earth as rain and snow.

Condensation. Water is stored in clouds.

Evaporation. Heat from the sun evaporates water in the oceans.

Infiltration. Rainwater soaks into the ground.

Surface runoff. Water flows to creeks, rivers, and lakes.

Groundwater discharge. Groundwater feeds springs, creeks, and rivers.

◀ **The hydrologic (water) cycle**

Storage. Groundwater fills the spaces between soil particles. Wells pump up groundwater.

mean we have to be in the future. Each greywater system, rain garden, and composting toilet is a step on the path away from reliance on dams and toward healthy, free-flowing rivers.

Let the Rivers Flow: The Undamming Movement

The largest dam removal in history is under way (at the time of writing), involving two dams on the Elwha River. This three-year removal project began in the fall of 2011. These early-1900 dams blocked fish passage a few miles from the sea, decimating salmon runs in what was once the largest salmon-bearing river in Washington state. The Lower Elwha Klallam Tribe fought for this removal project from the day the dams were built, and tribal restoration crews have been preparing for the salmon's return, restoring mile after mile of salmon streams. "The river is going to be given a second chance to restore itself," remarks tribal member Byron Bennett as an excavator tears into the Elwha Dam.

Nationwide, dam removal is booming. Roughly 1,100 dams have been removed in the past hundred years, and the rate has quickened more recently, with 800 taken out in the past 20 years. Most of these dams are obsolete, posing a danger to below-dam residents while also harming the creek or river ecosystem. The White Salmon River in Washington flows freely for the first time in more than 100 years; the

Marmot Dam on the Sandy River in Oregon and Horse Creek Dam in California went out with a bang. Michigan is embarking on the largest dam removal in its history, with three dam removals in the works on the Boardman River to restore natural river conditions and improve fishing. The removal of two dams on Maine's Penobscot River, in combination with adding fish passage to other dams, will open access to 1,000 miles of Atlantic salmon habitat, the result of years of hard work and collaboration between river restoration groups and the Penobscot Nation.

What happens to the river after the dam? After Maine's Edwards Dam (built in 1837) was removed in 1999, the first time an operating hydroelectric dam was removed in favor of restoration, "The Kennebec River has come to life magnificently over the past ten years, just as we knew it would if given a chance," said Brownie Carson, then executive director of the Natural Resources Council of Maine. "Evidence of the river's rebirth is everywhere. . . . Eagles, osprey, and sturgeon are spotted daily; seals have been seen chasing striped bass as far inland as Waterville; and this spring the river hosted the largest alewife run on the East Coast. The Kennebec's revival has been a true wonder of nature."

Rain: A Gift from the Sky

Our homes interact with water in two main ways: how water arrives and how it leaves. Most homes have

Dams Kill Salmon

In 1924, after the first Bullards Bar Dam was built on the Yuba River, the returning salmon encountered the dam for the first time. Unable to pass it, they died at the base. So many dead salmon floated downstream of the dam that the stench became unbearable. Pacific Gas & Electric Company workers resorted to torching the carcasses to alleviate the smell.

Dams built without fish passage prevent salmon from accessing their spawning grounds, while those built *with* passage present new challenges for baby fish. Salmon thrive in cool water; warmer water makes them more susceptible to parasites and disease. As water slows to a trickle in the reservoir behind the dam, baby salmon must navigate warm upper waters that are as lethal as the cold, oxygen-depleted deep waters below. The trip to the sea that once took a few days can now take more than a month.

Salmon populations have plummeted since the dam-building frenzy of the mid-twentieth century. Atlantic salmon are extinct in many rivers and surviving populations are a fraction of their historic numbers. Most Pacific salmon runs in the western states are between 2 and 5 percent of their historic sizes, with many stocks of wild salmon extinct and the remaining ones endangered.

two sources of water: the pipe flowing in with drinking water (from a well or a municipal supply), and rain or snow that falls from the sky. Similarly, water leaves our homes either via the sewer line flowing to the sewer treatment plant or a septic system, or as runoff, also called stormwater.

When we utilize water falling from the sky, we strike a balance with our natural water supply. Collecting and using rainwater have no negative impacts on another watershed. If we use that rainwater to grow food, create shade plants, and provide habitat, we improve our ecological landscape and thereby improve the health of our watershed. Chapters 6 and 7 will teach you how to catch and use rainwater.

When we ignore the rainwater falling onto our homes and rely on the second supply — the pipe — we connect our daily existence to a smörgåsbord of environmental and social problems. To avoid this, all we have to do is to look up to the sky and harvest the rain. It doesn't take much precipitation to be successful. As you will see, some people live modern and comfortable lifestyles relying on a mere 8 inches of annual rainfall.

Groundwater: Nonrenewable Fossil Water?

Around 30 percent of the Earth's freshwater is underground (**groundwater**). This water once fell as rain or snow and soaked slowly down through the upper layers of soil, filling cracks and pores in the soil. The **water table** is the boundary below which the soil becomes saturated with water (where all the air spaces between the rocks are full of water). An **aquifer** refers to an area where the ground holds a lot of water. It is both permeable and porous, enabling water to be pumped out.

Shallow aquifers are typically recharged quickly and have been a source of water for humans throughout history, particularly in arid climates. It wasn't until the 1950s that fossil fuel energy became widely available, enabling people to drill and pump from deeper and deeper wells. Today, groundwater supplies drinking water for two billion people and irrigates approximately 40 percent of the world's food supply.

If water pumped from the ground is replaced through infiltration from the rain, groundwater is renewable. Without that balance, groundwater can be as nonrenewable as oil. Much of the major reserves, like the giant Ogallala aquifer of the Great Plains, were filled in ancient times and receive little new supply. This paleowater of the Ogallala dates back to the last ice age and is being pumped ten times faster than it's filled. Residents of Maryland may have been surprised to find out they drink million-year-old water. A 2012 study by the U.S. Geological Survey found the Patapsco aquifer underlying Maryland, a vital freshwater supply for the area, to be ancient: the water has been underground for tens of thousands to more than a million years.

Pumping groundwater faster than it recharges causes groundwater depletion. All across North America and the world, communities struggle to cope with the consequences. A lower water table means wells dry up, streams stop flowing, riparian plants die, biodiversity is lost, and saltwater intrudes into coastal freshwater aquifers. To restore a balance, communities can increase infiltration to recharge the aquifer while simultaneously reducing withdrawals. Groundwater contamination is another threat to this important water supply; our groundwater needs to be protected against everything from fracking to septic systems, hazardous waste leaks to coal ash and perchlorate (from rocket fuel).

Why Is Water Scarce?

THE AMOUNT OF WATER ON OUR PLANET is both gigantic and finite. Every day about 80 trillion gallons of water fall onto the Earth as precipitation. That's enough for each person to have around 10,000 gallons a day. So why are so many people affected by water shortages? Here are some reasons:

- Rain and snow aren't evenly divided up around the world and conveniently parceled out over the year. It may come all at once in one place, or skip over a watershed entirely.

- Rainfall is unpredictable and, if climate change models are accurate, it is likely to become more so.

- Population growth and industrialization increase the demand on water supplies while the location of accessible freshwater is shifting.

- If rain doesn't fall in a watershed to flow into a river and fill a town's reservoir, the town can run out of water. Similarly, if snow doesn't fall in places like the Sierra Nevada mountains, there is no reserve of snowpack to sustain agriculture and cities during the dry California summers.

- Groundwater is being used more quickly than it's replenished. Those who rely on overdrawn groundwater will experience dry wells.

Water scarcity is a regional phenomenon and occurs all over the globe. A grim symptom of water scarcity is dry rivers: the mighty Colorado, the Rio Grande, the Indus in Pakistan, and the Ganges in Bangladesh are some of the largest rivers that run dry before reaching the sea. There are thousands and thousands more.

Drought

A drought gets people's attention on water. The year I spent writing this book was hot and dry. More than half of the continental United States was in severe to extreme drought conditions. Kemp, Texas, experienced the worst-case scenario when the town's water supply went dry. City officials resorted to giving out bottled water at City Hall to desperate residents until the supply tanks slowly refilled. The corn and soy belt of the Midwest was decimated. Visible effects of the drought were fish deaths, hot rivers, dry rivers, forest fires, and barges unable to operate due to low river flows. Five hundred million trees died.

To a farmer who relies on rainfall to grow crops, drought is obvious. No rain, no crops. But what is a drought in a desert city that receives 8 inches of rain a year, full of people using 200 gallons per day?

When our water system is not capable of supplying the demand placed upon it, we experience a shortage, or a human-created drought. Over-allocations of rivers, unchecked growth, and over-drafting of groundwater all create shortages.

The conventional response to water shortages is to divert more river water, build more dams, and drill more groundwater wells. It's becoming obvious that these aren't long-term solutions. With the added stress of climate change on our already maxed-out systems, millions of people will face water insecurity. By the end of this century the American Southwest is

Winnemem Wintu and the Raising of the Shasta Dam

ANYONE WHO EATS California-grown food is connected to the Shasta Dam. The keystone of the massive Central Valley Water Project, the dam and reservoir divert northern California rivers to irrigate agricultural land in the south. When the Shasta Dam was built in 1945, it flooded most of the Winnemem Wintu Tribe's ancestral homeland. Current proposals to raise the dam another 18 feet could flood the remaining sites.

The Tribe describes itself and its position as:

> . . . a traditional tribe who inhabits our ancestral territory from Mt. Shasta down the McCloud River watershed. When the Shasta Dam was constructed during World War II, it flooded our home and blocked the salmon runs.
>
> The salmon are an integral part of our lifeway and of a healthy McCloud River watershed. We believe that when the last salmon is gone, humans will be gone too. Our fight to return the salmon to the McCloud River is no less than a fight to save the Winnemem Wintu Tribe.
>
> As salmon people and middle water people we advocate for all aspects of clean water and the restoration of salmon to their natural spawning grounds.
>
> — *Sawal Mem, Sawal Suhana*
> *(Sacred Water, Sacred Life)*

The Bureau of Reclamation's study proposing to raise the Shasta Dam to increase storage for agriculture and urban use in southern California is fraught with problems. Raising the dam would flood the remaining sacred sites of the Winnemem, destroy miles of wild trout habitat, drown thousands of acres of National Forest land, and flood 1.5 miles of the McCloud River, protected under California's Wild & Scenic Rivers Act. It would cost more than a billion dollars. The same quantity of water could be acquired more cheaply with conservation or reuse without harming fish habitat, sacred sites, or forestland.

predicted to experience the largest decline in precipitation in the country and could lose up to 10 percent of its annual rainfall. An unfortunate consequence of water moving through a hotter, drier climate is that more water will be lost through evaporation and more moisture soaked up by dry soil in riverbeds, further decreasing river flows.

If you live in a western state, drought and water conflict are nothing new. If you're from the southeastern U.S., the recent droughts and interstate water conflicts have brought water supply issues to everyone's attention. Interestingly, the "killer drought" of 2005 to 2007 was actually mild compared to past droughts, according to researchers at Columbia University. They attribute the havoc this drought caused to booming populations and lack of planning, which left water suppliers unprepared to handle any reduction in their water supply. In the aftermath, short-sighted Southeastern towns are planning dam and reservoir projects, not just conservation and reuse. Georgia alone is proposing 20 new reservoirs.

Given past experience with drought, it should be apparent that building a dam and reservoir does not guarantee a new water supply. Reservoirs are weather-dependent infrastructure. If it doesn't rain and there isn't water in the river, a new dam or reservoir will do little good. It will also create an enormous evaporation pool, losing scarce freshwater to the atmosphere — on average, every acre of reservoir area evaporates one million gallons of water each year.

The Case of the Colorado

The Colorado River Basin is a sobering example of water shortages. The river is over-allocated; more water is promised than actually flows in the river. In the early 1920s, the men who divided up water allocations from the river did so during an unseasonably wet period that they mistook for normal. Today, 40 million people depend on the Colorado, and climate models predict reductions of flow in the river of 6 to 20 percent by the year 2050. Reservoirs on the Colorado River already lose an estimated 1.8 million acre-feet of water to evaporation each year, more than 10 percent of the total annual flow.

Thirsty cities like Los Angeles, San Diego, Denver, Las Vegas, and Phoenix compete for Colorado River water with Western farmers and ranchers who

Largest Irrigated Crop in the Country: Lawns

Italian-born NASA scientist Christina Milesi was shocked to see what Americans did to maintain a green lawn. She decided to find out how many resources we pour into our lawns. Using satellite images, aerial photos, and census data, she estimated we grow more than 63,000 square miles of lawn (three times more than corn), which guzzle 19 trillion gallons of water each year.

irrigate approximately 15 percent of the nation's food. Mexico receives about 10 percent of the river's flow and diverts it all for human use, to supply water to Tijuana, other northern cities, and agriculture. In 1922, conservationist Aldo Leopold described the magnificent Colorado River delta, which covered 3,000 square miles as, "Verdant walls of mesquite and willow . . . a hundred green lagoons. . . . The river was everywhere and nowhere." Now, this once diverse ecosystem is no longer. In its place is an enormous wasteland of cracked, dry mudflats.

Modern-day conservationists, like Osvel Hinojosa Huerta, director of the Water and Wetlands program for the Mexican nonprofit Pronatura Noroeste, fight to restore the Colorado River delta. For more than a decade he's been working to return water to the delta — even agricultural runoff or treated wastewater can help renew wetland and estuary life. Currently, the largest marsh wetland (40,000 acres) in the region is fed by drainage water from nearby farms. Experts predict that restoring just 1 to 3 percent of the river's flow would reconnect it to the sea and could restore around 200,000 acres of delta wetlands.

Cities dependent on the Colorado are planning for the future. Disappointingly, instead of stepping up conservation efforts and investing in reuse programs, some pursue costly and energy-intensive desalination plants. Removing salt from seawater is one of the most energy-intensive water supply options, requiring two to ten times more energy per gallon than treating wastewater for reuse. San Diego bought into the one-billion-dollar Carlsbad desalination plant that will supply around 7 percent of the region's water needs. The city has promised to buy at least 48 million gallons per day from the plant, hardly an incentive to pursue conservation or reuse.

With dozens of similar projects proposed along the California coast, it's a key time to promote more sustainable options. Orange County is not looking for a new supply of water; instead officials are planning to increase their water recycling plant's capacity from 70 to 100 million gallons per day. This system treats wastewater to nearly distilled water quality, for less than one-third the energy required to desalinate seawater and less than one half the energy needed to import water from Northern California.

Climate Change

Climate change experts predict the historic hydrologic cycle will be intensified. Dry areas will become drier and wet areas wetter. Storms will become more intense. Precipitation is more likely to fall as rain rather than being slowly released as melting snow. Heavy rains can overwhelm the soil's ability to absorb rainfall, contributing to increased flooding.

It's obvious how our water supply system is impacted by climate change: droughts reduce the supply while floods can contaminate it. Our wastewater treatment plants are vulnerable in a different way. These plants are located near the coast or rivers, and they often fail during storms and hurricanes. Flooding and power outages cause sewage overflows. And even during normal weather, our sewer plants don't always function as designed.

Sewage Treatment and Stormwater Pollution

RETURNING THE FOCUS BACK to your house: as mentioned, water leaves a home either through a sewer pipe or by rainwater (stormwater) that runs off the site. If you are connected to the sewer, all the household greywater from sinks, showers, and washing machines mixes with the toilet water, then joins the sewer pipes of all your neighbors, local businesses, and industries in your town and flows to the wastewater treatment plant.

When sewer plants aren't threatened by sea level rise or superstorms, they are fascinating places to visit. I remember the first sewer plant I visited, in San Francisco. A river of dark, dirty water pours in, 24 hours a day. What a gargantuan task: to remove all the trash, soaps, debris, feces, urine, and dirt we put in the water. Screens take out the trash; settling tanks sink the heavy stuff. Liquid effluent is injected with oxygen so microbes can consume the nutrients. (Even the most modern plant relies on these little bugs to clean the water.) The liquid effluent is heavily bleached to kill pathogens before being dumped into the nearest river, bay, or ocean.

Even though we've spent billions of dollars to construct this massive system, the nation's sewer infrastructure received a "D" on its most recent report card from the American Society of Civil Engineers. As noted on the *2013 Report Card for America's Infrastructure,* "D" represents *At Risk:* "The infrastructure is in poor to fair condition and mostly below

Rainwater Harvesting Revives Dry Rivers

||||||||||||||||||||||||||||||||||||||||||||||||||||||||||||||||||||||||||||||||||||||||||||||||||||||||||||||||||||||||||||||||||||||||||||

PROBLEM: The wells in Rajasthan's Alwar District in India had dried up. Then the streams and rivers dried up. Deforestation, resulting from Britain's hunger for timber, caused erosion, filling up the traditional rainwater collection structures, which in turn caused monsoon rains to run off the land instead of being collected to recharge the aquifer. This environmental degradation quickly transferred to the loss of social structures. The revival of traditional rainwater collection brought water back to this dry land.

SOLUTION: Hundreds of villages in this district have built and repaired thousands of small earthen check dams to conserve rainwater, and are reforesting denuded lands. Sixteen years later they boast of raising the groundwater table by almost 20 feet, reviving 800 dry wells, increasing forest size by 33 percent, and restoring five dry rivers to flow all year long. This small-scale, community-guided practice was good for the land, good for the people, and good for the pocketbook: the project created agricultural revenues that were four times greater than the costs of the improvements.

standard, with many elements approaching the end of their service life. A large portion of the system exhibits significant deterioration. Condition and capacity are of significant concern with strong risk of failure."

On a good day the nutrients and pathogens are removed from the water before discharge. Many days, however — especially when it rains or there is a power outage or a mechanical or human error — untreated sewage is released from the plant and flows into waterways (rivers, lakes, oceans). The infrastructure is aging, ailing, and expensive to fix; cost estimates are 300 billion dollars over the next 20 years.

Think how much work it is to rip up all the city streets and lay new sewage pipe. It seems as though keeping pollutants out of the water in the first place would be a lot cheaper and easier, and that using soil microbes to treat greywater as it irrigates our landscapes would make a lot more sense.

What's Wrong with Our Sewer System?

My personal laundry list of our sewer system problems is rather long. Below is a summary of the key issues. Notably, this doesn't include the secondary problems related to energy required to operate the plants.

Sewage plants fail. In the United States, an estimated 900 billion gallons of untreated sewage flows into waterways each year. The EPA estimates that up to 3.5 million people become sick from recreational contact with raw sewage, and this is just the reported illnesses. Beaches are closed due to sewage contamination: for three years in a row there have been more than 20,000 beach closure days in the United States. Malfunctioning sewage plants discharge nutrient-rich water, causing algae blooms and toxic red tides. Algae blooms can be hazardous for people and deadly for other aquatic life, robbing the water of oxygen. Dead zones, like those in the Chesapeake Bay, have water so depleted of oxygen that aquatic life forms die if they enter it.

Sewage treatment plants (even the most modern) don't remove many harmful chemicals from the water. Endocrine disruptors found in plastics, disinfectants, and birth control pills interfere with the reproductive organs of fish and other aquatic life. Downstream of wastewater treatment plants, eggs are found in the testes of male fish.

Sewage treatment plants are an environmental justice issue. No one wants one in their backyard, so treatment plants — along with incinerators, toxic waste dumps, and chemical plants — are disproportionately located in low-income, immigrant, or otherwise disenfranchised communities that lack the political clout to refuse them. An array of odors waft from the plants: a cocktail of hydrogen sulfide, ammonia, methane, aerosols of microorganisms, and possibly industrial solvents and petroleum derivatives from industrial wastewater. The stink is unpleasant, as well as potentially harmful. An EPA-sponsored study found that residents living near a sewage plant near Chicago, Illinois, suffered from an increase in skin diseases, nausea, vomiting, general weakness, and shortness of breath. (Other studies have not found detectable increase in disease for nearby residents, though plant workers do have increased risk for many diseases.)

Any water leaving our home through the sewer pipe contributes to this costly and damaging sewer infrastructure. Instead, we can reuse greywater for irrigation and waterless toilets for sanitation, to turn our sewer woes into a free and available water supply to beautify our home landscapes.

When Rain Pollutes: Stormwater

THE SECOND WAY water leaves our homes is through rainwater runoff. This stormwater currently is the largest source of pollution in waterways. As our cities and towns urbanized, roofs and roads replaced forests and grasslands. Instead of soaking into the land, rain runs quickly off this hardscape, causing flooding and erosion downstream.

Cities have responded by constructing systems specifically for channeling the stormwater off the streets and into creeks, culverts, and rivers to flow to the sea. In some municipalities, this stormwater system connects to the sewage system, and sewer treatment plants can become overwhelmed when it rains, frequently causing overflows of untreated sewage. This is called a *combined sewer system*, and the overflow a *combined sewer overflow*, or CSO.

Stormwater runoff moves pollutants from the land into the water. Pesticides, herbicides, oil, brake fluid, polychlorinated biphenyls (PCBs), and heavy metals make their way from our urban hardscape into rivers, bays, and oceans. A sad example of urban runoff pollution's devastating effect on wildlife is the endangered orca whale of Puget Sound. Runoff from the Seattle area has introduced so many toxins into the food chain that these whales are the most contaminated wild creatures on Earth. The salmon they eat are contaminated with PCBs, which accumulate in the orcas' fat and suppress their immune systems. Once widely used in industry, PCBs have been banned in the United States and Canada since the late 1970s, yet these chemicals continue to contaminate waters through runoff from contaminated sites, scrap yards, and landfills.

PCB contamination is just one problem pollutant: lead, mercury, pesticides, flame retardants, and oil — more than six million gallons each year — wash off the streets and into the Sound. Now, Seattle and surrounding cities are using rain gardens and living roofs to prevent urban runoff pollution.

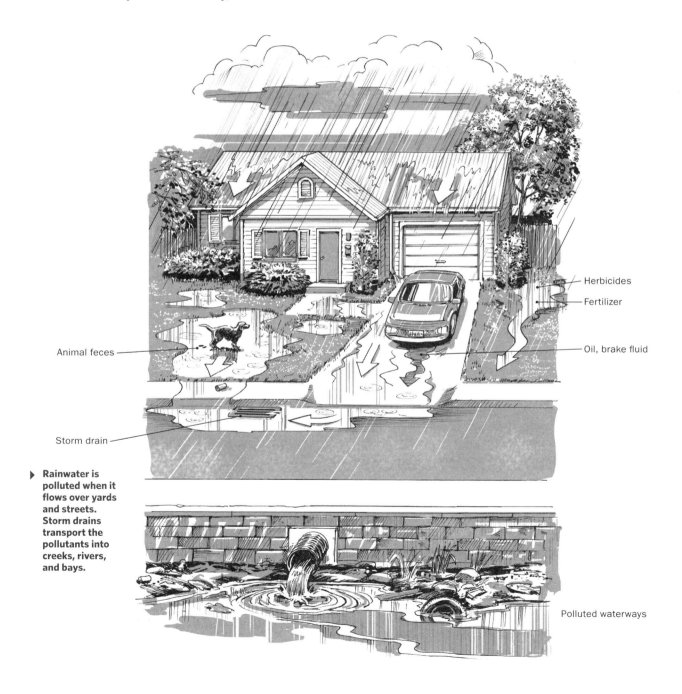

Herbicides

Fertilizer

Oil, brake fluid

Animal feces

Storm drain

▶ **Rainwater is polluted when it flows over yards and streets. Storm drains transport the pollutants into creeks, rivers, and bays.**

Polluted waterways

A Better Water Future

IT IS EXCITING TO SEE INDIVIDUALS all across the country rethink and redesign their home water systems. It's even more exciting to watch it scale up when a city or water agency invests in green infrastructure and promotes decentralized systems. From Portland, Oregon, to San Francisco, California, from Tucson, Arizona, to Chicago, Illinois, large-scale change is happening.

Water suppliers such as the San Francisco Public Utilities Commission, Tucson Water, and the City of Santa Rosa offer financial incentives for both grey-water and rainwater systems, as well as educational resources. In San Francisco, qualified homes even get a free on-site consultation with a local greywater expert through the city's greywater incentive program.

Many Hands Make Light Work

You may be lucky and live somewhere with free education, rebates, or incentives to support your home's transformation. Or you may need to approach your water district for support. In the meantime, other types of support can be cultivated. Seek out like-minded people in local watershed groups, permaculture guilds, or green-gardener-type programs. Invite your friends and family to help out with your projects. Host work parties to share the information as well as the digging. This book gives you the technical info to begin.

As you dive into the how-to portions of this book, I hope you will keep the larger implications of these systems in mind. The values of equity, environmental justice, restoration, and long-term sustainability can guide our communities to answer pressing questions such as:

- How do we balance our human needs for clean water with the needs of healthy aquatic ecosystems?

- How can we secure equitable water rights so all people have access to clean water and healthy watersheds for drinking, fishing, and cultural uses, and communities have collective control of their local water sources?

- How do we create water systems that restore and regenerate the environment rather than destroying and degrading it?

- In times of water shortages, who will decide how water is allocated?

Starting at Home

Our local water problems differ, but we can all find a solution appropriate for our situation. The ecologically mindful solution to our large-scale, one-size-fits-all infrastructure is to seek out regionally appropriate solutions that work in tune with natural water systems. Your own house is a perfect place to start.

Reducing Rainwater Runoff

At the household level, it's simple to solve the stormwater pollution problem. A simple rain garden, for example, can intercept runoff and prevent stormwater pollution while creating a lovely landscape feature. Or you can attempt a more ambitious project.

At the time we bought our house in Oakland, 80 percent of rainwater ran off the property into the

The Living Building Challenge

The Living Building Challenge™ is the most rigorous and forward-thinking of all sustainability certification programs. For a building to qualify it must be energy- and water-neutral, promote car-free living, and be designed with beauty in mind. It also can't use any chemicals on the "red list" (such as PVC).

One example is the Bullitt Center in Seattle, Washington, a six-story office building that opened on Earth Day 2013. This multistory, 50,000-square-foot commercial building is designed to be energy- and water-neutral. A 56,000-gallon rainwater tank collects rainwater below the building for use in the building's showers, sinks, and drinking fountains. Greywater is filtered and purified with plants before soaking into the ground. Composting toilets (Phoenix brand foam-flush models; see page 212) compost the human waste generated in the building.

PRE-REDESIGN

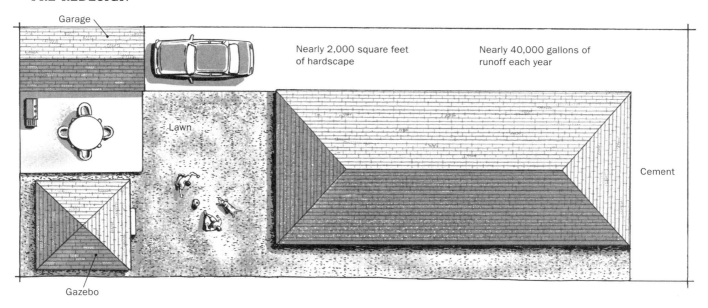

Garage

Nearly 2,000 square feet of hardscape

Nearly 40,000 gallons of runoff each year

Lawn

Cement

Gazebo

POST-REDESIGN

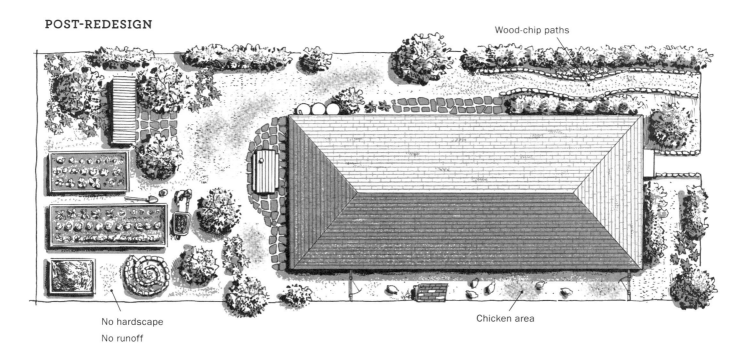

Wood-chip paths

No hardscape
No runoff

Chicken area

▲ **My home in Oakland, pre- and post-redesign**

stormwater system, ultimately contributing to pollution of the San Francisco Bay. We reduced this runoff rate to zero through a full landscape redesign — and all for less than a thousand dollars: The previous owners had paved most of the yard. We depaved it. It took two weekends, with a rented jackhammer ($200) and lots of help from our friends, followed by months of getting rid of the piles of concrete, ending with a dump truck rental ($250). We trucked in manure from a local stable and a few loads of wood chips from a tree trimmer to boost the organic matter in the compacted clay soil. Then we planted more than a dozen fruit trees, kiwi vines, a berry patch, native perennials to attract beneficial pollinators, flowers, and several vegetable garden beds ($500 in plants). The landscape became a lot more attractive and useful. Over time, the hardworking roots pushed their way down into the ground, aerating and loosening the earth, increasing the absorption capacity of our yard.

Reducing Consumption

Over the course of a few years, my household in Oakland reduced its total water consumption to 10 gallons per person per day (10 gpcd), a scant 7 percent of our region's 140 gpcd average. Our composting toilet used no water. Our greywater systems enabled us to redirect our 50 gallons per day (5 people × 10 gpcd) out to the yard (minus a few flushes of an ultra-low-flow toilet): 350 gallons a week of irrigation water. In addition, we infiltrated all the rainfall — around 50,000 gallons each year — into the land. Our yard was lush and productive while consuming very little potable water.

Our homes are microcosms of the larger world of water issues. When the scale of water problems feels overwhelming, I return to practical solutions in my home. I feel encouraged knowing my dishwater flows to irrigate passion fruit, guava, and tree tomatoes. The relative simplicity of reconfiguring a home plumbing system or replacing a flush toilet with a composting model makes the bigger, global problems feel more manageable.

Disconnecting from the System

||||||||||||||||||||||||||||||||||||||||||||||||||||||||||||||||||||||||||||||||||||||||||||||||||||

PROBLEM: Portland's combined sewer system has long been a source of contamination of the Willamette River.

SOLUTION: In the early 1990s Portland began a plan to reduce stormwater pollution and combined sewer overflows. Green streets, ecoroofs, and downspout disconnects, all strategies to reduce stormwater runoff, have already reduced sewage overflows by 35 percent. Through a Downspout Disconnect program, more than 50,000 houses have detached their downspouts from the combined sewer to divert nearly one billion gallons per year of stormwater from the river and soak it into the ground.

In 2008 the city committed to spending 55 million dollars to invest in green infrastructure projects. To date, they've planted nearly 30,000 new street trees, 800 streetside rain gardens, and more than 10 acres of ecoroofs. An ecoroof is a low-maintenance, vegetative roofing system used in place of a conventional roof. It captures rainwater, reduces stormwater runoff, improves air quality, helps insulate the building (which lowers heating and cooling costs), and provides habitat for wildlife. The city also provides financial incentives for harvesting rainwater and offers free classes and technical information on rainwater catchment and greywater reuse.

Saving Water in the Home and Landscape

A **WATER-WISE HOME CONSUMES A FRACTION** of the water used in a conventional home — without sacrificing modern comforts. In this chapter I will discuss a variety of techniques to create a water-wise home, including efficient fixtures, water-wise landscaping, greywater reuse, rainwater harvesting, and waterless toilet systems, as well as simple behaviors that help save water. For each technology I'll cover how much water you'll save, how much it costs, and the pros and cons of each technique.

The best way to start is by simply increasing the efficiency of your house so that you use less water for the same everyday tasks. This is the most economical and environmentally friendly strategy of all of these water-saving methods (strategies requiring fewer materials, particularly plastics, use fewer resources). The next step is to replumb the pipes and downspouts to supply your productive, vibrant, time- and water-saving landscape and to help prevent stormwater pollution and sewer overflows.

IN THIS CHAPTER:

Cultivating a Water-Conserving Ethic

INCREASING OUR AWARENESS OF WATER helps us to conserve it. When we wash our hands, turning the faucet on halfway accomplishes the same goal as running it full blast. When we're washing dishes and someone sparks up a conversation, we can chat with, or without, the faucet still running. We should never use precious potable water to accomplish a task in the name of convenience; for example, using water to clean driveways (the job for a broom), or running water over frozen foods to speed thawing. All of us can benefit from reflecting on water awareness, of seeing water, of noticing when it's used — or not used — and for what purpose. I invite you to find new ways to conserve in your daily life, and model a water ethic of respect and conservation; it will be noticed by your friends, family, and coworkers.

You may be thinking, "*I* don't waste water. The problem is my _____." (Fill in the blank with your teenager, spouse, roommate, etc.) Since we can only change our own behavior, the water-saving systems outlined in the rest of the book will save water in your home regardless of your housemates' habits (see Talking About Wasting Water, below).

Unfortunately, lack of water awareness is prevalent in our society at large and often leads to wasteful behavior. During times of acute shortages, the effects of personal behavior become an obvious community issue. What can you do if your neighbor is flagrantly wasting water during a drought and strict rationing is in place? First, assume best intentions; maybe they're unaware. A friendly conversation about your local water situation may help. Or, share

Talking about Wasting Water

Whenever I'm around someone wasting water, I have to bite my lip to not say something. Sometimes I say the right thing, sometimes the wrong thing, and other times I keep quiet. This is what I've found is often helpful:

- Approach someone blasting the faucet for five minutes while washing one dish. Say, "Can I show you something I do?" Model how to wash and rinse with a small stream of water.

- Approach someone washing a tiny load in the laundry. Say, "Oh, I have some laundry too. Mind if we combine ours to run a full load?"

- Approach someone washing a car with the hose running. Say, "Want to borrow my hose sprayer? It saves a lot of water and makes it easier to get the car clean."

- Talk about or show where the water comes from. Hang a beautiful photograph of the river supplying your town's water above the shower/sink.

- Consult a resource. Sometimes talking about behavior or cultural changes can be difficult. This book is a useful tool: *Difficult Conversations: How to Discuss What Matters Most* by Douglas Stone, et al (see Resources).

some effective techniques you've implemented, and even offer your help. For example, if they have an irrigation system spraying water onto the street, you could offer to help fix it. If you have a neighborhood organization, bring up water as a larger community issue and discuss strategies for your neighborhood to reduce consumption. Sometimes a little indirect pressure helps people change behavior without feeling attacked.

Eco-etiquette blogger Jennifer Grayson offers a great community-building suggestion to a reader in the Huffington Post:

> . . . why not use this as an opportunity to organize a neighborhood green watch? Invite everyone on your street to a backyard potluck barbecue and ask them each to bring one dish and one idea for bettering the block. As you're smiling and handing out margaritas, casually bring up your pet project: water conservation. I'm sure you're not the only one dealing with H_2O offenders, and the group might come up with some creative solutions to other environmental issues as well (people not recycling, doggie doo left on the sidewalk, etc.).

Recently, at an irrigation store in Los Angeles at the beginning of a dry summer, an employee was spraying down the concrete in front of the store. I

HOW MUCH WATER DO WE USE?

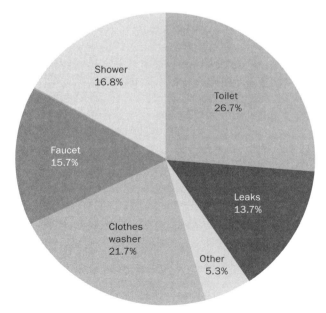

Toilets, showers, and clothes washers typically use the most water in a home. Leaks can consume almost as much as faucets.

said to him with a smile, "Hey, isn't that illegal or something?" Other workers overheard me and said to the water-waster, "Ya, come on Dave, go get the broom washer. We're supposed to be setting a good example here." He stopped spraying and got out a wet-broom attachment for the hose and finished washing the concrete using much less water than before.

Fix the Leaks!

A sad fact: leaks waste an average 14 percent of total home water use. The toilet alone is capable of wasting thousands of gallons a day — think entire swimming pools full of wasted water every year. If you see drips in your faucet, hear the toilet running mysteriously, or find swampy areas in your irrigation system, you have leaks.

Conduct a Leak Check

Some leaks are silent and hidden. Conduct a leak check by observing the water meter (if you have one). First, turn off all faucets and irrigation systems. Next, go outside to the water meter, usually located in front of your house near the curb. Carefully lift the concrete or metal cover to expose the meter inside the meter pit. Look for a needle on the meter's dial. If there are multiple windows or needles, use the smallest (labeled "one foot"). Mark the location of the meter by laying a toothpick or similar object over the needle. Check back in half an hour; if the needle moved, you have a hidden leak. Check with your water district if you need help reading the meter.

Leaking Toilet?

Have you ever heard water running in the bathroom when no one has used it recently? Have you noticed water move in the toilet bowl? If so, you have a toilet leak. Not sure? It's easy to check. Remove the lid of the tank and drip a few drops of food coloring inside. Wait about 15 minutes, then check the bowl of the toilet. If you see any color in the bowl, you have a leak.

Fixing Toilet Leaks

Toilets typically leak under the flapper (the rubber trapdoor-like flap on the bottom of the tank) or over the fill, or overflow, tube (the open-ended tube extending up toward the top of the tank). First, clean the

bottom of the tank and flapper; sometimes dirt prevents the flapper from closing fully, so water leaks under it into the toilet bowl. If water is leaking over the top of the fill tube, you can adjust the float or float arm on the fill valve so it lowers the water level (this is a simple adjustment, but the proper method

TWO TYPES OF TOILET GUTS

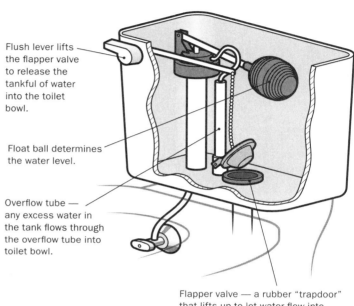

Flush lever lifts the flapper valve to release the tankful of water into the toilet bowl.

Float ball determines the water level.

Overflow tube — any excess water in the tank flows through the overflow tube into toilet bowl.

Flapper valve — a rubber "trapdoor" that lifts up to let water flow into toilet bowl. If the flapper doesn't seal well, water leaks under it into the toilet bowl.

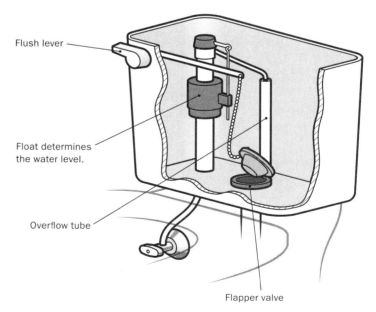

Flush lever

Float determines the water level.

Overflow tube

Flapper valve

▲ **Toilets often leak under the flapper or over the overflow tube.**

depends on the type of fill valve, also called a ball cock). If these don't fix the leak, you may need to replace the flushing mechanism. The Internet is full of detailed tutorials for replacing toilet parts and fixing leaks (see Resources).

Fixing Leaky Faucets and Showerheads

Drip, drip, drip. A leaky faucet wastes hundreds of gallons a month, adding up to thousands per year. Usually a dripping faucet can be fixed by replacing one or more washers, gaskets, or O-rings. On cartridge- and disc-type faucets, often it's best to replace the offending cartridge or disc. Faucet parts are inexpensive and commonly available at hardware stores and home centers, but it's important to get exact replacements. Take the old washer or other part to the store to prevent repeat trips.

Fixing a leak from a showerhead can be tricky because the leak actually occurs at the shower faucet, the valves of which tend to be recessed inside the wall. A cheap and easy "fix" to a drippy showerhead is to add a ball-valve shutoff before the showerhead. This is similar to the water-saving shower shutoff valve (see page 31); the difference is the ball valve completely shuts off the flow, whereas the other lets a drip through for anti-scalding protection. Keep the shutoff valve closed when you aren't using the shower.

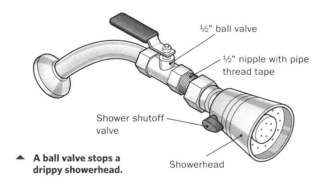

½" ball valve

½" nipple with pipe thread tape

Shower shutoff valve

Showerhead

▲ **A ball valve stops a drippy showerhead.**

Leaky Irrigation?

A drippy irrigation system typically wastes between 50 and 75 percent of all the water the system normally uses. Yikes! Have you noticed an unexplained rise in the water bill? Dry or wet patches in the yard, or otherwise poor performance of the system? If so,

you may have a leak. Irrigation systems in cold climates are especially prone to developing leaks, as any water left in the system can freeze in the winter and rupture tubing and other parts.

Check the supply lines of a drip irrigation system; they're often on the surface of the ground or under a shallow mulch layer. Turn on the irrigation system, and repair leaks by tightening loose clamps, plugging small holes, or cutting out damaged sections and reconnecting the tubing with repair couplings. Repairing leaks in an underground sprinkler system can be a more difficult task. Sprinkler owners could take this opportunity to upgrade to something more efficient, such as a drip irrigation system.

The Mini Makeover

A SIMPLE "MINI MAKEOVER," such as switching out water-guzzling fixtures and appliances for efficient models, can lower total household water use by up to 35 percent. These water savings translate to energy (and money) savings, and lower your home's carbon footprint.

Imagine a nice hot shower. Spend five minutes under a standard 2.5-gallon-per-minute (gpm) showerhead, and you'll use 12½ gallons of water. Spend five minutes swapping out the showerhead to a more efficient model using 1.5 gpm, and the next shower will use 7½ gallons, a 40 percent reduction in water

AVERAGE U.S. DAILY INDOOR WATER USE VS. AVERAGE USE IN WATER-EFFICIENT HOME (35% REDUCTION)		
Use	**Average Gallons per Capita**	**Average in Water-Efficient Home**
Showers	11.6	8.8
Clothes washers	15	10
Dishwashers	1	0.7
Toilets	18.5	8.2
Baths	1.2	1.2
Leaks	9.5	4.0
Faucets	10.9	10.8
Other domestic use	1.6	1.6
Total	69.3 gallons	45.3 gallons

Sources: *Residential End Uses of Water* (Denver, CO: AWWA Resource Foundation, 1999); *Handbook of Water Use and Conservation*, Amy Vickers (WaterPlow Press, 2012)

Water-Saving Tips

There are many options for saving water. Here are some simple solutions you can implement in your home, including relative cost and amount of water savings for each method.

💧 = small water savings		◯ = Free	
💧💧 = medium savings		$ = low investment	
💧💧💧 = large savings		$$ = larger up-front investment	

SHOWER

💧💧💧	Install a low-flow showerhead (1 gpm or 1.5 gpm).	$
💧💧💧	Install a shower shutoff valve. How it works: A manual shutoff valve on the showerhead allows you to turn the water on and off between soaping and rinsing without having to mess with the shower's faucet valves; the water temperature stays the same.	$
💧	Catch "clear water" in a bucket as the shower heats up. Use the water for plants or to "bucket flush" the toilet (pouring water swiftly into the toilet bowl creates a flush).	◯
💧💧	Take shorter showers.	◯

BATH

💧💧	Take fewer baths. If you take baths for health reasons, consider investing in a soaking tub that uses less water.	◯
💧💧	Share the bathwater with your family.	◯
💧💧	Fill the tub up partway.	◯

BATHROOM SINK

💧	Install a low-flow aerator (often available free from local water agencies) on sink faucets. A low-flow aerator typically replaces a standard aerator and reduces the flow of water.	$
💧	Turn off the water while shaving. Fill the bottom of the sink with a few inches of water to rinse the razor.	◯
💧	Don't turn the faucet on full blast; halfway gets the job done.	◯

TOILET

💧💧💧	Install a low-flow or dual-flush toilet. Water companies often give rebates for these.	$$
💧💧	Make your own "low-flow" toilet: Reduce the amount of water in the tank by putting a river rock or a plastic bottle, weighted down with water and rocks inside, in the toilet tank reservoir, ensuring it doesn't impede the flushing or filling mechanisms of the toilet. (This doesn't work as well as a low-flow toilet, so install a real one if you can.)	◯
💧💧	Flush judiciously: "If it's yellow let it mellow. If it's brown flush it down."	◯
💧💧💧	Get a waterless toilet.	$$

KITCHEN

💧💧	Don't turn on faucet full blast.	◯
💧	Use a dishpan in sink for hand-washing dishes.	$
💧	Use less soap on dishes to avoid unnecessary rinsing of excess soap.	◯
💧	Install a shutoff switch on the faucet. It allows you to quickly turn faucet on and off by flipping the switch up or down.	$
💧	Run dishwasher only when completely full.	◯
💧💧	Experiment to see how little you need to clean the dishes before putting them in the dishwasher. If you have to practically wash them before the dishwasher does, you will save water and energy by skipping the dishwasher altogether. Or, to save water when "pre-washing," thoroughly scrape food scraps into the compost, then use a basin of cold water to rinse dishes before placing them into the dishwasher.	◯

OTHER

💧💧💧	Convert your swimming pool to a rainwater harvesting tank and visit the local pool when you want to swim.	$$$
💧💧💧	Use a pool cover if you must have a pool; covers reduce pool water loss by 30 percent.	$$
💧💧💧	Remove the lawn and replace with beautiful perennials adapted to your climate or fruit trees grown with greywater. (Instead of tearing up the turf, simply cover it with cardboard, add compost on top, then wood chips. Plant directly through the cardboard.)	$$
💧💧💧	Choose a type of grass suited for your region to lower the need for lawn irrigation.	$$

WHOLE HOUSE

💧💧	Do you have to run the water for several minutes before it heats up in the shower? Install a recirculating pump to avoid wasting water while it heats up. This pump recirculates water in the pipe until it's hot.	$$

and energy. Each person using the shower will save around 1,300 gallons of water each year.

Upgrading your washing machine can save even more. An old top-loading washing machine uses around 40 gallons per load, while the most water-efficient front loaders use around 12. The Alliance for Water Efficiency estimates a family of four could cut its washing machine water use to half, or less, with an efficient machine — from 12,000 gallons a year to 6,000 gallons a year.

The chart on page 30 offers a glance at 35 percent savings on everyday household fixtures and appliances. How much you use in your home may differ from these numbers. In chapter 4 you'll calculate your personal water use.

Daily Water Use

The United Nations recommends that each person on Earth have 13 gallons of water per day for drinking, cooking, and cleaning. Per-capita water use varies greatly around the world, even among rich countries.

- United States — 100 gallons
- United Kingdom — 40 gallons
- Germany — 51 gallons
- Mozambique — 1 gallon

Does Your Landscape Have a Drinking Problem?

MANY LANDSCAPES DO. They drink a lot, and they drink the wrong stuff: the potable, treated, and pressurized water. Many homes use as much water in the yard as for all indoor purposes: 50 percent inside, 50 percent outside. In hot, dry climates an even higher portion is used outdoors. Reducing water used in the landscape is critical for a water-wise home. This section provides an overview of design and techniques to save water in your landscape. Many methods can be used in conjunction with rainwater harvesting and greywater reuse.

Water-Smart Landscaping

A water-smart landscape does not rely on freshwater irrigation to thrive. Plants are adapted to local climate conditions and grow well without fertilizers or pesticides. Plants that require frequent irrigation, like a vegetable garden, optimize water use through healthy soil and mulch, while supplemental irrigation comes from rainwater or greywater instead of the tap. Water-smart landscapes should also be ecological, minimizing use of resources, such as gas mowers or trimmers, herbicides, or imported building materials, and focusing on plants that improve the productivity of the land by providing food, building materials, shade, natural fences, or wildlife habitat.

Well-designed landscapes prevent stormwater pollution, recharge groundwater tables, and require less input from people than a lawn or rose garden does. They are friendly to our oceans, bays, rivers, creeks, and salmon; they protect local watersheds. All of us, whether we live in the desert or get 60 inches of rain a year, can create beautiful, productive landscapes that consume no water from the tap. And they most certainly will not all look the same.

The Landscape Problems

- On average, most homes in the U.S. use the same amount of water outside for irrigation as they do inside the home for all other uses.
- Irrigating with drinking water wastes chemicals and energy (that were used to treat the water and transport it to your home).
- Conventional landscapes require water, fertilizers, and often pesticides to survive. These pollute waterways when they're washed away in the rain.
- Many irrigation systems waste enormous quantities of water as they over-irrigate.

The Landscape Solutions

- Pick the right plants for your region. We don't expect the weather to be the same in Phoenix and Seattle; why should we see the same backyard landscapes?
- Group plants by their water needs
- Irrigate in the morning or evening to prevent evaporation loss
- Replace spray irrigation with drip irrigation. Spray irrigation loses water to evaporation and runoff.

- Use smart controllers that run on current weather data or use soil moisture sensors, instead of standard programmed controllers that tend to over-irrigate (they don't know when to shut off or reduce irrigation as the weather changes).

- Improve soil health to improve the plants' health. Healthy plants look better and won't tempt you to give them extra water because they look sickly.

- Use rainwater and greywater as the primary sources of irrigation water

Designing a Water-Wise Landscape

WHETHER YOU'RE DESIGNING an entirely new landscape, redesigning your existing yard, or making simple water-wise improvements over time, incorporate water-wise techniques from the start. Design the garden so plants requiring frequent irrigation are near a greywater or rainwater source and, once established, the remaining plants thrive without irrigation.

Most people will start small and make incremental changes to transform an existing landscape. If this is your plan, start by creating an overall landscape design as a guide. It will help you prioritize projects and envision how the pieces will fit together. This is a strategic time to consult with an ecological landscaper. Even a one-hour consultation with a professional can be extremely valuable. Find someone who specializes in sustainable practices with a focus on the type of landscape you love, be it native plants, butterfly gardens, food forests, or edibles.

Water-Wise Landscaping Techniques

Choose plants adapted to your climate. Every place has a wide array of locally adapted (native) plants that evolved to live and thrive in that bioregion. Once established, these plants require no water and no fertilizers. Exotics from a similar climate also grow well with little water or inputs. Also, choose plants adapted to the location you will plant them. For example, native wetland plants will not do well without irrigation since they have adapted to living in a wet area.

Right plant, right place. Choose the proper location for each plant. For example, sun-loving plants don't do well in the shade, and large trees planted right next to the house will only cause problems. Remember to plan for the mature size of the plant and give it the necessary room needed to grow to its full size.

Marvelous mulch. Add an organic mulch cover of wood chips, straw, or other similar material, several inches thick. Mulch acts as an insulating blanket, shades the soil, reduces evaporation loss, and suppresses weeds. In the vegetable garden use thick straw mulch — it's easier to move out of the way to harvest and plant.

Arrange plants by water needs. Organizing your landscape into groups of plantings with similar water needs, called **hydrozoning**, facilitates water-efficient irrigation.

Locate high-water-use plants, such as vegetables, near the house where they can be irrigated with greywater or rainwater.

Moderate-water-use plants require some supplemental irrigation. Plant them where they can be irrigated with rainwater or greywater.

Low-water-use plants — native plants, or exotics from a similar climate — grow without supplemental irrigation. Use them to vegetate the rest of your landscape with no supplemental irrigation other than the rain falling from the sky.

Feed the soil. Healthy soil grows healthy plants. Adding compost is an easy and effective way to improve the soil. Compost improves the structure of soil, increasing aeration and water-retention characteristics as well as providing nutrients for plants.

Keep your overall goals in mind. You may need to remove poorly suited plants from the landscape (water hogs, sickly or disease prone ones, etc.). Don't feel bad about replacing them with more suitable plants. Try to think of your landscape as an ecosystem instead of as individual plants.

Create rain gardens to infiltrate rainwater into the soil to irrigate sections of the landscape.

Install greywater systems to irrigate plants requiring supplemental watering.

A Note about Natives

A native plant from your area is adapted to thrive in your local climate, with only rainfall and snowmelt for irrigation. However, there is a large variation between microclimates and bioregions; many native plants are identified as broadly as by what state they are from. A native plant from my state, California, could be from the desert, a high-elevation alpine meadow, an oak savanna, a coastal riparian stream, or a wetland marsh. You can imagine these plants have very different needs and water requirements, and many would not thrive in my yard in Los Angeles.

A native-plant nursery (especially one specializing in very local plants) is a great place to find water-thrifty plants suited for your yard. Native plant societies also might offer guidance, or you can head out to a nearby natural area to observe local specimens in their wild habitats. Seek out places similar in exposure, soil type, and moisture to your yard. You'll see natives and locally adapted exotics, as well as some pushy, invasive plants (don't plant these!).

Also notice how the plants change with the seasons. Many plants do not stay green all year long: landscaping expectations of year-round green and flowering plants are contrary to nature and the seasonal changes of plants. Fall browns and yellows are beautiful, too. Tall, elegant seed stalks and their natural die-off remind us of the cycle of life and death. And if you decide you only want greenery, find the evergreen natives from your climate, be it ocotillo cactus or juniper hedges.

Steps to Designing Your Water-Wise Landscape

A full landscape (re)design is a big project. The changes required to make your landscape water-wise depend on your current landscape, your goals, and your budget. Below I'll go over some basic steps and considerations for designing a landscape (see Resources for additional information).

Always keep your goals in mind throughout the process: What do you want from your landscape? Talk to your family and housemates about their wishes. Start with the big picture and leave details, like plant selection, for later on in the design process. Remember to consider (and notify) your neighbors if anything in your plan will affect them, such as removing trees, adding tall plants that could shade their yard or house, etc., and don't shade their home in a negative way (e.g., block the winter sun). There may be legal requirements around this also; check with your local government.

1. **Meet your yard.** Bring a comfy chair and a beverage. Sit. Look around. Listen. Smell. (Don't write, yet.) Move the chair around and sit in various parts of the yard. Find places that feel good to spend time in. Notice what plants are currently growing in the yard. Are they healthy? Productive? Useful? Notice how the sun moves overhead and when different parts of your yard are sunny, shady, cool, or warm. Think about your neighbors and how they affect your experience in the yard. For example, are there people you'd like to easily converse with, or others you'd like a little privacy from?

2. **Make lists.** Write down all the things you'd love to have in a landscape. Next to them write ideas of features in the landscape that could meet these goals. For example, if you wrote down "child's play area" you could meet that goal with a swing set, a weeping mulberry bush (to hide under and pick berries), or a sandbox. When you get to the decision-making phase, you can revisit this list and choose the features that work best in the overall design. If you have a small yard with limited space, you can prioritize landscape features that have multiple functions, such as the weeping mulberry, which can provide a habitat for birds in addition to delicious berries and a child's play area.

3. **Sketch the property.** Depending on the size of your project, the size of your landscape, and your ability to visualize, you can either draw a simple "bubble diagram" sketch, or you can

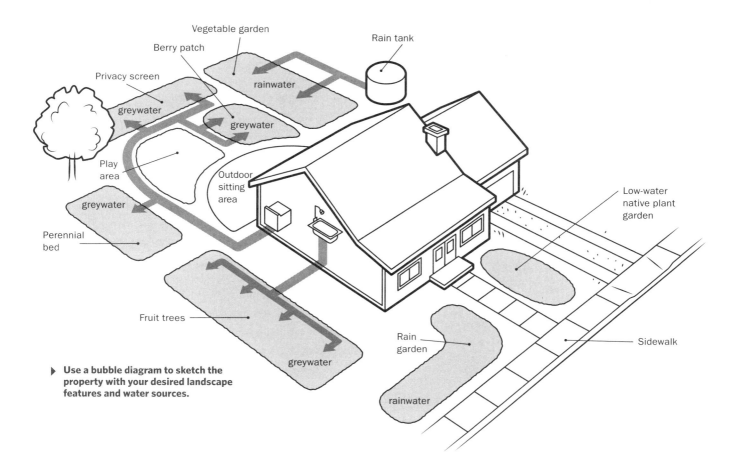

Vegetable garden

Berry patch

Rain tank

Privacy screen

rainwater

greywater

greywater

Low-water
native plant
garden

Play
area

Outdoor
sitting
area

greywater

Perennial
bed

Fruit trees

greywater

Rain
garden

Sidewalk

rainwater

▶ **Use a bubble diagram to sketch the property with your desired landscape features and water sources.**

draw a detailed landscape plan. Another easy option is to use Google Earth, a free program you can use to print an aerial image (with measurements) of your property.

4. **Think more.** Think about how you currently use the yard, and how you'd like to use it. Do you want an outdoor eating area? Do you want to spend time gardening and growing annuals? Or would you prefer a perennial landscape needing less frequent maintenance? Where will your compost pile go? Do you need a privacy screen from the neighbors? Does your house need summer shade? Are there colors you'd love to see on your way to the front door?

5. **Where is the water?** Identify the areas that can be irrigated with greywater and rainwater (see chapters 4 and 6 for guidance). Locate plants needing supplemental irrigation in these areas.

6. **Experiment with layout.** Use a bubble diagram to locate the features you want to include in the landscape. Think about the yard like rooms in

your house. Draw bubbles showing where each of these outdoor "rooms" will be. Avoid using impermeable surfaces, like concrete, or energy-intensive materials to meet your needs (e.g., if you need a retaining wall, consider using urbanite, pieces of recycled concrete, instead of new material). You may photocopy the original sketch of the property and do multiple bubble diagrams, or cut out the bubbles and move them around on top of a sketch of the property, before finalizing the design. Find what works best for you.

7. **Zoom in for details.** Try out different designs. Look at books for ideas. Walk around your neighborhood. See what specific plants may thrive in your yard. Visualize how these ideas would look. Make lists of plants you'd love to grow. Find out if they do well in your area and would fit in your chosen site. Think about what existing plants in your yard you want to keep and which ones you don't.

8. **Get real.** Now that you have all your ideas and dreams in one place, think about your time and budget constraints. Prioritize things that are feasible for you. Make decisions and "finalize" your sketch. Note that nothing is truly final in a landscape; things are constantly changing.

9. **Take your landscape plan outside.** Now you want to really "see" how your plan will look once implemented. Using the plan, mark out the boundaries of planter beds, pathways, etc. with flour (some people use spray paint, which is very visible but not very eco). Place landscape flags (or make your own flags out of stakes) to indicate where your trees, shrubs, or other large plants will go. Remember to account for the mature size of each plant and give it enough room to grow. If you plan to have any patios or outdoor kitchen areas, mark them off with stakes and string. Visualize how this will all look and feel. Make changes as necessary.

10. **Start small.** Plants and natural environments are dynamic and always changing. Start in the area of highest priority for you. Starting small is doable, and quick and easy successes help motivate you to work up to bigger changes.

When to Consult a Professional or Local Experts

A full landscape redesign is a big investment (of time, and often money). If you're not familiar with local plants and are inexperienced with landscaping, I encourage you to seek out further resources to help ensure your success. Budget permitting, find a landscape professional or permaculture designer (with experience with your preferred type of landscape) to help you with the design process. Or, seek out local cooperative extension offices, master gardener chapters, or trusted nurseries for free help. Many water districts or local nonprofits have public demonstration gardens to highlight local water-wise landscapes. Or check out the U.S. Environmental Protection Agency's (EPA) Water Smart website (see chapter 4 Resources), which includes water-wise plant info for every state.

Irrigation Systems

UNTIL YOU CAN DESIGN YOUR LANDSCAPE to rely on greywater and rainwater alone, your plants will most likely require potable water irrigation. And even your drought-tolerant sections of the yard may need water to become established. There are several options for how to deliver water to the plants, from simple hand watering with a hose to automated drip irrigation systems.

Hand watering and low-tech "drip" systems (a drippy bucket placed near a plant) are low-cost and require very few materials. You also get to spend time outside, getting acquainted with the plants. However, since this method is relatively time-consuming, it's less practical for those with large landscapes.

If you need to invest in a permanent irrigation system, choose drip irrigation instead of spray irrigation. Drip emitters deliver small amounts of water directly to the root zone of the plants. Spray irrigation uses sprinklers or micro-spray emitters, which waste water as some of the tiny droplets blow away or evaporate before soaking into the soil.

Drip Irrigation and Controllers

A drip irrigation system can be controlled manually, or with a basic timer or a more sophisticated automatic controller. With a simple wind-up timer you go outside and turn on your system for a set amount of time (say 20 minutes), then it shuts off by itself. This prevents the system from being left on unintentionally, but it won't irrigate while you're on vacation. If you get an automatic controller, it's a good idea to invest in a "smart" controller, which uses current weather data or soil moisture levels to determine how much water to deliver to the plants. This is a much more water-efficient option than conventional timers that don't reduce irrigation as the seasons change, unless someone remembers to go change them (most people don't). Look for a controller certified by the EPA's WaterSmart program, or talk to a local irrigation specialist for recommendations.

Drip irrigation is suitable for irrigating with rainwater; I'll talk more about this in chapter 7. Greywater systems typically are not compatible with standard drip systems and require a separate irrigation system. See Manufactured Greywater Systems on page 122 for more info.

Soil Food Web

Healthy garden soil is teeming with life. Soil life keeps your plants healthy, making water and nutrients available to them. A cup of soil contains billions of tiny microbes (bacteria and protozoa) and beneficial fungi, as well as earthworms and insects. Referred to as the "soil food web," plant health is directly connected to soil health. Damaged soils can be repaired by reintroducing soil biology through compost, compost tea, or other beneficial soil bacteria–containing organic fertilizer. Nutrients and organic matter in greywater feed these microbes that feed your plants!

Pros: Drip Irrigation

- Delivers water to the root zone of plants; keeps paths and areas between plantings dry

- Saves time

- Timers allow system to work even when you're away, and to water at night when evaporation is relatively low.

- No runoff; water is applied in small quantities to each plant

- No trenching required for the installation

Cons: Drip Irrigation

- Made of plastic (petroleum-based, non-renewable, usually ends up in the landfill)

- Can waste water if a weather-sensitive timer isn't used. Simple timers won't shut systems off during a rainstorm, or reduce usage as daylight shortens.

- Can be damaged by careless digging and rodents; leaking wastes lots of water.

Other Irrigation Tips

When gardening in hot climates, plant closely together so plants shade the soil and reduce evaporation losses, or use a shade cloth over the garden bed during the hottest part of the day. Add compost to increase the water-retention characteristics of the soil. Always heavily mulch!

Over-watering? If your landscape requires supplemental irrigation, learn more about how much to irrigate to avoid over-watering. Using the evapotranspiration rates (ET) — a local weather-based measurement of how much water plants require and how much is lost from the soil — you can fine-tune irrigation to conserve water. See How Much Water Do My Plants Want? (page 65) for details, contact your water department or cooperative extension service for more information, or consult a landscape professional.

Low-Tech Irrigation Systems

Help establish the roots of your new plantings with a low-tech **drip system**. Fill a large plastic jug (1 to 3 gallons) with water, poke a small hole in the bottom, and set it next to the plant. Loosely attach the lid so air can enter and the water slowly drips out. Refill as needed. Another method uses unglazed clay pots for subsurface irrigation. This **olla** (pronounced "oy-yah") **irrigation** is an extremely efficient technique that's been used agriculturally for thousands of years in arid climates. Bury an unglazed bottleneck-shaped pot next to the plant, and water will "leak" out into the root zone, with plant roots sucking it out through hydrostatic pressure as they need it. In the vegetable garden, ollas are best for large annuals like beans, greens, and squash.

▲ **Olla irrigation**

Greywater, Rainwater, and Waterless Toilets

THE REMAINDER OF THIS CHAPTER will introduce you to greywater, rainwater, and waterless toilet systems. I'll discuss how they work, how much water you'll save, how much systems cost, and their general pros and cons. Subsequent chapters teach you how to design and build these systems.

Greywater

Greywater is used water from sinks, showers, baths, and washing machines; it is not wastewater from toilets or laundry loads containing poopy diapers. Plants don't need clean drinking water like we do! Using greywater for irrigation conserves water and reduces the energy, chemicals, and costs involved in treating water to potable quality.

Reusing water that we already have is a simple and commonsense idea. Just use "plant-friendly" soaps (those without salts, boron, or bleach), and you have a good source of irrigation water that's already paid for. Greywater systems save water and more. They can extend the life of a septic system, save time spent on watering, act as "drought insurance" (a source of irrigation during times of extreme water scarcity), and encourage the use of more environmentally friendly products. They also use less energy and fewer chemicals than other forms of wastewater treatment. Chapters 4 and 5 provide how-to instructions for installing a greywater irrigation system in your home.

▶ **House using greywater for irrigation with simple laundry-to-landscape and gravity-fed systems**

Water Savings from Greywater

You can expect to save between 10 and 20 gallons per person per day (or more) from a greywater system, though this number can fluctuate greatly. Studies estimate savings of between 16 and 40 percent of total household use. How much you actually save depends upon how much you currently irrigate, whether you use greywater on existing plants or you plant new ones, and how many greywater sources you can access.

Types of Greywater Systems

There are many types of greywater systems, ranging from simply collecting water in buckets to fully automated irrigation systems. I'll group them according to their relative level of complexity and briefly explain how they work.

"Low-tech" systems for irrigation are the lowest in cost, simplest to install, and easiest to obtain permits for. Common types include **laundry-to-landscape (L2L)** and **branched-drain** systems.

"Medium-tech" systems for irrigation incorporate a tank and pump to send greywater uphill or to pressurize it for drip irrigation (filters are cleaned manually).

"High-tech" systems provide automated drip irrigation or toilet flushing in high-end residential houses and larger-scale commercial or multifamily buildings.

Hurray for the Washing Machine!

Washing machine water is typically the easiest source to reuse; direct greywater from the drain hose of the machine without cutting into the house's plumbing. Each machine has an internal pump that automatically pumps out the water and can be used to direct greywater to the plants.

No-Fuss Gravity Systems from Showers and Baths

Showers and baths are excellent sources of greywater, though accessing the drainpipes may be challenging, depending on their location. A diverter valve placed in the drain line of the shower allows greywater to be diverted to the landscape. Gravity distribution systems are usually cheaper and require less maintenance than pumped systems, and distribute greywater through rigid drainage pipe. Greywater flow is divided into multiple irrigation lines to irrigate trees, bushes, vines, or larger perennials via mulch basins (see Mulch Basins on page 62).

Pumped Systems: Filtered and Unfiltered

Pumped systems push greywater uphill or across long distances. Greywater is diverted into a *surge tank*, from which it's pumped to the landscape. Adding a filter allows greywater to be distributed through smaller tubing, increasing the potential irrigation area but also increasing the cost and maintenance of the system.

Pros: Greywater Systems

- Greywater is produced every day, all year long and is a reliable source of irrigation.

- Simple systems recycle tens of thousands of gallons a year, for a relatively low cost.

- Systems take up little space; often all the pipes are buried and invisible.

- It's easy to irrigate fruit trees, shrubs, and large annuals and perennials.

- It's an automatic watering system, saving time and ensuring plants get watered.

- It reduces wastewater going to the sewer or septic system.

Cons: Greywater Systems

- Accessing greywater may be challenging, depending on how your house and landscape are designed.

- Greywater reuse is not legal in some states.

- Requires use of "plant-friendly" products in the house.

- Small plants, or plants spread out over a large area, are more difficult to irrigate with the simplest systems, though pumped and filtered systems will work.

Cost of Greywater Systems

Materials for simple greywater systems typically cost a few hundred dollars. If you're handy, you can install a system yourself in a day or two. Professional installations range from around $1,000 to many thousands of dollars, depending on the type of system and your site. Chapter 5 includes more details about specific system costs.

Rainwater Harvesting

Collecting rainwater for irrigation or indoor use reduces home water consumption, prevents water pollution, and utilizes a free source of pure water delivered right to the house. The benefits of harvesting the rain are achieved in two ways: By shaping our landscapes to soak rainwater into the ground, we nourish plants, recharge the groundwater table, and prevent urban runoff pollution. By collecting rainwater from our roofs, we rely less on groundwater or limited surface water supplies. Rainwater is the only true source of water "income" to supply our homes, enabling water independence. Looking to the rain as a primary source of water is what societies around the world have done for millennia, and many still do today.

There are two main ways to harvest rainwater: in a tank and in the ground. Roofwater collection directs rainwater or snowmelt into a tank or a barrel. Harvesting rain in the landscape, with rain gardens, directly irrigates plants and recharges the groundwater table. Chapters 6 and 7 lead you through planning, designing, and installing several types of rainwater harvesting systems.

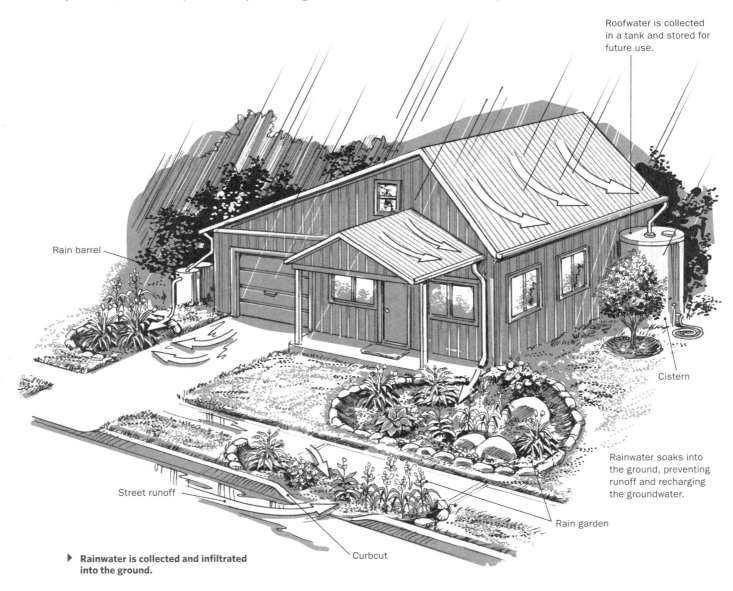

Roofwater is collected in a tank and stored for future use.

Rain barrel

Cistern

Rainwater soaks into the ground, preventing runoff and recharging the groundwater.

Street runoff

Rain garden

Curbcut

▶ **Rainwater is collected and infiltrated into the ground.**

Rain Gardens

What happens when rain falls onto your roof? Where does the water flow? Next time it rains, go outside and watch where the water goes and what it does. There are many strategies to "slow, spread, and sink" rainwater in the landscape, including installing rain gardens and reducing concrete and other impervious surfaces. This improves water quality, recharges groundwater, and reduces peak flood flows. These systems are simple, merely creating space in your yard to allow rainwater to stay.

A **rain garden**, also called a water-harvesting basin or earthwork, is a sunken area of the landscape designed to collect, temporarily store, and infiltrate water into the ground during a rainstorm. Rain gardens work with nature, relying on soil microbes and plants to filter, hold, and soak rainwater into the ground. They are both beautiful and useful; you choose the specific plants to create the aesthetic you want. The plants can provide habitat, grow food, or create color and textures you enjoy, and all the plants are adapted to your climate so they don't need supplemental irrigation.

Roofwater Catchment: Rain Barrels, Tanks, and Cisterns

Rainwater can be stored in any watertight container. The most common types are barrels, tanks, and cisterns.

Rain barrels. The classic 55-gallon rain barrel can be purchased or constructed out of repurposed food-grade barrels. Direct a downspout into the top of the barrel, create an outlet with a garden hose bib at the bottom, make an overflow to the rain garden, and you have a rain barrel system. Connect rain barrels together to increase storage capacity.

Tanks and cisterns. The most basic system collects roofwater via the gutters and stores it in a large tank. Screens keep out leaves and mosquitoes, an overflow directs excess water to a rain garden, and an outlet at the bottom of the tank directs rainwater to a garden hose or drip irrigation system. Some systems use pumps and are equipped to filter water for indoor use. Tanks can range in size from 50 to 50,000 gallons and are typically made from plastic, fiberglass, metal, ferrocement, or wood. Using rainwater indoors saves much more water than using it for irrigation only, but the setup is more complicated and more expensive.

Water Savings from Rainwater Systems

Millions of people around the world, including in the U.S., get all their water from the rain. Even places with low annual rainfall can collect rainwater; you can collect 1,000 gallons from every inch of rain on a 1,500-square-foot house. If you have the space, the rainfall, the money, and the will, you can get off the "water grid" completely with a rainwater-harvesting system — a 100-percent water savings from a municipal or well system. However, most systems are designed to supplement a home's municipal or well supply.

Michael Reynolds, visionary designer of Earthships, believes that anyone can live comfortably on 8 inches of rainfall a year. He practices **multiuse water management**, collecting rainwater for household use, reusing it as greywater for toilet flushing, and using septic effluent for irrigation. The sky is the limit!

Pros: Rainwater Harvesting in the Landscape (Rain Gardens)

- Prevents stormwater runoff and protects waterways

- Conserves water; reduces the amount of irrigation the landscape requires from supplemental supplies

- Cleans soil; rainwater can leach salts in contaminated soils to below the root zone area.

- Promotes groundwater recharge

- Reduces peak flows, mitigating flooding

- Reduces erosion

- Rain gardens are inexpensive and easy to build.

- Gardens serve as visual reminders of the connection between our homes and the health of the watershed.

Pros: Roofwater Catchment

- Free source of water, delivered to your home.

- Great water quality for irrigation; water is distilled and purified as it evaporates from oceans.

- Reduces amount of rainwater delivered to storm drains, minimizing stormwater runoff.

- Reduces amount of water your house consumes.

- Provides emergency water supply.

- Facilitates water self-reliance.

- Rainwater doesn't contain minerals that "hard" groundwater often does, so softening systems are not needed if water is used indoors.

Cons: Rainwater Harvesting and Roofwater Catchment

- Requires space in the yard to infiltrate water.

- Above-ground roofwater catchment requires space for storage containers.

- Some types of systems are expensive and require special skills to install.

- Roofwater catchment systems aren't legal in some places.

Costs for Rainwater Systems

The costs of rainwater harvesting systems vary greatly. If you do the work yourself, you can create rain gardens for the cost of the plants and soil amendments. Larger projects may require the help of a contractor and/or an excavator, or a lot of friends with shovels!

Roofwater harvesting can also be very low-cost if you acquire used storage containers and do the work yourself. If you buy a new tank, costs typically range from 50 cents to one dollar per gallon of storage; larger tanks cost more but usually have a lower dollar-per-gallon price than smaller tanks. Plastic tanks tend to be the lowest in cost, but this depends on your site specifics. Indoor-reuse systems cost more up front, require a skilled installer, and may involve permitting challenges depending on where you live; costs range from $1.50 to $3 per gallon of storage.

Waterless Toilets

Waterless toilets, also called **dry** or **composting toilets**, turn human pee and poo into fertilizer, using microbes and bacteria to break down and digest the material. They can replace flush toilets to save water, protect the environment, and reconnect nutrient cycles. Waterless toilets work in both rural and urban homes and don't rely on expensive sewer infrastructure or septic systems. For most homeowners, a composting toilet requires a fundamental shift in thinking about waste: it doesn't get flushed away. (Have you ever wondered: where is "away," anyhow?)

Waterless toilets require more attention than flush toilets, which may cause some people to feel uncomfortable, but it's actually not bad at all. Anyone with the experience of raising a child is more than qualified for managing a toilet; it's easier than dealing with poopy diapers! I've heard from many composting toilet users that they quickly became comfortable with their toilets, and that this experience has changed their notion of what they consider disgusting. How gross is mixing everyone's poop together with drinking water and commercial and industrial wastewater, then dumping it (often untreated) into a bay, lake, river, or ocean where people swim and fish? Chapter 8 provides detailed how-to info on choosing, constructing, and maintaining composting toilets.

Types of Toilets

Composting toilets range from a simple homemade sawdust bucket toilet to a manufactured toilet complete with a special chamber that heats and mixes the material to speed up the natural decomposition process. From the most simple to the most complex, all composting toilets rely on natural processes to "compost" the waste. Toilets differ in size, style, and aesthetics. Some toilets divert urine, others don't. Some use electricity, others don't. Some require maintenance weekly, some monthly, and others even less often. Composting toilets can also be used in commercial-scale applications.

Sawdust bucket. If you're looking for a low-cost toilet and don't mind a weekly chore, consider the sawdust bucket toilet. It's simple, straightforward, and easy to maintain. Developed by Joseph Jenkins, composting toilet researcher and author of the classic book *The Humanure Handbook* (see Resources), the sawdust toilet is used all over the country, from urban San Francisco to rural homesteads. How it works: The toilet seat sits above a 5-gallon bucket that collects pee and poo. (A pretty wooden box conceals the bucket.) Add wood shavings after each use and empty the bucket when it fills up into an outdoor compost chamber to process. For higher-use situations (like large parties or festivals), a larger container, such as a wheeled garbage bin, collects the material. Read how to build a sawdust toilet on page 230.

Manufactured composting toilets. Manufactured toilets range from small, seasonal-use toilets to porcelain models that "flush" with a few ounces of liquid, flowing urine and feces to a large composting chamber below the bathroom. Chapter 8 discusses manufactured toilets in detail.

Water Savings from a Composting Toilet

The conventional flush toilet is one of the largest water users in the home, accounting for up to one-third of all indoor water use. Depending on your toilet and flushing habits, you'll see savings of 18 to 30 percent of total indoor consumption.

Pros: Composting Toilets

- Save water, up to one-third of indoor use

- Prevent pollution of waterways by keeping nutrients like nitrogen and phosphorus on land and out of the water

- Function anywhere; they are autonomous from sewer and septic systems.

- Create a cultural shift, demonstrating a respect for water

- Promote public health; prevent infections by keeping waterborne pathogens out of water where people swim

Cons: Composting Toilets

- Space restraints may limit toilet options in some houses.

- Some designs require space outside for composting area.

- Require maintenance by someone comfortable managing excreta

- Visitors and guests may not be accustomed to a waterless toilet and need education (although this is also a potential benefit).

- Having pee and poo in the home may represent downward mobility to some, particularly people who grew up without indoor plumbing.

Costs for a Composting Toilet

You can make your own sawdust bucket toilet for 20 dollars using salvaged materials, spend a few hundred dollars on a nicer-looking model, or invest thousands on a large manufactured toilet system. The cost depends on several factors: whether you need the toilet for seasonal or year-round use, your site constraints, the aesthetics of the toilet, and how much maintenance you're willing to perform. Toilets for year-round use that look like a "regular" toilet and require relatively little maintenance will cost more.

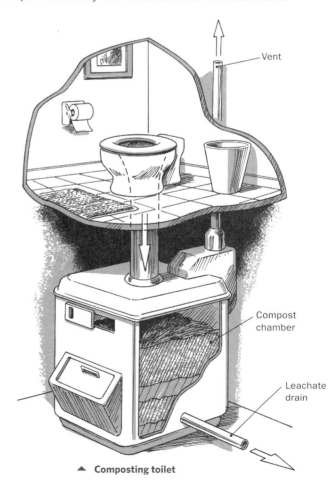

Vent

Compost chamber

Leachate drain

▲ **Composting toilet**

My Journey

IN AUGUST 2012 I sat in a radio studio talking about greywater with my former plumbing teacher, and Oakland's senior inspector, Jeff Hutcher, on American Public Media's *The Story*. When I met Jeff in 1999, I never would have imagined this moment. I was a student in his residential plumbing class, seeking to learn hands-on skills to build sustainable water systems. He was horrified to hear about my "Frankenstein" greywater systems and refused to answer questions about my then-illegal plumbing systems in class (he was, after all, a city inspector). Now, he and I work together to streamline permits and facilitate legal reuse of greywater.

For the past 15 years I've designed and built simple residential water reuse systems: greywater systems, rainwater catchment, and composting toilets. Once my friend and housemate Cleo Woelfle-Erskine and I cut into our home's plumbing to run the shower water outside, I couldn't imagine ever again letting this good irrigation water escape to the sewer. We taught our friends and wrote about the how and the why of it. Our group, the "Greywater Guerrillas," grew out of these projects. Later, we worked on an anthology, *Dam Nation: Dispatches from the Water Underground,* which placed greywater reuse, rainwater catchment, and composting toilets in the larger political context of water issues around the globe.

Some genuine plumbers joined our group: Christina Bertea, the first woman admitted into Local 159, Plumbers and Steamfitters Union, and Andrea Lara, then an apprentice. With their involvement we honed our skills and revamped our designs. Andrea, Christina, and I taught dozens of hands-on workshops all over the Bay Area and southern California. As our state entered a multi-year drought, we couldn't keep up with the demand. Every workshop filled up, along with the wait list. I gave talks at green-living festivals, universities, and churches, even high schools.

Since all our work was illegal, according to state plumbing code at the time, we became involved in changing the code. In 2009 the State of California overhauled its greywater code, making many greywater systems legal. That same year we renamed our group "Greywater Action: For a Sustainable Water Culture," to represent our goals and strategies to a diverse audience.

We continue to teach hands-on workshops, and have expanded to train professionals who want to offer these services to their clients. In our one-week class we teach people theory and hands-on skills, culminating with their installing a real system on the last day of class. Over a hundred people from across the U.S. and Canada have graduated and now champion greywater in their communities. Their systems, businesses, and workshops are the ripple effects.

Putting Hands — and Imaginations — to Work

Now I live in Los Angeles and my drinking water comes from far away. How do I teach my young child the importance of conserving water when he's never seen the source?

When he blasts the water to wash his hands or help with the dishes, I remind him, "What do the fishies say?"

"What?" he asks.

"They say, 'Hey! Stop wasting water! We need it in the rivers so we can swim and breathe.'"

We can use our imaginations to teach our children, and our hands to re-create our water systems. I look forward to the day when anyone who *doesn't* reuse greywater is on the fringe — when, after a rain, we all have full tanks and pooling rain gardens, rather than rivers in the streets.

PART 2

WATER-WISE SOLUTIONS

|||||||||||||||||||||||||||||||||||||||||||||||||||||||||||||||||||||||||||||||||||||||||||||||||||||||||||||||||||||||

Creating Sustainable Water Systems for Your Home

AFTER INCREASING THE WATER EFFICIENCY of your home and landscape, the next step is implementing one or more sustainable water systems: greywater, rainwater, and waterless toilets. Whether you do the work yourself or hire a contractor, there are many simple and effective options.

The chapters of this section will lead you through the planning, design, and implementation steps of several types of systems. Retrofitting a house with a greywater system is a very site-specific project: your home's plumbing configuration and your property's landscape have a big influence on what kind of system is most appropriate. Similarly, your rainwater system is influenced by your roof size, climate, and budget. Careful planning will help you choose the best system for your situation, the one that maximizes your reuse potential for the lowest cost and least amount of maintenance.

Now it's time to begin viewing your home and landscape through the lenses of a water harvester. From the interior plumbing to the roof and gutters to the yard's ground contours, you'll be assessing where water flows and how you can direct it to irrigate your productive, ecological landscape.

4

Greywater Reuse: Planning Your Home System

IF YOU'RE LIKE MOST PEOPLE, you wash clothes, take showers, and run water down the sink. Why let this good irrigation water go to waste? Surely you've heard the expression, "Don't throw the baby out with the bathwater." Now, let's stop throwing out the bathwater!

In this chapter I'll take you through the initial design and planning steps for building a greywater system that's tuned to match your water usage, your home's plumbing, and your landscape. You'll learn how to estimate how much greywater your home produces, identify the greywater sources you can tap into, and test your soil and size the mulch basins (to receive the greywater in your landscape). You'll also learn what plants grow well with greywater and which soaps and products are safe to use. After you've done the preparation work, chapter 5 will take you step-by-step through the installation of various systems.

Don't forget to start with efficiency. If you skipped chapter 3, go back to make sure your home is water-efficient. Remember, fixing leaks and upgrading fixtures can reduce indoor water consumption by around 35 percent.

IN THIS CHAPTER:

Identify Your Greywater Sources

IF YOU'RE HOPING TO USE GREYWATER from your existing home, you'll find that some greywater sources are easier to access than others. If you're building a new home, you have much more flexibility as to which sources you tap into — and where. Diverting greywater from drainpipes often requires installing a diverter valve (called a 3-way valve) that enables you to switch the water flow between the drain line (leading to the sewer or septic system) and the greywater system. Diverter valves can be operated manually or remotely, via an electrical switch. First we'll look at the primary potential sources for greywater in a home, then we'll discuss the details of tapping into a home's drain system.

Clothes Washers

Washing machines are the easiest source of greywater to reuse. The machine's internal pump pushes greywater out through the machine's drain hose; from there you can reroute it to the landscape without changing the existing drainpipes. I've worked on hundreds of laundry greywater systems, and they're consistently the easiest and simplest of the greywater options.

In most homes, a greywater pipe begins its route toward the landscape by exiting the laundry room through the wall or floor. Think about how you could send a new pipe from your washing machine out to the landscape. Can you go out through the wall or down into a crawl space and then outside? If your house has a concrete slab foundation and your machine is in a room with interior walls, the only way to send the water outside is to run the pipe through another room in the house, perhaps hidden under shelving or along a baseboard.

It is easy to live with a laundry greywater system. There are several commonly available greywater-compatible detergents that allow you to safely irrigate plants with the greywater from regular laundry loads. For times when you want to use bleach or wash soiled diapers, just turn the valve located next to the washing machine and redirect the water to the original drain.

Showers and Baths

Showers and baths produce large volumes of good irrigation water, although diverting it to the yard may be tricky, particularly in existing homes. The next section will help you navigate your drainpipes to identify these potential greywater sources. If you are inexperienced with plumbing, this aspect may feel confusing; consider finding a handy friend or plumber to be your reading buddy. Or, read on to develop your greywater sleuthing skills: it can be fun and empowering to uncover the mysteries of the household plumbing system.

Greywater or Graywater?

People often wonder why *greywater* is spelled two different ways. All around the world greywater is spelled with an e, except by a few groups in the U.S., mostly regulators who write state codes (though some states, like Washington, use the e spelling). I like the e spelling to intentionally connect greywater to the global movement around water.

Bathroom Sinks (Lavatories)

Bathroom sinks typically produce such small quantities of greywater that they don't warrant a big investment for a system, though sometimes it's easy to reuse the water. In my house the downstairs sink was easy to divert to irrigate a nearby pomegranate bush and male kiwi vine, whereas the upstairs sink would have been more involved, so we just detached the drain to "bucket-flush" the toilet (we were careful to plug the drain line to prevent sewer gases from entering the bathroom).

Easy options include:

- Combine the sink greywater drain with the shower/bath drain and divert the greywater after both sources have combined.

- Install a diverter valve under the sink and direct water to one or two nearby plants in a tiny branched drain system.

- Alternatively, disconnect the sink drain and collect greywater in a bucket to bucket-flush the toilet. Experiment to find out how much water it takes to flush your toilet: empty the bucket directly into the toilet bowl (not the tank), and the toilet will flush.

- Install a SinkPositive system: a faucet and tank that replace the toilet tank lid (see Resources). When you flush the toilet, fill-water flows out the sink so you can wash your hands as the toilet tank refills.

There are manufactured greywater systems designed to collect, filter, and disinfect bathroom sink greywater below the sink and then pump it into the toilet tank for flushing. I know a few people who have tried these systems, and each had numerous problems with them. Consider other options first if you plan to reuse sink water.

Kitchen Sinks

Kitchen sinks usually produce a plentiful supply of water that can be diverted from the sink drain inside the house. Kitchen greywater tends to contain food scraps and grease, so it takes more effort to maintain the system than with other greywater sources.

Some states consider kitchen water "greywater," while others consider it "blackwater," like what comes out of the toilets. If your state doesn't call kitchen water "grey," a legal installation will be more challenging. With determination and an open-minded building department, it's possible to get an experimental permit or use the "alternative materials and methods" section of your state's code.

Divert kitchen water directly below the sink for easy access to the pipes and diverter valve. The greywater pipe needs a route to the landscape, and you can send it below the floor or directly out of the house, depending on your situation and climate. Local code may require the diverter valve be located downstream of the vent connection.

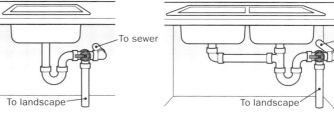

▲ **Single sink basin with diverter valve**

▲ **Double sink basin with diverter valve**

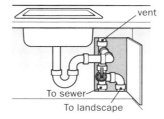
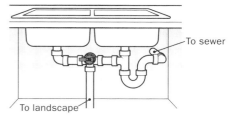

▲ **Installation of diverter valve after the vent connection**

▲ **Double sink basin with one side of sink connected to greywater system**

Filtering Kitchen Greywater with Mulch Basins

The challenge with a kitchen sink greywater system is the gunk. First, make sure you have a fine screen in the sink to catch food BEFORE it goes down the drain. If you have a double sink, consider plumbing just one side to the greywater system and using the other side for the dirtiest, greasiest dishes. Next, think about where the food particles that make it past your screen will end up. Do you want to have a pre-filter before the irrigation system to catch them? A wood-chip biofilter? Wetland filter? Sand filter? Screen? Worm bin? If these sound like good ideas, think again. Whatever you use to catch the organics will quickly clog, causing a backup or overflow of greywater, plus more maintenance to clean it.

Kitchen greywater creates a unique type of gunk that is merciless on filters. For years I pre-filtered the kitchen water as part of my greywater system. For years I cleaned out disgusting screens, sand, wood-chip filters, wetland filters. The last straw: I came home from a particularly long day at work to see that my wood-chip biofilter had clogged (again) and kitchen sink water was pouring out the top of the filter and running down the side of my house.

Then I found a simple solution: mulch basins (see page 62). These are depressions in the soil, filled with wood chips that catch organic matter and infiltrate greywater into the soil. Instead of sending all the water to one basin, divide up the flow to multiple basins. This **branched drain system** requires less frequent maintenance since each basin receives only a portion of the total flow. Organic matter in the greywater decomposes in the basins and is eaten by earthworms.

The first time I dug under my kitchen sink outlets, I was amazed to see the soil beneath the mulch swarming with earthworms. In the past, I'd only seen failed experiments in which the kitchen water flowed directly through a worm bin before the irrigation system. It's hard to keep worms happy when they're doused with water on a daily basis; they leave or die. In the mulch basin system, worms can come and go as they please, eating organic debris from the greywater. Eventually the wood chips will clog and decompose, slowing the infiltration. Maintenance is easy: grab a shovel, dig out the decomposed material, and replace with fresh wood chips.

Other people have had success sending unfiltered kitchen water to large, underground "infiltration galleys" (see Sewerless Homes on page 126 for more details).

Your Home's Drain, Waste, and Vent System

YOUR HOME PLUMBING SYSTEM is actually made up of three different systems: the water supply, the drainage/waste system, and the venting system. Drain pipes and vents are connected and commonly referred to as the **drain-waste-vent (DWV) system**. *Water supply pipes* are much smaller in diameter (typically ¾ inch and smaller) than drainpipes (1½ inches and larger) and are full of pressurized water — not a pipe you want to cut into by mistake! *Supply pipes* are commonly made of copper or galvanized steel pipe or CPVC or PEX plastic tubing. *Drainpipes* may be made from cast iron, galvanized steel, copper, or PVC or ABS plastic pipe.

The drain or waste system carries wastewater away from the fixtures to the sewer line or septic system. The venting system is composed of pipes traveling up through the roof, to safely release sewer gases away from your living space and to introduce air into the system. The air prevents a suction effect that can slow the travel of water (think of how holding your finger over the end of drinking straw "magically" keeps the liquid suspended inside the straw; without venting, the same thing can happen in a drainpipe).

Drainpipes serving sinks, tubs, and other fixtures have **traps**, simple devices to separate the open end of the drain from the sewer end, keeping sewer gases from rising into the living space. The U-shaped section of pipe under your bathroom or kitchen sink is called a **P-trap**. Toilets have traps built into their bases. The bend in a trap retains enough water at all times to seal off the drainpipe; it's self-replenishing and refills every time water flows through the pipe. Allowing air into the system via vents maintains an equilibrium in the pipes so the water in the traps isn't siphoned out. Before homes were plumbed with vents, sewer stench (as well as the occasional explosion due to buildup of sewer gas) was commonplace.

If you look under your bathroom or kitchen sink, you'll see the P-trap between the sink outlet and a horizontal pipe leading to a hole in the wall. Behind the wall is the vent (going upward) and the drainpipe (sloping downward) connecting to other drainpipes and ultimately to the main drain of the house. Sewer gases rise up and exit the vent above the house, while greywater and blackwater (from the toilets) flow downward to the sewer or septic system. All the drainpipes should have a **cleanout**, a Y-shaped fitting (or a short section of pipe) with a removable cap so you can get inside the pipes to clean out clogs in the system.

For a well-functioning DWV system it's important that the pipes and vents are large enough to accommodate the flows inside them and that they are sloped properly to avoid blockages. Greywater drainpipes typically are 1½-inch pipe and larger (the outside pipe diameter will be closer to 2 inches), while toilet pipes are 3 inches or larger. Each fixture must be vented, either with its own vent or through a secondary vent connected to the main vent (the uppermost portion of the main drainpipe, sometimes called the "stack"). In general, any reference to pipe size (for example, a "2-inch pipe") refers to the *inside* diameter of the pipe: the *outside* diameter is larger and varies depending on the pipe material. The outside of a 2-inch copper pipe is smaller than a 2-inch cast iron pipe, even though they have the same inside diameter.

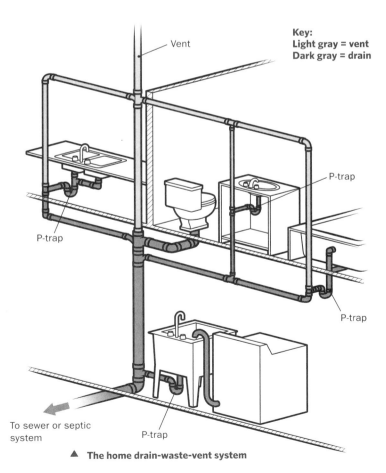

Vent

Key:
Light gray = vent
Dark gray = drain

P-trap

P-trap

P-trap

P-trap

To sewer or septic system

P-trap

▲ **The home drain-waste-vent system**

Examining Your Pipes for Diverter Valve Locations

While some older houses (in mild climates) may have exterior drain and vent pipes, most homes have internal piping running inside the wall and floor structures. Drainpipes for greywater systems often are accessed in a basement or crawl space. Unfortunately, houses with slab foundations have their greywater pipes buried in concrete; these pipes are much more difficult to access. If you live in an old house, keep in mind that it may not be properly plumbed. For example, you may find the water from two showers flowing out a drainpipe that is sized for just one bathroom sink. Always confirm you have identified the right drainpipe by running hot water in the fixture you believe it is connected to. The drainpipe will feel warm if your sleuthing is correct.

Diverter Valve Basics

As you assess pipes for potential greywater use, focus on finding a location for the diverter valve. To install the valve you'll remove a section of the drainpipe and essentially splice the valve into the pipe. The best location for the valve depends on the source of greywater (sink, shower, etc.) and your home's plumbing configuration. In most situations, the valve should be installed after the vent extends upwards and it **must** be installed **before** the connection to the

toilet drain, a 3-inch or larger pipe. You'll need about 7 inches of straight pipe to fit the valve in.

If there is not a large enough section of straight pipe to fit the diverter into, you'll need to reconfigure the plumbing to create room. If you're new to plumbing, this is an excellent time to get assistance from an experienced plumber.

Houses with Internal Plumbing

To identify first-floor shower pipes, go into the crawl space or basement and look for a P-trap. You may even see part of the bathtub above the P-trap. To make sure you have the correct pipe, run hot water down the drain of the tub or shower and feel which pipe heats up. Second-floor shower drains are commonly combined with the toilet drain before dropping down to the crawl space in a 3-inch pipe — but not always. Check for 2-inch pipes below an upper-story bathroom; run hot water in the shower and feel if the pipe heats up.

The DWV system of some homes is plumbed inside the walls, with no convenient crawl space to access the drains. During a remodel, or by removing a section of the wall, a diverter valve can be installed with an access hatch, to direct greywater to the landscape. In the lower image opposite, the shower drain is inside the wall and combines with the toilet drain.

Stay safe in the crawl space: The crawl space may not be the safest place, especially if your house is old. Before crawling under, check for potential hazards lurking below such as mold, damaged asbestos pipes, standing water or wet areas that could cause electric shock if the wiring is improperly installed, spiders, or animal presence (you don't want to encounter an angry raccoon when you're crawling on your belly with no quick escape route!). After you have identified potential hazards, take the necessary precautions to stay safe (gloves, respirator mask, eye protection, thick clothing covering all your skin, flashlight, turn off the power, etc.). If wild animals nest under your house, wait till they've left, then board up their entrance before you begin looking for potential greywater sources.

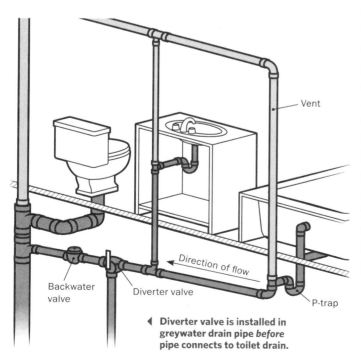

Vent

Direction of flow

Backwater valve

Diverter valve

P-trap

◀ **Diverter valve is installed in greywater drain pipe *before* pipe connects to toilet drain.**

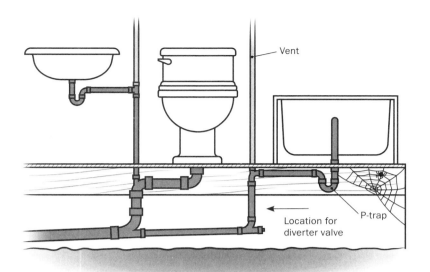

Vent

Location for diverter valve

P-trap

▲ **Internal plumbing. Plumbing is accessible in the crawlspace under this first-floor bathroom. Note potential location for diverter valve.**

Houses with External Plumbing

If you see pipes running up and down the outside of a wall near a bathroom, these are likely to be exterior vent and drain pipes. Exterior pipes make it easy to identify greywater sources, and you can divert the water without slithering under the house.

Since exterior pipes from a bathroom may contain any combination of sink, shower, and toilet, take care to properly identify what fixtures flow into the pipes. For example, a 2-inch or larger pipe that you believe is the shower drain may also contain the sink water. Test the pipes by running hot water from both fixtures. Also, note where the fixture's drainpipe enters the exterior pipe. Sometimes this isn't obvious. The tee fitting may be buried in stucco or covered with siding. If you accidentally cut into the pipe too high you will be in the vent, where no greywater flows.

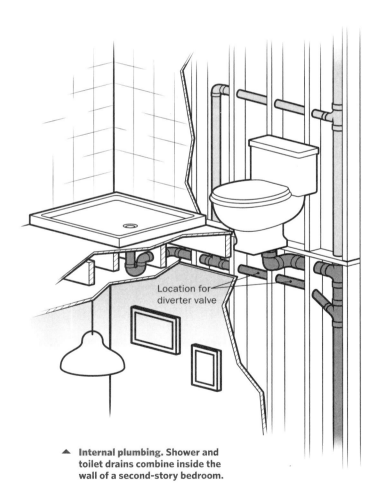

Location for diverter valve

▲ **Internal plumbing. Shower and toilet drains combine inside the wall of a second-story bedroom.**

Solutions for Greywater Pipes Buried in the Wall/Floor/Ceiling

It takes more effort (and cost) to access greywater pipes inside the wall or floor. Often this requires cutting a section out of the floor/wall/ceiling to access the pipe and install the valve, as well as making an inspection hatch or access door so you can get to the valve to control the flow of greywater. An alternative for a bathtub drain is to elevate the tub on a platform to create room for the valve in the drain before it goes into the floor; however, this is a big project.

If your shower pipes are buried in a concrete slab foundation, you have a few options. During a remodel, keep the shower pipe separate from the toilet until they're outside the house, where you can install a valve in a subsurface access box. Or, elevate the tub and install the valve in the drain before the pipes enter the slab.

If you can't feasibly access the pipes, consider using buckets or siphons, or installing an alternate shower that is greywater accessible.

Notice in the left-hand drawing below the shower drainpipe combines with the toilet drainpipe before exiting the wall. To divert this shower, a diverter valve would be located under the floor of the bathroom. The shower drainpipe in the drawing on the right exits the house separately from the toilet drainpipe. Locate the diverter valve anywhere along the drainpipe. Place the valve to collect from the desired fixtures, and in the most accessible location.

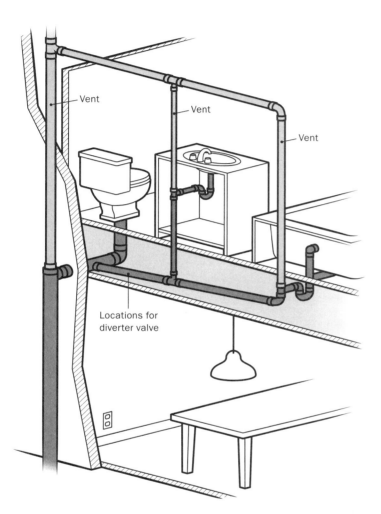

Vent

Vent

Vent

Locations for diverter valve

▲ **External plumbing. Shower and toilet drains combine in the floor.**

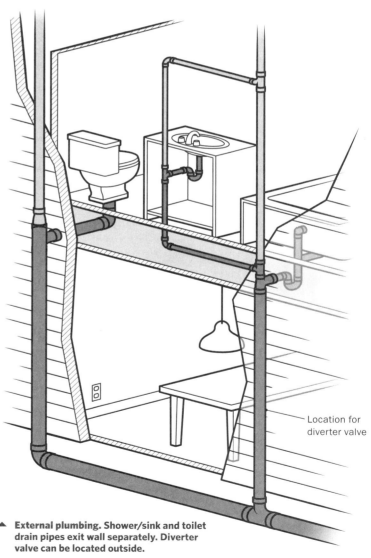

Location for diverter valve

▲ **External plumbing. Shower/sink and toilet drain pipes exit wall separately. Diverter valve can be located outside.**

Undesirable Greywater Sources

Not all sources of household water are appropriate to reuse in a backyard system. Don't use:

- Dishwasher drain water. Dishwasher detergents are high in salt. If you don't have a sewer/septic option, send the dishwasher water to irrigate salt-tolerant plants.

- Water drained from any sinks that receive chemicals, such as in darkrooms

- Softened water from a sodium-based water softener; such water contains salts that are harmful to plants. Use a potassium-based softener or magnetic softener instead if you want to reuse the greywater.

- Water softener backwash; also high in salts

- Toilet wastewater. *Never* put toilet wastewater into a greywater system.

Summary of Greywater Sources

Here's a quick rundown of the major greywater sources, including the advantages and disadvantages of using each source.

Clothes Washer

Advantages: The washer's internal pump and flexible drain hose make accessing water easy and allow you to tap into the system without altering the existing plumbing. It's usually easy to send a new greywater pipe outside, either through a crawl space or through a wall. It's also easy to turn off the system if there is too much water or you want to use bleach in a wash load.

Disadvantages: The machine's internal pump is not strong enough to pump water uphill or across long distances, and the system is unable to distribute water over a large area.

Notes: If the laundry is in an interior room and there is no crawl space or basement, sending a pipe outside can be relatively difficult or impractical. Many states do not require a permit for a washing machine system that does not alter the existing household plumbing.

Showers and Baths

Advantages: Often the largest and cleanest source of greywater.

Disadvantages: Installing the diverter valve can be tricky, depending on the configuration of the existing plumbing. There must be room to access and alter the drainage plumbing, either in a basement or crawl space or below the floor.

Notes: If you have old plumbing or a tricky install, or you are not experienced with plumbing, consider hiring someone to install the diverter valve. Installations on showers on a concrete slab or in a second-story bathroom can be difficult or impractical. Consider an outdoor shower if you are unable to capture from the indoor shower(s).

Bathroom Sink (Lavatory)

Advantages: Easy access to greywater from under the sink. Often easy to combine the sink drain with the shower drain under the bathroom

Disadvantages: Small quantity of water with relatively high concentration of soap

Kitchen Sink

Advantages: Able to access water under the sink. Organic matter from food particles creates compost and is good for gardens.

Disadvantages: Because there is additional organic matter in kitchen greywater, the systems are more prone to clogging.

Notes: Some states don't consider kitchen greywater "grey"; they classify it with the toilet wastewater and don't allow legal reuse. If the sink is a double sink, consider hooking up just one side to the system (the side without the garbage disposer, if there is one).

Estimate Your Greywater Flows

HOW MUCH GREYWATER YOUR HOME PRODUCES depends on the number of people in your house, your water use habits, and your fixtures and appliances. On average, each American produces between 20 and 40 gallons per day of greywater. It's important to get the most accurate estimate you can

Greywater Pioneer: Art Ludwig

ART LUDWIG IS AN ecological systems designer with 30 years of experience in the field. He has studied and worked in 22 countries, authored books on greywater and water storage, and created the first "greywater-compatible" soap, designed to break down into plant nutrients (see Resources). His book, *Create an Oasis with Greywater,* often referred to as the greywater bible, shares decades of experience along with original designs of the popular laundry-to-landscape and branched drain systems.

What advice do you have for people wanting to install a greywater system?

Choose the simplest possible approach and implement it as well as possible.

What's your all-time favorite greywater system?

My favorite greywater system is the first branched drain system I built. I thought it would fail in a day, but it didn't. If fact, I couldn't get it to fail no matter what I did. Even after putting pure kitchen sink water down and then removing the screen in my sink and dumping compost scraps down it, nothing failed (except the sink trap clogged). Everything that made it past the trap flowed out to the mulch basin via a "free flow outlet," with no odors, no clogging, and no problems.

before designing your system, to avoid over- or under-watering your plants.

If your project involves a permit, you may be required to use a method specific to your state or local code (see Sample "Code-Type" Estimate for Greywater Production on facing page). Yet even if you use a code method, it's a very good idea to also use the method described below, because it's specific to your habits and therefore gives you the best estimate for how much irrigation water is available.

State codes tend to overestimate greywater flows. This ensures the system is large enough to handle volume increases — not a bad idea if your in-laws decide to move in. The downside is that when the home produces less greywater than estimated, the system will be overbuilt, cost more, and may not irrigate properly. In places with tiny yards, this could prohibit a legal installation due to an insufficient landscape area to accommodate the oversized system. If your system does not involve a permit, you're better off avoiding the code method since it's not very accurate.

To estimate how much greywater your household produces, you'll need a few pieces of information:

1. The flow rates of your fixtures.

2. The bathing and laundry habits of everyone who lives in your house (number and length of showers per week, number of baths per week, and loads of laundry washed).

3. Information regarding future changes in occupants or habits. For example, are you about to have a baby? If so, laundry use will increase. Are your kids leaving for college soon? If so, shower use will decrease.

Design your system using the most accurate estimate for the foreseeable future, and consider ways to adapt for future changes. For example, a greywater shower system may be a perfect fit with kids leaving for college and new trees needing irrigation: the young trees will benefit from the extra greywater while the kids are still at home, and once the trees are established they can survive on less when the kids leave. If your usage is going to increase, think about how you might expand the system or create another zone to utilize more water.

Calculating Weekly Greywater Flows

Use the following formulas to calculate your weekly greywater output. Also see Find the Flow Rates of Showerheads, Faucets, and Washing Machines (page 56) to determine actual flow rates of your fixtures.

Washing machine: *Weekly production: ___ gal/load (the rating of your washing machine) × ___ loads/week = ___ gal/week.*

Also calculate the maximum daily flow from your washing machine so you can appropriately size the landscape area to avoid pooling or runoff of greywater. For example, if you do all the laundry on Saturdays, you'll need a larger infiltration area than if you spread out the laundry over the week.

Maximum daily flow from washing machine: ___ gal/load (the rating of your machine) × ___ loads on a typical laundry day = ___ max gal/day.

Showers: *___ gal/min (or gpm, which is the flow rate of your showerhead) × ___ min/shower × ___ # of showers/week (if people in the house take different lengths of showers, alter this formula accordingly) = ___ gal/week. (Repeat this formula as needed for each person in the home.)*

Typical shower flow rates are 1.5 gpm to 2.5 gpm.

Baths: *___ gal/bath (typically between 30 and 45 gallons) × ___ baths/week = ___ gal/week.*

Bathroom sinks: *___ gal/min × ___ min/use × ___uses /day × = ___ gal/day × ___ 7 (days in week) = ___ gal/week*

Bathroom sinks are typically 2 gpm to 2.2 gpm, or 2 gallons per person per day (gpcd).

Kitchen sinks: *___ gal/min × ___ min/use × ___ uses/day = ___ gal/day × ___ 7 (days in week) = ___ gal/week.*

Kitchen sinks are typically 2 gpm to 2.2 gpm, or 3 to 8 gallons per person per day (gpcd).

Sample "Code-Type" Estimate for Greywater Production

Note: This example uses the California plumbing code; other states may use different numbers.

Step 1: Determine the number of people in the home based on the number of bedrooms. Count two occupants for the first bedroom and one occupant in each additional bedroom. It doesn't matter how many people actually live in the house.

Step 2: Calculate daily water use. Showers, bathtubs, and bathroom (lavatory) sinks (combined) produce 25 gallons per day (gpd) per occupant. Washing machines produce 15 gpd per occupant.

Step 3: Multiply the number of occupants (based on Step 1's result) by the water use (per occupant) to determine the total estimated greywater produced daily:

Number of occupants × greywater flow per occupant = total estimated greywater flow

For example, a three-bedroom home would produce:
Number of occupants: Four (two in first bedroom, one in each of the other bedrooms)
Shower water use: 25 gpd × 4 occupants = 100 gallons per day or 700 gallons per week
Washing machine greywater: 15 gpd × 4 people = 60 gallons per day or 420 gallons per week
Total greywater = 160 gallons per day or 7 × 160 = 1,120 gallons per week

If two people lived in this home, they would probably produce much less greywater than 160 gallons per day (1,120 gallons per week), especially using water-efficient fixtures. To comply with a code using this method, the occupants would size the infiltration area of the system to accommodate 160 gallons per day of greywater. Some codes allow alternative estimation methods, such as reduced estimates in homes with water-efficient fixtures.

Find the Flow Rates of Faucets, Showerheads, and Washing Machines

Most fixtures have their flow rates printed on them in small type, though their actual flow rate may be different due to variations in water pressure. Finding the actual flow rate is easy, especially if you have a helper. If you find that your showerhead uses more than 2.5 gpm, replace it!

MATERIALS

Large container, such as a 5-gallon bucket or large pot

Timer that measures seconds

Container that measures gallons (such as a gallon-size milk jug)

Calculating Faucet or Showerhead Flow

1. Turn on the shower or sink faucet full-blast.

2. Using the timer, fill the large container for exactly 1 minute.

3. Pour the water into the 1-gallon container to find the flow rate. Round to the nearest ¼ gallon. This is your fixture's flow rate in gallons per minute (gpm).

Calculating Washing Machine Gallons per Load (using one of the following methods):

1. Get a large container (or several smaller ones) and fill it from the drain hose of the machine as you wash a load of laundry. (You must first remove the drain hose from the standpipe or utility sink and detach anything holding it in place.) If you have a top-loader, be prepared to collect up to 50 gallons of water!

2. Call a retailer or manufacturer that carries the same brand machine you have and ask them the typical gallons per load of your machine. This info is not easy to find on the Internet. Keep in mind that many machines now adjust water use based on the size of the load, which makes it harder to determine a "typical" load.

Compare Your Results to a Water Bill

After calculating your weekly water use, compare the results to a winter water bill, a time of year when you do not irrigate. Greywater is typically 75 percent of total indoor use. For example, if you estimated 80 gallons of greywater per day, and your December water bill shows 110 gallons per day, your estimate is close to 75 percent (110 gallons × 0.75 = 82.5 gallons). If your number is not close to 75 percent of the winter bill, go back and check your results. If you feel confident your usage estimates are accurate and your estimate is much lower than what the bill shows, you may have a water leak.

Sample Calculation of Greywater Irrigation Potential

Here's an example of how four people in a household can calculate their total gallons-per-week greywater output, and thus their irrigation potential.

Shower: Two people take one 3-minute shower every day. Two people take 8-minute showers four times a week. The showerhead's flow rate is 2.0 gpm.

2 gpm (showerhead flow rate) × 3 (minutes) × 7 (showers per week) × 2 (people) = 84 gallons

2 gpm (showerhead flow rate) × 8 (minutes) × 4 (showers per week) 2 (people) = 128 gallons

Total gallons per week = 84 + 128 = **212 gallons per week**

Bathroom sink: 1.5 gpm × 1 minute per person per day.

1.5 gallons × 4 (people) × 7 (days in week) = **42 gallons per week**

Washing machine: The entire household does five loads of laundry each week. Their machine uses 20 gallons per load.

5 (loads per week) × 20 (gallons per load) = **100 gallons per week**

Kitchen sink: Flow rate of the sink is 2 gpm. The household estimated that each day they use the sink for 4 minutes on breakfast dishes, and use dishpans for the dinner dishes (2 gallons to wash and 3 gallons to rinse).

2 (gpm) × 4 (minutes) + 5 gallons (tubs) = 13 gallons per day

13 × 7 (days in week) = **91 gallons per week**

Total Weekly Greywater Flow: 445 gallons

RECORD YOUR HOME'S GREYWATER OUTPUT				
Fixture	Typical usage (for reference)	Gallons per use (gal/load or gpm × min/use)	× Uses per week	= Weekly greywater (gallons)
Washing machine	Top-loader 40–50 gallons/load			
	Top-efficient 20–30 gallons/load			
	Front-loader 12–25 gallons/load			
Shower	Low flow = 8 gallons/person/shower			
	High flow = 12 gallons/person/shower			
Bath	30–50 gallons per bath			
Bathroom sink	1–5 gallons/person/day			
Kitchen sink	3–8 gallons/person/day			

Diverting 100 Percent of Your Greywater

A home's sewer or septic drain needs enough wastewater flowing in the underground pipe to get the poop and toilet paper (the solids) from the toilet to the city's main sewer line (or a private septic tank) without clogs. In a properly functioning home system, each toilet flush carries the solids all the way to the main line. Unfortunately, many homes' sewer drainpipes are not sloped properly and/or have root intrusion or other issues that affect their performance, and greywater (from showers, sinks, etc.) picks up the slack, helping to carry the solids through the pipe.

NO GREYWATER "BACKUP"

My house diverted all greywater to the landscape, and only one ultra-low-flow toilet was connected to the sewer. For a few years there were no problems. Then the house's sewer drain clogged. A plumber unclogged it and said it clogged because we didn't have enough water flowing through the system. We ignored him. It clogged again. We redirected one shower to the sewer. It clogged again. Finally, a company sent a camera down the sewer line and discovered the old clay sewer pipe was collapsed, missing in parts, and had roots inside it. Our problems were unrelated to low greywater flows, but rather resulted from a 100-year-old broken clay sewer pipe. After our new, properly sloped sewer line was installed, we diverted all the greywater to the yard problem-free (about four years have passed now).

The lesson: If you divert all your greywater to the yard and don't abandon the sewer completely with composting toilets, be prepared to troubleshoot sewer issues that come up. Otherwise, regardless of the true source of the problem, your greywater system will get blamed.

THE BIGGER PICTURE

What happens to the entire sewer system if lots of people reuse greywater? Massive sewage clogs? Probably not. In the *Study of the Effects of On-Site Greywater Reuse on Municipal Sewer Systems* (2011; see Resources) researchers found the sewer system operated with large fluctuations in flows, with two major peaks occurring each day (morning and evening). Reusing greywater would have the largest impact on the system during these peak flow times (imagine lots of morning bathing water going into the yard instead of the sewer). Widespread reuse of greywater would reduce the peak flows, but would have almost no impact on the system during the current lowest-flow times of the day (when toilet flushing is the major source of water in the system).

Because the sewer system currently operates at these low-flow times, and these flow rates would not be affected, researchers concluded that widespread reuse of greywater should not increase blockages. In fact, they hypothesized that sewer systems could experience positive effects from greywater reuse, with an increase in capacity.

SEPTIC CONSIDERATIONS

A septic system also needs sufficient wastewater to function properly. Is it okay to remove all greywater from the septic? Some people say no, that it will cause septic failures. Yet many homes have done this without problems. In fact, diverting greywater from the septic helps solve the most common problem with failing systems: too much water. According to ecological wastewater designer Bill Wilson, "By tapping out the greywater, all you are doing is greatly extending the retention time. This makes for better primary treatment, not worse." One system Wilson designed for a winery tasting room sent water only from a very efficient dishwasher, foam flush toilets (3 ounces of water per flush), and waterless urinals, all discharging directly into a properly designed septic tank — problem-free. A properly designed system has an effluent filter and sufficient distance between the inlet and outlet to assure good separation of liquids and solids, among other important details.

Note that there is an alternative to reusing greywater system for homes on septics: reusing septic effluent directly from the tank. See page 131 for more information.

Soil Structure and Type

HEALTHY PLANTS REQUIRE HEALTHY SOILS.
The soil in your yard is composed of different types and sizes of particles. If you crush a handful of dry soil in your hand, you may notice mineral particles (from broken-down rocks) of different sizes — some very tiny and others, such as sand grains, larger and visible to the naked eye. The soil texture, the size of the soil's mineral particles, is static: you cannot change it.

In your handful of soil you'll also notice organic particles from decomposing leaves, sticks, and roots. These mineral and organic particles are held together to form clumps of soil, called **aggregates**. In between the clumps are air spaces, which allow oxygen and water to move through the soil. A suitable soil structure, with enough air spaces between soil clumps, is important for plant health.

What holds these soil particles together? Soil microbes. These little creatures not only break down organic matter and make nutrients available to plants, but they also excrete a glue-like substance that holds soil particles together, building soil structure. Soils that have poor structure, either from compaction or lack of organic matter, can be improved by adding compost and planting deep-rooting plants to increase aeration in the soil.

Test Your Soil

It is important to know your soil type, or *soil texture*, when designing a greywater irrigation system. The soil type affects how quickly or slowly water soaks into the soil.

Soils are made up of clay, sand, and silt particles. Clay particles are the smallest, smooth to the touch, and hold together when wet. Sand particles are the largest and are loose and grainy whether dry or wet. Water moves more slowly through clay soils than sandy soils; greywater irrigation in clay soils requires a larger infiltration area than in sandy soils because it will take longer for the water to soak through clay. If the infiltration area is too small, the soil could become saturated, resulting in greywater pooling on the surface before all the water can seep in.

You can identify your soil type with a simple "ribbon" test. However, be aware that some local codes require a specific method to meet permit requirements, such as a laboratory analysis (see Resources).

Identify Your Soil Type with a Soil Ribbon Test

Soil type can be highly localized, meaning a home landscape can have different types in different areas. For best results, test your soil directly in each area you plan to irrigate with greywater and below any amended soil; for example, if you've added a layer of compost over the native soil. In most cases, test to a depth of 8" to 12", as this is how deep your mulch basins (page 62) may be.

TOOLS

Trowel

Water

Ruler

1. **Use the trowel to loosen the soil** and take a walnut-sized sample into your hand. Remove any rocks or roots from the pile, adding more soil if needed.

2. **Moisten the soil slowly,** kneading as you add water until it reaches the consistency of bread dough, not a slurry. If the sample gets too wet or dry, adjust with more soil or water. Mix the paste around on your palm and notice if the soil is mostly sandy, has a fine gritty feel (which means it has silt), or is very smooth (which means it is rich in clay). Keep mixing and kneading the soil for a minute or two until it is uniform and any lumps of clay have been thoroughly wetted. You may need to add a little more water to it.

3. **Make a ball out of the soil,** then try to form a ribbon: place the ball in your hand between your thumb and forefinger, gently squeeze the soil, and push it upwards into a ribbon, extending the ribbon as long as it will go before breaking from its weight. Don't try to mold the soil into a ribbon by rolling it in your palms. **Note:** If the soil will not make a ball, it is **sand**; if it makes a ball but not a ribbon, it is **loamy sand**.

4. **Identify your soil type** based on the length of the ribbon:

   ◆ If the ribbon breaks into pieces that are less than 1" (2.5 cm) long, you have some kind of loam. If you can feel many sand grains, it is a **sandy loam**; if not, it is **loam**.

   ◆ If the ribbon is more than 1", perhaps even 2", you have a **clay loam**. If it is sandy-feeling, it is a **sandy clay loam**.

   ◆ If the ribbon is more than 2" long, it is **clay**. It will probably be shiny when wet. If you can feel many sand particles, it is **sandy clay**.

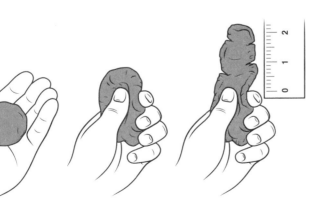

▲ **Soil ribbon test**

Conduct an Infiltration Test

How does water flow through your soil? If you're directing greywater to a planted area you currently irrigate, you probably already know that water infiltrates there, so this test may be unnecessary. But if you're new to the landscape or are directing greywater to a previously unlandscaped area, conduct a simple infiltration test to make sure the site is suitable for greywater irrigation. Surprises may await you a few feet underground. For example, you might discover that someone has buried a concrete slab underground, preventing water from soaking through; thus, a bad location for greywater.

Sending greywater to a poorly draining area isn't good for the plants or the irrigation system design. Plants don't like soggy roots (unless they're wetland plants), and a slow infiltration rate leads to pooling or runoff of greywater. If you can't direct greywater elsewhere, focus on improving the infiltration of the soil; add compost, use large mulch basins (see page 62) to soak up greywater and release it slowly, and plant deep-rooting plants to open the soil.

TOOLS

Shovel

Marker

Ruler or stick

Source of water

Timer

1. **Dig a hole,** about 12" deep and as wide as your shovel, in the area you plan to infiltrate greywater. Insert a ruler or stick marked with inches into the hole.

2. **Fill the hole with water.** Let the water soak into the soil, then repeat. The goal is to saturate the surrounding area, and this usually takes at least three fillings (or conduct the test after a rain).

3. **Fill the hole with water and measure the level** with the marked stick. Record how long it takes for the water level to drop several inches. If water drops 1" per hour or faster, you have sufficient drainage for irrigating the area with greywater. If it takes longer than 2 hours for the water level to drop 1", or if all the water in the hole doesn't drain all day, this is not a good location for greywater irrigation.

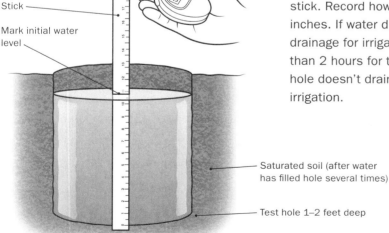

Stick

Mark initial water level

Saturated soil (after water has filled hole several times)

Test hole 1–2 feet deep

▲ **Infiltration test**

Mulch Basins

A MULCH BASIN IS A SUNKEN AREA in the landscape filled with mulch (wood chips, straw, or other organic material). It's designed to absorb greywater, infiltrating it into the ground and preventing it from pooling or running off. Most of the greywater systems described in the book, except drip irrigation systems, use mulch basins. Food particles and organic matter stick to the mulch and decompose. The size and type of mulch used depends on what's available locally, as well as how long you want it to last. Larger wood chips decompose more slowly than finely shredded material and won't need replacing as often. Typically, large wood chips will last one to three years.

Sizing Mulch Basins

Suppose you've worked out how much greywater you have, and you decide to irrigate 10 trees. Will your 10 mulch basins be large enough for all the water? To calculate the necessary size of the infiltration area, you need to know the soil type and how many gallons per day of greywater will enter the system. As an example, if you have clay soils, you'll need about 1 square foot of infiltration area per gallon of greywater. The Soil Type and Infiltration Area chart below lists basic area requirements for other soil types.

Multiply the gallons per day of greywater your home generates by the number corresponding to your soil type. This square footage represents the minimum size of the total mulch basin area your system requires. For example, if a home produces 60 gpd of greywater and the irrigation site has clay soil, the minimum infiltration area required is 60 square feet (60 × 1 = 60 square feet). Since the

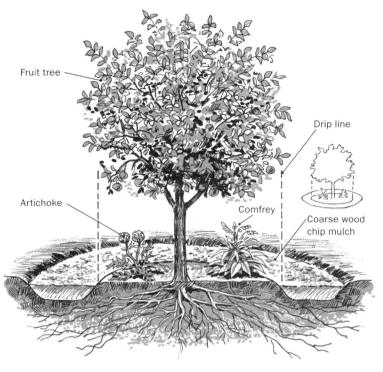

▲ **Mulch basin around a fruit tree**

system irrigates multiple plants, the 60 square feet of infiltration area can be spread out across the yard. For example, to irrigate 10 trees, each would need 6 square feet of infiltration area.

Keep in mind this calculation doesn't consider the plant water needs (see How Much Water Do My Plants Want? on page 65). Also note that systems that use drip irrigation won't use this calculation because the water is spread out over a much larger area; therefore ponding and runoff are rarely problematic.

Size Basins for the Future

Will you be selling your house? Is your household size increasing? If so, size your infiltration area large enough to accommodate increased flows. If you'll be selling your home, it's a good idea to size the system based on the number of bedrooms, since you won't know how many people may move into the home (see Sample "Code-Type" Estimate for Greywater Production on page 55).

SOIL TYPES AND INFILTRATION AREA	
Soil type	**Area needed to infiltrate each gallon of greywater (per day)**
Sand	0.25 square foot
Sandy loam	0.4 square foot
Loam	0.5 square foot
Sandy or loamy clay	0.6 square foot
Clay	1 square foot

Protect Groundwater and Drinking Water Wells

Greywater has the potential to contaminate a shallow groundwater table, and in many areas groundwater is used as a local water supply. To prevent this, greywater should infiltrate through at least 3 feet of soil before reaching a water table.

Not sure how deep the groundwater is where you live? Get the shovel out and dig a 3-foot-deep hole at the lowest point of your proposed system. If there is no visible water seeping into the hole, then the area is safe to irrigate with greywater. If you see water in the hole, the groundwater table is too shallow for greywater irrigation in that area. In places with seasonally high groundwater, use greywater only during the dry, irrigation season, and divert back to the sewer in the rainy season. (Homes on septic systems may also be legally required to divert back during the rainy season, though this practice is not protective of groundwater because septic leach fields discharge deeper underground than do greywater irrigation systems.)

To protect drinking water wells, don't irrigate too close: codes often require 50 to 100 feet of horizontal distance between greywater irrigation and the well.

Choosing Plants for Greywater Irrigation

A WELL-DESIGNED SYSTEM finds a balance between the amount of greywater available and the irrigation needs of the plants. Since the amount of greywater and plant water needs both fluctuate, your design goal is to find an optimal match: irrigate as many plants as possible while keeping them healthy. During rainy times when your plants don't need irrigation, either turn off the greywater system or, in well-draining soils, keep it on. The amount of greywater going through a system is minuscule compared to a rainstorm.

If you have an existing landscape, follow these steps:

1. Decide what area of the landscape is easiest to direct greywater to. Be open to changing the landscaping, if necessary.

2. Determine if the plants in this area are appropriate to irrigate with greywater.

3. Estimate how much water the plants require (see How Much Water Do My Plants Want? on page 65). Remember, this is estimating their peak irrigation needs; they don't need this much water most of the year.

4. Compare the amount of greywater available with the irrigation needs of the plants. Do they match up? Try to stay within 30 percent of their irrigation needs. You may find your plants thrive with less water, and if they occasionally become water stressed you can supplement with rain or tap water.

Greywater-Compatible Plants

Larger plants are better suited for greywater irrigation than smaller ones. A tree or bush with a large root area can withstand fluctuation in water much better than small plants can. Large plants also need more water than small ones, making it easier to distribute more greywater to fewer plants. As you look at your landscape, identify the easiest plants to irrigate. Most houses exhaust their greywater supply before the entire landscape is irrigated. If you end up with extra greywater, consider planting something new.

Some landscape areas aren't well suited for greywater irrigation, such as lawns or areas full of small plants (although high-tech systems can irrigate these types of plants; see page 131 for more info). Consider these techniques to improve a landscape for simple greywater irrigation:

- Remove a section of the lawn and plant perennials. Or, remove a strip of lawn around the edge for new plantings.

- Plant more greywater-compatible plants in the area. Consider taking the other plants off irrigation and, if they die, replace them with something suitable to your climate.

- Redesign the landscape so it is compatible with greywater irrigation (see chapter 3 for ideas).

Note: If you're wondering whether hot water from a shower or washer may harm the plants, don't worry; it won't. By the time hot water flows down the pipes, soaks through the mulch, and reaches the roots of plants it's not hot anymore.

Fruit Trees, Bushes, Vines, and More

These are the easiest plants to irrigate with greywater:

Trees. Fruit trees (or any trees) adapted to your local climate thrive with greywater irrigation.

Bushes and shrubs. Bushes and shrubs suited to your region are easy to irrigate with greywater. Consider fruiting varieties, or find ones that create bird and beneficial insect habitat.

Vines. Edible vines, like passion fruit or kiwi, are attractive and produce fruit.

Larger perennials. Perennial vegetables, which produce year after year without needing replanting, are a productive addition to any landscape (see Resources for ideas). Flowering plants provide bird and butterfly habitat.

Large annuals. Large annual plants, both edible and nonedible, can be irrigated with an L2L or pumped system; for example, tomatoes, corn, zinnias, squash. (Remember, you can safely irrigate food crops so long as the edible portion is above the ground and greywater doesn't touch it.)

Smaller plants growing closely together can be irrigated in the middle of the planting area, so their roots share the water. Or, create distribution channels to move greywater toward the plants, like a "sun" mulch basin.

Mulch basin

▲ **"Sun" mulch basin. Greywater flows out from center of basin toward smaller plants.**

Plants for Ecological Disposal (Wetland Plants)

If you have ample irrigation water and don't need to be water-conscious in your landscape, consider growing water-loving wetland plants; they thrive with frequent and plentiful greywater irrigation. Or, if a lush wetland is in your garden design, dedicate some of your greywater for it. It's a lot easier to direct a portion of the greywater to irrigate a wetland than to flow all the greywater through it before an irrigation system. (Wetlands are used to process greywater in places without irrigation need or sewer/septic options, and these designs flow all greywater through the wetland.) Backyard wetlands are prone to clogging, which prevents greywater from passing through.

Native and Low-Water-Use Plants

Use greywater to irrigate drought-tolerant and native plants, but be careful not to over-irrigate them. These plants can survive typical droughts in their climate, but they may look better during the dry times with a little extra water — the reason many people irrigate them. Design a greywater system to spread out water as much as possible through the landscape. If you're looking for ideas for appropriate native or low-water-use plants for your climate, visit the EPA's website to find local sources of information (see Resources). Water districts and local extension services may also provide this information.

Inform Your Landscaper or Gardener about Your Greywater System

Anyone working in a landscape with a greywater system should understand how the system works and where the components are located; otherwise, they may unintentionally damage the system. Show your landscaper or gardener photos of pipe and outlet locations (pre-burial) and make sure they understand the importance of maintaining the outlets and mulch basins, never covering them with soil.

How Much Water Do My Plants Want?

Many people have no idea how much water a plant needs. I'll start with a rough estimate of how many fruit trees you could irrigate from a simple washing machine system, assuming there is no rain to supplement the greywater irrigation. Determine your irrigation potential by multiplying the first number (one load per week) by the number of loads you do each week:

Cool Climates (65–75-degree summers)

- Front-loading machine (one load a week): 1 to 2 trees
- Top-loading machine (one load a week): 3 to 4 trees

Warm Climates (75–85-degree summers)

- Front-loading machine (one load a week): 1 tree
- Top-loading machine (one load a week): 2 to 3 trees

Hot Climates (85–100+-degree summers)

- Front-loading machine (one load a week): ½ tree
- Top-loading machine (one load a week): 1 to 2 trees

With the above estimates in mind, perform some basic calculations to determine more accurately how much to irrigate your plants. There are many factors that affect plant water requirements, including climate, exposure (e.g., southern or northern), wind, shade, mulch, type of plant, and plant size.

Next, I'll show you two methods for estimating how many gallons per week a specific plant should receive. The first is a quick, rule-of-thumb estimate and is accurate enough to keep your plants healthy and happy. Use this method to guide your system design. For those of you wanting more detail, the second method (which incorporates evapotranspiration, or ET, rates) can help you fine-tune your design, though this level of precision is not essential and the calculation is considered optional.

Keep in mind that these methods, as with any technique for determining irrigation needs, provide only *estimated* amounts. Always observe your plants: they can receive a wide range of irrigation amounts and still grow healthily, so long as the soil doesn't become waterlogged. Try to maximize your greywater potential and irrigate as many plants as possible; you'll save more water if you under-irrigate and add supplemental water occasionally, as opposed to consistently over-irrigating.

Rule-of-Thumb Estimate of Weekly Irrigation Need

Determine the weekly irrigation need of a plant based on its size and the climate. The plant size is measured by the area under its canopy; for trees and bushes, this area is shaped like a circle. Planted beds or hedgerows have a rectangular area. Use the area of a circle: multiply π (3.14, or round to 3.0) by the circle's radius (r) squared (area = π r²). Find the area of a rectangle by multiplying the length by the width.

To determine the irrigation needs (in gallons per week), first find the number of square feet of planted area, then divide by:

- 1 in a hot, arid climate
- 2 in a warm climate
- 4 in a cool climate with coastal summer fog

For example, here's the calculation for an apple tree that measures 4 feet from the trunk to the outer branches:

Area of circle = π × r² (rounding π to 3) = 3 × 4² = 48 square feet

Area of tree's footprint = 48 square feet

4 feet

▲ **Find the area under a tree using A = πr².**

To find the estimated peak irrigation need, divide 48 square feet by the number for the climate:

In a hot, arid climate: *48 ÷ 1 = 48 gallons/week*

In a mild climate with warm summers: *48 ÷ 2 = 24 gallons/week*

In a cool climate with coastal summer fog: *48 ÷ 4 = 12 gallons/week*

This rule-of-thumb estimate is most accurate for plants with moderate water use, like fruit trees. Water-loving wetland plants would like more water, while drought-tolerant or low-water-use plants require less. If you are irrigating a low-water-use or drought-tolerant plant, divide your estimate (gallons/week) in half again.

Estimating Water Requirements Using Evapotranspiration Rates (ET)

Evapotranspiration, or ET, is the combined effect of water evaporating from the soil and being used (transpired) by plants. In relatively warm, dry climates plants lose more water than in cooler, moister climates. This method assumes that all moisture by evapotranspiration will be replaced though irrigation. It factors in the type and size of the plant as well as the climate. You'll need the following information:

1. **The area of the plant(s)** in square feet (see previous page).

2. **The species factor of the plant(s).** The plant species factor indicates high (0.8), moderate (0.5), or low (0.2) water use. Garden books typically provide this information and often represent it with a water droplet; a full drop is high, half-full drop is medium, and empty drop is low. Most fruit trees are moderate-water-use plants. If you can't find this info in a general reference book, look in the Water Use Classification of Landscape Species (WUCOLS; see Resources).

3. **The ET rate for your area.** The rate depends on climate conditions. Typically, ET is given in inches per month or per day. This can be converted to inches per week, which is what's needed for the formula. You can find ET rates online, or ask your local cooperative extension program or water district.

The EPA's Water Sense website has a tool you can use to find your peak irrigation month and subsequent reference ET rate (see Resources). The tool also provides average rainfall for the peak irrigation month so you can adjust your irrigation estimate accordingly. Visit their website and simply enter your Zip code. Keep in mind that this data is for the peak irrigation month and you don't need to irrigate this much all year long. Usually if you stay within 30 percent of this number, either lower or higher depending on your available greywater, the plants should be happy.

Use this formula to calculate weekly plant water requirements:

0.62 (conversion coefficient to change inches/week to gallons) × ET (weekly) × species factor × plant size (square foot)

The following examples look at irrigation requirements for a living fence made of pineapple guava bushes (moderate-water-needs plant; species factor: 0.5) covering a 100-square-foot area using peak irrigation (as reported by the EPA Water Sense website):

Los Angeles, CA. *Peak ET July 6.73 inches/month or 1.68 inches/week: 0.62 × 1.68 × 0.5 × 100 sq ft = 52 gallons/week (irrigating within 30 percent of this would be 36 gallons/week)*

Tucson, AZ. *Peak ET June 12.42 inches/month or 3.1 inches/week: 0.62 × 3.1 × 0.5 × 100 sq ft = 96 gallons/week (irrigating within 30 percent of this would be 67 gallons/week)*

Seattle, WA. *Peak ET July 5.42 inches/month or 1.36 inches/week: 0.62 × 1.36 × 0.5 × 100 sq ft = 42 gallons/week (irrigating within 30 percent of this would be 30 gallons/week)*

Miami, FL. *Peak ET April 6.65 inches/month or 1.66 inches/week: 0.62 × 1.66 × 0.5 × 100 sq ft = 51 gallons/week (irrigating within 30 percent of this would be 36 gallons/week)*

These estimates don't take into account summer rains; obviously plants won't require as much water during the week if it rains. You can subtract average rainfall from the ET rate for this calculation, although, depending on the rainfall frequency, this rain could come in one heavy storm, or be spread out evenly over the month, and this will impact how much water plants would like during the week.

A Greywater Pond?

My first two greywater systems flowed through a bathtub wetland into a greywater pond, overflowing with water hyacinth. I loved the 8-foot-tall cattails that filtered shower water clear and odorless. It took a few years before I realized this wasn't a greywater reuse system, rather an ecological disposal system; the cattails were sucking up the water that could have been irrigating my thirsty garden. (Once mature, the plants literally sucked up an entire shower on a hot day — not a drop overflowed out of the wetland to the garden.)

Though technically easy and also beautiful and fun, using greywater for a backyard pond is not something I recommend. If your goal is to save water, a greywater pond isn't the right choice. The quality of greywater is unsuitable to fill a pond, it must be filtered by wetland plants first (unless you want a pool of disgusting, stinky greywater). These thirsty plants remove nutrients and organic matter from the water, which your garden could have benefited from; less greywater flows out of the wetland than in.

A water-wise choice for anyone with both a pond and a landscape is to irrigate with greywater and fill the pond with freshwater (or rainwater), bypassing the need for the water-loving wetland filter. Separately, greywater ponds epitomize the concerns of the regulatory world. Their list of potential hazards includes: drowning risk for children, potential for direct contact with the water, mosquito breeding grounds, and overflow to a neighbor's yard or storm drain. Ponding greywater is prohibited by even the most lenient codes.

Permaculture centers take pride in their greywater ponds. Shining photos of rural greywater-fed ponds frequent blogs, books, and magazines. Not often emphasized is the fact that these ponds typically fill with rainwater; just a fraction is "grey." People who try to replicate them are disappointed when their backyard greywater pond is a slimy, stinky algae pool. A backyard rainwater pond won't cause such headaches! (See Resources for info on rainwater ponds.)

System Design Considerations

What part of the landscape should you irrigate — the lawn uphill from your house or the fruit trees downslope? Before getting to specifics, I'll cover general design principles to help you narrow your options and define your goals. Start with the following basic considerations.

Can you have a gravity irrigation system? First, consider areas of your yard close to the greywater source that require irrigation and are NOT uphill or across large areas of hardscape. Gravity-based systems typically last longer, cost less, use fewer resources, and require less maintenance than pumped systems.

Does water infiltrate well in the area where you plan to use greywater? If this is an area you don't already irrigate, you should perform an infiltration test (page 61) to make sure greywater will soak into the soil without pooling.

Will the location of the greywater system cause any unforeseen problems? Maintain setbacks from the house's foundation, neighbors' yards, retaining walls, streams and lakes, groundwater table, and water supply wells. See the chart below for some standard setback distances (based on California code). Setback requirements vary by area; check with your local code authority for a permitted system. Codes often include setbacks for septic tanks and leach lines, although it seems illogical to require a setback from a leach line, since greywater would have been in the leach line if it wasn't diverted from the septic system.

EXAMPLE SETBACKS FOR GREYWATER IRRIGATION AREA (MINIMUM DISTANCE)	
Building foundations	2 feet
Property lines	1.5 feet
Water supply wells	100 feet
Streams and lakes	100 feet
Water table	3 feet above
Retaining wall	2 feet

In addition to the basic elements shown in the chart, greywater surge tanks also may have setback requirements. If your project requires a permit and you need a tank, ask your local building department for their thoughts on tank placement. Other cases may involve special situations that require modifications to the setback requirements. For example, if your neighbor's yard is lower and covered with hardscape (e.g., a concrete patio), a 1.5-foot setback may not be enough distance to prevent leaking of greywater onto the neighbor's patio. Increase setbacks any time the greywater-irrigated landscape is elevated above any type of hardscape, such as sidewalks, patios, walkways, or roads.

Greywater 101 (or How to Avoid Common Problems)

- Don't store greywater! Nutrients in greywater break down over time, causing a stink. To avoid odor problems with surge tanks (in a pumped system), make sure the tank is vented, can be cleaned, and is located outside of the living space. (And don't send greywater to mix with rainwater in a rainwater tank; the tank will become contaminated.)

- Don't allow greywater to puddle or pond up. It is nonpotable and people shouldn't contact it. Ponding also creates mosquito breeding grounds.

- KISS (Keep It Simple or you'll be Sorry). The more components and parts used, the more potential for system failure. At the residential level, simple systems tend to work best, last longest, and cost less than complex setups. Many systems do not require a tank, pump, or filter; use these components only when necessary.

- Plan carefully to match your greywater production with the needs of your plants.

- Use plant-friendly products (those without salts, boron, or chlorine bleach).

- For specific system problems and solutions, refer to chapter 5.

Plan Greywater Systems into New Home Design

If you plan your house with the greywater system in mind (not to mention rainwater catchment and waterless toilets), you'll have more options and an easier system to install. Here are some planning tips:

- Locate the house above the landscape area when possible.

- Keep the plumbing accessible (no concrete slab). If you will have a slab foundation, design an accessible location for diverting greywater, and don't join greywater and blackwater pipes below the slab.

- Design the landscape to fit with your greywater (and rainwater) supply.

- If you are not planning to install the greywater system immediately, put in the diverter valve with a "greywater stub out," or create a place to easily add it in later.

Plant-Friendly Soaps

GREYWATER CAN EITHER BENEFIT or harm plants, depending on what soaps and detergents you use. Its quality as an irrigation source is directly connected to what you put down the drain. Luckily, it's easy to choose soap products that are plant-friendly, avoiding the following ingredients:

- **Salt and sodium compounds.** Salts can build up in the soil and inhibit plants' ability to take up nutrients and water. Minimize and avoid salts.

- **Boron.** This plant microtoxin is damaging in small amounts. Do not use any products that contain boron, including the laundry additive Borax. Because it is nontoxic to people, boron is found in many ecological products.

- **Chlorine bleach.** Bleaches containing chlorine kill microorganisms, including beneficial soil microbes. Hydrogen peroxide bleach can be used instead, or you can turn off your greywater system when using bleach.

- **Alkaline compounds (optional).** Some products raise the level of pH, making the water more basic (or alkaline). This isn't a problem for most plants, although some types (such as blueberries and azaleas) prefer acidic conditions and basic water may not suit them. In general, liquid soaps do not increase the pH of the water, whereas bar soaps do. Cleaning products can also be extremely basic (alkaline). If you are using greywater from a source where only liquid, pH-neutral products are used, greywater can irrigate any plants, including acid-loving ones. Refer to garden books, extension offices, or local nurseries to determine whether your plants are acid-loving.

Product Recommendations

Following are some products that have been used successfully for many years in greywater systems. This list is not exhaustive, and you may find others that are free of boron and salts. Additionally, you can look up the ingredients for personal care products at Environmental Working Group's *Skin Deep Cosmetic Database* (see Resources).

- Washing machine: ECOS, Biopac, Oasis, Vaska. (Powdered detergents are never okay; only use liquid detergents.)

- Showers: Aubrey Organics (most types), Everyday Shea, Dr. Bronner's.

- Sinks: Oasis all-purpose cleaner, Dr. Bronner's liquid castile soap, most glycerin-based soaps.

- Cleaning products: Use vinegar-based products, not white powders. Or, turn off the greywater system if you use salt-based powder cleaners.

Salts

The amount of salts you can send into your yard without damaging your plants depends on your climate, soil, and plants. If you live in a place with heavy, frequent rainfall, rain will leach salt out of the soil before it can build up to harm plants, so the occasional salty product won't matter. On the other hand, places with salty tap water (such as groundwater or Colorado River water) and a dry climate are more prone to salt buildup, requiring more care to avoid additional salts from greywater. And keep in mind that fertilizers are high in salts, and salt tolerances of plants vary considerably. In arid climates direct rainwater into greywater basins as well as rainwater basins to flush salts from the soil.

When Greywater Is *Not* a Great Idea

OUTDOOR GREYWATER IRRIGATION SYSTEMS are not always appropriate. Here are some situations where greywater reuse may not be suitable:

Not enough space for plants and irrigation systems. With a very small (or nonexistent) yard, there may be not enough landscape area to infiltrate greywater.

Too close to a creek or drinking water well. Setbacks range from 50 to 100 feet.

Unstable slope. Adding extra water to a steep or otherwise unstable slope could cause a landslide.

Uninterested and uncooperative people living in the home. If people won't use plant-friendly products or maintain the greywater system, it could harm the landscape (unless the landscape is designed with salt- and boron-tolerant plants, and an outside person does the maintenance).

Difficult-to-access drainpipes. When it's an awkward situation, such as a house on a slab foundation with all greywater sources in the middle of the home, money may be better spent on things like ultra-efficient appliances and rainwater systems.

Very poorly draining soil. If you live in a swamp, it will be hard to infiltrate greywater into the native soil and you won't be saving water; swamps don't need irrigation. Consider an ecological disposal system, like a constructed wetland, or an indoor greenhouse greywater system.

If you can't use greywater for irrigation, investigate options for indoor reuse, such as for toilet flushing, or focus on rainwater catchment or composting toilet systems.

Using Greywater to Flush

FLUSHING THE TOILET with pure drinking water offends common sense and ecological awareness. Why not flush with nonpotable greywater instead? In the right situation, flushing with greywater is a great idea. However, in many situations there are better ideas to implement first. It's typically cheaper and easier to set up an outdoor greywater irrigation system. It's also easier to install a rainwater system to flush the toilet, rather than a greywater one. But if your site doesn't need irrigation, there are systems that filter greywater to flush the toilet.

Challenges with Toilet Systems

Toilet-flushing greywater systems usually require frequent maintenance, manual cleaning of filters, and chemical disinfectant to prevent odors in the bathroom. They also tend to be relatively complicated, and it's critical that they be designed and installed properly. A few companies sell systems, while some greywater professionals design their own. Studies and system users report that lower-cost systems ($3,000–$5,000) have maintenance issues, while the better-functioning ones have a steep price tag ($8,000–$9,000). In general, it costs far less to purchase an ultra-low-flow toilet and showerhead than invest in a toilet-flushing system.

Getting a permit tends to be more difficult for indoor reuse of greywater, although a few states, such as Florida, make it easier than outdoor reuse. Some tinkerer types create functional methods to flush, but these are never up to code. A study on 25 toilet-flushing systems in Guelph, Canada, found an average savings of just 4.5 gallons per person per day (gpcd). Toilets using treated greywater tend to require more maintenance and internal parts wear out, causing wasteful leaks.

Recommendations

Use shower water first for indoor systems, since it has fewer particles to filter out. You'll need to access

Is Greywater a Hazard to Your Health?

Some people hold the mistaken belief that greywater is hazardous, on par with sewage. There are many studies on the quality of greywater with respect to public health. Here are some key points:

- **Don't drink greywater!** It is of lower quality than drinking water and unsafe to ingest.

- Greywater-irrigated soil is not safe to ingest, nor is soil irrigated with tap water. The City of Los Angeles conducted a study comparing greywater-irrigated soil and non-greywater-irrigated soil. Both were found unhealthy to ingest.

- Many studies have found fecal indicator bacteria present, demonstrating the potential for greywater to contain fecally transmitted pathogens. A problem with using indicator bacteria, like fecal coliforms, is that the bacteria are present in all mammals' feces and can multiply outside the body, resulting in inaccurate estimates of fecal matter in greywater. Other studies tested greywater for a cholesterol found only in the human gut, unable to grow outside the body, and found the levels of feces reported in the other studies using indicator bacteria were 100 to 1,000 times too high. Does this matter? Some people still believe greywater isn't much cleaner than sewage and don't know that the methods used to test greywater were grossly inaccurate.

- Few studies have found actual pathogens in greywater. Testing for specific pathogens is expensive, and pathogens are found only if someone in the home has the illness and germs get into the water. Some studies that tested for pathogens didn't find any, while others found common pathogens like *Cryptosporidium* spp. and *Giardia* spp., which are also found in most surface waters in the U.S. When people are sick they infect others by living together, directly touching, and sharing dishes; the chance of infection through a greywater system is extremely unlikely.

- There are no documented cases of illness resulting from greywater, while there are over three million documented cases of illness each year (just in the U.S.) from recreational contact with water contaminated by legal sewage treatment plants that overflow.

Is greywater hazardous to your health? No. Most likely, greywater use improves public health by reducing waterborne illness, since the only people potentially liable to exposure already live together and greywater is kept out of sewer systems that often fail.

the drainpipes to install the diverter valve, and install a tank with a filter. Lastly, do a reality check to make sure you are ready to do the necessary maintenance for this type of system to function well. Or consider a simple system like SinkPositive, a retrofit for your toilet tank lid that turns it into a sink.

Health and Safety Considerations

A PROPERLY DESIGNED greywater system is safe for you and your family, as well as the environment. As you design your system, keep the following considerations in mind:

- Greywater is not safe to drink or ingest.

- Greywater can harm aquatic ecosystems.

- Avoid direct contact with greywater; your system should not create a puddle, pond, or any standing water that would create a hazard to unsuspecting children and a place for mosquitoes to breed.

- When watering food plants, don't let greywater contact edible portions of the food (to avoid direct ingestion). Don't irrigate root vegetables, and use subsurface irrigation for growing edibles near the ground.

- Never use greywater in sprinklers where the spray could be breathed in.

Polluting Aquatic Ecosystems

The nutrients found in greywater help your garden, but harm lakes, streams, and oceans. In the garden, the nutrients are fertilizer, sent to your plants each time you do laundry. If, instead of soaking into the soil, greywater runs into the storm drain and out to a river or bay, the nutrients pollute the water, feed algae, and rob oxygen from aquatic organisms. This is how the gigantic "dead zones" are created in our bays and oceans, usually by fertilizer runoff and sewer overflows. Don't let your greywater contribute!

Hazardous chemicals should never be used with a greywater system (or anywhere); they will contaminate your yard. When sent to the sewer plant they usually aren't removed either, and will end up in a river, lake, or ocean.

California DPH Supports Greywater Reuse

Public health officials supported California's revised greywater code. At the public hearing for adopting the 2009 greywater code, Dr. Linda Rudolph of California's Department of Public Health spoke in favor: "We believe that the proposed standards are adequately protective of public health and may provide substantial water conservation benefits and decrease demand on existing water supplies. We think this guidance will improve public health protection. . . ."

Codes and Regulations

UNDERSTANDING YOUR LOCAL greywater codes is important for a few reasons. If your project requires a permit, understanding the perspective of your regulatory agency will help you work together. If you're working on policy change, you must figure out how to have a functional code that simultaneously addresses concerns of health and safety officials. Read more tips from code-changing pioneers in Greywater Action for a Sustainable Water Future (page 72), The Environmental Health Perspective: Rob Kostlivy (page 76), and Compost Toilet Pioneers Legalize Site-Built Toilets: David Omick and ReCode (page 221).

Historically, plumbing codes did not distinguish between greywater and blackwater (from toilets). Greywater was required to be collected together with blackwater and sent to the sewer or septic systems, and reusing greywater was illegal. This began to change in the early 1990s when drought-prone California realized this potential source of irrigation water was being wasted. The state plumbing code changed to allow legal reuse. Greywater advocates from that time will tell you how this code, though a positive first step, was practically useless. It treated greywater like septic water, requiring a small septic-type system to dispose of it deep underground (with a tank and gravel-filled leach lines). People interested in irrigating with greywater still had to build illegal systems. California alone had an estimated 1.7 million unpermitted systems. States like Arizona, which followed California's example code, had a similar experience.

Greywater Action:
For a Sustainable Water Future

GREYWATER ACTION (the group I helped start) educates about greywater, rainwater, and composting toilet systems through hands-on workshops and presentations. Prior to 2009 our name was The Greywater Guerrillas, and all the greywater work we did was illegal, primarily due to an overly restrictive state code. After teaching hundreds of Californians how to install simple systems, we worked to legalize the practice. Responding to strong public support, millions of illegal systems, and a statewide drought, California changed the greywater law.

What advice do you have for other groups wanting to offer greywater education?

Start by gaining practical experience; install a system in your own home. People want to know what it's like to live with a system. How do the plants respond? Do greywater-friendly detergents really get the clothes clean? It takes time to gain experience, so the sooner you can start the better. In the meantime, collaborate with experienced people, attend trainings, and find partners to combine skills (plumbers, handypeople, permaculturists, landscapers).

How can people promote greywater in places without a code?

Regardless of legality, firsthand experience and working local examples are critical. Many regulators have never seen a greywater irrigation system, which makes it challenging to get a good code in place. Install systems based on designs proven in other regions as demonstration sites. Invite regulators for an "unofficial" visit to see them. Policy change requires effort at both the state and local level. Local regulators are hesitant to allow something not sanctioned by the state. Also, you'll need buy-in at the local level to accept a new state code and promote it. Here are some examples of what we've found successful.

- Build a support base. In the two years leading up to our state's code change we led hundreds of people through the installation process of diverting laundry and shower water to irrigate the landscape as part of our one-day workshop model. It was fun, empowering, connected the home to larger water politics, and left an enthusiastic homeowner with a greywater system. These were the people who flooded state policy makers with letters, e-mails, and calls demanding that greywater be legalized. Regulators commented that the code change meetings were the largest they'd ever seen, with the most public comments.

- Find an influential ally to go through the permitting process (or pilot project if the code hasn't changed yet): a city council member, water department employee, or someone in the building department. Find the perfect site: very simple to install, nothing tricky or questionable, a model system. Ideally this would be at the home of your influential ally, or your own home.

- Let the city monitor the system if it's a pilot project. Get lots of press. Conduct tours.

- To influence state policy, first find out how greywater is regulated in your state. If the department in charge isn't open to change, find a supportive congressperson. Though state legislation doesn't write codes, it can require the responsible agency to rewrite the code.

- After code change, get permits for various types of systems and work with the building department to create a simple permit application and checklist for future permits. And pressure the water district to incentivize greywater.

Arizona Breaks New Ground

In 1998 greywater pioneer Val Little, director of Water Conservation Alliance of Southern Arizona (Water CASA), conducted a survey in southern Arizona and found that 13 percent of residents used greywater, all illegally. The overly restrictive code prevented her from teaching people how to reuse greywater properly, so she worked to change the regulations. The end result was a performance-based code that outlines health and safety requirements (see Greywater Codes: Performance and Prescriptive, below). Residential greywater systems that follow the guidelines are legal — without permits, fees, or inspections — so long as the system produces less than 400 gallons per day. Now water departments, NGOs like Water CASA, and the state environmental health department can offer advice, brochures, classes, and financial incentives to encourage safe, legal greywater reuse. Arizona's success was emulated by other states, including New Mexico and Wyoming. Eventually (in 2009), California upgraded the state code to remove some permitting barriers for irrigation systems.

The Current State

Greywater codes still don't exist in many parts of the country. At the time of writing, some states regulate greywater like septic water and require a septic disposal system for it. Others, like West Virginia and Massachusetts, allow greywater systems only in houses with a composting toilet. Florida bans outdoor greywater use but allows it for flushing toilets. Georgia allows you to carry greywater in buckets to the plants, but you can't get a permit to build a simple greywater irrigation system. Washington state's code allows very small systems built without a permit (following performance guidelines), but all other systems have quite stringent requirements. Oregon requires an annual permit fee.

Many barriers still exist for legal greywater systems around the county, but the tendency is toward better, friendlier codes. To find out how greywater is regulated in your state, look at the state's plumbing codes or the state environmental health department; greywater is either regulated by the plumbing code (building department) or the department of the environment. Or, contact your local building department, environmental health department, water district, or environmental groups, though they may not be up-to-date on the code if a recent change has taken place.

Having Trouble Getting a Permit?

Getting permits is important to mainstream greywater reuse, as well as to keeping your home up to code. Unfortunately, it's not always easy to get a permit, especially in places lacking precedent. Early adopters seeking permits work hard and often are forced to build a more costly and complicated system than necessary. Even in states lacking a greywater code, permits may be obtainable through the "alternative methods and materials" section of the code. Some homeowners have had success using their home as a "pilot" project that allowed local regulators to issue an experimental permit and then monitor and learn from that system.

Greywater Codes: Performance-Based and Prescriptive

Performance-based codes describe health and safety requirements for greywater systems. Systems that meet the requirements are legal; those that don't are not. Performance-based codes don't typically require inspections or fees, yet provide legal grounds for a city to take action against a problem system. For example, "no pooling or runoff" is a common guideline that prevents exposure to greywater, but many codes don't specify how to meet this requirement. Performance-based codes are written in simple, straightforward language. States and local jurisdictions can provide further guidance, such as how to size a system to avoid pooling and runoff, but the more specific details are left out of the code.

Prescriptive codes specify exactly how to build a greywater system including what materials and parts can be used. Instead of stating "No pooling or runoff allowed," they may estimate greywater production based on number of bedrooms in the house and size the irrigation area based on soil type.

Greywater Pioneer: San Francisco Public Utilities Commission (SFPUC)

THE SFPUC PROVIDES WATER to 2.6 million people in the San Francisco Bay Area, operates a combined sewer system, and treats more than 80 million gallons of wastewater a day. A leader in on-site reuse of alternate water sources, including greywater, rainwater, stormwater, blackwater and foundation drainage, the SFPUC has developed technical assistance materials to help developers reuse water in large commercial and mixed-use residential properties.

Along with San Francisco's Non-potable Water Ordinance, the SFPUC provides financial incentives to buildings over 100,000 square feet to reuse water for irrigation and toilet flushing. Their new headquarters, located at 525 Golden Gate Avenue, in the heart of downtown San Francisco, consumes 60 percent less water than similarly sized buildings. The on-site wastewater treatment system uses a "living machine" to clean greywater and blackwater to be reused for toilet and urinal flushing, treating 5,000 gallons a day to supply 100 percent of the nonpotable building water needs. The building's 25,000-gallon rainwater harvesting system provides irrigation around the building.

I spoke with Paula Kehoe, director of Water Resources with the SFPUC, about their sustainable water programs:

What advice do you have for other water agencies interested in promoting on-site water reuse in urban areas?

Cities are on the front line and can create pathways to encourage innovation in water use. Water agencies are working hard to increase water efficiency and to diversify their water supply.

Encouraging the reuse of nontraditional water supplies, such as graywater and blackwater, expands our options and decreases the potable water used for flushing toilets and irrigation.

Water agencies can provide leadership to address concerns with these projects by engaging with local health and building departments to establish standards for local oversight that ensure public health protection. Consistent and ongoing communication with local agencies is the key to developing successful programs.

What are your goals for San Francisco's water systems?

Our overall goal for San Francisco's water use is to maximize efficiency and decrease potable water consumption. One strategy is to maximize the on-site reuse of alternate water sources on multiple scales in all new developments in San Francisco, including building, block, district, and neighborhood scales.

What aspects of the program do you think can be successfully replicated in other areas?

The Non-potable Water Program (2012) coordinated three City agencies to streamline the permitting process for on-site systems; it's a great model for other municipalities. We worked with the City's Departments of Building Inspection (SFDBI) and Public Health (SFDPH) to develop a regulatory pathway to approve alternate water source projects. The SFDBI oversees construction; the SFDPH prescribes water quality criteria and oversees operation (including permitting the treatment systems); and the SFPUC provides cross-connection control services, technical guidance, and financial incentives up to $250,000 per project to encourage on-site reuse.

A detailed code that spells out how to construct a greywater system will result in safer, better-built systems, right? Unfortunately, that's not the case. Greywater systems are complex; they interact with the living world of soils and plants, and are influenced by water-use habits, fixtures, climate, and physical layout of the house and landscape. Unless the code considers all these variables (and in fact it never does), it results in overly restrictive requirements, adding unnecessary cost, or creates an inefficient irrigation system. When a code is out of touch with reality, people ignore it and build illegal systems, with no guidance. After all, since it's common sense to reuse the water we already have, why should it be difficult to get a permit, or the fees be expensive?

National Codes and Standards

Wouldn't it be great if there were just one code for the whole country, so each state didn't have to reinvent the wheel around greywater law? The International Association of Plumbing and Mechanical Officials (IAPMO) writes codes that are adopted across the nation, and it has a new one on greywater (find it in the Uniform Plumbing Code). Unfortunately, this UPC code isn't very good. States who adopt it will need to alter it — like California did for its 2013 plumbing code — or risk minimal compliance from the public. The International Code Council (ICC) also writes codes adopted by many states; its greywater code, found in the International Plumbing Code (IPC), is even worse than the UPC. (States that use the IPC should write their own code instead of adopting the greywater chapter.)

National standards for indoor reuse systems are being developed. NSF International recently released water quality guidelines as part of their standard for nonpotable indoor reuse (toilet flushing). NSF 350: Onsite Residential and Commercial Water Reuse Treatment Systems is, according to NSF, "a revolutionary standard that sets clear, rigid, yet realistic guidelines for water reuse treatment systems." By meeting these testing requirements and receiving certification, companies (who can afford the expensive certification) should find it easier to gain permits, a positive step for indoor reuse and large-scale commercial greywater systems.

Summary Characteristics of Optimal Greywater-Friendly Regulations

- Easy to follow

- Performance-based. Guidelines outline health and safety requirements. For example, no pooling or runoff, minimize contact with greywater, keep all greywater on the property where it's generated, etc.

- Do not require a permit or fee for the safest situations; for example, single-family homes where all greywater is used for irrigation in the yard

- Permit required only for more risky or complicated situations; for example, large flows, indoor reuse, or multifamily dwellings

- Code is statewide with a mechanism in place to educate local regulators.

Water Utility Perspective

Susie Murray, water resource specialist with the city of Santa Rosa, California, discusses the cost-effectiveness of promoting greywater:

"From a water utility perspective, offering an incentive for greywater is cost effective. In 2012 wholesale water cost approximately $700 per acre-foot (af), while buying it back from our account holders through a greywater rebate program costs about $450 per acre-foot. Greywater also works well in combination with other conservation incentive strategies." In addition to greywater rebates the city offers other incentives, such as for turf removal and switching to low-flow showerheads.

Ask your water district for an incentive! Water districts around the country offer financial incentives for reusing greywater. Tucson Water, in Arizona, offers a rebate for one-third the cost of the greywater system (up to $1,000), and offers free educational workshops and online resources (see Resources). In California, San Francisco's water department has a free manual instructing residents how to build simple systems, offers free workshops, and subsidizes parts for constructing a washing machine greywater system. Other towns, including Santa Rosa, Santa Cruz, Goleta, and Monterey, offer rebates for installing a system.

The Environmental Health Perspective: Rob Kostlivy

ENVIRONMENTAL HEALTH DIRECTORS have a big job. They regulate food production, solid waste, water supply, vector control, hazardous materials, milk and dairy products, air sanitation, noise control, rabies and animal disease — the list goes on. Greywater falls under their charge, though most receive no formal training in it. At the very first California Greywater Conference, Rob Kostlivy, director of the Tuolumne County Environmental Health Department, gave the keynote welcome speech. He explained why environmental health departments have often blocked legal greywater reuse, and how he's working to change that. I spoke with Rob about his work in Tuolumne County. (Note: Environmental health departments have different names state by state, including variations such as Department of Ecology or Department of Environmental Quality.)

Why are environmental health departments often a barrier to legal greywater reuse?

The fear of the unknown has been a driving force that has plagued environmental health departments across the state for many years. We were taught that greywater is blackwater, virtually the same standard as septic system waste. Without the proper training and education, most jurisdictions chose to fear greywater in lieu of trying to understand it or become educated in the subject.

Tuolumne County has permitted a lot of greywater systems and sponsored the first California Greywater Conference. Can you talk about how your department is promoting safe reuse of greywater?

I looked at the literature from other places using greywater, like Australia. When I read reports from their environmental agencies, it helped me become comfortable with greywater. As a result, we permitted the largest greywater project in California at Evergreen Lodge, more than 50 interconnected and independent systems at that facility. We worked closely with a local installation company to ensure health and safety precautions were in place, while simultaneously educating ourselves about different types of systems and reasonable safety precautions; we didn't want to force an over-engineered or overly costly system, but we still wanted to ensure that we protected public health. Now that this large system is entering the third year of operation, we are continuing to look at the monitoring reports to get a big snapshot of how the system is working, looking at what worked and what needs to be improved.

To promote greywater, Tuolumne County partnered with Sierra Watershed Progressive to create California's first greywater conference. My intentions were simple; I wanted the *regulated* to sit across from the *regulators*. I knew we had a lot to learn from each other and felt it was important that the curriculum at the conference to be conducted by the experts in the field, the grassroots organizers, educators; I also wanted the greywater community to hear the regulator perspective as well. I felt that we needed to work together to help develop resolutions in solving our statewide water crisis. I received feedback from my environmental health colleagues that this conference was a success and that they will continue to learn and work at promoting a smart, sensible and scientific approach to permitting greywater. In my humble opinion, this is a great turnaround in attitude by the regulators. It shows how with partnership, we can accomplish great things!

Installing Your Greywater System

GET YOUR GLOVES ON and the measuring tape out — it's time to design and build your system. By doing the preparation work in chapter 4 you learned about how much greywater your home generates, your soil type and the size of infiltration areas needed, and the plants you'd like to irrigate. In this chapter you'll learn everything you need to know about planning and installing a few of the most common types of greywater systems. You'll also find an overview of other types of systems — either more complicated or less common.

IN THIS CHAPTER:

- Choosing a Greywater System
- Laundry-to-Landscape (L2L) System
- Installing an L2L Irrigation System
- Irrigation Options
- Branched Drain Gravity-Fed System (Without Storage)
- Installing a Branched Drain System
- How to Wire an Actuator
- Greywater System with Tank and Pump
- Building a Pumped System
- Manufactured Greywater Systems
- Other Types of Greywater Systems
- Greywater in Freezing Climates
- Plumbing Basics for Greywater Installation

Choosing a Greywater System

GREYWATER IS a unique type of irrigation water, distinctly different from rainwater or potable water from the tap. To choose the best greywater system for your situation, you'll need a basic understanding of how different types of systems work and their advantages and limitations, as well as a clear understanding of your site: the landscape, plumbing configuration, your budget, and how much maintenance will realistically be done to keep up the system. Much of this information you gathered in chapter 4, and the remaining considerations will be covered here.

Combine Greywater Sources or Keep Them Separate?

One big consideration is whether to keep the greywater flows separate and install a system for each fixture, or to combine the flows together and install one larger system. For example, will you combine the showers with the washing machine greywater or keep them separate? What's best depends on your situation: the layout of your home, the type of system you want to install, and what types of plants you plan to irrigate. In general, if you are installing a system in your current home and are not doing a major plumbing remodel, it's most practical and economical to keep the greywater sources separate and build a different system from each fixture. In new home construction, or during big remodels, you could combine flows together and install one larger system.

When Separate Systems Make Sense

- Your house is already built and you don't want to do extra plumbing work.

- You want a simpler and lower-cost project.

- You plan to use gravity systems for showers/sinks and a laundry-to-landscape system for the washing machine.

- You need irrigation water near the various greywater sources. For example, one shower is close to the front yard, while the washing machine is near the backyard.

Tip: Even if you combine some flows, consider keeping the washing machine separate. A separate valve next to the machine will let you control the laundry flow without shutting off the entire system.

When Combining Flows Makes Sense

- You plan to incorporate a pump or filter.

- You want to include fixtures that aren't used frequently, for example, a guest bathroom.

- You want multiple irrigation zones. You'll typically need more than one fixture to generate enough water for multiple irrigation zones.

Tip: If you plan to reuse your entire household's greywater and have multiple bathrooms in the home, consider keeping one bathroom off the system. Guests can use that bathroom without sending their soaps to your yard, or forcing you to turn off the entire system.

Other Considerations

Permits and their requirements are other significant factors. Some types of systems are much easier to get a permit for than others, and many local authorities impose rigid permitting guidelines, which will impact your system design. In addition, most homes and landscapes were not planned with a greywater system in mind, so the best greywater system for you may not be quite what you originally imagined. You may discover your site presents logistical challenges

Operation and Maintenance Manual for your Greywater Systems

You will need an Operation and Maintenance (O&M) manual for each greywater system (and most codes require you to have one). This manual explains:

- what types of soaps and detergents can be used

- when the system should be shut off

- how much greywater it was designed for

- maintenance requirements

- basic troubleshooting tips

- a site plan of the system with photographs of the unburied pipes to help locate them if you plan future alterations or landscape work.

Place the O&M manual in an easy-to-find location, such as inside a plastic sleeve and taped near the diverter valve or greywater fixture (for example, on the side of the washing machine). Show the manual to any house-sitters or house guests, and pass it on to new owners if you sell the house. Some local municipalities, either the city or water district, can provide you with an O&M manual to adapt; or you can download one from the website of a nonprofit such as Greywater Action (see Resources).

or your landscape plants aren't suitable. Being flexible and open to change, particularly landscape changes, will help you find an affordable and suitable system.

Greywater Systems at a Glance

In this chapter I'll explain how to design and install four common systems: the laundry-to-landscape (L2L) system, branched drain, and pumped systems (both with and without a filter). The Greywater Systems Overview chart on the facing page summarizes the costs and capabilities of these systems.

Laundry-to-landscape systems typically are the lowest in cost and easiest to install. Because the installation doesn't alter the household drainage plumbing the system often doesn't require a permit.

Gravity-based branched drain systems require the landscape to be lower than the plumbing and are best suited for larger plants — and they're low-maintenance; a great choice for irrigation of trees and bushes.

Pumped systems, both filtered and unfiltered, are designed to move greywater uphill and are capable of spreading the water over large areas. These systems typically are more difficult to get a permit for and may require backflow prevention (see page 117). Check with your local building authority, as specific requirements can add significant costs to the system.

Which System to Do First?

A common order of installing systems — for people retrofitting existing homes, as opposed to new construction or major remodels — is to start with the laundry-to-landscape system, then install gravity or pumped systems from the other fixtures. A kitchen sink system requires more frequent maintenance than other sources of greywater due to higher organic matter in the water, so it's best to include one after the easier-to-maintain systems are installed.

When to Turn Off the System

If you have a functional sewer or septic system, direct your greywater that way whenever:

- using chlorine bleach, hair dye, harsh cleaners, or other toxic substances.

- using non-plant-friendly products (those with salts or boron).

- washing to remove toxic or hazardous chemicals from clothing, such as gasoline or paint thinner spilled on your shirt.

- washing diapers or clothing containing fecal matter.

- there are puddles in the yard or any visible signs of greywater surfacing.

GREYWATER SYSTEMS OVERVIEW

Type of system	Laundry-to-landscape (L2L)	Branched drain	Pumped — no filter	Pumped — with filter
Fixtures	Washing machine only	Showers/baths, sinks, kitchen sink, washing machine	All fixtures	All fixtures (kitchen sink typically is not recommended)
Materials cost (excluding permit)	$100–$300	$250–$500	$500–$1,500	$1,000–$4,000
Cost of professional installation (excluding design fees for any permits)	$700–$2,000	$800–$4,000	$1,500–$4,000	$2,000–$4,500
Skills needed for typical installation	Basic landscaping and construction; basic plumbing	Basic landscaping, construction, and plumbing. Plumbing can be complex.	Basic landscaping, construction, plumbing, and sometimes electrical. Plumbing can be complex.	Basic landscaping, construction, plumbing, and sometimes electrical. Plumbing can be complex.
Able to move water uphill?	No more than a few feet	No	Yes	Yes
Suitable for trees and shrubs?	Yes	Yes	Yes	Yes
Suitable for smaller plants?	Yes, though front-loading machines can't distribute water to many locations.	Not usually. Possibly if plants are clustered and irrigated in the center of the group.	Yes, though not able to spread water out as far as with drip irrigation.	Yes; also suited to drip irrigation.
Suitable for lawn?	No	No	No	Possible, though more challenging.
Maintenance	Annual	Annual	Annual	Every 1–2 months, possibly less often (depending on the site and system specifics).

Using Greywater without a System: Tips for Renters and Homeowners

It would be great if all landlords were water-conscious and supported the efforts of their water-wise tenants. Some are, but many still don't want tenants changing the house, which makes installing a greywater system more challenging. If you're a homeowner, perhaps you aren't ready to install a dedicated system, or you just want some simple solutions for reusing greywater right away. Here are a few ideas for reusing water without altering the house. Don't forget to check with your landlord about these projects; they may want to pay for the parts or learn more.

"Laundry drum" system. Simply stick the hose of the washing machine out a nearby window (nearby window required), drain it into a drum/small tank (about 50 gallons), then connect a garden hose to the bottom of the barrel.

Laundry-to-landscape system with no hole in the wall. Attach a piece of wood, such as a 2×4, to the bottom of a nearby window and drill through the wood instead of the wall. The window closes against the wood and the pipe exits the house with no holes in the house. Alternatively, if your landlord allows a hole in the floor (and you have a crawl space), drill through the floor and run the pipe outside via a screened vent.

Outdoor washing machine. Set up your washing machine outside on a covered deck or porch (requires above-freezing temperatures). Connect the machine to an outdoor spigot, and run only cold-water loads.

Bucket or siphon. Collecting greywater in buckets builds muscle and provides a visceral awareness of how much water you use. Collect shower greywater by plugging the tub to bail out the water, or simply shower over a bucket. And don't forget to collect the "clear water" while your shower heats up. If the landscape is lower in elevation than your tub, you can siphon the water outside (with a hand pump and garden hose). Kitchen sink water can be collected in a dishpan in the sink.

Loose connection allows air flow out of drum

Mulch basin

Large drum   Strap   Garden hose

▲ Constructing a laundry drum system is similar to converting a 55-gallon barrel into a rain barrel (see page 178). The key difference is there is no shutoff on the bottom, since greywater should not be stored. Directly attach a garden hose to the barrel and place the hose in a well-mulched part of the yard near thirsty plants that will soak up the greywater.

Laundry-to-Landscape (L2L) System

INVENTED BY GREYWATER PIONEER Art Ludwig, the laundry-to-landscape (L2L) greywater system is one of the most popular types of systems in the U.S. I've helped install hundreds of these in workshops and trainings and can't imagine living without one. It can be built with off-the-shelf parts, doesn't alter the household plumbing, and doesn't require a permit in many states. The system captures greywater from the drain hose of the washing machine, connects to a diverter valve so you can easily switch the system on or off, and then distributes greywater into the landscape through a main line of 1-inch irrigation tubing and ½-inch branch lines that feed specific plants. It is one of the easiest systems to construct, and is very easy to change. **Note:** The washing machine has an internal air gap, which keeps it (and the L2L system) safely separate from the potable water pipes.

Designing Your L2L System

To prepare for constructing the system, you'll determine where to run the pipe from the washing machine out to the landscape, what plants are easiest to irrigate, and how many plants you can irrigate based on your home's greywater production. By choosing nearby plantings or those downhill of the home, you'll design the system so the washing machine's internal pump is not overtaxed. The type of washing machine you have will impact the system: conventional top-loaders can distribute greywater to more locations than front-loading machines and most high-efficiency top-loaders.

Note: If your home generates large volumes of greywater, be sure to read Got a Lot of Greywater? Don't Dig One Big Basin (page 103) for advice on appropriately distributing larger flows.

Adding Gravity Feed?

If you're planning to install a gravity-fed branched drain system as well as an L2L system, it's wise to first plan the irrigation portion of the gravity system before deciding what to irrigate with the L2L system. The reason? It's much easier to distribute water from an L2L system than a gravity one, and you'll have more options for the L2L. For guidance on designing a branched drain system, see Site Assessment, on page 103. In general, if one area in the landscape will receive greywater from both types of systems,

Diverter valve

TO SEWER

Washing machine

1" irrigation tube

½" outlets

▲ **Laundry-to-landscape system**

DISTRIBUTING WATER WITH AN L2L SYSTEM

Upward slope: Don't irrigate uphill from the washing machine.

Flat yard: Irrigate within 50 feet.

Berm

Downward slope: Serpentine the tubing to slow the water flow.

Irrigate on upper side of plant. Build a berm to create a flat mulch basin.

direct greywater from the branched drain system to irrigate the closest trees and bushes, and use the L2L system to serve slightly more distant plants or smaller plants in the vicinity.

Distribution Limitations

The washing machine pump pushes greywater through the L2L irrigation system at low pressures. Each time the machine pumps it sends all the water inside the washer drum to the landscape, then the pump turns off. Because of this, the system is limited in how many outlets it can have; if there are too many, it's impossible to get water to come out them all. Below are general guidelines on the limitations of different types of machines. You can always have fewer outlets, but including more may require a lot of adjusting to achieve an even flow of water.

- Regular top-loading machines can distribute water to about 20 locations (19 tees and one open end of the tubing).

- Water-efficient machines can distribute water to about 8 locations (7 tees and one open end

of the tubing) for a front-efficient machine, and 10 for a top-efficient machine.

Assessing Your Site

Identify planted areas suitable for L2L irrigation (trees, bushes, larger perennials, or large annuals). Then, consider where the irrigation pipe from the washing machine can exit the house, either through the wall or crawl space. Is the exit near a suitable irrigation area? If not, are there other exit options (for example, crossing to another side of the house through the crawl space)? Also consider landscape alterations to make the installation easier; for example, planting trees or bushes in an accessible part of the yard.

How High and Far Can the Washing Machine Pump?

The washing machine pump can send greywater directly to the landscape, but not too far away or up a hill. Overworking the machine's pump could damage it. (Since replacing a washer pump is a lot cheaper than buying an effluent pump, some people whose yards are gently sloped choose to overwork their machine's pump slightly rather than installing a pumped system.) These general guidelines will help you select an appropriate part of your landscape, but remember that each situation is different; change the system if you notice problems with the machine. If your machine doesn't drain well or has other pump problems, fix them before installing an L2L system.

- Upward-sloped yard: Don't distribute water uphill of your washing machine, meaning the yard should not be higher in elevation than the machine. The pump in the machine is not designed for this.

- Downward-sloped yard: On downhill slopes the greywater distribution piping can extend as far as necessary. Don't run tubing straight down a steep slope, though; the water will rush to the bottom, making it difficult to irrigate the upper portions. Instead, snake tubing down the hill in an S or serpentine pattern, like a switchback trail, to slow the flow of water.

- Flat yard: Most machines can pump water across a flat yard for up to 50 feet without problem. Traveling farther risks pump damage; friction in the tubing increases pressure on the pump. Elevating the machine can help give a little more oomph in the system.

Subsurface or Surface Irrigation?

There's a wide range of recommendations among different state greywater codes regarding where to direct greywater — either on the surface of the landscape or delivered deep belowground. Because most of the plants' roots, as well as the soil microorganisms that clean greywater, are found in the upper 1 to 2 feet of soil, surface irrigation is usually better. (Remember, greywater must land onto mulch, never bare soil.) It's also a lot easier to observe and maintain the system when greywater outlets are aboveground; people are less likely to forget to check the outlets since they're visible, and maintenance is easier as well.

Surface irrigation isn't always possible, though. Some codes don't allow it, and often gravity branched drain systems must have outlets below grade due to the slope of the land. Whenever you need to irrigate subsurface, try to stay as close to the surface as you can. Some states require that outlets are covered but not necessarily below grade.

Washing Machine Warranties

If you are purchasing a new washing machine, you may be wondering whether installing this system could affect your washing machine warranty. The answer: Perhaps, but probably not. My personal and anecdotal experience is that washer repair people don't question the greywater system or attribute any washer problems to it. I know of just one instance when the company's installer of a new washer didn't want to hook it up to the pre-installed 3-way diverter valve, claiming it would void the warranty on the machine. Others have experienced the opposite: the installer helpfully hooked up the new washer to the valve.

Surface Irrigation
▼ Greywater drops through the air and lands onto mulch, where it's quickly soaked up.

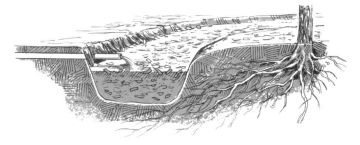

Subsurface Irrigation
▼ A mulch shield protects the greywater outlet and water is released below the surface of the mulch.

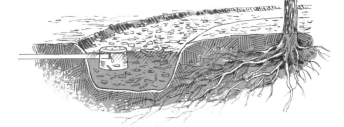

▼ Greywater lands onto mulch at the surface and is covered with a solid shield.

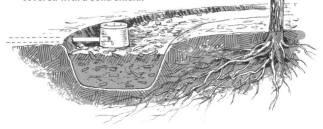

Call Before You Dig!

Call 811 (or visit www.call811.com) several days before starting a project to find out where your underground utilities are located. The hotline will route your call to your local utility call center. You'll tell the operator where you're planning to dig and they'll notify the utility providers in your area, who in turn will mark any underground utility lines on your property. You can also hire a private locator to find lines inside the property; this might be advisable if you have outbuildings, such as sheds and guest houses, that may be supplied by electrical and water lines from your house but aren't officially within the purview of utility companies.

In addition to having all utilities marked, it's up to you to make sure you don't put a pickax through a buried service line, which could be a deadly mistake. Use extreme caution when working anywhere near buried lines. Or better yet, avoid these areas entirely.

Sketching and Documenting Your System

As you're determining where you'll send the water — and before beginning construction — make a detailed diagram of the entire system, including the number of bends, length of pipe, etc. This will save you a few trips to the store when you build. Remember that the end of the main tubing is an outlet and should be located in a mulch basin near a plant to be irrigated. After you've installed the system, edit this drawing as necessary to document the "as-built" system. This document, along with the pre-burial photographs, will help you find the buried tubing and outlets in the future. Add all final drawings to your Operation and Maintenance manual (O&M) manual (page 78).

Hardscape in the Way?

Greywater pipes can't run over hardscape. If you need to pass through a driveway, stairs, or a patio to run the pipe to the landscape, you can:

- Remove the hardscape.

- Go under it. If the sidewalk is just a few feet wide and there is enough room to dig on both sides, tunnel under. First dig a hole on each side of the hardscape, then start digging under it with a trowel. Connect the holes with a steel rod or other ramming tool. Use rigid 1-inch PVC pipe instead of tubing under the hardscape if you think the tubing could be damaged when you shove it under. Tape off the end of the pipe so soil doesn't get inside, then hammer the pipe through the tunnel. Or use a water-jet to tunnel under, though it makes a giant mud puddle.

- Cut a groove out of the hardscape, using a masonry blade on a circular saw, or a concrete saw. Fill the groove with concrete patching material or cover it with gravel, sand, or decorative tile.

- Run the pipe on top of the concrete, then build a small ramp cover for the pipe (so it's not a tripping hazard).

- Find an alternate route — perhaps along the house to the edge of the hardscape. This may alter your irrigation plans.

- Run the pipe snugly against a stair riser to avoid creating a tripping hazard. Use 1- or 2-hole straps to attach the pipe snugly.

System Design Example

Here is an example of an L2L system for a three-person household in Austin, Texas. They wash four loads of laundry a week at 25 gallons a load and never wash more than two loads on any given day. This is the basic information they need to design the irrigation and infiltration area for their system:

- Greywater produced: 100 gallons a week (25 gallons × 4 loads)

- Daily max: 2 loads (50 gallons); this will help determine the size of their mulch basins.

- Soil type: Sandy clay (coefficient 0.6; see page 62); *0.6 × 50 = 30 square feet of mulch basin*

- Plot plan of house yard: Washing machine on east side; plants on the south side. They can run the pipe under house to reach the south side.

Clean the Pump Filter

Many washing machines have an internal filter to keep large particles out of the pump. Over time the filter clogs, which adds strain on the pump and can prevent it from evacuating all the water from the machine. Before installing a greywater system, and any time the machine struggles to pump out the water, clean the pump filter. Remove the front cover to reach it, unscrew the filter cover, and be prepared for a few gallons of water to spill out. Clean out the filter and put it back in place. You can find instructions online for various brands of washing machines by searching with "how to clean your pump filter," or you can consult a washing machine repair person for assistance.

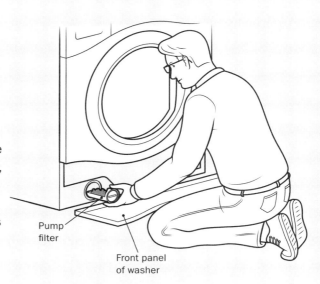

Pump filter

Front panel of washer

When they assessed the site, they found that their existing irrigation system had three zones. One of the zones irrigated five small trees (3-foot radius from trunk to drip line), which were the most suitable plants for an L2L system (the other plants were small and spread out). They could slope the pipe downward as it traveled under the house, then run it 10 feet to reach the first tree; all the trees were within 50 feet of where the pipe traveled flat. This zone of trees seemed to be easiest to irrigate, so they checked to see if the greywater production was a good match for the trees (was it too much or too little water?). In terms of irrigation amount, each tree would receive 100/5 = 20 gallons per week. Austin gets some summer rain to supplement greywater during the hottest time of the year.

They calculated the plant water requirements using both methods from chapter 4 (page 65).

Using the "rule of thumb" method, a small tree requires:

$\pi r^2 = 3 \times 3 \times 3$ feet = 27 square feet

27 square feet × 1 (hot climate) = 27 gallons per week

Using the ET method, a tree of this size in Austin requires:

0.62 × 27 square feet × 0.5 × 8.21 (ET) = 69 gallons/ month or 17 gallons/week

This demonstrates that 20 gallons a week is a good amount of irrigation water for each tree in this climate.

Next, they determined how large each mulch basin should be to infiltrate greywater into the ground. Based on the soil type and gallons per day calculated above, the system requires 30 square feet of mulch basin area. Since the water will be divided among five different trees, each tree needs a basin at least 30 ÷ 5, or 6 square feet.

▼ **A simple sketch of the L2L system**

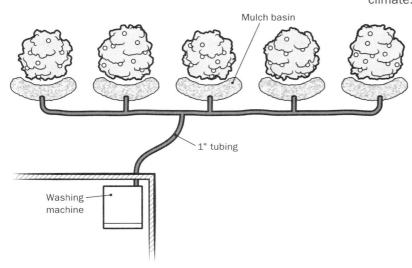

Mulch basin

1" tubing

Washing machine

Installing an L2L Irrigation System

Installing an L2L system requires very basic plumbing and landscaping skills. You'll be working with plastic pipe and tubing, which are easy to cut and assemble. In general, the most difficult aspect of the installation is drilling the exit hole for the pipe. If drilling through the wall or floor of your home feels daunting, get help from a knowledgeable friend or hire a handyperson to help you. Most systems take a day or two to install, though with help can go much quicker. Make sure to source the materials for your system a few weeks before you plan to install it. Depending on what your local hardware and irrigation stores stock, you may need to mail-order a few of the parts; see Resources for online retailers. See Plumbing Basics for Greywater Installation (page 135) for details on parts and basic techniques. You can also build a PVC-free system using BluLock fittings (see Resources).

MATERIALS

Interior Plumbing

Pipe thread tape

Two 1" PVC male adapters

One 1" PVC male × barbed adapter (or 1" male × ¾" barbed adapter if your washer hose is smaller; measure the inner diameter of the end of your washing machine drain hose to determine which size you need)

One brass threaded 3-way valve (full-port valve; see step 2)

One 1" hose clamp

Two 1¼" 2-hole straps with screws

1" schedule 40 PVC pipe (as needed)

1" PVC 90-degree and 45-degree elbows (as needed)

One air admittance valve (AAV) or auto-vent

One 1½" × 1" PVC reducer bushing

One 1½" PVC female adapter (slip × FPT)

One 1" PVC tee

PVC cement (glue)

1" PVC couplings (as needed)

1" 2-hole straps with screws (as needed)

Landscape Irrigation

One 1" barbed × slip (or barbed × insert) transition coupling

1" HDPE tubing

½" PE tubing (as needed)

1" × ½" barbed reducing tee (one for each "irrigation point," or branch from the main line to each mulch basin)

1" × 1" × 1" barbed tee (quantity as needed; one for each branch from the main line)

Large garden staples (for ¾" or 1" tubing; use one every few feet)

½" green- or purple-backed ball valves (full port ball valves; quantity as needed, usually 2 to 4)

Exterior house paint

Construction-grade sealant (see step 15)

Optional (for flushing the system): One 1" PVC slip union and one brass female hose thread × ¾" male hose thread fitting (see step 12)

TOOLS

Drill and ¼" pilot bit (long enough to go through your wall or floor)

1½" hole saw (optional: masonry bits for stucco)

Two tongue-and-groove pliers (or two large wrenches)

Hex-head driver

Permanent marker

PVC pipe cutter or handsaw

Level

Shovel

Mattock or pickax

Narrow trenching shovel

Tubing cutters or large clippers

Hammer

Thermos (full of hot water) and a cup

Painting supplies

Finding Parts to Build an L2L System

Gathering parts for your system will take you to several stores (irrigation, plumbing, and hardware) or online retailers (see Resources).

Tubing. Find 1" tubing, either high-density polyethylene (HDPE) or polyethylene (PE, or "poly"). HDPE is stronger and less likely to kink than PE. Irrigation stores sell several types of HDPE tubing, all suitable for greywater. Don't use tubing that is visibly kinked or seems easy to kink (try bending it to see). In urban areas the only 1" option typically is *Blu-Lock*; find a distributor on the manufacturer's website (Hydro-Rain).

3-way valve. Brass 3-way valves, used in hydronic heating, often are hard to find locally. Larger plumbing supply stores carry them, and sometimes general building supply stores or irrigation stores will order them. Get a *full port* valve, available from brands such as Legend Valve and Red-White. The inside of a full port valve is not reduced in size, whereas *regular port* valves are a pipe size smaller inside, which creates more friction in the system. Banjo makes a suitable full port 1" plastic valve.

Air admittance valve (AAV). Use either an official AAV ($20) or a lower-cost auto-vent or in-line vent ($4). Both are available from plumbing suppliers and hardware stores. Note that the cheaper one isn't allowed in standard plumbing applications but often is okay to use in an L2L system because it's connected only to the irrigation system, not the household plumbing.

Mulch. Use chunky wood chips (1 to 1½") from a local tree trimmer. One-half of a cubic yard is usually plenty. Or, buy wood chips from a landscaping store (loose or bagged).

1" barbed fittings. Find these at irrigation stores or online (for example, dripworks.com).

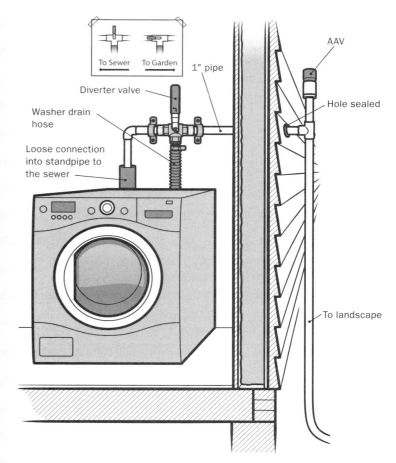

▲ **Washing machine connected to diverter valve; water flows either to landscape or to sewer/septic.**

1. Make an exit hole for the pipe.

To exit the house you need a 1½" hole, either in the wall or floor. Identify the best location for the hole. Exit through the wall if you don't have a basement or crawl space, the area you plan to irrigate is adjacent to the wall, or the washing machine is on the second story and there is living space below the floor. Exit through the floor if you have an accessible basement or crawl space and can run the pipe out through a screened vent or other opening (you won't have to drill a hole in an exterior wall or foundation wall).

Before you drill, look for hidden obstacles in the wall, such as electrical wires, pipes, or studs. Drill a

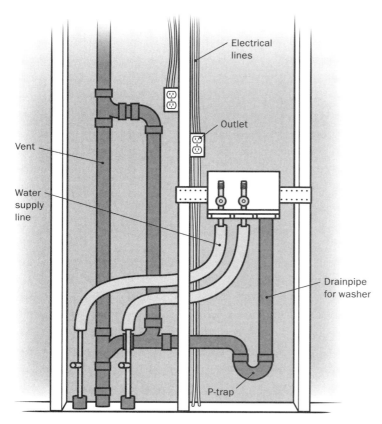

Electrical
lines

Outlet

Vent

Water
supply
line

Drainpipe
for washer

P-trap

▲ **Watch out for plumbing and electrical inside the wall
when you drill.**

¼" pilot hole with a long, thin drill bit (called a pilot bit) that can pass through the entire wall or floor. With a stucco or fiber cement board siding you can use a special masonry hole saw bit, but these are expensive. Drill carefully; stop if you hit anything in the wall. If necessary, try different spots until you exit freely. Check the exit hole from the outside to see if it's a good location, for example, not right next to the window frame. Since the pilot hole represents the center of the 1½" hole, make sure there's at least ¾" clearance around all sides of the pilot hole.

When you're confident you're drilling in the proper location, use the pilot hole as a guide and drill the exit hole with a 1½" hole saw. To make a clean-looking hole on both sides of the wall, drill from both the inside and the outside. When drilling through several wall layers, the hole saw will get filled up and you'll need to remove the "cookie" that forms inside the

bit (using a screwdriver) before you're able to drill all the way through.

If your wall's exterior siding is wood, vinyl, or plastic, use a regular hole saw bit for the hole. If the siding is stucco or fiber cement board, you can use a special masonry hole bit, but these are expensive. Alternatively, trace the outside of a scrap piece of 1" PVC pipe on the wall with a marker, then drill around the hole with a smaller masonry bit. Chip out the circle with a hammer and chisel, then snip the lath or wire behind with metal snips. After the stucco is removed, drill the rest of the way using a standard hole saw.

Note that some building codes require exit holes to be "fire rated" if they are within a certain distance from another building; for example, 5 feet. If other homes are very close to yours, check with your permitting agency about fire rating requirements.

2. Prepare the 3-way valve.

Wrap pipe thread tape clockwise around the threads of the two 1" male (non-barbed) adapters (clockwise as you face the open end of the threaded side), wrapping tightly three times around. Screw the adapters into the right and left sides (opposite ends) of the 3-way valve. Start gently by hand to avoid cross-threading. (If you cross-thread, the metal threads will strip the plastic threads and will leak.) The fitting should turn easily at first, then get harder. Do the same with the 1" male x barbed adapter in the middle outlet of the valve. Tighten the fittings snugly with tongue-and-groove pliers. Don't overtighten, or the fitting could crack.

Place the hose clamp over the washing machine drain hose. Then push the hose over the barbed fitting on the adapter. Tighten the hose clamp over the hose and barbed fitting, using a flathead screwdriver or hex-head driver.

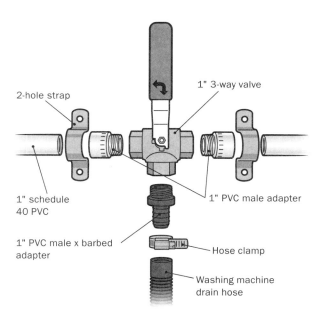

2-hole strap

1" 3-way valve

1" schedule
40 PVC

1" PVC male adapter

1" PVC male x barbed
adapter

Hose clamp

Washing machine
drain hose

▲ **Parts to connect 3-way valve to washing machine drain hose**

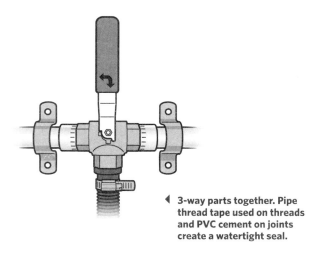

◀ **3-way parts together. Pipe
thread tape used on threads
and PVC cement on joints
create a watertight seal.**

NOTE: Some hoses have a hard end portion that
can be cut off. Take care not to cut too close to
the ribbed portion — you'll need about one inch of
smooth hose end to slip over the barb. Other hoses
have a rigid U-shaped piece of plastic attached
to them, which can be removed. If the hose is too
short or otherwise unsuitable, replace it (it's easy
to do). If it's hard to fit the hose over the barb,
soften the hose by heating it with a hair dryer or
sticking it into a cup of hot water; when hot, the
hose should fit on. Check this connection for leaks
after you finish the system.

3. Mount the valve.

Decide where to mount the 3-way valve. The valve
must be above the **flood rim** of the washing machine
(the highest place water could fill) and have enough
clearance so you can easily turn the handle. The
valve must be strapped to a stud or other piece of
wood mounted behind. (If there is no stud, attach a
piece of wood behind the valve location.) Mount the
valve with 1¼" 2-hole straps or plumbers tape (if
you strap over the pipe, use 1" straps).

4. Plumb to and from the 3-way valve.

Next, plumb the most direct route from one side of
the valve back to the sewer/septic (where the hose
previously drained). At this stage, you're just dry-
fitting the parts. If your hose previously drained into
a utility sink, direct the PVC pipe into the sink in an
out-of-the-way location. If your hose drained into a
standpipe, plumb the PVC pipe so it extends a few
inches into the standpipe. The standpipe should
be larger than the PVC pipe so that there is room
around the sides for airflow. If your existing standpipe is undersized, consider upgrading it.

Plumb the other side of the valve to the exit hole
to the landscape. Use 1" schedule 40 PVC and
either 90- or 45-degree elbow fittings. Measure, cut,
and dry-fit (without glue) the PVC together to get
an idea where the pipe will go. With glue, the pipe
will slide farther into the fitting, up to the lip on the
interior; take this into account when measuring so
you don't end up short. Leave several inches of pipe
sticking out of the 1½" hole (outside the building or
below the floor).

Locate the air admittance valve, or AAV (see
page 87). This must be at the highest point of the
system. Position the AAV at least 6" above the flood
rim of the washing machine and in a visible and
accessible location.

If you pipe through the floor or drop down to exit
lower than the 3-way valve, locate the vent inside the
laundry room. If the pipe travels directly out of the
wall, at the height of the 3-way valve, the AAV can
be outside. The AAV may need protection in freezing
climate; confirm that the specific valve you use is

3 LOCATIONS FOR AAV

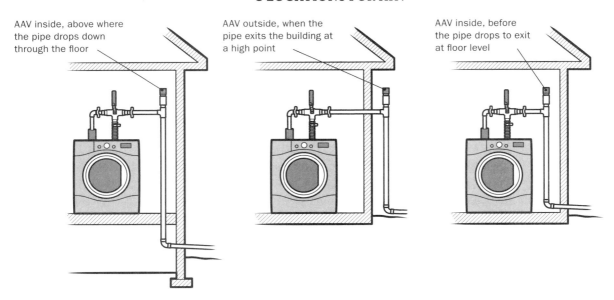

AAV inside, above where the pipe drops down through the floor

AAV outside, when the pipe exits the building at a high point

AAV inside, before the pipe drops to exit at floor level

rated for outdoor use, or install it inside. In any case, the tee and AAV assembly will be located above the point where you drop the pipe down (either through the floor or, if outside the house, down to the soil).

NOTE: If the plumbing to the sewer/septic feels tricky (i.e., a lot of tight turns), use a second washer hose instead of rigid pipe. Attach it to the valve via a second male pipe thread x barb fitting and slip it into the standpipe instead of plumbing with PVC. You can buy a washer hose at most hardware stores.

OPTIONAL: Add a union fitting into the pipe in any location where you may want to easily disconnect it — for example, if you plan to paint the wall behind the valve and want to easily disconnect and reconnect the system, or to send a plumber's snake down the standpipe to clean out a clog.

5. Assemble the air admittance valve (AAV).

Glue the 1½" × 1" reducer bushing into the slip side of the 1½" female adapter. Take care that the glue doesn't drip onto the threads on the other side of the adapter. Wrap pipe thread tape on the threads of the AAV, screw it into the threaded side of the female adapter, and hand-tighten the valve. Cut a 2" to 3" piece of 1" PVC pipe. Glue one end of the pipe into the 1" side of the bushing and the other end into the top of the tee.

AAV ASSEMBLY, SEPARATED AND GLUED TOGETHER

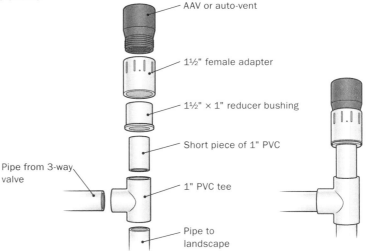

AAV or auto-vent

1½" female adapter

1½" × 1" reducer bushing

Short piece of 1" PVC

Pipe from 3-way valve

1" PVC tee

Pipe to landscape

6. Complete the interior pipe runs.

Now you're ready to glue the interior PVC piping. Before gluing, number and mark the fittings and pipes (with a permanent marker) so you'll know what goes where after you disassemble the parts to apply the glue. Plan the best order to glue and avoid "gluing yourself into a corner." Some of the glued joints allow for more flexibility than others; for example, the last two pieces in an assembly need space to be separated and pushed together.

7. Complete the remaining PVC pipe run.

Depending on your site, at this point you may have a short section of PVC remaining to reach the landscape, or you may need to pipe under the house through the crawl space before reaching the landscape. If the AAV is located outside, attach it to the pipe sticking through the house wall, and pipe down to the landscape. If the AAV is inside, connect it to the pipe extending through the floor and continue to the landscape. Try to maintain a downward slope whenever possible, and minimize fittings to reduce friction in the pipe. In the crawl space, strap the pipe to floor joists or available beams every 5 feet or so. Use 1" couplings as needed to connect long runs of pipe, and glue all joints.

Outside the house, use the 1" barbed x slip (or barbed x insert) adapter to transition between PVC and the irrigation tubing. The tubing will slip over the barbed side of the fitting. This often is the most convenient place to disconnect the irrigation portion of the system to flush the line. Either use a union so it's easy to detach, or simply leave this connection unglued (it usually doesn't leak, but if a small leak would be problematic don't use this method).

8. Prepare the landscape: dig the mulch basins.

To irrigate trees, bushes, shrubs, and larger annuals, dig a mulch basin in the drip line of the plant. See How to Dig a Mulch Basin (page 96) for details. If you are irrigating garden vegetables or herbs, see Irrigating Raised Beds (page 100) for advice on preparing the soil. You'll either dig very small mulch pits or cover the soil with straw and irrigate onto the straw.

9. Trench to each basin.

In most sites, you'll dig a trench for the tubing and bury it. Sometimes you can run the tubing on top of the soil in shaded locations; for example, along the edge of a fence, under a deck, or other out-of-the-way locations. Tubing can be in the sun, but it will last longer if it's not. You may also leave it above ground once it's inside garden beds.

Plan the run of irrigation tubing from the PVC pipe to all the mulch basins. Take the most direct route you can, with no sharp turns. Never kink or squish the tubing, which restricts the flow of water and could damage the washing machine pump. The tubing should run parallel to the basins but a few inches offset from each basin, so when you install the tee the ½" tube will enter the basin (see Tubing detail, page 92).

If there are any areas where the tubing may become damaged, such as under a swing set, transition back to rigid PVC in those locations.

Note: Avoid using barbed 90-degree elbows for turns. Instead, make a wider-radius turn with the tubing. The tight turn in a barbed 90-degree elbow restricts the flow of water and creates a place for debris to get stuck.

Trenches should be about 4" deep and level or sloping downward. If the tubing runs up and down, it will be harder to distribute water evenly to the plants.

10. Install the main line and greywater outlets.

Roll the 1" HDPE main-line tubing to all the mulch basins (see Tips for Working with Irrigation Tubing on page 139). Make sure the main-line tubing isn't inside of the basin; it should be a few inches offset, on top of solid earth. At each irrigation point cut the tubing and insert a 1" × ½" barbed reducing tee. Dig a small trench into the basin and run a short piece of ½" tubing from each tee and into the center of each mulch basin.

Optional: If your site requires the 1" main-line tubing to reach multiple areas, use 1" × 1" × 1" barbed tees as needed. Run a 1" line anytime you would need more than a few feet of ½" tubing to reach the plants.

You may discover that it's much more convenient to run tubing inside of a basin; for example, when irrigating along a narrow strip of land that isn't wide enough for the basin and tubing side by side. In this situation, run tubing inside the outer edge of the basin and securely stake it against the side wall of the basin, as high up as possible, as shown. Never run the tubing in the middle of your basin, because it can be damaged or wiggled by people stepping on it.

Stake the tubing down with long garden staples so it doesn't wiggle out of the trench. You will bury the tubing later, after you've tested the system.

▲ **Avoid running tubing inside the basin.**

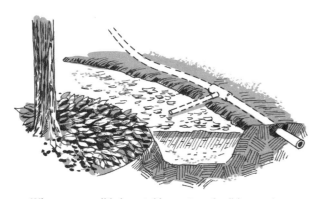

▲ **Whenever possible keep tubing on top of solid ground next to the basin.**

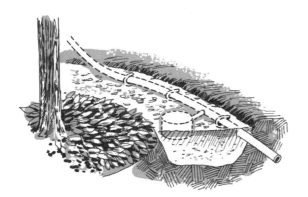

▲ **If tubing is inside the basin, stake it securely to the upper side of the basin wall.**

11. Prepare the greywater outlets and add mulch.

For surface irrigation: Add mulch to fill the basins. Place a flat stone or brick under the greywater outlet to help locate it in the future and prevent it from being inadvertently covered with mulch. You'll need to be able to find the outlets easily for annual maintenance.

For subsurface irrigation: Fill each basin partway, then add a mulch shield to the end of each outlet, including the end of the main line (see How to Make a Mulch Shield on page 98). Next, fill basin the rest of the way with mulch.

Mark the greywater outlets. This is where you'll do the annual maintenance to ensure the outlet doesn't clog and greywater flows freely onto the mulch.

12. Add a connection to flush the system (optional).

You may include a garden-hose connection to test or flush the system. If you do this, make sure that it's not possible to connect a garden hose without fully disconnecting the greywater pipe coming from the washer. That would be considered a cross-connection and is not allowed. To temporarily connect a garden hose, either pull apart the joint where the tubing connects to the PVC adapter, which may be a little difficult, or install a union with some adapters to more easily disconnect the system.

Here's how. To flush the system, open the union and insert a brass female hose thread x ¾" male hose thread fitting into the side going to the garden. Do this by firmly pushing the brass threads into the plastic (see image) and turning — the metal will bite into the plastic enough to hold the fitting in place. Then connect the garden hose and flush the line.

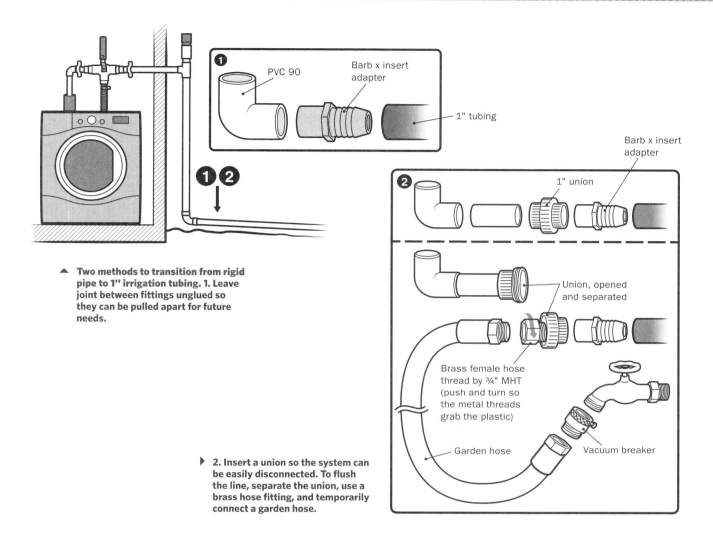

❶ PVC 90   Barb x insert adapter   1" tubing

❶ ❷

Barb x insert adapter

❷   1" union

Union, opened and separated

Brass female hose thread by ¾" MHT (push and turn so the metal threads grab the plastic)

Garden hose   Vacuum breaker

▲ **Two methods to transition from rigid pipe to 1" irrigation tubing. 1. Leave joint between fittings unglued so they can be pulled apart for future needs.**

▶ **2. Insert a union so the system can be easily disconnected. To flush the line, separate the union, use a brass hose fitting, and temporarily connect a garden hose.**

13. Test and tune the system.

Now you'll check to see if water comes out evenly from all the outlets. The first step is to get water running through the system, and there are two ways to do this. One is to run a washer cycle (or two or more), which works well with a conventional top-loading machine or in a small system with a water-efficient machine. The other method is to temporarily connect a garden hose (see step 12), and turn on the hose to a medium flow. Be sure to check the flow again with only the machine running to adjust for differences in pressure and water quantity.

NOTE: The first few gallons of water will fill the lines and wet the plastic tubing, and water may not come out for a few moments (possibly not until the second cycle of the machine).

If your yard is flat, you'll probably have more water coming out the first few outlets than the last ones. To tune, or balance, the system, first adjust the angles of the tees. Orient them slightly downward to get more water out of the ½" branch, or upward to slow the flow. You can also spin the ½" tubing so that the curve increases or decreases the flow.

If the flow is still uneven, add a ½" ball valve to the first outlet and close the valve slightly to reduce the flow, allowing more water to continue to other outlets. Be sure to use "green" or "purple back" ball valves. These are full-port valves with no restriction inside the valve; regular ball valves restrict the flow inside and will clog up.

Add valves until water comes out evenly, but only use them as needed. Do not add valves to all the outlets! They are clogging and maintenance points. If you have more than a couple of valves, you probably need to redesign the main line instead of adding more valves.

Take photographs before burying any tubing. Put them in your O&M manual (see page 78) so you know where to avoid digging in the future.

After you've tuned the system, bury the tubing as needed. Double-check each mulch shield (if you have them) to make sure there are several inches of air space between the outlet and the surface of the mulch.

WARNING: Leave the end of the 1" main line open. Never use a valve or plug at the end to stop water flow. Restricting the main line can back up the washing machine or damage its pump if outlets clog over time. The exception to this rule is when a system has multiple 1" lines. For example, if you used a 1" × 1" × 1" tee and have two different main lines, one can be restricted, as long as the other one stays fully open.

If you used a garden hose to test the system, disconnect it and reconnect the irrigation tubing to the PVC pipe. Run a load of laundry and observe how water flows through the system. You may need to make a few more adjustments to get water flowing out all outlets evenly.

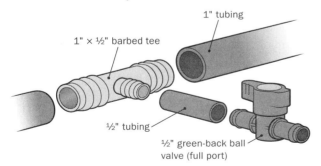

1" tubing

1" × ½" barbed tee

½" tubing

½" green-back ball valve (full port)

▲ **Green-back ball valve installed on outlet line to control flow**

14. Check for leaks.

With the water still flowing through the greywater system, check all of your glued joints in the house (on both the greywater and sewer/septic side). Carefully check the connection from the washing machine hose to the 3-way valve. If it leaks, tighten the hose clamp or add a second clamp. If it's still leaking, disconnect the hose and use a short piece of vinyl tubing to create a bridge. Clamp the tubing to the washing machine drain hose and to the barbed fitting.

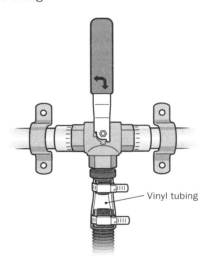

Vinyl tubing

▲ **Bridge of vinyl tubing between washer drain hose and 3-way valve to stop a leaky connection**

15. Paint the pipe and label the system.

Paint any exposed exterior PVC pipe with exterior latex house paint to protect it from sunlight, which makes bare pipe brittle over time. Seal any holes in the wall or floor with a construction-grade sealant that is waterproof and adhesive to protect your home from water damage. Sikaflex is a common brand. Regular silicone caulk can peel away over time. Label the 3-way valve. Even though the valve comes pre-labeled with a small arrow indicating the direction of flow, it's not always obvious where the water is going. Make a clear label, or take a photo of the valve with the handle in both positions and label the photo. Prominently post the label near the valve.

NOTE: Many codes require aboveground pipes to have labels saying "Caution: Nonpotable Water, Do Not Drink" placed every 5 feet.

Put your O&M manual in a visible place; for example, inside a plastic sleeve taped to the washing machine.

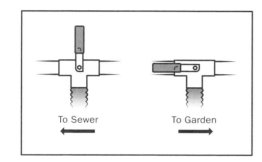

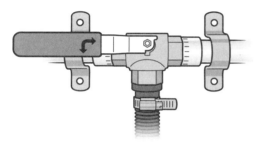

▲ **Labels for diverter valve**

Checklist for L2L Installations

Did you remember to:

- Install the 3-way valve above the flood rim of the machine, in an accessible location, with a label?

- Put the AAV on the greywater side of the 3-way valve and at the high point in the system, in a visible and accessible location?

- Use 1" pipe and tubing with 1" × ½" tees to direct greywater to specific plants?

- Leave the end of the 1" main-line tubing fully open, with no valve or cap?

- Protect your machine by not overtaxing it with long irrigation runs? Remember to stay within the general safe distances for your washing machine (see page 82).

- Check that all greywater soaked quickly into the mulch? If there was pooling or runoff, enlarge mulch basins or add more outlets.

- Follow any necessary setbacks? (See Example Setbacks for Greywater Irrigation Area on page 67.)

- Irrigate based on how much greywater you produce and how much the plants need?

Maintenance and Troubleshooting

Laundry-to-landscape systems need maintenance about once a year, in addition to routine visual inspection of the plumbing parts and connections near the washing machine.

3-way valve and AAV. Do a quick visual check for leaks frequently (and make sure label is in place). Replace the AAV if it's leaking.

Piping and tubing. If damaged, cut out the damaged section and replace with a coupling (for tubing use a 1-inch barbed coupling).

Greywater outlets. Check for even distribution. Unclog lint or hair built up in the outlet. Open ball valves and unclog with a small stick (there may be a glob of gunk in the valve). If needed, flush the system with a garden hose (see instructions on page 92.

If an entire section of the system is not receiving water, there may be a clog or kink in the main line; a clog could occur at a tee or 90-degree elbow. Dig up the area where the fitting is located, remove it, and check inside for debris. Or, examine the tubing anywhere it may have been kinked or damaged.

Mulch basin below greywater outlet. Check for signs of pooling. As mulch decomposes, the basin will drain more slowly. Remove and compost decomposed mulch and replace with new mulch.

Washing machine doesn't evacuate all the water. Determine if the problem is connected to the greywater system or if it also occurs when the washing is discharging to the sewer/septic system. Divert greywater to the sewer/septic system and observe the machine. If the problem still occurs, it's not related to the greywater irrigation system. If you suspect the 3-way valve itself may have clogged, disconnect the washer hose to unclog the valve. If the problem is not the valve and occurs on both the sewer/septic and greywater systems, the most likely cause is the internal pump filter on the machine has clogged; clean the pump filter (see page 85). If the problem occurs only when the greywater system is turned on, check the outlets and end of the line for clogs. Also review your design and ensure you didn't overwork the pump by using too-small tubing (anything less than 1" for the main line) or by traveling too high uphill, or too far.

Irrigation Options

BOTH THE L2L and branched drain system use mulch basins to soak greywater into the ground to irrigate plants. This section will discuss how to construct a mulch basin for both types of systems, how to use a second 3-way valve in the landscape to create two zones, and (L2L only) how to irrigate in raised garden beds.

How to Dig a Mulch Basin

Dig mulch basins in the "drip line" of the plant you'll irrigate, the area under where the branches end. Basins can be shaped like a circle, a semicircle, a trench, or sun shape, depending on where your plants are located. Plants growing along the fence or property line will have a semicircular or trench-shaped basin, whereas a tree in the middle of the yard may have a circle around it. Greywater spreads out in the bottom of the basin; larger basins wet more of the root zone.

Note that the drip line of young plants will change as the plant grows. You can locate the basin at the current drip-line, or locate it a few feet away and overhead-irrigate the plant for the first year (until the roots reach the greywater).

If you encounter large roots, dig around or under them. Damaging small roots is like pruning small branches; it won't hurt the plant. Use the soil dug out of the basin to make a berm, creating a wall around the basin. The berm defines the area and reduces digging — increasing the height of the berm increases the depth of the basin. Stomp on the berm to compact the soil.

Alternatively, if you don't want a berm, put the soil in an out-of-the-way location or consider using it to elevate the surrounding area, since sunken basins are more water-efficient. Keep the bottom of the basin flat, or gently sloping downward, to encourage water to spread through it.

Remember, more basins are better than one larger basin, and if you want to oversize the basin for an added safety margin, make sure to add more outlets to spread out the water.

In downward-sloping yards, dig a trenched-shaped mulch basin on the uphill side of the plant; use the excavated soil to create a berm on the downslope, making a flat area uphill of the plant to infiltrate greywater. See Distributing Water with an L2L System, page 82.

Add finishing touches to your basin: the sides of sunken basins can be stabilized with rock or other locally available materials (wood, sections of tree trunk, etc.).

Though L2L and branched drain systems both irrigate in a mulch basin, there are some specific differences:

L2L basins typically are 6" to 12" deep, with the deeper (12") basins for larger plants receiving more water.

Branched drain basins typically are 8" to 18" deep, based on the depth of the greywater pipe where it enters the basin. Dig 8" to 10" below the pipe so there is enough space for greywater to fall through an air space and land on a thick mulch layer. These basins are usually deeper than those for an L2L system because the branched drainpipe is usually buried deeper (due to the downward-sloping pipe). You may need to deepen the basin depending on where the pipe enters, since you dig the basin first, and run the pipe to it.

Remember that the total area of the mulch basins must be sufficient to soak all your greywater into the ground; the size is determined by your soil type and the amount of greywater your home generates (see Sizing Mulch Basins on page 62 for details).

▼ **Three variations of mulch basins (filled with wood chips when complete)**

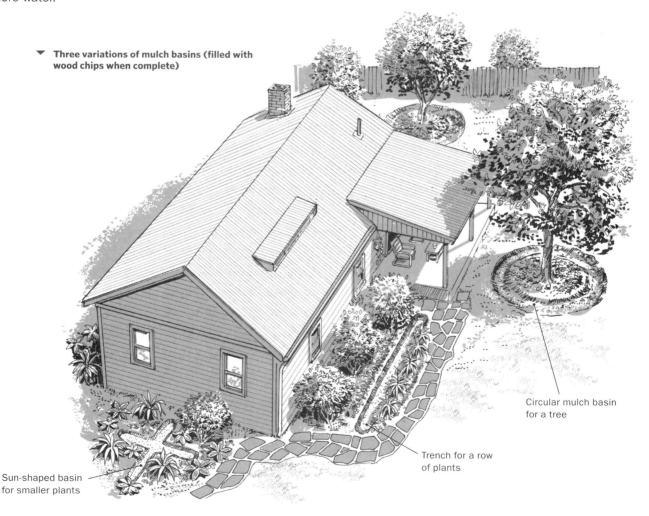

Circular mulch basin for a tree

Trench for a row of plants

Sun-shaped basin for smaller plants

How to Make a Mulch Shield

When greywater is distributed subsurface, roots can grow up the pipe and clog it. To prevent this, use a mulch shield to create an air space around the outlet; roots won't grow through air. Try to keep subsurface irrigation as close to the surface as possible — deeper is not better (see Subsurface or Subsurface Irrigation? on page 83).

The specific depth of distribution is determined by your state's code; for example, California requires each greywater outlet to be 2 inches below a mulch shield. Use a manufactured irrigation valve box for a sturdy, long-lasting mulch shield. A free and eco-friendly alternative is to use repurposed 1-gallon plastic pots, though these will collapse if stepped on and won't last many years. You can also use small

sections of a wide-diameter (3 inches or larger) plastic drainpipe. Water-efficient washing machines can use smaller mulch shields than top-loading machines, since each outlet will receive less water.

The important thing is to make sure greywater falls through *air* for several inches and onto several inches of *mulch*. Prepare the shield as described, then fill the mulch basin with a few inches of mulch. Place the mulch shield inside the basin, on top of mulch. Insert the greywater tube into the shield and fill the basin to the top with mulch. Maintain the air space between the outlet and mulch to prevent future clogs. You can add a flat paving stone or a garden statue on top of the mulch shield for aesthetics and to make it easier to find the outlets for annual maintenance.

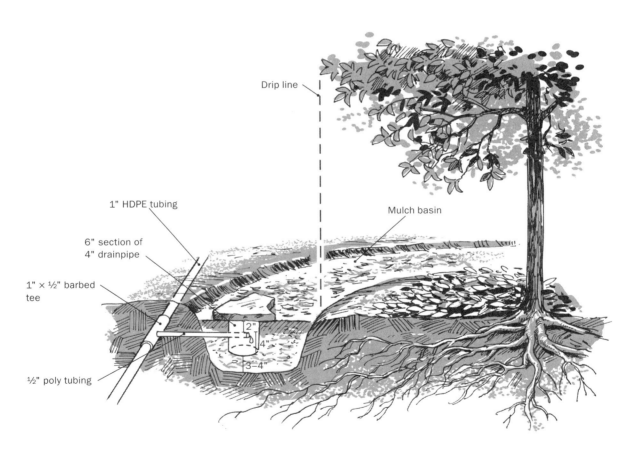

Drip line

1" HDPE tubing

6" section of 4" drainpipe

1" × ½" barbed tee

½" poly tubing

Mulch basin

2"

4"

3–4"

▲ **Mulch shield from a piece of drainpipe. Cut the pipe into 6" lengths, then drill a hole 2" down from the top edge to insert the greywater tubing. Put something on top to cover it, like a flat rock. This can be used with water-efficient washing machines.**

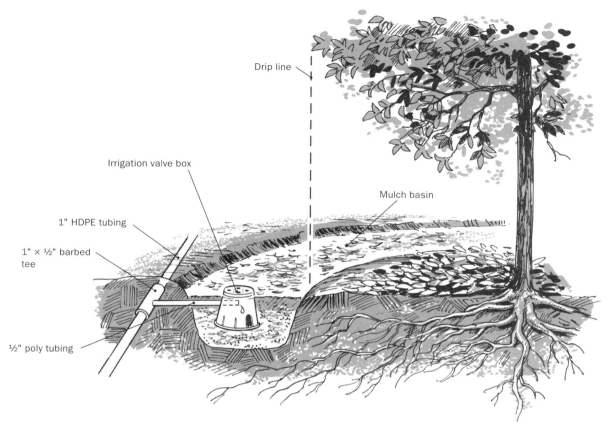

Drip line

Irrigation valve box

1" HDPE tubing

1" × ½" barbed
tee

½" poly tubing

Mulch basin

▲ **Mulch shield from a valve box or sturdy plastic pot. Position the pot or valve box so the wider end is down. Drill a hole large enough for the tube 2" below the top of the mulch shield. Cut off excess plastic below the hole. Usually 4" to 6" below the hole is desirable.**

If using a sturdy pot: Cut a hole, wide enough to fit your hand inside, in the bottom of the pot (now positioned at the top). Cut without compromising the strength of the pot. Place a flat rock or paver above the mulch shield to cover it.

Multiple Irrigation Zones

If your house produces lots of greywater and your plants are spread over different areas of the yard, consider two irrigation zones. Zones spread greywater over a larger area, but require manual switching. If switching between zones on a regular basis for the next ten years seems unrealistic, skip the zones and add more plants to benefit from the extra water (or divert excess to the sewer).

To install the second zone for a L2L system, place a 1" 3-way valve where it's easy to access (for switching between zones). Use three 1" male adapter x barb fittings, wrapped with pipe thread tape, and threaded into each side of the valve. Connect the greywater line from the machine to the middle port, then connect zone 1 and zone 2 to the right and left

sides of the valve. It is possible, though more complicated, to install this second valve inside your house.

Note: A similar technique can be used in a branched drain system. Use the larger 1½–2" valve.

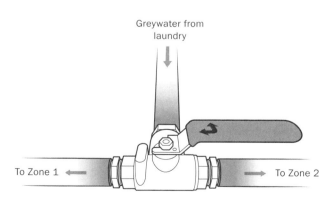

Greywater from
laundry

To Zone 1   To Zone 2

▲ **Two-zone valve**

Irrigating Raised Beds

Since raised beds are harder to irrigate with an L2L system than in-ground plants, only include them if other plants do not need irrigation. Take care to avoid kinks when directing tubing up into a bed: you may need to use two 1" barbed 90-degree elbows to safely enter the bed. If you plan to irrigate other plants in addition to the raised bed, send the 1" line into the bed and then back out, since water reaching a tee before the bed will take the lower route and not travel up the tube into the bed.

There are two common ways to irrigate raised beds. The first method is to use 1" × ½" tees, as described for other plants, directing water into mini-mulched areas in the bed. Plant large annual vegetables around the outlets (never root crops). The second method requires frequent maintenance (every few months), so is less desirable: Run the main line into the bed, cover the bed with straw, drill ¼" holes into the 1" tubing, and cover the whole thing with a half of a 3" corrugated drainpipe, as shown. This method allows greywater to be distributed over a larger area. However, the ¼" holes will clog and have to be cleaned out by hand — not something I want to spend my weekend doing.

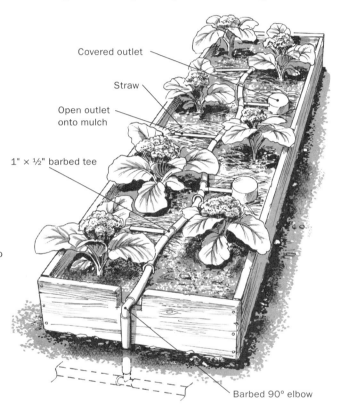

Covered outlet

Straw

Open outlet onto mulch

1" × ½" barbed tee

Barbed 90° elbow

▲ **Mini-mulch basins inside raised bed. Greywater outlet can be covered with a mulch shield for code compliance.**

Half of a 3" corrugated drainpipe

¼" holes drilled into 1" tubing

Straw

▲ **Maintenance-intensive option. Drill ¼" holes into 1" tubing. Holes clog over time and require manual declogging. Cover tubing with drainpipe for code compliance.**

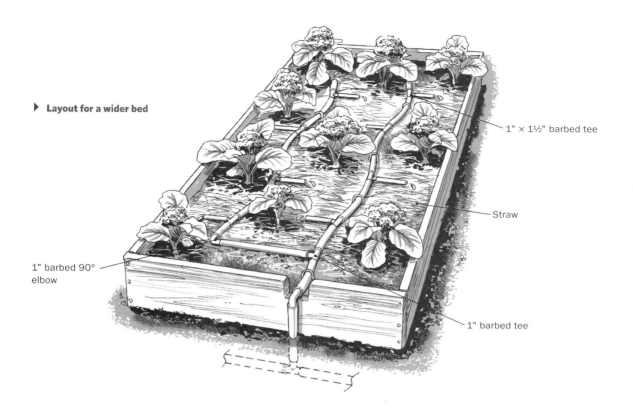

▶ **Layout for a wider bed**

1" × 1½" barbed tee

Straw

1" barbed 90° elbow

1" barbed tee

Installing a "Second Standpipe" for a Washing Machine

A "second standpipe" system is another option for a washing machine greywater system. It includes a secondary standpipe installed near the washing machine to drain by gravity to the landscape. To switch between the greywater and the sewer/septic systems, you manually move the washing machine's drain hose from one standpipe to the other.

Second standpipe systems are most commonly used in hot climates that have relatively high water requirements per tree, because it's harder to distribute greywater to many plants. The irrigation portion of the system is installed with a branched drain configuration system (see Branched Drain Gravity-Fed System on page 102 for installation details).

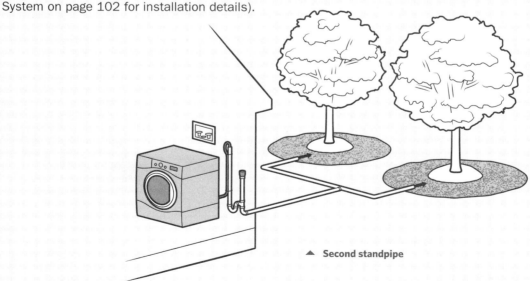

▲ **Second standpipe**

Branched Drain Gravity-Fed System (Without Storage)

A BRANCHED DRAIN SYSTEM (also developed by Art Ludwig) conveys greywater by gravity to the garden. This system is commonly used with showers, sinks, or combined flows. A diverter valve taps into a greywater fixture (e.g., a shower or sink) in the drainage plumbing located beneath the fixture. One side of the valve is connected to the sewer/septic pipes and the other side is plumbed out to the landscape. The user can control the flow of greywater by turning the valve, either manually or remotely. Rigid, 1½-inch or 2-inch ABS pipe delivers greywater throughout the system.

Once in the landscape, the pipe divides repeatedly to distribute the water into multiple mulch basins to irrigate specific plants, including trees, shrubs, or large perennials. The cost and difficulty of installing branched drain systems vary greatly.

Sometimes major plumbing work is required to access the greywater, while other times it is quite simple to divert the water.

Branched drain systems are well suited for kitchen sink greywater (note that not all states allow reuse of kitchen water). Be aware that kitchen greywater is more attractive to raccoons, bears, and other wildlife, and they may dig up your basins. Distribute kitchen greywater to multiple outlets to minimize maintenance; see pages 47 and 48 for more information.

Designing Your Branched Drain System

The design of your branched drain system will be largely determined by your site factors, including where you tap into the plumbing, where the pipe exits the building, and which plants you will irrigate. A careful assessment of your site in combination with understanding how the system functions will help you design a well-functioning system for your

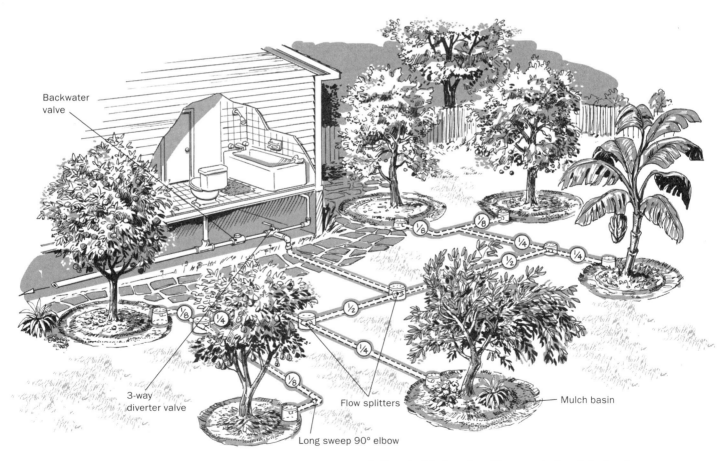

Backwater valve

3-way diverter valve

Long sweep 90° elbow

Flow splitters

Mulch basin

▲ **Branched drain system. Shower water here irrigates six fruit trees. Fractions show how the flow splitters divide greywater flow into halves, quarters, and eighths.**

Got a Lot of Greywater? Don't Dig One Big Basin.

A common mistake for new greywater installers is to direct lots of greywater into one giant mulch basin. It may seem like digging one larger basin would be just as good as two smaller ones, but it's not. The reason? Though a large basin has lots of area, greywater flowing out one outlet will decompose mulch and slow the infiltration in the area surrounding the outlet, which can result in pooling greywater. To provide extra capacity in a system, it's better to divide the flow to more outlets, rather than to dig larger basins around fewer outlets.

home. A successful design really pays off; once installed, these systems are extremely easy to use and maintain. The following section discusses each aspect of the system design to prepare you for construction.

Site Assessment

A branched drain system relies on gravity. This means that all of the irrigation piping must slope downward, and the landscape must be lower than the greywater drain pipes in the house. The minimum slope for the pipe is 2 percent, or ¼ inch of drop per 1 foot of distance traveled. This requirement can make it difficult to go under or around patios or walkways due to elevation loss. It's much easier to install this system in downward-sloping yards than in flat yards. With the latter, you can opt to irrigate near the house, within 20 feet or so, but keep in mind that the pipe gets deeper and deeper the farther it travels.

Branched drain systems are best for irrigating trees, shrubs, and large perennials. If you have extra water, consider planting more to benefit from the greywater.

Ask yourself these questions to determine whether your site is suitable for a branched drain system:

- Can you access the greywater source, install a diverter valve, and exit the house to reach the plants? Valves located in the crawl space can be

turned by a motor (called an actuator) controlled with a switch in the house.

- Identify what plants you will irrigate with the system (e.g., trees, bushes, larger perennials).

- Look for design challenges, like sidewalks, large tree roots, or buried sewer, gas, or water lines.

Then, identify the plants to irrigate based on the quantity of greywater and the plants' water requirements (see How Much Water Do My Plants Want? on page 65).

Diverter Valve and Pipe Runs

There are many different plumbing configurations and potential challenges for installing the diverter valve. The basic steps are covered here, and you can adapt the concepts to fit your situation. If you are a plumbing novice, this is a great time to get help or hire someone to install the valve.

First, determine where to locate the valve and where you can exit the house with the greywater piping. This may limit your irrigation options. Also decide whether you need an actuator (the valve should be readily operable, so if you'd need to slither in the crawl space to reach it, install an actuator). After you've determined the valve location and where the greywater pipe will exit the house, confirm that it's still feasible to irrigate the plants you've planned to irrigate. If not, reassess the landscape.

Warning: Always divert greywater *before* a connection to a toilet drain.

If the drainpipes are in a crawl space and the system does not require a permit, install the diverter valve high enough so the greywater pipes can exit the house above the foundation. For permitted systems you must install the valve after the vent and P-trap. Some local authorities may allow you to deviate from this if you have a compelling reason, but most likely they won't.

In some situations the diverter is more convenient to install in the drain or trap arm (before the trap or vent), such as:

- When there is not enough elevation drop for the greywater pipe to exit above the foundation; for example, if the crawl space is very shallow. If the greywater can't travel by gravity over the top of the foundation, you will need to core-drill through the foundation wall, adding cost and time.

- When the plumbing is old, made of metal, or otherwise difficult to alter. It may be easy to put the valve in the drain before the trap, but it's extremely complicated to install it downstream.

- In a sink-only system: the valve can be installed under the sink in the tailpiece or trap arm. This allows you to operate the valve from inside the house. Alternatively, open the wall and install the valve in the vertical drain just below the vent, and keep it accessible by creating an access hatch (greywater codes typically will permit this). See drawing on page 50.

The diverter valve is about 6½ inches long and needs a little extra room for the transition couplings, so plan to remove about 7 inches of pipe to install the valve. However, it may be easier to remove a whole section of pipe than to cut into it, especially if the pipe is cast iron. If space is an issue, purchase a "space saver valve" (made by Jandy; see Resources); it's a few inches smaller than the standard model.

Ideally, the greywater pipe exits the building above the foundation (for ease of installation). Remember, the pipe must drop at least ¼ inch per foot of horizontal run. Measure the distance in feet from the valve to where you will exit the house, and divide by 4. This represents the number of inches of drop required. For example, if you have 20 feet between the valve and the house exit point, the pipe run needs 5 inches of drop. Use a laser level or measure down from the floor joists to determine whether you have enough room for the elevation drop. If you can't exit above the foundation, reconsider the valve placement or plan to core-drill through the foundation wall (you can hire a company to do this, or rent equipment to do it yourself).

Permit Troubles with 3-Way Valves

Sometimes inspectors are hesitant to allow the 3-way valve because the valves are not made for drainage plumbing; they're designed for pool and spa applications. If your project requires a permit and your inspector brings up this issue, the following info may help (all inspectors I have worked with realized there is no alternative and allowed the valve to be used):

- The valves are certified (NSF/ANSI Standard 50; see Resources).

- No 3-way valves in North America are made for drainage plumbing or greywater.

- An alternative to a 3-way valve is to use two 2-way ball valves, but this would allow the user to leave both sides open or both sides shut — clearly less desirable than using a valve made for pools.

- These valves work. They're used all over North America for greywater with no apparent problems.

Splitting the Flow

Distributing water to the landscape with a branched drain system is different from other irrigation methods. A fitting called a **flow splitter** (also called a double-quarter bend, twin 90, or double-ell) divides water evenly in two directions. Use multiple flow splitters to divide the flow into halves, quarters, eighths, or sixteenths. For example, if 20 gallons of greywater from a shower flows through the system and is divided (via flow splitters) into eighths, each of the eight outlets discharges 2½ gallons.

A challenge with this system is that it's easier to send more water to the plants in the beginning of the system than the end. For example, a thirsty banana patch near the beginning of the system could get half the water from the first split. Make sketches of your system to plan how to divide the flow appropriately. Common wye or tee fittings also are able to divide the flow, but they don't necessarily do this evenly, so you won't know how much water the plants were receiving. If you can't find flow splitters, use tees instead. I recommend having one (or more) flow splitters on hand while you design the system; this helps with visualizing how to split up the flow appropriately. A common beginner's error is to use them like the tees used in a laundry-to-landscape system, inserting one into the line any time you want to irrigate. This won't work!

In order for the flow to split evenly, you'll need about 2 feet of straight pipe leading into the flow splitter. If the pipe curves just before the split, turbulence will send more water out one side than the other. In practice, it may not be possible to have exactly 2 feet, but do the best you can.

In most systems, a single shower should have at least four to eight outlets, a kitchen sink four to six, and a bathroom sink two to three, depending on usage (more outlets for more people/more greywater in the system).

Draw a sketch of your system as accurately as possible. After you install the system, return to this site plan and adjust it as needed so the "as-built" site plan accurately shows where the pipes and outlets are. Put this in your O&M manual (see page 78), along with photographs of the unburied system.

Backwater Valve

Permitted systems likely will need a backwater valve, a one-way check valve to prevent sewage from backing up into the greywater system. In practice, this is a redundant safety precaution; the 3-way valve physically blocks off the sewer side when it is turned to greywater. However, if the valve isn't shut properly, backed-up sewage could enter the system. If you install a backwater valve, keep in mind that a plumbing snake (used to unclog a sewer line) can't come back through the valve without breaking it; be sure to show the valve to any plumber working on the pipes in the future.

SITE PLAN OF DIVIDED FLOWS

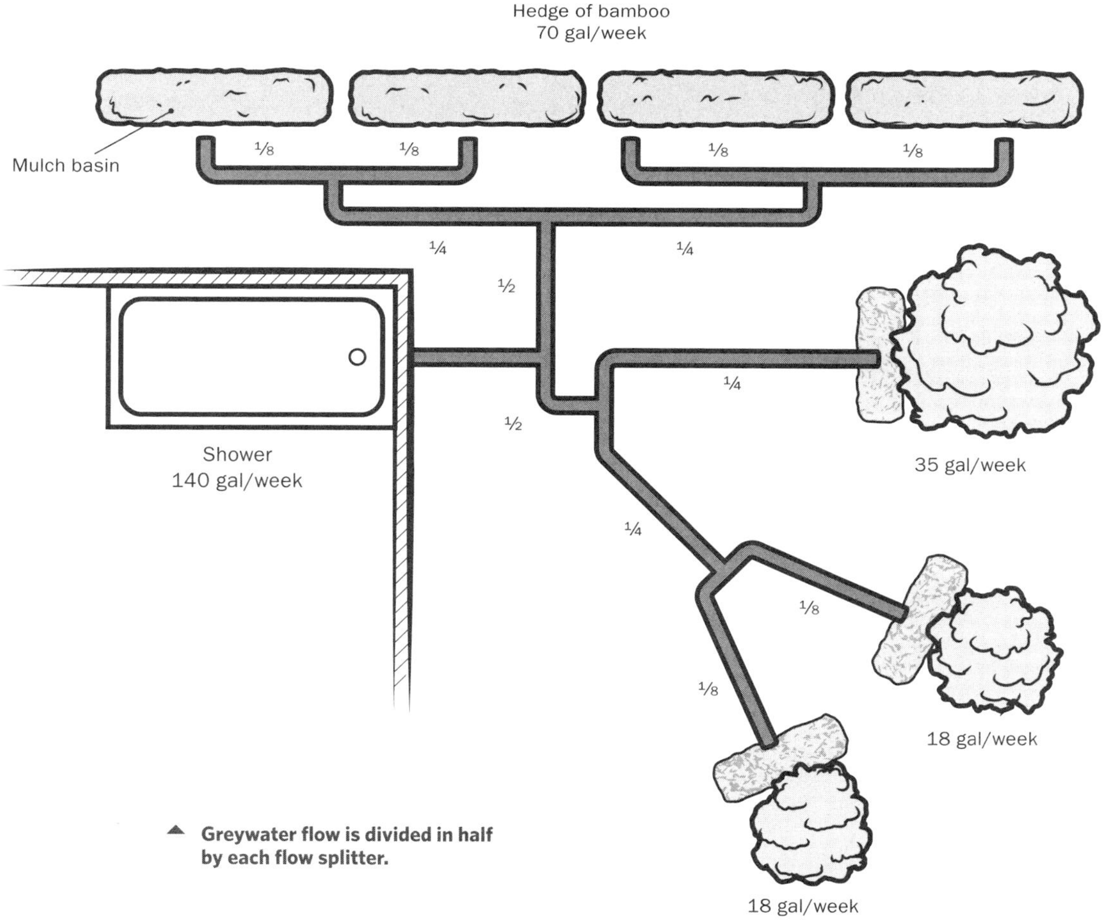
Hedge of bamboo
70 gal/week
Mulch basin
1/8
1/8
1/8
1/8
1/4
1/4
1/2
1/4
1/2
Shower
140 gal/week
35 gal/week
1/4
1/8
1/8
18 gal/week
18 gal/week

▲ **Greywater flow is divided in half by each flow splitter.**

Installing a Branched Drain System

This project walks you through the basic steps of installing a branched drain system. No two branched drain systems are identical, so you'll likely need to adapt the steps to fit with your home and landscape. Installing a branched drain system typically takes two or three times longer than installing a laundry-to-landscape system. Cutting into old plumbing can lead to unexpected complications, working in a crawl space is slow, and sloping the pipe is very time-consuming (plus it means a lot of digging!). Having friends or hiring someone to help will make the installation easier. The bulk of the materials you'll need are available at any plumbing store. However, the diverter valve and flow splitters most likely are not. Order those parts a few weeks before you plan to install the system. If you'll be getting free wood chips from a local tree trimmer, allow for a few weeks for the delivery. See Plumbing Basics for Greywater Installation (page 135) for details on plumbing parts and essential techniques.

MATERIALS

One 1½"–2" 3-way diverter valve (Pentair or Jandy brand)

One 1½" or 2" ABS backwater valve (as needed)

Transition couplings (to install diverter valve to your existing plumbing)

1½" or 2" ABS pipe and fittings (as needed)

ABS straps (to hang pipe in crawl space), or 2-hole straps or plumbers tape (to strap pipe to walls)

Cleanout plugs (as needed)

Flow splitters (twin 90s or double-quarter bends; see step 6)

Actuator and related parts (for remote switching via a switch inside the home; optional)

ABS cement

Irrigation valve boxes (as needed; see step 10)

Construction-grade sealant (see step 11)

TOOLS

Pipe cutter or hacksaw

Cutter compatible with your existing plumbing (see chart on page 136)

Hex-head driver

Tape measure

Permanent marker

2-foot grade level

Tin snips or drill, piloting bit, and hole saw (see step 4)

Digging tools (mattock, trenching shovel, digging bar)

Torpedo level

Painting supplies

1. Install the 3-way diverter valve.

Depending on your plumbing setup, you may want to alter the 3-way diverter valve to change the location of the inlet. The valves are preset to use the middle port as the inlet, but often it's more convenient for the inlet to be on one of the side ports. Take the valve to the drainpipe and determine if you should change the inlet. See 3-Way Valves for Branched Drain Systems (page 108) for installation instructions.

Measure and cut out a section of the drainpipe to insert the diverter valve. If you're using a backwater valve, consider where it will go before cutting the pipe. Most backwater valves must be installed in the horizontal position.

NOTE: If your house has old metal plumbing — prone to leaks when jiggled — make sure you feel confident to handle other plumbing problems that could arise from installing the valve.

Connect the valve with no-hub or transition couplings: Loosen the metal band and slide it over the pipe. Then, insert the rubber coupling over the pipe and valve, bending it back for a tight fit (see Installing a transition coupling on page 137). Slide the band over the coupling and tighten the band with a hex-head driver.

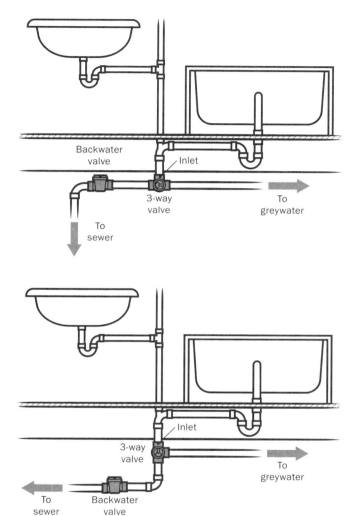

▲ **Top: Example of diverter valve using the present middle part for the inlet. Bottom: Example of valve adjusted to use a side port for the inlet.**

2. Install an actuator (optional).

Install an electronic actuator if the valve is not easily accessible for manual operation. See How to Wire an Actuator (page 114) for installation instructions.

3. Plumb to the exit point.

Complete the piping run from the diverter to the house exit point, using ABS pipe and following standard plumbing techniques and your local code requirements. Support the pipe every 4 feet, either with strapping fastened to something solid, or use ABS pipe hangers attached to the floor joists to prevent vertical and horizontal movement of the pipe. Maintain a minimum slope of ¼" drop per 1 foot of run, checking the slope with a grade level.

Install cleanouts (required every 100 feet of horizontal pipe, or after turning an aggregate of 135 degrees, such as with a 90 bend and a 45 bend). Use *long sweep* fittings for horizontal-to-horizontal or vertical-to-horizontal turns to avoid clogs. Use *short sweep* fittings only for horizontal-to-vertical turns.

4. Run the pipe outside.

When possible, exit through a crawl space vent. Cut a hole out of a corner of the vent screen that's large enough for the pipe, using tin snips. Or, drill a hole through the wall just large enough for the pipe (see page 87).

If the pipe is too low to exit above the foundation, you have two options:

- Bury a surge tank under the house and pump the water over the foundation. This is a good option if you have enough space for the tank and you need a pump for the rest of your system (if your landscape is uphill or you'll be filtering the water for a drip irrigation system). If the rest of the system can be gravity-fed, go with the second option.

- Core-drill through the foundation. Hire a contractor or do it yourself with a rented drill and core bit. This will add some cost and work to get the water out, but allows a gravity system instead of a pump.

3-Way Valves for Branched Drain Systems

Plastic 3-way valves are made with the inlet in the middle port and an outlet port on each side. Unlike the brass 3-way valves used in an L2L system, these larger plastic valves can be altered so the inlet enters any port (see instructions, below). These valves are made for the pool and spa industry and often have to be mail-ordered. Two common brands are Pentair and Jandy. They are "never-lube" valves, meaning they're self-lubricating. Each valve works with two sizes of pipe: the 1½"–2" size works for both 1½" and 2" pipe. Jandy also makes a 3" valve and a "space saver" valve for tight spots.

Whenever possible, use transition couplings instead of glue to connect pipes to the valve. This protects the valve from being made unusable if you glue in the wrong place. If a valve location is hard to reach, install an actuator to turn the valve remotely. However, all valves, even with an actuator installed, must be accessible for future repairs (see How to Wire an Actuator on page 114).

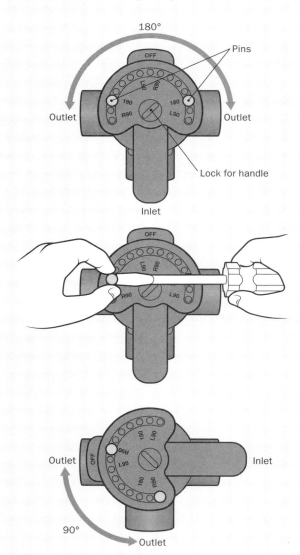

▲ **Modifying a Pentair valve**

How to Change the Inlet of the 3-Way Valve

Pentair and Jandy valves require different modification techniques.

Pentair valve. This is the easier of the two valves to change.

1. Remove the plastic "pins" on the handle, using a flathead screwdriver.

2. Position the valve so the handle shuts off an outlet port of your choice. The valve should turn 180 degrees when the inlet is in the middle, or 90 degrees with the inlet on a side. Place the pins in the desired location (right 90, left 90, or 180).

3. Test the valve by turning the handle and observing which port it shuts off. If it doesn't turn as desired, switch the pins (e.g., from the left 90 to the right 90 position).

Jandy valve. Be careful when adjusting this valve. If the handle and internal shutoff become misaligned, it can become tedious to fix.

1. Remove all screws on the top of the valve. Using a flathead screwdriver, break the seal and lift the faceplate off the valve.

2. Carefully position the valve so the "inlet" label on the faceplate faces your desired inlet and the handle "off" position is shutting off either the greywater or sewer/septic port.

3. Reinstall just a few screws, and test the valve. If it works as desired, add the remaining screws.

Note: After a Jandy valve has been altered, the valve handle will turn past the shut-off outlet. Label the valve clearly to prevent moving the handle too far.

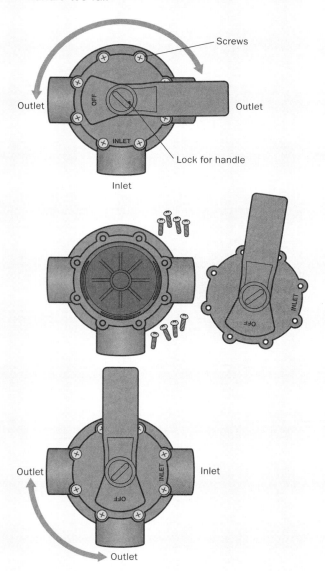

▲ **Modifying a Jandy valve**

5. Dig the mulch basins.
See How to Dig a Mulch Basin on page 96.

6. Mock up the outdoor pipe runs and dig the trenches.

On top of the ground, lay out the pipe and fittings to each basin. Cut pipe as needed to determine where the pipe and fittings will be located (don't dry-fit; just lay the materials out so you'll know where to dig the trench). Add cleanouts to the flow splitters: Purchase flow splitters with cleanouts pre-installed, or you can make your own. See Installing a Cleanout in a Flow Splitter (page 113) for instructions.

Remove the first section of pipe so you can dig its trench. Use a mattock and trenching shovel to dig to the first flow splitter. In flat yards, bury the pipe as shallow as possible at the beginning; it must slope downward continuously and will get deeper as you go. If the yard slopes downhill, you can bury the pipe deeper at the beginning because it can stay at a relatively constant depth.

If cars will drive over the pipe, make sure there is a foot of solid soil above the top of the pipe. If you're getting a permit, talk to the inspector about burial depths; standard depth for ABS pipe carrying sewage should not apply to an irrigation system. If the inspector disagrees, you must argue your case or risk not being able to install this system; it won't work if the pipe has to be 2 feet underground.

Tip: When trenching through a lawn, use a flat shovel and cut out pieces of turf that you can later replace, then dig the trench with a mattock. The end result will be cleaner than a messy trench through the lawn.

Level the trench so the bottom slopes ¼" per foot and is as smooth as possible. It's okay to slope more steeply, but in a flat yard the accumulated increase in pipe depth creates a *lot* more work. Check for slope using a grade level, or you can tape a 1"-thick block to the bottom of one end of a 4-foot level: when the level reads flat, the trench bottom is sloping ¼" per foot.

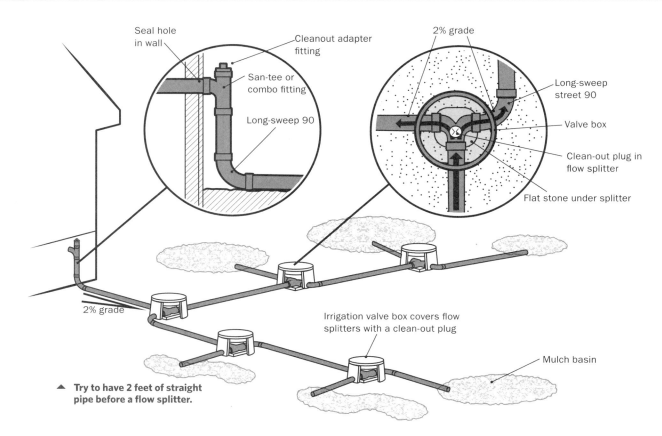

Seal hole in wall

Cleanout adapter fitting

San-tee or combo fitting

Long-sweep 90

2% grade

Long-sweep street 90

Valve box

Clean-out plug in flow splitter

Flat stone under splitter

2% grade

Irrigation valve box covers flow splitters with a clean-out plug

Mulch basin

▲ **Try to have 2 feet of straight pipe before a flow splitter.**

7. Dry-fit the pipe runs.

Assemble the pipe and fittings needed to reach the first flow splitter. Use long-sweep 90-degree bends (not short-sweep bends), 60-, 45-, or 22-degree bends to change direction in the pipe runs. To turn directly from a flow splitter, use a *street* fitting, which inserts into the hub of the flow splitter. If any pipe is warped, install it so the warp runs sideways (not up or down).

Position the flow splitter on a brick or flat stone to prevent it from tilting as the soil settles. The splitter must be perfectly level across the top; check it with a torpedo level. Slope the pipe out of the splitters: gently push the pipe downward with a level on it to get the proper slope.

Trench and dry-fit the next section of pipe. Continue trenching a section at a time until you've completed the whole system. You may need to weight down the middle of long, straight runs of pipe with soil or a large rock. Remember to maintain a ¼" slope the entire way. If you encounter roots or underground pipes, go under them: do not dip down

and up again, otherwise solids in the pipe will settle and clog. Check the depth of each mulch basin, and deepen any basin with less than 8" between the pipe and the bottom of the basin.

8. Test the system and glue the pipe runs.

Support the pipe by piling on mounds of soil or large rocks over the pipe at intervals to hold it in place. Run water through the system and check the outlets for even flows. Adjust the angle of flow splitters (tilt them as needed to adjust the flow) or the pipe until water flows evenly from each pipe. So long as you have an even split of water in the flow splitter, the two pipe runs out of the flow splitter are independent of each other; each pipe's slope and length won't affect the other pipe (e.g., If one side of your yard slopes downhill, that side won't get more water than the other).

Mark the pipe and fitting at each joint so you glue them in the right position. Mark which side of the pipe should go up (any warps should go left/right, not up).

Making a Mulch Shield for a Branched Drain System

Make a mulch shield from an irrigation valve box, or a 5-gallon bucket. Maintain a drop of several inches between the mulch and the pipe to prevent roots from growing into the pipe.

To create a mulch shield:

1. Put a layer of mulch under the outlet, about 4" to 6" thick.

2. Set the mulch shield on the mulch, and mark where the pipe will enter.

3. Drill a hole, slightly larger than the pipe, into the mulch shield with a hole saw. Carefully insert the pipe into the shield. Check the levels. Adjust the height of the mulch shield as needed; for example, if it raised up the pipe, wiggle the mulch shield down.

4. Mulch shields made from an upside-down plastic bucket need a hole cut in the bottom (which is now the top of your mulch shield) so you can see inside. Cut a hole large enough to see inside without compromising the strength of the bucket. Cover the hole with a flat paving stone.

After all mulch shields are in place, test the system again. If everything flows evenly, fill in the rest of the basin with mulch.

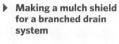

▶ **Making a mulch shield for a branched drain system**

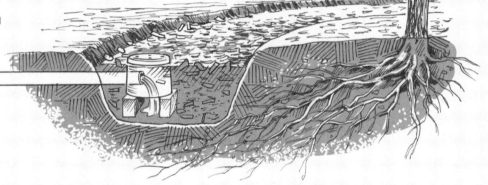

NOTE: If the pipe sits in the sun, it can warp; be aware of this if you don't bury the pipe right away.

Go back and glue everything from the top to the bottom. Keep the levels handy while gluing, making sure you don't over- or under-slope any sections. Do one more flow test before burying the pipe.

9. Add mulch shields or reinforce the outlet at the basin.

If the pipe enters the mulch basin below grade, add a mulch shield onto the end of the pipe to prevent it from clogging. The shield and pipe end extend into the center of the basin. See Making a Mulch Shield for a Branched Drain System (above) for instructions. (Local code may also require the outlet to be covered.)

If the pipe enters the basin above ground, reinforce the ground where the pipe emerges, using stones. The pipe should extend a few inches into the air to provide an air gap over the mulch.

10. Take pictures and bury the pipe.

Photograph the entire system while it's exposed. If the system is permitted, inspectors will want to see it unburied. Often they'll let you bury long straight runs of pipe with the fittings exposed, but be sure to find out; if you can't bury it, put large rocks or mounds of dirt in just enough places so the pipe won't move around.

As an optional step, you can wrap the pipe with wire so it's findable with a metal detector. Also consider using valve boxes with metal in the lid (most come this way).

Begin burying the pipe by packing fine, rock-free soil under and around the pipe, either with your hand or foot. If you bury it with loose dirt below, the pipe can settle and change the levels. Make sure you don't push up the pipe as you are packing the dirt. Double-check the levels before covering the pipe, making sure the top of the pipe is clean so dirt doesn't interfere with the level. Now bury the pipe while leaving the flow splitters exposed.

If you've included cleanouts in the flow splitters, make an access box for each. An irrigation valve box is easy to adapt for this: just cut notches in the bottom so it fits over the pipes and the flow splitter. Keep the lid of the valve box at the surface of the ground. If you haven't included cleanouts, you can bury flow splitters, but it's a good idea to mark the location in case you decide to alter the system in the future.

11. Check for leaks, paint the pipe, and add the labels.

Run water through the system and check for leaks. Pay special attention to joints under the house in places you won't frequently see. Turn the valve and check for leaks on the sewer/septic side.

Paint any exposed plastic pipe with exterior latex paint (the same color of your house) to protect it from sun damage. Add a label next to the 3-way valve, and (if applicable) at the switch for the actuator. Seal any holes in the wall or floor with a construction-grade sealant that is waterproof and adhesive to protect your home from water damage. Sikaflex is a common brand. Regular silicone caulk can peel away over time.

NOTE: For systems requiring a permit, inspectors typically want to see a "running test," with water flowing through the system. After the inspection, bury any exposed pipe.

Maintenance and Troubleshooting for Branched Drain Systems

A properly installed branched drain system requires very little maintenance. Each year you'll need to check the system for proper flow and replace mulch as needed.

Mulch basins. Check the mulch basin under each outlet annually. If there is pooling greywater, remove the decomposed mulch under the outlet and replace with fresh mulch. If pooling occurs frequently there may be too much water entering the basin. Enlarge the basin, add more plants to take up the water, or redesign the system so that less water enters that basin.

Outlets. Check outlets for flow annually. If the flow is uneven, check the flow splitters for clogs. Flush the system with a garden hose inserted into a cleanout, or blast water backwards from an outlet. If the pipes are under-sloped solids may settle and create clogs, especially if greywater is from a kitchen sink.

Raccoons digging up basins. Raccoons are attracted to earthworms below the greywater outlets. If they dig up the basin, shovel the mulch back inside. If they disturb mulch shields, drive a long stake into the ground next to the outlet shield and screw the shield to the stake.

Valve won't turn fully. Unscrew the faceplate of the valve and remove it. Clear out any debris. Replace the faceplate, making sure it's in the correct position so the valve shuts off the greywater or sewer/septic pipes as designed.

Installing a Cleanout in a Flow Splitter

Flow splitters are manufactured as a solid fitting but can be easily adapted to include a cleanout plug in the center of the fitting. Just drill a hole into the fitting to add a plug. A cleanout is a handy addition for two reasons: you can remove the plug and observe the water flowing while testing the system, and you can check for clogs or insert a hose to flush the system. Because this alteration isn't watertight (which doesn't matter because water is flowing on the bottom of the fitting and the plug is on the top) and it "mixes materials" — a PVC plug into an ABS fitting — inspectors generally don't approve of it; ask if your system will be inspected.

To install a cleanout:

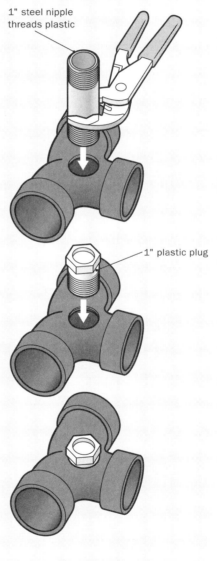

1" steel nipple threads plastic

1" plastic plug

▲ **Cleanout in a flow splitter**

1. Drill a 1¼" hole in the center of the flow splitter, using a drill and 1¼" hole saw (you have to secure the fitting before drilling so it won't spin; I step on it).

2. Cut threads into the hole by inserting a 1" metal nipple (a short piece of threaded steel pipe) and turning clockwise with tongue-and-groove pliers. Remove the nipple by turning it back out.

3. Screw in a 1" plastic plug.

How to Wire an Actuator

The actuator, essentially an electric motor, attaches to the face of the 3-way valve and allows you to control the valve by a switch located inside the house. The 24-volt actuator is wired to a plug-in transformer, which provides power, and a toggle switch to control the valve. Plan to locate the switch near any electrical outlet where you can plug in the transformer. Generally, the best location for the switch is near the fixture it controls, mounted on the wall of the bathroom or inside the vanity. Or, install it near any electrical receptacle with easy access to the switch; for example, at the entrance to the basement or inside a utility closet.

An actuator is needed on any diverter valve that is not readily accessible, such as in a crawl space, cluttered basement, or other out-of-reach location. The actuator must be accessible for repairs and not be buried inside a wall or under a floor (install an access hatch in these situations). Installing an actuator typically adds a few hundred dollars in materials, as well as a few hours of labor. If there is no available receptacle to plug in the transformer, you'll need to have one installed, following local code requirements (in bathrooms and utility areas you'll likely need a GFCI-protected receptacle.) Anyone with basic wiring skills can install an actuator, but professional assistance may be needed if your site requires a new electrical outlet.

If you're inexperienced with actuators or your situation requires that you adjust the actuator (see Step 1), it's a good idea to set it up inside the house and make sure it works properly before you attach it to the 3-way valve in the crawl space (either do this before you cut in the 3-way valve, or use a second valve to practice on). It's possible for an actuator to be defective, and it's a lot easier to discover this if you're working with everything inside the house.

MATERIALS

One actuator that is compatible with your 3-way valve (common brands include Goldline and Pentair)

One toggle switch (on-off-on)

One plastic electrical outlet box with solid cover

One ¾" × ½" reducing bushing

One waterproof strain relief cord connector

18 AWG 3-wire cable, 20 feet (or as needed)

One 24-volt transformer

Wire connectors (wire nuts)

Wire clips

TOOLS

Screwdrivers

Wire strippers

Needlenose pliers

Drill with driver and bits

1. Determine how the actuator should turn the valve.

Just as the 3-way valve was manufactured to make a 180-degree rotation (with the middle port on valve the inlet), the actuator does the same unless you change it. If you changed the orientation of your 3-way valve so that the inlet is on the left or right side (see 3-Way Valves for Branched Drain Systems on page 108), you need to change the actuator. Read the manufacturer's instructions on how to do this (typically, you'll open up the actuator and readjust the cams, which determine how far the valve turns in each direction). Since you can't test the actuator until it's mounted and wired, you may choose to wait until Step 6, Test the actuator, to make these adjustments.

2. Mount the actuator onto the diverter valve.

Attach the actuator to the face of the 3-way valve. Follow the manufacturer's instructions for more details. Typically, you take off the valve handle, unscrew four screws on the faceplate (these screws line up with the screw holes on the actuator), then screw the actuator onto the valve with longer screws, and reattach the handle. Make sure the actuator's switch is turned on. (Turning it on at this step will save you a trip into the crawl space later on.)

3. Run wires from the actuator to the electrical outlet.

Run the actuator's wires to the switch location. For example, if you plan to locate the switch inside the bathroom and the actuator is located in the crawl space below, drill a small, discreet hole in the floor (e.g., inside the vanity, where the wire will be hidden) and feed the wire up into the room.

4. Prepare and mount the switch box.

Choose a location for the switch box. This should be easily accessible and near the outlet where the transformer will be plugged in. (If your switch box will be located outside or in a damp location use a waterproof switch box.) Remove the cover from the switch box. Drill a hole in the middle of the cover, just large enough so the toggle switch fits through. Insert the toggle switch through the hole and secure it using the toggle switch's locknut. Thread the ¾" × ½" reducing bushing into the lower knockout of the switch box, then attach the strain relief cord connector to the bushing. Note: If your box doesn't have threaded knockout holes use a suitable strain relief cord connector that fits with your box. Finally, mount the box to the wall with screws. Don't put the cover on yet because you'll be connecting the wires inside the box.

5. Wire the actuator to the transformer and switch.

The final wiring connections will vary based on the type of actuator and transformer you have; follow the manufacturers' instructions. A sample wiring configuration is shown below for general reference only. Once you've made all the wire connections inside the box, confirm that the actuator switch is turned on for testing.

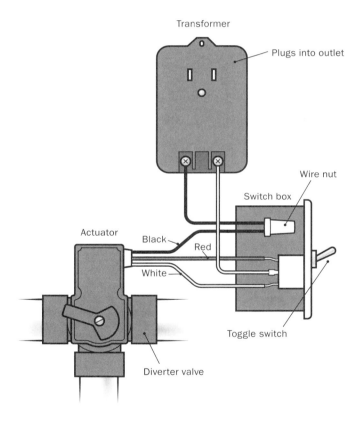

▲ **Sample wiring for actuator**

6. Test the actuator.

Snap the toggle switch up; the actuator should slowly turn the valve, stopping when it shuts off the desired port. Snap the switch down (it will click through the center location before it clicks again to engage the motor). The actuator should now turn the valve slowly in the opposite direction. Note where the actuator turns the valve; for example, switch up = greywater, and switch down = sewer/septic (or vice versa). If the actuator doesn't turn the valve,

first check to make sure it's getting current, then check the wiring. Lastly, adjust the cams (see step 1) if the valve is not turning appropriately.

When you've confirmed that the actuator turns the valve correctly, attach the faceplate to the switch box. Label the switch and secure the actuator and transformer wire as needed (using wire clips). Remember to unplug the transformer if you need to change the wiring.

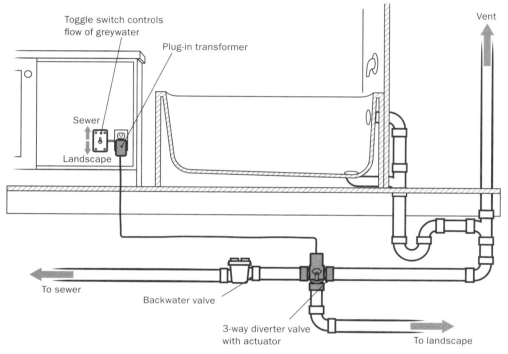

▲ **Actuator installed**

Greywater System with Tank and Pump

CAN'T INSTALL A GRAVITY SYSTEM? Pumps can easily send greywater uphill to your plants. Here's how: Greywater is directed to a small tank, called a surge tank, and then pumped to the landscape. The water is not stored for more than a day — 24 hours typically is the longest you're allowed to store it legally, and stored greywater stinks! The system requires access to the plumbing to install a diverter valve, room for the tank, and an electrical outlet to plug in the pump. Permitted systems may also need an electrical permit if the system requires a new outlet.

Pumped systems offer a few advantages over gravity-based systems. They can send water uphill and across long distances. They're also able to distribute water to more plants than gravity-based systems, and they're effective for combining flows and distributing the water around the landscape. As for the disadvantages, pumped systems use energy, and the pump will eventually need replacing, perhaps every ten years if you're lucky. You can use a pumped system for drip irrigation, but you have to filter the greywater and use special greywater-compatible drip irrigation tubing; otherwise the emitters will clog.

Design Considerations

The first question to ask yourself when designing a pumped greywater system is, "Does this system truly need a pump?" Many people assume that a greywater system needs a pump, when many don't. These situations, however, do require a pump:

- The only landscaped area needing irrigation is uphill of the greywater sources.

- There is a long flat area of hardscape that must be crossed before reaching the landscape.

- The yard is flat and the only irrigation needs are far from the house.

First identify where to install the 3-way diverter valve. See Diverter Valve and Pipe Runs on page 103 for details.

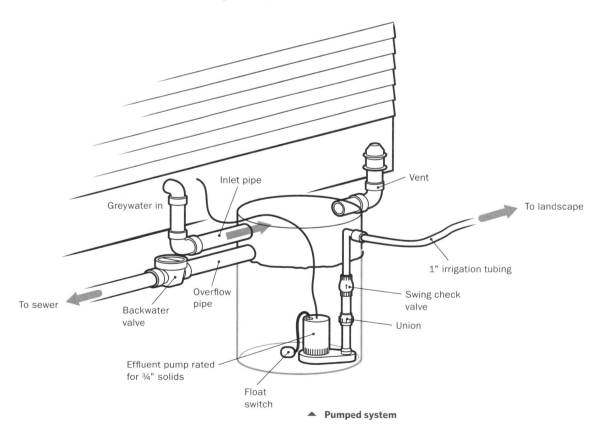

Greywater in — Inlet pipe — Vent — To landscape — 1" irrigation tubing — Swing check valve — Union — Overflow pipe — Backwater valve — To sewer — Effluent pump rated for ¾" solids — Float switch

▲ **Pumped system**

Planning the System

A pump can send greywater to any part of your land-scape, even into separate irrigation zones. Try to route as many greywater sources as you can into the tank. Tank capacity depends on how many fixtures flow into it; size it so there is enough room for all the water to enter and be pumped out without overflow. This is typically 30 to 100 gallons.

The tank needs an overflow drain in case the electricity goes out or the pump breaks. Ideally, the overflow drains into the sewer/septic and alerts you of any system failures, such as the pump going out. If your project requires a permit, an overflow to the sewer/septic likely will be mandatory. Sometimes it's not possible to overflow to the sewer/septic, in which case you can overflow into a nearby mulched area, or skip the overflow and find out that something is wrong when the shower stops draining.

Where to Locate the Tank?

Common tank locations are adjacent to the house, in a basement, buried outside the house, or buried in a crawl space. Some state codes have setback requirements for the tank location, so talk to your local permitting authority for details. Following are three basic setups.

House with a basement: Plumb greywater sources into the tank and locate the tank near an electrical outlet.

House with a crawl space: Place or bury the tank outside of the house. If overflow to sewer is impractical, create an overflow to a mulched area near the tank.

House with a very low crawl space: Either bury the tank under the house or, if you can't fit a tank into the crawl space, core-drill through the foundation to get the pipe outside and then bury the tank near the house.

If you get a permit for a pumped system, there may be additional requirements not included in the following instructions. Talk to your inspector early on to find out exactly what's required for your project. Some jurisdictions require backflow prevention with any pumped system — even those with no potable connection — to prevent problems due to future alterations to the system that may create a cross-connection. Installing a backflow prevention device will add $500 to $1,000 to the cost of your system, in addition to potential fees for annual inspections of the backflow prevention device.

How to Choose a Pump

A high-quality pump will last many years. Look for an **effluent** pump that's rated to pump ¾" solids (so it can pump out anything that gets down the drain), is fully submersible, and operates on 115/120-volt (not 230/240-volt) electrical power. A typical sump pump is not powerful enough for this system. Some people use smaller-sized pumps, rated to pump ⅜" or ½" solids, though they aren't as strong as ¾"-rated units. Note that most effluent pumps are designed for a larger discharge pipe than the 1" irrigation line used in this system. I'm not aware of any problems in the field with reducing the line to 1", though some pump companies may recommend against it.

Because this system is not the standard application for a pump, it can be harder to get help from a pump specialist. Irrigation system pumps typically are sized based on the combined factors of how high and far they will be pumping, as well as the pressure and gallons per minute (gpm) required by the irrigation system; for example, 30 psi at 15 gpm. Since unfiltered greywater doesn't have these pressure requirements, typical pump sizing calculations do not apply. In most situations any pump rated for ¾" solids will be more than powerful enough to irrigate a typical yard.

Building a Pumped System

This project provides an overview of pumped system construction. There are many variables that impact each specific installation, including the existing plumbing, tank location, permit requirements, and the landscape. The installation of the diverter valve can be identical to that of a gravity branched drain system, while the tank location determines where you plumb the greywater pipe and the overflow. Due to the variability of pumped systems, I'll cover just the basic process to give you a sense of what's involved; specific construction details will be dictated by your project requirements.

A few common challenges you may encounter when installing your pumped system are installing a below-grade tank, working in a small crawl space, tapping into old plumbing pipes, and (for projects requiring a permit) stringent permit requirements. For example, an inspector may ask for a drain on the tank, but if the tank is below-grade installing a drain is nearly impossible. Once the plumbing and tank are installed, the irrigation portion is much simpler, faster, and lower-cost (in materials) than that of a branched drain system.

1. Install a 3-way diverter valve.

Follow the same procedures as when installing a diverter for a gravity-based branched drain system (see page 106). This also includes the option of installing an actuator to control the valve remotely (see page 114).

2. Install the surge tank.

Surge tanks typically are 30 to 50 gallons for a single fixture, and 50 to 100 gallons for multiple fixtures. The surge tank must be near an outlet so you can plug in the pump. If you do not have solid, flat ground, you'll need to make a gravel or concrete pad for the tank. Some codes require concrete pads.

3. Plumb the greywater piping into the tank.

Identify where the greywater source(s) will enter the tank. Drill the appropriate size of hole in the top of the tank (not the lid) for the watertight fitting. See "Tapered vs. straight threads" on page 135 for options for a watertight connection (either a bulkhead fitting, Uniseal gaskets, or electrical conduit male adapter with female coupling and a washer). Use a hole saw to drill a clean hole.

Plumb the pipe into the tank. Do not screen the inlet or outlets. Screen will quickly clog and require frequent cleaning.

Alternatively, you can purchase a sewage basin made with preformed holes. Called "knock-outs," these can be conveniently punched out, so no drilling is necessary.

4. Plumb the overflow.

Overflows connected to the sewer/septic must be equipped with a backwater valve in the horizontal position to prevent the possibility of sewage backing up into your tank and getting pumped out to the garden. Locate the overflow slightly lower than the greywater inlet. Install a bulkhead-type fitting the same size as used for the inlet. If you plumbed more than one pipe into the tank, size the overflow to accommodate the total inflow.

Plumb the overflow either back to the sewer (for permitted systems and any system where this is possible) or to a mulch basin. Install a tee-type fitting to connect the overflow to the sewer pipe; the specific fitting will depend on your plumbing configuration. Install the backwater valve. An overflow to a mulch basin doesn't need a backwater valve here because there is no sewer connection.

5. Install a vent.

The tank must be vented. You can use a standard vent or an AAV (see page 87). Alternatively, if the tank isn't connected to the sewer (and doesn't require a permit), any loose seal will let air into the tank and function as a vent. If you connect to the household vent system, make sure you are above the highest sewer connection so a sewage clog couldn't backflow sewage down the vent and into your tank.

6. Install the pump.

See How to Choose a Pump (page 118) for help with pump selection. Place the pump in the tank and make sure the float switch can move freely; if it gets hung up on the tank wall, the pump won't turn on (or off). Drill a hole for the pump's cable, above the inlet and overflow. Use a waterproof cord connector if your system requires a sealed connection.

Run 1" PVC pipe from the pump to the outside of the building. You'll need a few fittings to connect the pump to the 1" pipe, and these depend on the type of pump you have. If your landscape is above the tank, install a 1" *swing check valve* in the 1" pipe in the tank. This prevents water from flowing back into the tank; if enough water flowed back in, it could cause the pump to cycle unnecessarily.

Adjust the float switch so the smallest amount of water is allowed to sit in the tank; that is, the pump stays on as long as possible.

If you are adding a filter to the system it would be installed here, after the pump and before the irrigation system.

7. Install the irrigation system.

The irrigation portion of a pumped system can be identical to that of a laundry-to-landscape system (page 81), with a couple of key differences. First, you can supply more outlets (20 or more) with a pumped system, although you'll need to consider how much water stays in the line if you have very long runs and a small surge tank. Secondly, you can cap the end of the main lines on a pumped system. You can also have multiple zones in a pumped system; see Irrigating with Multiple Zones (facing page) for ideas, keeping in mind that one zone is simplest. Zones that are controlled manually will require you to switch between them on a regular basis, while automatically controlled zones will add cost and complexity to your system. Remember to use mulch basins in the landscape to soak up greywater and slowly release it to the roots of plants, and to size the system based on your estimated greywater production and the plant water requirements of the landscape (see Estimate Your Greywater Flows on page 53 and How Much Water Do My Plants Want? on page 65).

8. Test and maintain the system.

Plug in the pump and run water through the system. Check for leaks and confirm that the pump turns on/off appropriately. Also check for even water distribution in the landscape. If necessary, fine-tune the system as described for an L2L (see page 93).

Perform the same regular maintenance on the irrigation lines as with an L2L system. In addition, check on the tank and pump annually, or as needed. Clean out the tank if the sludge layer builds up too much.

Irrigating with Multiple Zones

Standard timers, controllers, and irrigation valves used to create multi-zoned irrigation systems with potable water are not compatible with a simple greywater system. Often, thoughtful planning of the greywater system — and successfully directing different fixtures to distinct areas of the landscape — can obviate the need for multiple zones. However, there are several situations when you may want to spend the extra time and money to create a multi-zoned greywater irrigation system:

▪ You produce more greywater than you can logistically spread out over one area.

▪ You want to fully dry the soil in between irrigation periods.

▪ You want some areas to receive more water than others.

Greywater can be switched between zones by manual or automatic methods. The simplest method is manual: Add a second 3-way valve outside, in an accessible location. This creates two zones for which you manually turn the valve to switch back and forth (see Multiple Irrigation Zones on page 99). Before choosing a manual method, ask yourself whether it's realistic that you will switch this valve every week for the next ten years. If not, install a single zone or an automatic switching method.

Automatically controlled zones employ an indexing valve that distributes greywater to multiple zones (up to eight). Each time the pump turns on, the indexing valve rotates to a new zone, without need for a controller or power supply. Many indexing valves require high pressure to operate; try a lower-pressure one, such as Fimco's *Wastewater Hydro Indexing Valve* (10 psi; costs about $90), which requires minimal filtration. You may need to include a filter to use this valve. Orenco makes a mechanical distribution valve (about $270) that operates with their compatible pump (see Resources for manufacturer websites). While this valve is designed to require filtration (80 mesh), installers report it works without any. Consult with valve manufacturers for help with selecting a compatible pump.

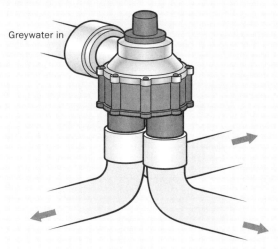

Greywater in

▲ **Indexing valve. Each time the pump turns on, the valve rotates to a new zone. (It requires an appropriate pump for the valve to function properly.)**

Manufactured Greywater Systems

THE HOLY GRAIL OF GREYWATER SYSTEMS: a low-cost "kit" that sends greywater into drip irrigation tubing without the need for regular maintenance. It works in every home and landscape. And it won't break in a year. Manufactured greywater systems attempt to do this, with varying degrees of success. The greatest challenges come from the fact that greywater systems are not one-size-fits-all, and they're a hybrid of plumbing and irrigation systems. You won't find plumbers or landscapers buying a "kit" when they plumb a house or install an irrigation system; there are too many variables for that to be feasible.

Manufactured Greywater Kits: Pros, Cons, and Costs

If you need a pump, or want drip irrigation, manufactured systems offer a convenient package with the necessary components: tank, pump, and filter. In addition, you can get technical support from the sales representative for help with installing the system. The main drawback with kits is that typically you end up with relatively low-quality parts and more frequent maintenance. These kits use parts made for other industries (there are no greywater-specific parts in North America), such as pool, pond, wastewater, or septic effluent equipment. Most systems require regular filter cleaning — an unpleasant task, and if forgotten it causes a system failure. Find out specifics about required maintenance on filters if you're considering installing this type of system. Or, pocketbook permitting, get a maintenance contract with an installer.

Greywater kits can cost $500 to $800, not including the diverter valve, plumbing parts needed to plumb greywater to the tank, irrigation components, or any associated preparation, labor, or permitting fees. Now we'll take a look at two systems currently on the market (see Resources for online suppliers).

Aqua2Use

This unit is housed in a small (approximately 2 × 1 × 2-foot) plastic box that has a series of filters (originally made for filtering fish pond water) and a low-capacity pump. It's rated to pump up to 16 feet at 14 gpm. Greywater is filtered to pass through a ¼-inch tube, so you could install an irrigation system with a ½-inch main line and ¼-inch branch lines or outlets to plants. If you want to use in-line drip irrigation, an additional 100-micron drip irrigation filter will be needed on the pump output. Use a disc-type filter, as these require less frequent maintenance than screen-type filters.

Pros: Aqua2Use

- Filtered greywater can be spread out over a larger area than unfiltered greywater.
- The system is preassembled and includes the tank, pump, and filter all in one package.

Cons: Aqua2Use

- Pump is small and not robust.
- Float switch can get hung up on tank edge and cause pump to cycle endlessly.
- Greywater storage capacity is small; when it gets backed up, greywater overflows to sewer and is wasted.
- Filters must be cleaned manually, about every six months. Any disc filter on this system will require inspection every month.
- A clogged filter makes all greywater flow to the sewer until the filter is cleaned; plants won't be getting water when the filter is clogged.
- Kit doesn't come with any irrigation components.
- Greywater is not filtered enough to be sent directly into drip irrigation tubing (it will clog the tubing over time). Additional filters (not included in kit) are needed.

IrriGRAY

The IrrigGRAY kit consists of a tank, pump, filter, and greywater-compatible drip irrigation line. You can purchase the components separately or all together. At the time of writing, IrriGRAY is coming out with several new products designed to automate the system, including a self-cleaning filter and a controller for 12 irrigation zones that can bring in freshwater if the greywater system doesn't have enough water. If these products work well, this could provide a more automatic and sophisticated system able to be installed by a handy homeowner.

Pros: IrriGRAY

- Filtered greywater can be used in greywater-compatible drip tubing and distributed over a much larger area than unfiltered greywater.

- Able to water small plants

- Kit contains all the parts you need for the tank, pump, filter, and irrigation line.

- Company has been very helpful and responsive in troubleshooting and providing installation advice.

Cons: IrriGRAY

- Filter must be manually cleaned (for systems using the non-self-cleaning filter).

- Clogged filter can cause pump to cycle continuously until it's noticed, or until the pump burns out (unless you install an alarm on it; see below).

- Drip tubing can get clogged over time, especially from washing machine greywater, and must be flushed.

I used this system for a two-year trial in my garden, with shower greywater. It was easy to install, and it was great to be able to irrigate the vegetables with the drip tubing. Cleaning the filter wasn't hard to do, but when I forgot it caused the pump to cycle endlessly — one time it pumped for two days before I noticed. Luckily the pump didn't burn out, though the tank was steaming from the heat! To address this issue, the manufacturer now offers an alarm that alerts you when the filter needs cleaning ($100+ for alarm). The tubing in my system didn't clog until the end of the two years, though a friend's system, using laundry greywater, clogged after six months. (Neither of us flushed the tubing until it clogged.)

IrriGRAY also sells a gravity-drip system for greywater. A filter attached to the outlet of a barrel sends greywater into the IrriGRAY drip tubing. This system is easy to install and an efficient form of irrigation, but it requires manual filter cleaning and regular flushing of the drip line to avoid clogging in the tubing.

Creating a Hybrid Kit System

One option for people willing to tinker with a system is to purchase the most useful components of the two kit systems and combine them. For example, buy Aqua2Use filters (not the kit) as a prefilter for your own pump and tank, then use an IrriGRAY foam filter to the IrriGRAY drip tubing. This combination of filters should last a year without cleaning, though it depends on how much greywater flows through and how dirty it is.

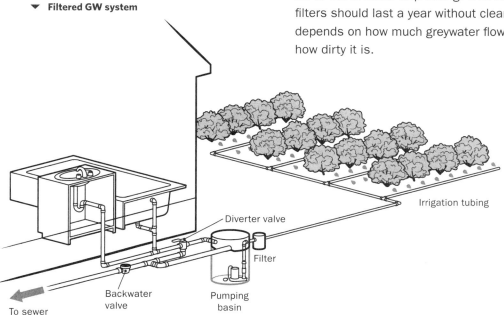

▼ **Filtered GW system**

Diverter valve

Irrigation tubing

Filter

Pumping basin

Backwater valve

To sewer

Other Types of Greywater Systems

GREYWATER SYSTEMS that aren't connected to a house, such as those drawing from an outdoor sink or shower, can be extremely simple and functional. Other types of systems have specialized functions, such as ecological disposal of greywater or supplying year-long irrigation in freezing climates by incorporating an indoor greenhouse.

Outdoor Shower

Simple and easy to install, an outdoor shower is a perfect way to irrigate nearby plants. Imagine a cool shower on a hot day, water flowing over your body and draining directly to nearby plants that adorn the shower structure. When you build the floor of the shower, use flagstone or a small concrete pad and slope it toward a well-mulched planted area adjacent to the shower — no need for a drain or plumbing. For elevated floors, slope the soil below and cover it with rock to move water toward the plants. Use a food-grade garden hose to supply the water. For a warm shower, use coils of black irrigation tubing to heat the water passively, through sun exposure.

Outdoor Sink or Drinking Fountain

Every community garden or outdoor seating area needs a sink for washing garden produce or dirty hands and for supplying drinking water. Greywater from the sink irrigates nearby plants via a small branched drain system. Supplying the sink from an existing spigot means the fixture isn't permanently connected to a building's plumbing system and therefore won't technically produce "greywater" or be illegal without a permit . . . in most cases; the legality of this is a "gray" area. Obviously it's not illegal to wash your hands using a garden hose and let the water run on the ground, but if you build a small structure and install a sink using the garden hose, will that produce greywater and require a permit? This legal ambiguity makes these systems attractive in schools or community centers where permitting greywater systems may be particularly challenging.

Subsoil Infiltration Systems

Subsoil systems use infiltration chambers to soak greywater into the ground, instead of mulch basins. Greywater flows to belowground chambers designed to fill up with an inch or two of water, then let it soak into the ground. Chambers are sized based upon

Sloped flagstone or cement

Basin with mulch and landscape plants

◀ **This outdoor shower directly irrigates the landscape.**

estimate flows; larger chambers accommodate more water flowing into them. Subsoil systems are used where subsurface irrigation is needed and where a lot of water must infiltrate into a small area. They're also incorporated into some types of greywater greenhouses (see page 126). These systems often are installed to comply with local regulations and are commonly used in combination with composting toilets in place of a septic system (for an example, see Sewerless Homes on page 126).

The cost of a professionally installed whole-house system ranges from $6,000 to $10,000 to replace a septic system. DIY installations using gravity flow to subsoil half-barrels may cost $200 to $300 in materials. There are a variety of materials available for subsurface irrigation:

Infiltrators. These are designed for septic systems. Use the shortest (in height) infiltrator possible so greywater will soak higher in the soil profile where there is more biological activity to process the water. Infiltrator Systems makes one that's 8" tall × 48" long × 34" wide (see Resources).

Box trough. Build your own infiltrators by creating a wooden box trough — essentially a rectangular box with no bottom. This allows you to customize the size and depth of the infiltrators to fit your site. Include an access hatch on top that opens for inspection and maintenance.

Half-barrels. Use salvaged plastic barrels, usually 30-gallon-size, and cut them in half. Drill an entry hole on top and cut out an inspection hatch.

Dosing tank. Professionally installed systems often use a dosing tank, which collects greywater and sends it all out to the infiltration area a few times a day. This allows the soil to re-oxygenate between doses. Dosing tanks can be pumped or work by gravity.

Pros: Subsoil Infiltration

- Keeps greywater below the ground surface, which is required by some state codes

- Able to send more water to a smaller area than with a branched drain system

- Meets code requirements for houses installing alternative wastewater systems, such as a composting toilet with greywater system

- Prevents groundwater pollution and recycles nutrients in upper levels of soil

- Professionally installed systems are ultra-low-maintenance.

Cons: Subsoil Infiltration

- Not a water-efficient method of distributing greywater; water is concentrated instead of being spread out to maximize its irrigation potential.

- Requires a lot of digging and possible disturbance of existing landscaping

Surge tank

Effluent pump

Infiltrators

▲ **Subsoil infiltration system**

Sewerless Homes

JOHN HANSON and his Maryland-based company NutriCycle Systems install whole-house systems (greywater with composting toilets) as an alternative to a septic or sewer system. He also designs greywater systems used worldwide for the composting toilet company Clivus Multrum. His systems are maintenance-free: he has ten-year-old systems that require no maintenance whatsoever.

His greywater systems satisfy health department concerns for approving no-septic homes or businesses (all sites must meet the percolation requirements of a conventional system for regulatory approval of an alternative one — this prevents development on a site unsuitable for a septic system). They are designed to prevent groundwater pollution and recycle nutrients; they are not specifically for irrigation.

Greywater is delivered to subsoil infiltrators either with a pump or gravity dosing tank (non-electric). John uses Orenco's *automatic distributing valve* to create multiple zones in the pumped systems. His systems have no filters, and all organic matter decomposes in the soil. In freezing climates pipes are buried deeper and never have standing water in the pipes. In most places he infiltrates 8 inches deep, though goes deeper (12 to 16 inches) in areas with extreme weather conditions.

The cost for a residential greywater ranges between $6,000 and $10,000. A Clivus Multrum composting toilet is $6,000 to $10,000. The total cost is between $15,000 and $20,000 — about the same as a new septic system.

John installed a Nutricycle system at his home in 1980, with two waterless toilets and one foam flush toilet (3 ounces per flush) connected to a Clivus Multrum toilet. The compost is removed once a year and used on the property. Household greywater is absorbed by a beautiful flower bed. You can visit John's website (see Resources) to see these systems in action and to contact him for an appointment.

John's advice to us: "Do it! Get involved, do something that is not polluting."

Greywater for Greenhouses

Greywater can be used to irrigate greenhouse plants. Common in cold climates, greenhouses extend the growing season and maximize the irrigation potential of greywater. There are two categories of greenhouses irrigated with greywater: stand-alone, outdoor greenhouses and integrated, indoor greenhouses that are attached to the house.

Stand-alone, outdoor greenhouses can be constructed anytime and the plants can be irrigated with a pumped greywater system. Irrigate larger plants with a simple pumped system (no filter) or, to spread out the water to irrigate numerous small plants, include a filter for a drip irrigation system. Always cover the soil with mulch (either wood chips or straw) to catch particles in the greywater and prevent clogging of the soil. See Greywater System with Tank and Pump (page 117) for help with system design and installation.

In some situations a laundry-to-landscape system can also irrigate greenhouse plants. The washing machine must be close enough to the greenhouse (within 50 feet in a flat yard, or farther in a downward-sloping yard), and the plants must be either in-ground, in small raised beds, or in very large pots (wine-barrel-sized). See Laundry-to-Landscape (L2L) System (page 81) for more information.

The cost to irrigate an existing outdoor greenhouse is the same as with the standard L2L, pumped, or filtered greywater system.

Integrated, indoor greenhouses irrigated with greywater are typically installed during new construction or a major remodel. **Earthships**, passive-solar houses made from natural and recycled materials (see page 145), incorporate greywater greenhouses that grow beautiful plants and also filter the greywater to be reused to flush toilets.

In cold climates an indoor greenhouse requires proper siting to maximize sun exposure and minimize the need for supplemental heating. The cost for a professionally installed indoor greenhouse and greywater system may range between $10,000 and $30,000, on par with putting a small addition onto a home. The cost for the greywater system represents a small portion of the total cost for the greenhouse.

Pros: Greenhouse System

- Greywater can be used to irrigate all year long in cold climates (when outdoor plants are dormant).

- Indoor greenhouses facilitate growing tropical plants in just about any climate.

- Can create zero-discharge systems as the plants evapotranspire all the water

- Can filter greywater for toilet flushing

Cons: Greenhouse System

- Building an indoor greenhouse is more complicated than simply installing a greywater system, and it requires proper siting (southern exposure in the northern hemisphere).

- Problems with indoor greenhouses can affect the living space (for example, a white fly infestation).

- Moisture levels and temperature of the greenhouse must be maintained.

- May require a pumped system to move greywater into the greenhouse

Composting and Greywater at Camp

Bar-T Mountainside camp, in Urbana, Maryland, once had approval to put in a one-million-dollar septic system for their capacity of 350 daily campers. Instead, they installed a greywater and composting toilet system, saving more than $500,000 (even with an overdesigned greywater system and the cost of building a new basement for the compost chambers). The system is six years old and has helped to teach thousands of children about nutrient recycling.

Inflow of greywater

Impermeable planter

Outflow

◀ **South-facing indoor greenhouse filters greywater and grows lush plants.**

Indoor Greywater Greenhouse (with Composting Toilet)

CARL AND SARA WARREN run a residential design-build contracting company in eastern Massachusetts. When they decided to convert their barn into an office, they found out the septic system wasn't large enough for increased flows. They decided to install an alternative, *zero-discharge* system. Composting toilets are an accepted technology and no problem for permits in their state. They chose a Phoenix composting toilet (Carl says they've had absolutely no problems with it and feel sorry for people who have to put up with the smell, water use, and cleaning hassles of a flush toilet). Getting a permit for a greywater system was harder and required approval from the state department of environmental protection; their system is monitored as a pilot project.

The system begins with water-efficient fixtures (washing machine, shower, bathroom and kitchen sinks) draining to a surge tank. Greywater flows by gravity to ¾-inch PVC pipes, spread throughout the greenhouse planters. The planters were insulated and lined with an impermeable rubber membrane (required by the state department of environmental protection) and filled with a combination of peat moss, vermiculite, loam, and compost. Carl was surprised at how tolerant the plants were, and they experimented to find ones that thrived and evapo-transpired the most water; bananas won. The beds transpire 50 gallons a day, even in the winter.

Maintenance includes trimming plants, annual cleaning of the grease interceptor (under the kitchen sink), biannual cleaning of the lint collector, and regular cleaning of strainers in the sink and shower drains.

Carl reflects that the greatest drawback to his system is the heating requirement. Because the greenhouse had to fit into an existing building, he wasn't able to orient it for passive heating. With proper orientation and an automatic insulating shutter system, he believes it could be 100 percent passively heated.

Cost
Greenhouse (12 × 21 feet): $20,000
Nighttime shutter system: $3,000
Greywater system: $700
Composting toilet (Phoenix- rs200, middle-sized): $6,000

Constructed Wetlands

A **constructed wetland** is a watertight planter, typically lined with a pond liner, filled with gravel and planted with wetland plants. The plants, gravel, and microbes around the roots filter greywater and remove nutrients. More common in wastewater treatment plants and commercial-scale greywater than in backyard systems, constructed wetlands ecologically "dispose" of the water, instead of efficiently reusing it. Constructed wetlands are well suited for homes that produce more greywater than is needed in the landscape. And, importantly, in places without sewer treatment, constructed wetland systems treat household greywater to prevent water pollution.

Anyone researching constructed wetland systems will read about the importance of retention time: how long each water molecule remains in the system. In a municipal-scale system that treats wastewater for discharge into a waterway, it's critical to have sufficient retention time to ensure all the nutrients are removed from the water. In a backyard wetland, retention time is not important: the nutrients in greywater will fertilize the garden, and the water won't be discharged into a waterway. Backyard wetland system designers should focus on clogging prevention and surge capacity rather than retention time.

Backyard constructed wetlands typically are used for ecological disposal of greywater in climates with ample rainfall or places without sewer treatment. With my own system, I learned that I could easily grow the wetland plants I love without the drawbacks of flowing all the greywater through the wetland prior to the irrigation system, by directing a portion of greywater to irrigate the wetland and using the rest for other plants. Costs for systems range from a few hundred dollars for a small do-it-yourself installation (or less if you use salvaged materials) to many thousands of dollars for a large, professionally installed system.

Here are a few things to keep in mind when designing a wetland system:

- How large? A very rough rule of thumb for sizing a wetland is ½ to 1 square foot per gallon (per day), with a depth of 1 to 2 feet.

- Use well-washed pea gravel for the substrate, and larger rocks around inlets and outlets.

- Use pond liner or an old bathtub to create a watertight planter. Sometimes wetlands are made out of cinder blocks or a strong wooden planter with a liner.

- Do not allow water to surface. Keep the outlet lower than the inlet to prevent surfacing greywater.

- Wetlands will require weeding and thinning of plants.

- Send the overflow to an appropriate location. For zero-discharge systems the overflow should be pumped back into the inlet of the wetland or any prior surge tank. Otherwise, send it to a well-mulched area.

- Don't plant fibrous-rooted plants near the inlet or outlet; they can clog up the system. Plant cattails, papyrus, equisetum, and canna lily or other plants well suited for your climate.

Pros: Constructed Wetland Systems

- Able to grow water-loving (and beautiful) wetland plants without using potable water

- Plants and microbes remove nutrients from water, ecologically cleaning it.

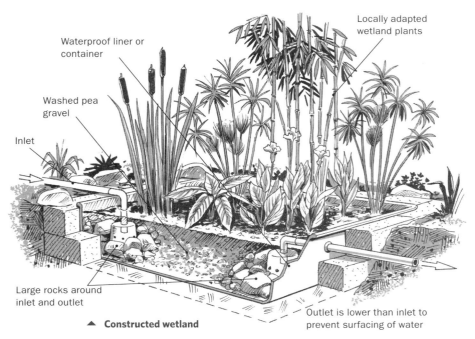

Locally adapted wetland plants

Waterproof liner or container

Washed pea gravel

Inlet

Large rocks around inlet and outlet

Outlet is lower than inlet to prevent surfacing of water

▲ **Constructed wetland**

- Water-loving plants consume lots of water, reducing the quantity of greywater to manage.

Cons: Constructed Wetland Systems

- Less irrigation water available if greywater passes through a wetland first

- Clogging can occur in wetland from overgrowth of roots that fill the air spaces in the gravel. This is time-consuming to remedy.

- If greywater contains salts, the wetland can increase their concentration. Wetland plants evapotranspire water but not salts, resulting in lower-quality irrigation water than domestic water.

Sand Filter to Drip Irrigation

Sand filters are used in both drinking water and wastewater treatment, and often there is confusion between the two processes. **Slow sand filters** clean water for drinking. Small quantities of nonpotable water slowly drain through sand, where microbes remove pathogens and contaminates from the water. It is a biological process. **Rapid sand filters** treat wastewater. Greywater, for example, is pumped rapidly through a sand filter where the hair, lint, and gunk stick in the sand; filtered greywater comes out (not drinking water quality!). Filtration is adequate for drip irrigation systems without clogging the small emitters. It is a physical process.

Casa Dominguez Multi-Family Greywater System

Casa Dominguez provides affordable housing to 70 families and transition-age youth exiting the foster care system, as well as a child-care center and health clinic. Greywater from the laundry irrigates a beautiful courtyard and the perimeter landscaping. The "sand-filter to drip irrigation" system was made by the company ReWater. Casa Dominguez is LEED platinum certified, the highest level of certification from the U.S. Green Building Council, and obtained the first permit for a multi-family building to reuse greywater in Los Angeles County.

Rapid sand filters, like those used in swimming pool systems, are employed in high-end greywater systems. These systems use pumps, tanks, controllers, and drip irrigation and are much more expensive than other types. In general, a sand filter to drip irrigation system is installed in whole-house greywater systems, in high-end residential, multifamily, and commercial-scale new construction.

In a typical rapid sand filter system all greywater from the house is plumbed to a surge tank, where the greywater is stored temporarily. Inside the tank an effluent pump, turned on by an irrigation controller, pumps greywater through the sand filter, then out to the landscape. The hair, lint, and other particles are filtered out in the sand, and greywater is distributed to plants via greywater-compatible irrigation tubing (made for greywater or septic effluent). If there is not enough greywater to complete the irrigation cycle, the system automatically supplements with domestic water. The controller automatically cleans the sand filter by pumping fresh water backwards through the sand, removing the lint, hair, and particles, and sending them to the sewer. The cost of this type of system ranges from $10,000 to $30,000.

Pros: Sand Filter System

- Very efficient form of irrigation

- Replaces other irrigation systems, since greywater can be supplemented with other water sources to meet any irrigation need

- Fully automatic; filter is self-cleaning.

Cons: Sand Filter System

- Expensive and requires a high skill level to install

- Relies on pumps and electricity

- Requires backflow prevention so the system can't accidentally contaminate potable water supply. This adds cost and permitting challenges.

- Filter doesn't remove salts, boron, or other substances potentially harmful to plants. It only removes large particles that would otherwise clog the irrigation system.

Reusing Septic Tank Effluent for Irrigation

Homes with a septic tank system may be able to reuse the septic effluent water for irrigation, with just a few alterations to the conventional system. A conventional septic system consists of a septic tank and a drain field, also called a leach field. Wastewater from the home flows into the buried septic tank. Solids in the water sink to the bottom and are decomposed by anaerobic bacteria while the liquids, called septic effluent, flow out the other end into the leach field. Leach lines are made from large, perforated pipe buried in gravel-filled trenches. The effluent flows into the leach lines, out the holes, and soaks down into the soil.

Homes with a septic system can adapt the tank to reuse all the effluent without separating out greywater flows. These systems treat septic effluent to irrigation quality, and often are used when a traditional septic leach field is not suitable (for example, if the land is rocky with poor infiltration) or to capture irrigation water. Some states allow this treated effluent to be reused for irrigation. Most systems add oxygen to the septic tank to feed aerobic bacteria which clean the effluent to a higher quality. Companies such as Orenco make whole systems designed for septic effluent reuse. Other products, like the *Sludgehammer Aerobic Bacteria Generator* (see Resources), are installed inside the existing septic tank. Reed-bed constructed wetlands are also used to treat the septic effluent for irrigation.

In terms of cost, if the local authority allows the septic leach field to be reduced or eliminated, the cost is comparable to that of a traditional system. By contrast, regulatory requirements could make the system more expensive than a traditional one if they require a conventional leach field system in addition. Typical costs for professional installation are $7,000 to $10,000. Materials only — for homeowner installations — run around $4,000.

Pros: Reusing Septic Effluent

- Able to reuse all water, even the toilet.

- Can be lower in cost than retrofitting all the fixtures to capture greywater.

Greywater Goes High-Tech

A HIGH-TECH GREYWATER SYSTEM not only irrigates the plants, it knows how much water your home is using and reusing. All info is uploaded to a web page, where you can monitor the real-time water use, daily greywater flow and municipal use, view charts of monthly usage, and get e-mail alerts for pipe breaks or leaks (this could save a lot of water!).

John Russell, owner of Water Sprout (see Resources), a design-build company specializing in greywater and rainwater systems, uses technology to automate and monitor his systems. John has fine-tuned his system over the past 10 years, using various filtering methods, all self-cleaning and operating with controls and make-up water.

He recently installed a system in a LEED-certified new home in Kentfield, California, collecting all household greywater (except kitchen sinks) for landscape irrigation, and rainwater for reuse in toilets and laundry. Greywater flows into a 300-gallon underground tank for temporary storage. The system pumps filtered greywater to the landscape drip irrigation. The filters are automatically backflushed once a week to reduce system maintenance to once a year.

John has more experience with greywater filters than anyone I know. His recommendation to those considering filters:

"Filtering greywater appropriately is probably the most challenging aspect of utilizing greywater. When purchasing systems it's important to understand how often the filters need to be maintained, and try to choose systems that require minimal maintenance. Who wants to spend their weekend cleaning greywater filters?"

Using Septic Tank Effluent for Irrigation

JEREMIAH KIDD AND HIS FAMILY reuse every last drop of water leaving the house in their landscape. Jeremiah is the owner of San Isidro Permaculture (see Resources), an ecological landscaping company specializing in greywater, rainwater, and edible landscapes in Santa Fe, New Mexico. In his own home Jeremiah decided to install a blackwater recycling system instead of the greywater systems he often installs. Why? The only growing options on his land were uphill from the house, he'd have to pump the water with any reuse system, and the blackwater system gave him more options and control over the irrigation system.

His home is plumbed conventionally; water from the shower, sinks, washing machine, and toilet flow together into the septic tank. The blackwater irrigation system begins in the second chamber of the tank with a Sludgehammer system (see Resources), pumping oxygen into the chamber to feed aerobic bacteria that clean the water. The treated septic effluent overflows into a pump tank where it's pumped out through a filter to subsurface drip irrigation designed specially for wastewater, using Netafim purple tubing for the irrigation lines. (New Mexico requires that tubing be buried 6 inches below grade.) Soil microbes further clean the water, and plants benefit from the nutrients. Jeremiah's system has four zones: two zones of native plants, providing habitat for birds and beneficial insects; and two zones of food production, food forest and fruit trees. He concentrates the water in those zones during the growing season.

"I think of this as a fertilizing system. It's not enough water for the entire landscape, but it reuses all the water from the home and sends nutrients to the plants," says Jeremiah.

They are a water-conscious family, using less than 20 gallons per person per day. With a large landscape (they garden around 10,000 square feet), their system covers only about one-third of the need. The other two-thirds is irrigated with rainwater and, occasionally, well water.

Jeremiah built the system himself (as well as the house). He spent around $4,000 for the parts. He was allowed to reduce his leach field significantly, from around 30 infiltrators down to 8. This is an accepted technology in New Mexico, and there were no problems with getting a permit. Maintenance is minimal: twice a year he cleans filters and once a year adds bacteria to the tank.

Cons: Reusing Septic Effluent

- Not typically suitable for installation by the average do-it-yourselfer

- Requires additional electricity use, and pumping of the water

- Not (yet) legal in some states

- Systems don't remove salts or boron from the water, which can harm plants. Plant-friendly products must still be used in the house, and there is no way to turn "off" the system.

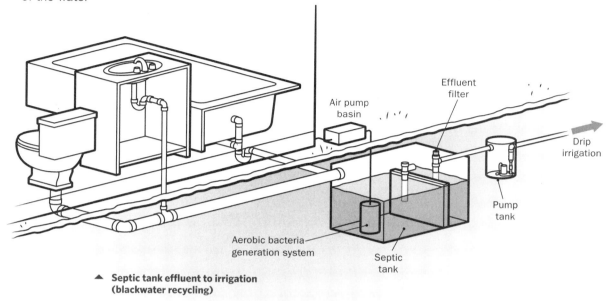

Air pump basin

Effluent filter

Drip irrigation

Pump tank

Aerobic bacteria generation system

Septic tank

▲ **Septic tank effluent to irrigation (blackwater recycling)**

Greywater in Freezing Climates

LIVE SOMEWHERE CHILLY? Maintaining a greywater system in freezing conditions requires additional planning and precautions:

- Gravity systems should drain completely. Standing water in the pipes could freeze and create a blockage, or potentially burst the pipe. Meticulously maintain proper slope throughout the entire system.

- Do not allow any standing water in lines from pumped systems. Ensure greywater will drain out or drain back into the tank.

- In a pumped or L2L system: If it's logistically difficult to prevent standing water in the line, create an automatic bypass at the beginning of the system. If the main line freezes, water will be forced out the bypass; for example, a tee fitting with a tube running high enough up so greywater

doesn't exit unless the line is blocked (if the tube is too short, greywater will come out like a fountain).

- Greenhouses irrigated by greywater (see page 126) can produce food and greenery year-round.

- Shut off the system (and drain down any places with standing water) until irrigation is needed. Install a drain-down valve at the low point of the system to empty the pipes for winter. Use a tee with a ball valve at the lowest point. Close the valve when using the system and open it to drain the line.

Note: Shutting off the system may be unnecessary, even with freezing, snowy weather. The warmth in greywater can keep lines open and the ground biologically active (see Cold-Climate Greywater: Evergreen Lodge on page 134).

Cold-Climate Greywater: Evergreen Lodge

EVERGREEN LODGE, in the mountains of Yosemite, California, recycles nearly a million gallons of water annually, thanks to the work of Regina Hirsch of Sierra Watershed Progressive and the lodge's environmentally conscious leadership. Over the past few years Regina and her crew installed dozens of systems at the lodge, both simple gravity-fed branched drain systems (in 55 guest cabins) and large automated systems from the commercial laundry and staff dorms.

"The system is a big win for the lodge," reflects owner Brian Anderluh. "We were able to take greywater out of our septic system and use it instead for our landscape beautification project, without requiring any more fresh water from our well."

Regina, an ecologist turned landscaper, notes, "Plant productivity at Evergreen Lodge has increased threefold since we installed these systems, and soil biota is on the rise."

Even though the lodge gets an average of 30 inches of snow annually, the systems operate problem-free all winter long. (They carefully designed each system so no standing water remains in the lines to freeze, and the soil remains biologically active from the warmth of greywater.)

"Branched drain systems far exceed the pumped systems; however, controller-based valved systems have been reliable for nearly three years with high demands due to drought conditions," notes Regina.

One system reused an existing irrigation system; they removed the emitters and sent filtered greywater through the ¼-inch tubing to landscaping in the main courtyard.

Regina adds, "Placing these systems in public view, especially when people are on vacation, is a powerful educational tool. Kids love going out and seeing the water from their shower draining to the trees outside, and the shower rinse water at the outdoor pool flow directly to mulched swales growing a garden before their eyes. It's so easy to understand what works when it is simple, effective, and in balance."

Plumbing Basics for Greywater Installation

TO INSTALL YOUR GREYWATER SYSTEM you'll need to be familiar with basic plumbing techniques, namely cutting, assembling, and attaching pipes. You'll also need to know what tools to use and understand how the components fit together. The following section will go over common terminology for plumbing parts, how to cut and connect materials, and some basic installation tips. If you're new to plumbing, I recommend getting a general reference book (see Resources) for support and for help with tackling any obstacles you may encounter.

Parts Primer

Understanding a few basic terms will help you find the parts you need when you're building your system. Standard plumbing parts are identified by their size and material and how they connect together. Here we'll also cover some of the not-so-common valves that are regularly used in greywater installations, including check valves, backwater valves, and air admittance valves.

Types of Threads

Wouldn't it be nice if plumbing parts all had the same type of thread, and they all connected to each other. Unfortunately for the beginner, standard or "normal" threads don't exist. Let's look at the most common types of threads you'll encounter when installing a greywater system.

Male vs. female. Male fittings have exposed threads; female fittings have internal threads. MPT = male pipe thread; FPT= female pipe thread.

Pipe thread vs. garden hose thread (vs. buttress thread). NPT (National Pipe Thread) is the most common type of thread found on standard plumbing supplies. Pipe threads are different from the threads on a garden hose. You cannot connect a female-threaded garden hose to a fitting that has pipe threads. Buttress threads, or "coarse threads," are commonly used in 30- or 55-gallon drums and IBC totes (more commonly used in rainwater collection systems than in greywater systems). Buttress threads are not compatible with NPT or garden hose threads. (You can mail-order adapters for them, or connect to the NPT thread options on the containers; see Working with Closed-Top Barrels on page 186 for details.)

Tapered vs. straight threads. NPT threads are tapered. If you try to connect a male-threaded adapter into a female-threaded coupling, the tapers on the threads will prevent you from connecting them fully together. Plumbing fittings have tapered threads. For a watertight seal, tapered threads must be wrapped with pipe thread tape. Plastic electrical conduit fittings have straight threads, so it's possible to fully connect a male to female adapter. This is useful as a lower-cost way to create an outlet in a barrel (just add a rubber washer in between them for a watertight seal) and can be used instead of a tank adapter or bulkhead fitting.

Check Valves (Swing vs. Spring)

A check valve is a one-way valve used to prevent water from draining back down a pipe after it's been pumped out and uphill. For greywater applications, use **swing** check valves, not **spring**. Swing check valves have a flapper inside that easily pushes open, requiring less pressure than the spring check valves. Swing check valves are used in pumped systems, though not typically for the laundry-to-landscape, since most L2L systems don't pump uphill. Don't

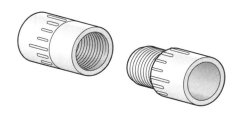

▲ **Female (left) and male threads**

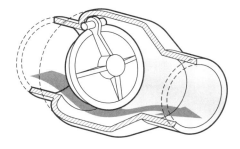

▲ **Swing check valve: water can flow in only one direction.**

use a check valve unless it's necessary, because it adds friction and is a potential clogging point. You can buy swing check valves at large irrigation or hardware stores.

Air Admittance Valve (AAV)

An air admittance valve (AAV), also called an in-line vent or auto-vent, is a one-way mechanical vent used in plumbing to replace the need for a conventional vent pipe to the roof. AAVs allow air into the system to prevent water traps from siphoning. In an L2L system the AAV is used to prevent a potential siphon in the washing machine as it tries to refill. In this application, the AAV is not connected to the drainage plumbing of the house and is not being used to vent the washing machine drain. Note that plumbing codes typically require a specific type of AAV, made for venting a drain (which costs around $20 or $30), but in an L2L system any mechanical vent is suitable, including the lower-cost "auto-vent" option (around $4). See Resources for more info.

Note: An AAV should not leak unless it is defective or breaks. If water ever leaks from the vent, replace it.

Backwater Valve

A backwater valve is another type of one-way valve designed to prevent a sewer backflow from entering the surge tank or greywater line. Install one on the overflow of a surge tank or on the sewer side of the diverter valve. A backwater valve is used for gravity flow and is serviceable (you can unscrew it and open the valve up for cleaning), unlike the swing check valve. Most backwater valves are installed horizontally, so plan accordingly. Plastic backwater valves are inexpensive (about $20 to $30) and are available from plumbing supply stores.

Union

A union fitting allows you to easily disconnect and reconnect the pipes. It can either be glued or threaded on a pipe. Install a union where you may want to disconnect the pipes; for example, to disconnect pipes to repair a pump. Unions are available at hardware and plumbing stores.

PIPE MATERIALS FOR DRAINAGE PLUMBING (AND HOW TO WORK WITH THEM)

Material	Options for cutting	Connecting joints
ABS (black plastic)	Tubing cutter with wheel for cutting plastic Handsaw for cutting plastic	Glue pipe to fittings with ABS cement
PVC (white plastic)	Tubing cutters with wheel for cutting plastic Large ratcheting cutters Handsaw for cutting plastic	Glue pipe to fittings with PVC primer and cement (or use Gorilla PVC, a less toxic self-priming cement)
Galvanized steel	Reciprocating saw with metal blade Grinder Hacksaw	Use appropriate transition coupling to connect to plastic pipe
Cast iron	Grinder Chain-snap cutter	No-hub couplings. Old cast-iron pipes were connected using "lead-and-oakum" joints.
Copper	Tubing cutter with metal wheel	Soldered joints. Use a transition coupling to connect copper pipe to the plastic valve.

Notes:

Plastic pipe is the easiest and cheapest to work with. Interface between PVC and ABS with transition glue or a transition coupling.

Steel pipe corrodes over time. Cut out as much old corroded pipe as possible and replumb. Be careful when cutting out a section of pipe; the vibrations can cause leaks in other pipe joints.

With old cast iron plumbing, don't disturb lead-and-oakum joints. They're sealed into the bell joint with molten lead, packed with horsehair or jute. You may need to replace a section of plumbing.

Copper is used for both water lines and drainage pipe. Water lines typically are 1 inch or smaller; drainage pipe is larger and has yellow markings. Don't accidentally cut into a water line!

Transition Coupling

Transition couplings are used to connect different sizes and types of pipe together. The size and thickness of the rubber inside the transition coupling compensates for the size difference (outside diameter) between the pipes and forms a watertight seal between them. The easiest way to get the proper coupling is to go to a plumbing supply house and ask for help. You will need to know the pipe size (the inside diameter of the pipe) and the material of the two pipes you want to connect together. For example, to connect a 2-inch copper pipe to the diverter valve, which is 2-inch plastic, you'll need a 2-inch copper to 2-inch plastic transition coupling.

Use a transition coupling to connect your 3-way diverter valve into the greywater drain. First, loosen the bands holding the steel jacket over the rubber coupling. Then, slide the steel jacket over the copper pipe. Slide the rubber sleeve over the pipe, then the diverter valve. (Make sure to orient the rubber sleeve correctly; in this example the copper side must go onto the copper pipe, and the plastic side onto the

plastic valve end.) You may need to roll back the rubber to fit the diverter in between the sections of rigid pipe, as shown. After the valve is in place, slide the metal sleeve over the rubber coupling and tighten the bands. Check this joint for leaks when you test your system (and tighten more if there is a leak).

Basic Installation Techniques

Following are some basic tips and guidance for connecting pipes to flow greywater out to the landscape. To learn more or to get hands-on training with plumbing basics, look for classes held at community colleges, home-improvement stores, or private schools; they can be a great place to learn tricks of the trade and gain tool confidence. Working with a knowledgeable friend is another way to learn your way around plumbing.

Connecting Threaded Fittings

To connect threaded fittings, wrap pipe thread tape around the threads; this helps creates a watertight seal. Wrap clockwise, as you face the open end with the threads, overlapping at least three turns. If you wrap the wrong direction, the tape will come off when you screw in the fittings; rewrap if this occurs. Carefully screw the fitting in clockwise. A trick to make sure you are not "cross-threading" the fitting is to first screw in the fitting to the LEFT until you hear a "click" and feel the fitting settle into place. Then screw the fitting to the RIGHT to tighten it. It should thread easily at first, gradually getting harder and harder. Plastic threads are easy to damage when threading into metal, so go slow and easy.

Cutting and Gluing Plastic Pipe (PVC and ABS)

Plastic pipe is easy to cut and connect. To construct your greywater system, you'll need to know how to measure, cut, and glue the pieces together.

Measuring. To measure a length of pipe, measure the distance between the fittings (see next page) then ADD the distance the pipe will slip into the fittings once it's glued (the glue lubricates the pipe so it slips into the fitting up to the lip). If you end up short, just cut the pipe and use a coupling to increase the length.

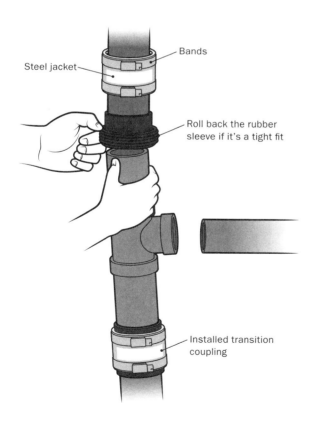

Bands

Steel jacket

Roll back the rubber sleeve if it's a tight fit

Installed transition coupling

▲ **Installing a transition coupling**

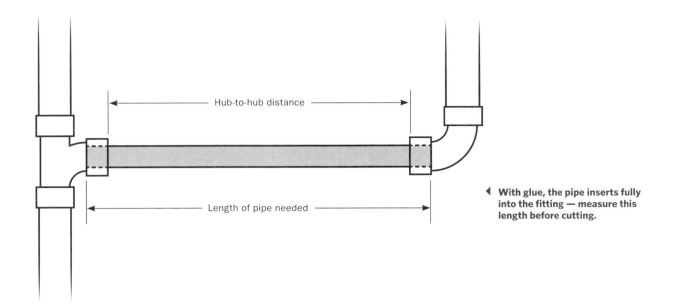

Hub-to-hub distance

Length of pipe needed

◀ **With glue, the pipe inserts fully into the fitting — measure this length before cutting.**

Cutting. You can cut rigid plastic pipe with a simple handsaw (with a blade for plastic), though ratcheting cutters for 1-inch pipe and tubing cutters (with plastic wheel) for larger pipe make a nice, clean cut. Cuts from a handsaw create burrs, little balls of plastic around the cut; always remove these with fine sandpaper or scrape them off with a utility knife before gluing the pipe.

Gluing. Dry-fit the pipe and fittings together, then mark the joints with 1-inch lines. When you glue, make sure the marks line up. Clean off the ends of the pipe with a rag before gluing. Connect PVC together using PVC solvent glue. Connect ABS pipes together using ABS cement. Use transition glue or transition couplings if you are connecting dissimilar plastics. Place old rags or newspaper on surfaces to protect them from dripping glue. Wear gloves. Apply glue on the inside of the fitting, then the outside of the pipe. Push the two together, lining up your marks. Hold for several seconds so the pipe doesn't push back out.

Tip: Gorilla PVC is less toxic than traditional PVC solvent glue and does not require primer like conventional solvent glue does.

▲ **Line up marks when gluing pipe.**

Tips for Working with Irrigation Tubing

Uncoil the tubing the day before and leave it out in the sun. Try to work on a warm day, as the tubing will be softer and more pliable. To make it easier to fit tubing onto barbed fittings, dip the ends of the tubing in hot water to soften the plastic (bring a cup and thermos). In general, work with the natural curves in the tubing, and don't try to straighten it. To irrigate multiple plants along a straight line, alternate curved pieces to maintain an overall straight trajectory. Always lay the curves sideways, not up or down. Rotate tubing on the barbed fittings to change the tubing's orientation.

Using a Grade Level

A grade level is a level with a second set of lines around the bubble to show 2 percent slope, standard drainage plumbing slope. It makes it easy to slope pipes: just touch the bubble to the second line to find proper slope.

"Tool Tight"

In greywater systems fittings should be "tool tight." Too loose causes leaks, and too tight cracks plastic. First tighten the fitting with your hands. Then use large wrenches or tongue-and-groove pliers to tighten until it is difficult to tighten more.

Tool Safety

Power tools make construction jobs faster but are dangerous if proper safety techniques aren't followed. Ask about tool safety if you're learning from someone else or using an unfamiliar tool. For example, if you're drilling a hole into wood and the drill bit gets stuck, the drill body will whip around and can smack you. With proper body positioning, a bruise is the worst that will happen. If you're unaware of where the drill may swing, you could be smacked in the face, knocked off a ladder, or get a broken wrist.

◀ **Hot water softens plastic.**

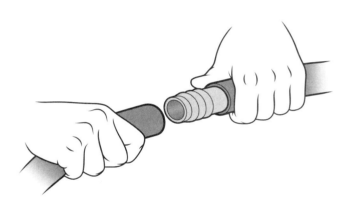

▲ **Dip end of tubing in hot water before pushing over barb fitting ridges so it fits over barbs with ease.**

6

Rainwater Harvesting: Planning Your System

CAPTURING RAINWATER for our homes and landscapes reduces our consumption and dependence on stressed freshwater supplies and dwindling groundwater, and prevents stormwater runoff pollution. If you think rainwater harvesting is suitable only for wet climates with year-round rainfall, think again. The practice of capturing the rain is thousands of years old, originating in the arid parts of the world: the Middle East, across Africa, and Native American communities in the American Southwest. People living in Mediterranean regions of Europe directed wet-winter rains into cisterns for use in the dry season. From simple shaping of the land by farmers to direct moisture to their crops to the creation of giant underground cisterns — navigable by boat — found under ancient cities like Istanbul, rainwater harvesting methods are as diverse as the cultures that practiced them.

Backyard rainwater systems can be quite simple and very effective. We can reshape our yards to prevent runoff and create a living, water-harvesting sponge to soak up the rain and sink it into the ground for our plants. And with roofwater collection tanks, we can store rainwater "for a sunny day."

IN THIS CHAPTER:

How Will You Use the Rainwater?

THE FIRST STEP IN PLANNING a rainwater harvesting system is getting clear on your personal goals for the system. This will help you determine what type of system is the best match for you. First, you'll decide whether you should harvest water in the ground with a rain garden or collect it for storage in tanks, or both. If your goal is to sustain a native landscape without supplemental irrigation, or you're concerned about water pollution from urban runoff, a rain garden will meet your needs. Directing rainwater into rain gardens and water-harvesting basins effectively slows water runoff and allows it to sink into the ground. Locally adapted plants thrive with these passive techniques; only exotics, fruit trees, vegetables, and other annuals need tank water.

If you are looking for a water supply for the vegetable or flower garden, or you need a new water supply for your home, plan a storage tank system. Size the system to collect enough water for the plants and/or your home. Properly sized rainwater tanks can provide 100 percent of a household's water needs. This chapter will help you determine your daily water usage, as well as your catchment potential based on where you live. Keep in mind that even if you have a tank system, you'll most likely need a rain garden as well to soak up the overflow water from your tank.

Keeping Rainwater in Your Landscape: Permeable Hardscape and Rain Gardens

START RESTORING natural water systems by reshaping your yard. Called earthworks, rain gardens, vegetated swales, bioswales, and more, these techniques give rainwater a place to soak into the ground, rehydrate soils, recharge groundwater tables, and refresh plants while preventing stormwater runoff pollution. Other strategies, such as removing hardscape, using mulch, and growing deep-rooted plants, keep rainwater in the landscape.

Dealing with Hardscape

How much of your yard is covered with concrete, flagstone, or buildings? As discussed in chapter 2, these impermeable surfaces are both wasteful and create

HARVESTING THE RAIN IN YOUR LANDSCAPE

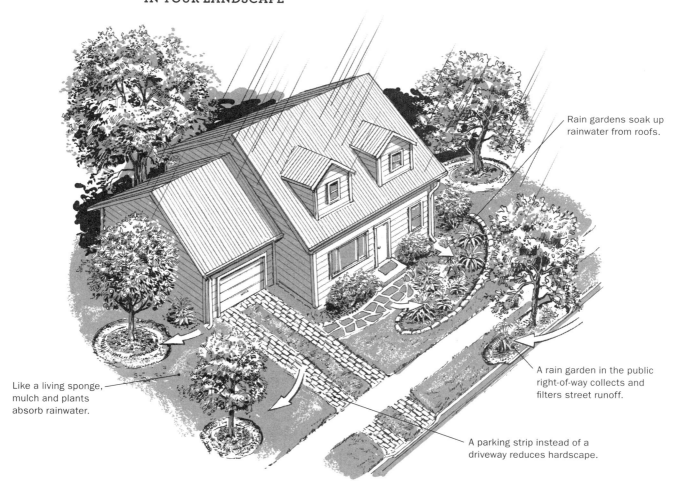

Rain gardens soak up rainwater from roofs.

A rain garden in the public right-of-way collects and filters street runoff.

A parking strip instead of a driveway reduces hardscape.

Like a living sponge, mulch and plants absorb rainwater.

pollution. Valuable rainwater flows away from the landscape and into the stormwater system, moving urban pollution into creeks, rivers, lakes, and oceans. You can take steps to increase the permeability of your yard and soak rainwater into the earth, rehydrating the landscape.

A Better Driveway

Driveways often are a major source of nonpermeable hardscape in a landscape, and in some cases, they're oversized or unused. Don't use your driveway? Convert it into beautiful and useful planting areas. Need somewhere to park the car? In many climates, all you'll need is two strips of concrete (under the wheels), the length of a parking space. Remove unnecessary concrete, then add compost, mulch, and plant. Permeable footpaths made from wood chips, gravel, or decomposed granite are low-cost and easy to build. There are also permeable hardscape surfaces, such as gravel, paving stones, interlocking pavers (with plants growing in between), turf blocks, and permeable pavement. Any "urbanite" (pieces of broken-up concrete) removed can be reused as material for walkways, terraces, benches, or garden beds.

Collect Street Runoff: Cut the Curb

Coax more water into your landscape and reduce street runoff with sidewalk-strip rain gardens. This involves removing a section of the curb in front of the rain garden, to allow street water runoff to flow into the planted garden basin. The City of Tucson has online designs for how to make a curb cut. Check with your own city about local requirements. In freezing climates, rain gardens fed by curb cuts must have salt-tolerant plants, due to a buildup of road salts in the soil.

Build a Rain Garden

It may not seem like much, but the thoughtful placement of a sunken basin, filled with plants and mulch, will protect your local waterways. Rain gardens collect runoff from impermeable driveways, patios, and roofs and slowly soak rainwater into the ground. They also reduce flooding, sewer overflows, and aquatic habitat destruction. Rain gardens are such a good idea, they are promoted by water agencies and environmental organizations all across the country.

Rain garden plants provide habitat for beneficial insects and birds.

Soil filters pollutants from lawns and roads, preventing pollution of local waterways.

The rain garden increases groundwater infiltration.

◄ **A rain garden absorbs rainwater, reducing downstream flooding, erosion, and street overflows.**

David Hymel: Rain Dog Designs

DAVID HYMEL IS ONE of the country's leading rain garden experts. He and Marilyn Jacobs own Rain Dog Designs, a company specializing in sustainable landscaping with a focus on rain garden education, design, and installation. Rain Dog Designs has installed more than 400 rain garden projects in the Puget Sound area over the past four-and-a-half years. They've collaborated with many cities and nonprofits to promote rain gardens and protect Puget Sound.

What advice do you have for people wanting to install a rain garden?

First think about your goals for the system. Some people want to improve their landscape, others want to do something for the environment. Then understand your skill level — can you do this on your own or do you need to hire a contractor? You should learn as much as possible about rain gardens, check out local resources, read books, and look at other rain gardens to get an idea how one will look in your landscape. If you're an avid gardener, choose plants that require more maintenance, more colorful ones. Otherwise, choose low-maintenance plants like grasses and sedum.

Can you talk a little about the neighborhood cluster installations you've been involved in?

Previously, we'd been putting in lots of single rain gardens around Puget Sound; with the amount of labor involved we thought it would be easier to put them in groups. In 2009 we worked with the City of Puyallup to pilot this idea; city staff was promoting rain gardens to meet their municipal stormwater permit. A local homeowner who'd attended a rain garden workshop was excited about the idea, and became the neighborhood advocate — a key to the project's success. He found six other homeowners on the block who wanted rain gardens. Neighbors who barely knew each other now worked and helped each other toward a common goal. In two weekends we installed seven systems, had 100 volunteers show up to help, hosted a live radio show in the neighborhood, and had a picnic and party afterwards. It was magical, and inspired the homeowners to go to the next level.

Not satisfied with just seven rain gardens, the neighborhood organized around green infrastructure to solve their seasonal roadway flooding problems. They encouraged Puyallup city officials to apply for a state grant to do a green street. But in order for the city to move forward with the grant request, there had to be buy-in from the majority of homeowners on the block, because the project would rearrange on-street parking — a very touchy subject in most neighborhoods. They got the buy-in, and the project was completed in March 2013.

Along the street, 8th Avenue NW, there are now: 20 residential rain gardens, including a school and an apartment complex; 11 roadside rain gardens in the City right-of-way with over 2,700 native plants; 100 percent infiltrating porous asphalt roadway; and pervious concrete and permeable paver sidewalks. We've completed cluster rain garden projects in 12 neighborhoods across Puget Sound.

What benefits have you seen in the Puget Sound area from rain gardens?

Rain gardens can be a very effective stormwater management tool, and the results are measurable. A shipping company at the Port of Tacoma installed three rain gardens at their terminal with four stormwater outlets into Commencement Bay. The rain gardens infiltrate runoff from 90,000 square feet of hardscape, almost 2 acres; this has removed outflow completely from one of the four outlets, a 25 percent reduction in total runoff from their 45-acre site. And now they're achieving their required benchmark for allowable levels of zinc and copper in the runoff water.

Is there a growing demand for rain gardens?

In the next few years the EPA is requiring cities (over 50,000 population) with combined sewers to reduce sewer overflows, ideally with Low Impact Design (LID) tools, like rain gardens (happening in 200 jurisdictions in the country). In the Seattle area there is a huge push to install rain gardens with the RainWise program — 20,000 of them in the county — to reduce stormwater into the sewer system and meet Clean Water Act requirements. This will create a huge new green construction market.

Roofwater Collection

ROOFWATER COLLECTION SYSTEMS collect and store rainwater for later use, either for irrigation or for use inside the house to flush toilets, wash clothes, or supply the shower and sinks. Collection systems are popular everywhere water is scarce, and indoor reuse systems are particularly desirable where groundwater is hard, salty, or absent. From coast to coast, and on islands, rainwater systems deliver soft, clean water to households. An estimated 30,000 to 60,000 people in Hawaii live entirely off rainwater, mostly on the big island of Hawaii. Entire subdivisions were built with no water supply, and since drilling a well through volcanic rock isn't an option, residents either catch the rain or pay to truck in water.

To plan a roofwater system, first calculate your rainwater potential — how much rain falls on your roof each year. Then, decide what you'll use it for (irrigation or indoors) and determine what size of tank to use and where to install it.

How Much Rain Can You Catch?

Calculate your rainwater potential based on the square footage of the roof and your annual rainfall. To find the square footage of the roof, measure the **footprint** of the roof; the slope or pitch of the roof planes doesn't affect the roof's catchment potential. If your house is square or rectangular, measure the length and width at ground level (under the roof) and multiply the two dimensions. If you have multiple roof sections, do this for each section and add them up. This square footage should be very similar to the square footage of one story of your home.

Theoretically, each square foot of catchment surface collects 0.623 gallon per inch of rain, or 623 gallons on a 1,000-square-foot roof. In reality, not every drop makes it to the downspout; some is lost through evaporation and leaking or plugged gutters. A more realistic calculation assumes a 90-percent efficiency, or 560 gallons per 1,000 square feet of roof (0.56 gallon per inch of rain per square foot of catchment surface).

To find the annual collection potential of your roof, multiply the square footage of the catchment surface by 0.56 gallon per inch of rain and then by

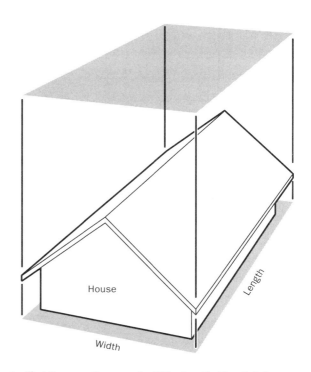

▲ **Find the area of your roof: width × length. The pitch does not affect the catchment area.**

Annual Collection Potential* on a 2,000-Square-Foot House in U.S. Cities

Phoenix, AZ: 8 inches = 8,960 gallons

Denver, CO: 16 inches = 17,920 gallons

Honolulu, HI: 18 inches = 20,160 gallons

San Francisco, CA: 22 inches = 24,640 gallons

Wichita, KS: 30.4 inches = 34,048 gallons

Seattle, WA: 37 inches = 41,440 gallons

Boston, MA: 43 inches = 48,160 gallons

Atlanta, GA: 50 inches = 56,000 gallons

Little Rock, AR: 51 inches = 57,120 gallons

Memphis, TN: 55 inches = 61,600 gallons

Miami, FL: 59 inches = 66,080 gallons

*Based on average annual rainfall for each area

your annual rainfall. There are many online resources for rainfall data, including the website of the National Oceanic and Atmospheric Administration (NOAA); see Resources.

For example, a 2,000-square-foot roof in an area with 20 inches of rainfall would collect:

2,000 × 20 × 0.56 = 22,400 gallons per year

Catchment Potential

Climate has the largest impact on your rainwater potential. A house in soggy Hilo, Hawaii (128 inches/year), collects 42 times more rain than the same size of house in bone-dry Calexico, California (3 inches/year). The chart below shows catchment potential of various roof sizes and rainfall rates.

RAINWATER CATCHMENT POTENTIAL

Roof size (in square feet)	Gallons per 1 inch of rainfall	Gallons per 20 inches of rainfall	Gallons per 40 inches of rainfall
1,000	560	11,200	22,400
1,500	840	16,800	33,600
2,000	1,120	22,400	44,800
2,500	1,400	28,000	56,000

Other Considerations

Annual rainfall data helps you estimate how many gallons you expect to collect each year. However, the frequency of the rainfall is also important to consider. Is the rain spread out evenly over the year? Or, does it all fall in a few months? These rainfall patterns influence the size of the catchment tank since you store rainwater for the dry times between rains.

We often don't have the "average" year reported by NOAA; keep this in mind when designing your system. If rainwater is your only water supply, plan your system for the worst-case-scenario year (or be prepared to truck in water during a drought).

Finally, if you live in a place affected by forest fires, the local fire department may have water storage requirements. Talk to them about how to best utilize your water system for fire protection.

Earthships

Developed by visionary (former) architect Michael Reynolds, Earthships are off-grid and energy- and water-neutral homes; that is, they produce all their own energy and collect all their own rainwater. A few thousand Earthships have been constructed all over the world. Sustainable features include passive solar design, rainwater catchment, greywater reuse, and indoor year-round food production, and nearly half the construction materials are recycled.

In the desert near Taos, New Mexico, Earthship residents have lived for 10 years strictly off the 8 inches of annual rainfall, using around 20 gallons of water per day. Rainwater and snowmelt are collected in tanks and supply all indoor water needs. Greywater flows to indoor planters in a south-facing greenhouse. The plants clean the greywater for toilet flushing while providing food and beauty inside the home. Toilet blackwater flows into a conventional septic tank outside. When local regulations permit, the septic effluent flows into an outdoor **biocell**, a planted area where plants process the blackwater. When local regulators prohibit this, the effluent flows into a conventional leach field.

Water is used at least three times in an Earthship: first in the fixture (sink, shower, clothes washer), second in the planter as irrigation, and third in the toilet (and perhaps fourth in the biocell).

Brad Lancaster: Water Harvester

BRAD LANCASTER IS THE AUTHOR of the best-selling, award-winning books *Rainwater Harvesting for Drylands and Beyond,* Volumes 1 and 2, and creator of an information-packed website (see Resources). Living on an eighth of an acre in downtown Tucson, Arizona, where rainfall is less than 12 inches annually, Brad practices what he preaches by harvesting about 100,000 gallons of rainwater a year. Brad Lancaster is a permaculture teacher, designer, consultant and cofounder of Desert Harvesters (see Resources). I spoke with Brad about rainwater harvesting.

What is your favorite RWH system?

In general my favorite systems are passive systems, like a rain garden, which will work if I'm home or not and cost no more than the cost of a shovel if I do the work myself. They're very accessible. These systems have much greater capacity than a tank ever could have. The capacity increases the more plant and soil life there is in the system. It's alive! A passive harvesting system is not a conservation strategy, but a production strategy: using 100 percent on-site resources, the system of plants, mulch, and soil microbes produces more than what I had before the system existed. That's what I find really juicy about it.

What advice do you have for people wanting to install rainwater-harvesting systems?

First, figure out what you want the water for. People often put in tanks before they even know what they're going to use the water for, and sometimes they find out they didn't really need a tank. For example, if your site has low-water-use native plants that don't need tank water, they'll be more lush and thrive on a passive system for less money. Other plants, like those in a vegetable garden, need supplemental water (in which case a tank likely makes sense). Try and get some kind of guesstimate of how much water you need so you can size the tank to fit your plants' needs. I find people tend to install a really small rain garden, or just a rain barrel, then discover they have nowhere near the capacity they need or wanted. With just a little planning and calculating they could enhance their harvests multi-fold, save a lot more water, and generate a lot more on-site resources.

(See Big, Really Big, or Enormous? (page 158) for sizing your rainwater tank, and see page 166 for help with determining the size and shape of your rain garden.)

Brad's rule:

I will not plant a fruit tree until I've installed on-site greywater within a rain-and-greywater garden from which that fruit tree will then draw its water. This ensures I get good fruit production without using virgin utility water — even in dry seasons and drought. The other cool thing about this rule is it limits how far I can send the water (by gravity or a laundry-to-landscape system) so all my oasis-producing fruit trees are within 30 feet of the house, close enough so I harvest the fruit instead of the wildlife, and I maintain the trees and greywater.

On the periphery I grow hardy multiuse food-bearing natives that crank on passive rainwater harvesting alone. And I mulch the surface of the soil around all these plantings, prioritizing the delivery of highly fertile composted kitchen scraps and humanure to the fruit trees. Keeping the lusher plants and greater fertility close to me (and freely irrigated by the greywater and rainwater from my home's drains and roof) creates the feeling, and the reality, of living within a sustainable oasis.

Basic Components of a Catchment System

EVERY RAINWATER CATCHMENT SYSTEM is made up of the same basic components regardless of its size or complexity:

- **Catchment surface,** typically the roofs of houses, sheds, garages, or rain barns

- **Gutters and downspouts,** to direct rainwater from the roof to the tank

- **Screens,** to keep dirt, debris, and leaves out of the tank

- **First-flush system** (optional) diverts dirtiest water away from tank

- **Storage tank,** in the form of cisterns, tanks, or barrels

- **Delivery system,** either gravity-fed or pumped; sends rainwater to irrigation or to house

- **Treatment or purification system** (optional; typically only potable water systems filter and disinfect the water)

Smaller and simpler systems won't use all these components, particularly the filters. Only pressurized systems require pumps, while many rainwater systems for irrigation operate on gravity alone. Now we'll take a closer look at each of the main system components.

Catchment Surface (the Roof)

Most roofs are suitable for collecting rainwater, especially when the water is used for irrigation. Avoid materials that could leach toxins into the water, such as lead flashing or fungicides in wood shingles. Some roofs can be painted to cover a less-desirable material, such as asphalt, and improve the water quality, like with Weather Barrier Raincoat 2000, a roof coating certified for potable-water catchment systems. A 2010 study by the Texas Water Development Board on the effect of roof material on water quality found metal, composite (asphalt) shingles, concrete tile, green, and cool roofs (those that reflect sunlight and keep the building cooler inside) were all suitable for rainwater collection, though the water would require treatment to meet drinking water standards. The study did not find that any one roof

material is superior to the others in regard to water quality (they tested rainwater after it flowed on the roof and past a first-flush diverter).

Suitable Roof Surfaces for Roofwater Collection

- Metal

- Composite shingles (check the MSDS if you plan to drink the water as some composites contain toxins)

- Clay/concrete tile, slate

- Green roof (living roof; may discolor water, therefore may be less desirable for indoor reuse)

Less Suitable or Unsuitable Roof Surfaces for Collection

- Flat roof with tar and gravel (can be improved with material like Raincoat 2000)

- Any roofing material containing asbestos

- Wood treated with fungicide

- Any roof with lead washers (sometimes used with fasteners on very old roofs) or lead flashing (can be improved by replacing/sealing lead components)

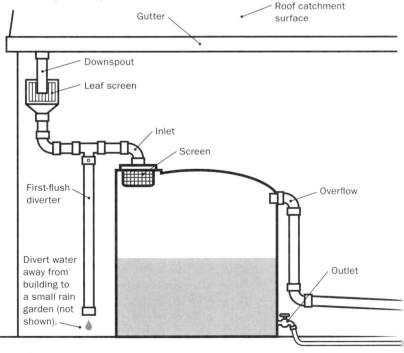

▲ Catchment system

Gutters and Downspouts

Gutters transport rainwater to the storage container. (Install them if your roof doesn't have any.) If you combine downspouts to direct more roofwater to the tank, size them adequately so they aren't overloaded in a rainstorm. Some old metal gutters contain lead; test yours if you plan to drink the water.

There are two methods to convey water from the gutters to the tank. One is to send a pipe from the downspout directly to the inlet at the top of the tank. This works if your tank is located next to the building. The second method can be employed if there is no room for a tank close to the house (or this placement is undesirable), so the tank is located away from the house. Since water seeks its own level, you can run the pipe down to ground level, along the ground to the tank (this could be buried or run along a fence line), and back up again to the inlet of the tank. (Yes, this really works.) So long as the inlet of the tank is lower than the gutter, water will seek its own level and travel up to the tank. Water traveling through pipe creates friction, and long runs of pipe need a greater height difference between the gutter and tank inlet to compensate for this "friction loss"; a foot is usually enough.

The latter method is called a "wet" system because rainwater sits in the ground-level pipe. The other system is "dry." A wet system requires a drain at the lowest point of the pipe run to drain and clean out accumulated organic matter, as well as to prevent damage to the pipe in freezing conditions.

Screens

Leaf screens can be installed over the entire length of the gutter, in the downspout, or at the tank opening. For small systems, such as those with rain barrels, a simple leaf screen at the inlet should be sufficient. The types of screens required in a rainwater system depend on the type and quantity of debris entering the system from the roof:

Screens over gutters. If you're installing new gutters, consider screening them; otherwise, use other screening methods. (Gutter screens, such as the brand Gutterglove, are pricey, around $8.50/foot of gutter.)

Strainer baskets above downspout. Leaf guards sit inside the gutter over the downspout and screen out large debris.

Leaf screen below downspout. A leaf screen sits below the downspout and screens out large debris.

In-line downspout filter. Vortex-type filter inside of the downspout swirls water so dirt falls out.

Leaf screen in tank. Plastic tanks often come with a strainer-basket filter to catch leaves and large debris before water enters the tank.

First-Flush or Roof-Washing System

Before clean rainwater fills the tank, it must travel over the roof and flow through the gutter system, where it may get dirty. Dust, leaves, and possibly animal poop accumulate on the roof during dry weather and are washed off with the next rain. To avoid collecting this dirty water, a *roof washer*, or *first-flush*

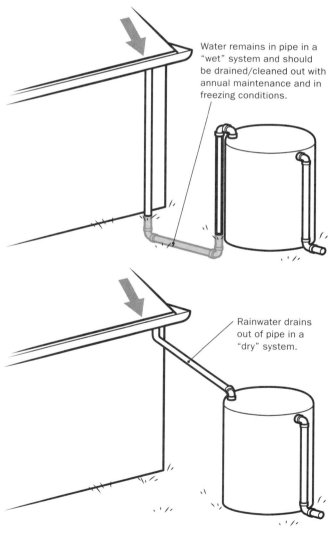

Water remains in pipe in a "wet" system and should be drained/cleaned out with annual maintenance and in freezing conditions.

Rainwater drains out of pipe in a "dry" system.

▲ **Wet and dry rainwater systems. Note: a wet system requires a drain in the line (not shown in image, see pages 193–194).**

diverter, shunts it away from the tank. These systems typically are used in climates with long, dry periods between rains, as well as in some potable rainwater systems.

The most common first-flush diverter is a tall standpipe that fills up with the dirty rainwater washing the roof before clean water can flow to the tank. The standpipe drains automatically between rains through a drip-tube at the bottom. A ball inside the standpipe floats up and plugs the top when the standpipe is full, preventing dirty water from mixing with the clean water flowing past. Kits cost around $40, or you can build your own for less. Places with frequent light rains lose a lot of water with this system because it drains after each rain and must refill before any water can enter the tank (see Installing a First-Flush Diverter on page 197).

A vortex, or centrifugal, downspout filter installs vertically in-line with the downspout and swirls water so dirt falls out and clean water flows to the tank. This is an alternative to a first-flush diverter and often is used with indoor rainwater systems, but does not come cheap.

Other options, such as a "roof washer," consist of a small tank or box with internal filters that clean rainwater as it passes through to the tank. These cost more ($400 to $900) and require more maintenance than a first-flush diverter.

Storage Tank

From the iconic 55-gallon rain barrel to the 5,000-gallon plastic cistern or even the 15,000-gallon ferrocement tank built on-site, there are many options for rainwater containers. Regardless of the size or material, all tanks should:

- be opaque, to prevent algae growth (you can paint or cover translucent tanks).

- have all openings screened to prevent mosquitoes from breeding.

- be located on firm and level ground.

- have an overflow to direct excess water out of the tank to a rain garden or other suitable location.

- be vented (an "empty" tank is actually full of air — if air can't exit, rainwater can't enter).

- be installed safely (large tanks need safety devices to prevent accidental drowning).

See Rainwater Containers (page 152) for a detailed discussion on common types of storage containers, the pros and cons of each method, and the general costs.

Delivery Systems

Delivery systems can send water to the landscape for irrigation or to the house for indoor use. Irrigation systems can often be delivered by gravity, either manually with a hose or via a gravity-fed drip irrigation system. Indoor systems (and elevated landscapes) require pumps.

Irrigation Delivery

With a rain barrel you can irrigate by hand, scoop water out the top of the barrel with a watering can, or attach a garden hose (with a shutoff valve) near the bottom of the barrel. Larger tanks and multiple-barrel systems also can use a hose or can be connected to a simple gravity-fed drip irrigation system. Uphill-sloping and larger sites may need a pump to deliver rainwater to the irrigation area.

Pumped or Gravity Systems

Rainwater used inside the home typically is pressurized with a pump to deliver it from the tank into the home, supplying fixtures and appliances. Rainwater systems use either a pressure tank and pump or a pressure-sensitive pump that automatically activates when a hose, faucet, or irrigation system turns on.

However, pumps aren't always used to deliver the rain inside. Cabins and other rural buildings sometimes can use an elevated tank to provide pressure for the fixtures. (The tank inlet must still be lower than the gutters for this to work.) Sinks and showers don't require high pressure — they flow relatively slowly under lower pressures — but appliances require specific pressure levels for proper operation (city water pressure is 30 to 40 psi, equivalent to the pressure produced by a tank that's 70 feet high). The Occidental Arts and Ecology Center, in Occidental, California, has a few cottages supplied by gravity-fed rainwater systems, with on-line design plans available (see Resources).

Using the Rain Indoors

USING RAINWATER INDOORS is the best way to maximize water savings, especially in Mediterranean climates where there's no outdoor irrigation need during the wet season. Indoor rainwater systems are more complex than irrigation systems, and it's important to seek professional advice. However, if you have professional experience or are a very handy DIYer, there is good technical information available (see Resources) to help you with the installation, although a consultation with an experienced installer is recommended.

Treatment or Purification Systems

All over the world rainwater is used for washing, cleaning, and drinking, without filters or disinfection. However, in the U.S. and Canada most potable systems do include filtration and disinfection. An increasingly popular option in homes connected to a municipal water supply is to use rainwater for non-potable indoor uses: toilet flushing and washing

EXAMPLE OF FILTERS USED IN A POTABLE RAINWATER SYSTEM

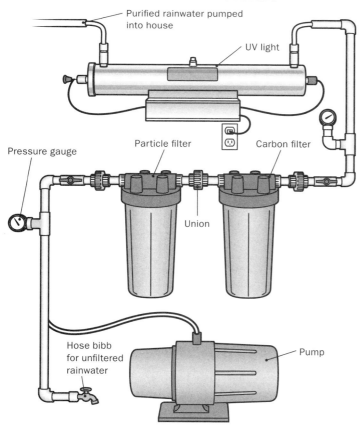

Purified rainwater pumped into house

UV light

Particle filter

Carbon filter

Pressure gauge

Union

Hose bibb for unfiltered rainwater

Pump

Want Design Help?

If it feels daunting to design your own rainwater harvesting system, seek out local installers for professional advice. The American Rainwater Catchment System Association (ARCSA) accredits installers; search their website for someone in your area (see Resources). Check their experience and talk to past clients. Some professionals, like the company RainBanks, offers design and phone consultation anywhere in the country.

machines. These systems are easier to get permitted, cost less, and don't require as much treatment as whole-house potable water systems.

For nonpotable use of rainwater (e.g., irrigation or toilet flushing), filters remove particles in rainwater to prevent clogging in a pump, drip emitter, or plumbing fixture. Nonpotable indoor systems also require filtration to prevent odor or discoloration in toilets or washing machines. Drinking water systems require filtration as well as disinfection so there are no disease-causing organisms in the water.

Types of Filters for Indoor Water

NSF International (NSF) certifies filters and provides a list of drinking water treatment units with NSF certification (see Resources). Drinking water systems typically use three types of filters:

Particle filters to remove sediment and grit from the water. Particles in rainwater are filtered out by cartridge filters. Rainwater is pumped through a filter that captures particles of different sizes. Installed in a row, each filter screens out smaller and smaller particles.

Carbon filters to improve taste and eliminate odors. An activated carbon filter captures microscopic particles in the filter's small pores, removing odors and color as well as some types of organic compounds, contaminants (e.g., pesticides and solvents), and volatile organic compounds (VOCs).

Ultraviolet (UV) disinfection for potential disease-causing organisms. UV disinfection is a widely used technology that destroys bacteria and viruses without any chemicals. Class A UV filters are installed after particle and carbon filters. Water must be sediment-free for UV light to be effective, because pathogens can be shielded by particles in unfiltered water. UV disinfection requires maintenance (cleaning the quartz sleeve) and annual lamp replacement. UV lamps are rated according to the gallons per minute they disinfect. There are other disinfection options, such as chlorine, though it's toxic to produce and forms carcinogenic trihalomethanes if it combines with organic matter. Ozone and sand filters are other options, as are under-the-sink drinking water filters.

City Rain: Clean or Not?

Rain is distilled water, free of pollutants. As raindrops fall through the atmosphere, they dissolve the carbon dioxide in the air, forming a weak acid with a pH of 5.7 or so. When rain falls through polluted air, it picks up particles of soot, dust, and smoke. If the air is polluted where you live, using rainwater catchment for irrigation is of no more concern than the rain falling directly from the sky and landing on your garden; the same pollutants will end up in the garden either way. However, with a roofwater catchment system, you should use a first-flush diverter (page 148) to minimize the introduction of additional pollutants from the roof to the garden. Any drinking water system requires additional filters to remove particulates.

Sample Treatment Methods for Indoor Use of Rainwater

Specific filtration and disinfection requirements are determined by local regulations and installer preferences, but here are some common treatment methods for different end uses:

Toilet

- Filtration: Minimum 50-micron sediment filter (prevents grit from interfering with toilet valves)

- Optional: Carbon filter to address any color or odor issues

- Permitting agencies may require 5-micron filters and disinfection

Washing Machine

- Minimum sediment and 5-micron carbon filter

- Permitting agencies may require disinfection

Potable Use (showers, sinks)

- Sediment filter

- 5-micron carbon filter

- 0.5- to 1-micron filter

- Class A UV disinfection

RAINWATER FILTERING METHODS		
Type of filter	**Function**	**When typically used**
Gutter screen	Covers the open tops of gutters to keep out leaves and debris	When new gutters are being installed, if many large leaves will enter system
Downspout screen	Screen above downspout to keep leaves and large debris out	In most systems that don't have gutter screens
First-flush diverter (or roof-wash system)	Diverts first few gallons of rain, which "wash" the roof and are dirtiest, away from the collection tank	In places with long, dry periods between rains, and in drinking water systems
Downspout filter (vortex)	Keeps particles out of the tank, acts as a first-flush system	Indoor systems
Particle filter	Removes particles from the water	Used for irrigation and indoor systems
Activated carbon	Removes organic contaminates (improves taste, odor, and color), chlorine, and organic chemicals	Indoor household systems
UV disinfection	Destroys disease-causing pathogens	Drinking water systems after filtration
Clay or slow-sand filter	Removes pathogens	Low-tech, low-cost method for drinking water purification. Very common globally

Slow-Sand and Ceramic Filters

Internationally, the low-tech filtering option of slow-sand and ceramic water filters is widely used for drinking water treatment. The group Potters for Peace teaches people how to construct these low-cost and highly effective ceramic filters. Simply pour water through the filter and collect purified water below with a jug. Regarding permits, this filter falls outside plumbing codes — it's like using a portable water filter to purify creek water while camping.

Potable Systems: Test the Water

Before drinking from your rainwater system, it's a good idea to test it. Tests may include bacteria (total coliform and fecal coliform), pH, and turbidity. Instead of relying on expensive testing for common pathogens like giardia and cryptosporidium, use filters that will remove them. Choose a certified lab and follow their collection methods so you obtain accurate results. For more information, visit the Safewater website (see Resources).

Backup Water for a Rainwater System

Some rainwater systems are connected to a supplemental water supply, typically a well or municipal water. In these systems, when the rainwater tank empties, the system switches over to use the second supply (called "make-up" water). The backup system can engage automatically, using a float switch or a digital controller, or it can be manually switched over.

The simplest method is for the backup supply to refill the tank, with an air gap to prevent any potential mixing of water in the tank with the backup supply. Unfortunately, this wastes energy, since the pressurized water from the backup system loses its pressure in the tank and must be repressurized by the rainwater pump. An energy-efficient alternative is a direct backup system with a 3-way valve that switches from rainwater to the secondary supply. When such a system is directly connected to a municipal supply, it requires backflow prevention to protect the municipal system from potential contamination by the rainwater system.

Rainwater as an Emergency Water Supply

Rainwater can be a great emergency water supply if you design your tank so it never empties. Have a separate tank for emergency use, or install two outlets on a tank, the higher one for regular use, the lower one for emergency use (and keep it shut off unless there is an emergency need for it). Plan a gallon of water per person per day for basic needs. Be sure to include means for purifying the water, such as a backpacker-type water filter, iodine drops, or boiling.

Rainwater Containers

RAINWATER CONTAINERS RANGE IN SIZE, shape, and material. Repurposed options include 55-gallon barrels that you can convert to rain barrels, and 300-gallon IBC totes, both of which can be connected together to increase storage capacity. Plastic and fiberglass tanks, with pre-installed screened inlets and outlets, are the simplest type of tank to install. Other options include metal or concrete tanks, and site-built ferrocement or steel culvert tanks.

Rain Barrels

Rain barrels typically are made from 55-gallon plastic barrels, either new or repurposed. Wooden barrels look nice, plastic ones are easy to work with, while metal ones rust over time. A single rain barrel can supply water for houseplants. Connect them together for additional storage (10 barrels hold 550 gallons) and tuck them under the deck or behind the garage; this is a great way to utilize otherwise unproductive strips of land. The cost of rain barrels can range from nothing to $100 each. Fittings to turn a standard barrel into a rain barrel cost between $10 and $20 per barrel.

10,000-gallon tank located away from the house

3,000-gallon tank near the house

8 rain barrels connected together for 400 gallons of storage

Single rain barrel

▲ **Types of rainwater containers**

Pros: Rain Barrels

■ Easy to install and a small investment of time and money

■ Increase water awareness

■ Provide good-quality water for potted plants

■ Easy to connect barrels together to increase storage capacity, up to several thousand gallons

■ Fit into places larger containers won't

Cons: Rain Barrels

■ Typically a small amount of storage

■ Can be hard to find salvaged barrels

■ Pre-made rain barrels are often poorly designed (see Common Rain Barrel Errors on page 179).

Tanks and Cisterns — for Larger Water Storage

Rainwater storage tanks come in many sizes, from a few hundred gallons to tens of thousands of gallons, and a variety of materials. Some include a screened inlet, outlet, and overflow, while other containers have to be modified with these components. I'll go over the most common ones below with the general price per gallon. Like rain barrels, some tanks can be modular, so that you can connect a few smaller tanks together. At the other end of the spectrum, large cisterns may be hard to install on an urban or suburban lot, particularly if the entryway into a backyard is small.

There are two main categories of tanks: prefabricated and site-built. Prefabricated tanks usually are made from plastic, fiberglass, or metal. They come in a range of storage capacity and sizes, starting at a few hundred gallons. Site-built tanks are typically larger, made from concrete, ferrocement, or steel. In new construction, concrete tanks can be incorporated into the structure of a building, deck, or patio, or installed underground. In the past, handmade stone and wooden cisterns were common, nowadays less so because they're expensive.

As you research tank types, keep in mind some logistical factors that influence the best tank for your situation: Consider where the tank can be located and if there are height or width limitations. Would one large tank be best, or multiple smaller tanks? Think about any potential natural disasters that may influence your tank selection; for example, if you live in a high-fire-risk area, choose a fire-resistant tank.

Prefabricated Fiberglass Tanks

Fiberglass tanks for rainwater collection come in both vertical cylinder for aboveground, and horizontal cylinder for belowground. Tanks for potable water use are coated on the interior with an approved food-grade resin, while the exterior is given a UV-resistant

Cold Climate Considerations

There are many examples of successful rainwater harvesting systems in freezing climates, though they do require extra precautions to avoid freezing and damage to equipment. (Hundreds of homes in Ketchikan, Alaska, are supplied entirely by rainwater.) To plan a system in a freezing climate, contact installers who work in climates similar to yours for the best advice. In general, tanks must withstand the snow load, be large and insulated so they don't freeze, and have all pipes insulated or buried below the frost line (the depth to which the ground freezes in winter). Heat tape often is used to prevent pipes and tanks from freezing, or tanks are installed in a heated structure. The Alaskan Building Research Series HCM-01557, *Water Cistern Construction for Small Houses* and the *Alberta Guidelines for Residential Rainwater Harvesting Systems* both have design details for freezing climates.

Concerns with Leaching

Rainwater will leach, or draw out, some components from whatever material it contacts. Materials that contact the water for longer lengths of time, like the storage tank, have more potential to leach into the water than components with minimal contact time, like gutters. Drinking water systems should use materials rated for potable water whenever possible. Use HDPE plastics instead of PVC, or at a minimum, keep PVC out of sunlight (paint or shade it) as sunlight promotes leaching.

layer that inhibits algae growth. Fiberglass can be repaired, and it can be painted with latex house paint. Typical tank sizes are 500 to 40,000 gallons; cost is $0.50 to $2 per gallon of storage capacity.

Pros: Fiberglass Tanks

- Durable and long-lasting
- Repairable
- Low cost in dollars per gallon for larger tanks
- Fittings, an integral part of the tank, don't typically leak.

Cons: Fiberglass Tanks

- Not locally available in all areas
- Smaller tanks cost more in dollars per gallon than plastic tanks.

Plastic

Plastic tanks are made with polyethylene or polypropylene materials and come in sizes from 50 to 10,000 gallons. Available at most farm, ranch supply, and large landscaping stores (as well as through mail order), they are probably the most common type of tank sold in North America. Costs are $0.35 to $1 per gallon.

Rainwater vs. the Big Pipe

Brad Crowley's master's thesis compared home-based rainwater harvesting to the $1.4 billion "Big Pipe" program planned to upgrade Portland, Oregon's combined stormwater and sewer system. He found that harvesting rainwater on-site may cost less and have greater benefits than the Big Pipe. He explored whether rainwater could replace potable water use inside the house and reduce stormwater runoff. In Portland, just a few hundred gallons of storage could supply the toilet flushing water for most homes. He concluded that home-scale systems would be a better option for Portland. Unfortunately, the Big Pipe went in anyway. Fortunately, Portland has made permitting easier for indoor rainwater harvesting and is actively promoting it. Now Brad installs rainwater systems professionally with his business Harvest the Sky (see Resources). He believes people will save the most water in Portland with indoor rainwater systems and outdoor greywater irrigation systems.

Pros: Plastic Tanks

- Available in most places

- Light and easily maneuverable

- Durable

- Often sold with inlet, outlet, overflow, and screens pre-installed

Cons: Plastic Tanks

- Water can heat up in warm climates if the tank is a dark color.

- Some people find them unattractive.

Site-Built Ferrocement and Concrete Tanks

Ferrocement tanks are built on-site using wire lath around a steel framework. The tank is coated with a thin layer of cement (technically a thin, sand-based concrete mixture), requiring less material than a concrete tank requires. Concrete tanks are thicker-walled, enabling them to be incorporated into the building structure or to be built underground. Cement (present in both concrete and ferrocement mixtures) raises the pH of rainwater, which can be helpful for indoor systems since rainwater is typically acidic and can corrode metal pipes. These tanks are also fire-resistant, an advantage in fire-prone regions. The cost of ferrocement and concrete tanks ranges from $0.30 to $1.25 per gallon.

FERROCEMENT TANK

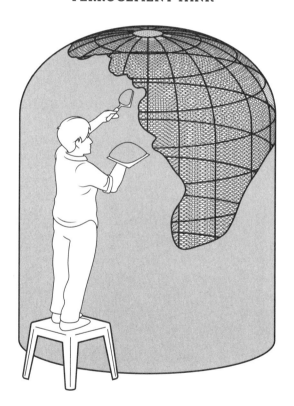

Pros: Ferrocement Tanks

- Low-cost, if you can do the work yourself; materials are inexpensive, but tank construction is labor-intensive.

- Constructed from readily available materials (cement, wire lath, steel rebar)

- Repairable

- Flexible in shape, can be curved

- Fire-resistant

Pros: Concrete Tanks

- Can be integrated into a building or built underground

- Repairable

- Fire-resistant

- Constructed from readily available materials

Cons: Ferrocement and Concrete Tanks

- Require skilled installer familiar with this type of construction

- Permanent installation, not movable

Galvanized Steel Tanks

Steel tanks can be prefabricated or site-built. They are durable and come in a large range of sizes. Metal rainwater tanks come with an approved coating or liner for potable use and to prevent rust and corrosion. They must be properly grounded to deal with an electrical charge in the event of a lightning strike. The cost of galvanized steel tanks runs from $0.70 to $3.00 per gallon.

Pros: Steel Tanks

- Many people find them more attractive than the plastic tanks.

- Can be constructed on-site by bolting panels together, enabling a large tank to be quickly constructed in an area inaccessible to large trucks

- Fire resistant

- Steel is recyclable (though tanks should last for many decades).

Metal Culvert Rain Tank: The Icon of Tucson

The Watershed Management Group (WMG), based in Tucson, Arizona, has been installing rain gardens, cisterns, and greywater systems since 2006. Through their co-op model, volunteers help construct systems, learn in the process, and earn the ability to host a workshop at their own home. In 2012, Tucson's productive Green-Living Co-op installed 21 rain gardens, 11 greywater systems, 9 rain tanks, and 7 rights-of-way projects, creating over 52,000 gallons of rainwater-harvesting capacity and nearly 70,000 gallons of greywater-reuse capacity.

When they're not installing rain gardens or greywater systems, WMG constructs sleek and attractive metal culvert rainwater tanks, fondly referred to as "The Icon of Tucson." Catlow Shipek, one of WMG's founders, explains why they prefer them over plastic tanks: "The metal culverts hold up better in the hot desert sun than plastic ones. They also hide all the plumbing, leaving a cleaner look. All the pipes enter and exit the tank through the concrete base." Learn more by visiting WMG's website (see Resources).

Cons: Steel Tanks

- If unlined, can rust and leach zinc into water.

- If improperly designed, tanks corrode and fail (e.g., water flowing over top, wetness at base of tank, or use of incompatible metals that leads to corrosion).

Aboveground or Belowground Tank?

In my grandparents' generation, underground cisterns were commonplace in American homes (and still are in other countries, where they're often built with simple hand tools and local materials). Now, aboveground tanks are more common because they're easier and cheaper to install. If you use a prefabricated tank belowground, make sure it was constructed to withstand the pressure of soil. Proper installation also is critical; unanchored tanks can literally float out of the ground if they're empty and the soil becomes saturated

Pros: Aboveground Tanks

- Lower in cost than belowground tanks
- Easier to install
- Easier to monitor and fix
- Less pumping required
- Potential for gravity-fed irrigation
- Less likely to become contaminated (belowground tanks can be contaminated by surface runoff if not properly installed)

Pros: Belowground Tanks

- Out of the way, saves aboveground space
- Can be installed under a patio or deck
- Protected from freezing

Rain Cubes: A Belowground Tank Alternative

You can create an underground reserve of water without a tank by using rain cubes. A rain cube resembles a heavy-duty milk crate. The system consists of

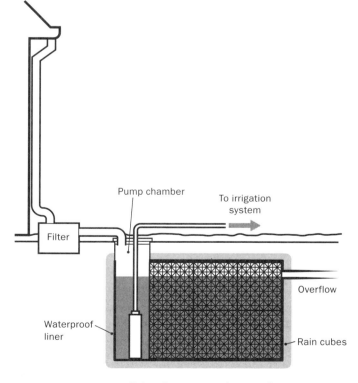

▲ **Rain cubes create underground water storage.**

a large hole, lined with a waterproof membrane (such as a pond liner), and filled with rain cubes, preserving 90 percent of the hole's capacity. The ground can be covered with a deck, patio, landscaping, or driveway surface. Rain cubes can also be used to convert a swimming pool into a rainwater tank (see page 206). One drawback with this type of system is that you can't access the inside of the system to inspect, clean, or repair it without entirely disassembling it.

Rainwater Pillows: Fit in the Crawl Space

Rainwater pillow tanks look like large waterbed bladders and are designed to fit into small areas, such as a crawl space. They typically cost more than rigid tanks but allow for more storage options when there aren't suitable locations for an outdoor tank. Sizes range from 50 to 50,000 gallons.

One Tank, or Two (or More)?

Some systems store rainwater in multiple tanks. Here are some reasons why:

- In a small yard, it can be easier to accommodate two small tanks than one large tank.
- If there is a problem with one tank, the other tank can still be used.
- To avoid permits: Often tanks under 5,000 gallons don't require building permits, while larger ones do.
- Multiple water-quality needs: Water collected from a dirtier roof is used for irrigation, while water from a cleaner roof is used indoors.

Components of a Tank System

To convert a tank into a rainwater storage system you need an inlet, an outlet, service access, a drain, an overflow, critter-proofing, and venting.

The inlet. Rainwater enters the tank through the inlet, commonly at the top of the tank. The force of the water falling into the tank can potentially stir up the sludge layer on the bottom. Use a "calming" device to diffuse the force of falling water, such as a basket screen below the inlet, or an extension inlet pipe running from the top of the tank toward the bottom, ending in an upward J shape.

The outlet. Rainwater exits the tank through the outlet. Keep the outlet as low as possible, to maximize storage capacity, but a few inches above the bottom to avoid withdrawing the sludge layer that can build up. Tanks used in drinking water systems often use a floating filter outlet, discussed below. All tank outlets need a shutoff valve.

Floating intake filter (for drinking water systems). A floating intake filter withdraws water from the cleanest water in the middle of the tank. (A sludge layer builds up on the bottom and debris floats on top.) These filters are mainly used in potable systems, since more prefiltering helps prolong the life of subsequent filters in the system.

Service access. Large tanks need access for repairs and cleaning. The service access must be closed and lockable to prevent people from falling in and drowning, especially with in-ground tanks. Install an internal ladder for climbing out in case someone does fall in.

Drain. A drain empties the tank for repairs or cleaning. Ideally it empties the entire tank quickly and is lower than the outlet.

The overflow. An overflow diverts excess water to a safe location after the tank fills. Make sure the overflow:

- Is placed to maximize storage space (as high up as possible).

- Is the same pipe size as the inlets so the flow isn't restricted.

- Is screened and critter-proofed. The overflow can be screened with fine-mesh ¼-inch non-corrosive material (or ¹⁄₁₆-inch for mosquitoes), but screens can reduce the flow of water and may require cleaning. Another option is a one-way flapper valve with a screen (sold as a rainwater tank accessory) or a backwater valve. Rats are especially talented at climbing up an unprotected overflow and drowning in the tank.

- Directs water to a rain garden or other appropriate area. Ensure the overflow will not erode the tank foundation.

Water-level indicators. How full is the tank? Options to monitor the water level include opening the lid to check, as well as an array of home-built or purchased devices ranging from simple gauge or weight-and-pulley indicators to high-tech digital devices with remote monitoring capability.

Big, Really Big, or Enormous?

"I love my rainwater system. I just wish it were bigger." To avoid feeling this common regret, install the largest tank possible in your situation (and make sure there is enough rain to fill it). If your system

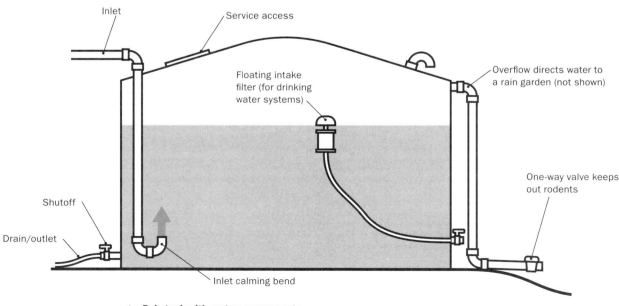

▲ **Rain tank with system components**

Have Land? How about a Rainwater Pond?

Rural areas that aren't too hot and dry can use an in-ground pond for water storage. Ponds cost less per gallon than a cistern does, and they provide wildlife habitat and a place to swim and raise fish. The drawbacks: ponds need more land and require heavy equipment to dig. They also tend to have lower water quality, requiring more filtration for indoor use. Art Ludwig's book on water storage (see Resources) includes information on pond construction.

supplements another water source, the main factors determining tank size are likely to be your budget and space limitations. But if rainwater will be your only water supply, you'll need to calculate how much water you use and how much you have available from rainfall:

1. **How much water does your home use?**

   Check a water bill or estimate your daily usage for greywater (see chapter 4) and add toilet water, or use the values given in Average Indoor Water Use in the U.S. (page 160) to supplement other calculations.

2. **How much rain can you catch?**

   Calculate your roof size and average rainfall (see page 144).

3. **Compare the available supply with your usage.**

   Do you have enough? If not, lower your consumption or increase your catchment size by installing a rain barn (a carport-like structure designed to catch rainwater).

As a general rule, you should store enough water to last through the typical dry spell in your area. In Mediterranean climates it typically rains for a few months and is dry for rest of the year, requiring much larger tanks than in places with annual rainfall spread out over the year.

Looking at Your Supply-Demand Balance

The following calculations can give you a general sense of your rainwater situation.

Daily potential. Compare your daily needs with your supply potential: Divide your annual rainwater potential (in gallons per year) by your daily household usage (in gallons per day). Do you use more or less than the daily gallons available?

Tank size. The amount of water you consume during a typical dry spell is approximately equal to the size of your tank: Multiply your daily use (in gallons) by the length of a typical dry spell in your area (in days). The result indicates how many gallons you would need to store for the dry spell. If the system is for irrigation or indoor nonpotable water, do a similar calculation based on your irrigation/indoor needs.

Here's an example of a home in Portland, Oregon. It's a 2,000-square-foot house with four people using 30 gallons per person per day (gallons per capita per day, or gpcd): whole-house need, irrigation only, and nonpotable indoor need:

Whole-House Need

Annual potential (37 inches/year × 0.56 × 2,000 square feet) = 41,440 gallons/year

Daily potential (41,440 ÷ 365) = 114 gallons per day (gpd)

Daily household usage (4 people × 30 gpcd) = 120 gpd

This household uses more water than it has available from rainwater. The family needs either to use less water or to increase their roof size to balance the supply and demand. Rainfall is typically spread out over the year, but much less rain falls in the summer months. Assuming a four-month (120-day) dry period, the household has the following storage needs:

120 days × 120 gpd = 14,400 gallons of storage.

Irrigation-Only Need

If the family wanted a system for irrigation only, a very rough calculation might look like this (irrigation needs: 200-square-foot vegetable garden and 10 medium-sized fruit trees).

■ 200-square-foot vegetable garden, using a rule-of-thumb calculation for plant water requirements from page 65:

Warm climate; 0.5 gallon/square foot/week. 200 × 0.5 = 100 gallons/week.

If they have a 7-month (28-week) irrigation season, they'd need:

28 weeks × 100 gallons/week = 2,800 gallons

■ 10 medium-sized fruit trees (radius 4 feet, area 48 square feet):

48 × 0.5 = 24 gallons/week × 10 trees = 240 gallons/week for 28 weeks = 6,720 gallons

■ To irrigate the vegetable garden and fruit trees, they'd need around 10,000 gallons of storage.

Alternative option would be to use greywater for the trees and irrigate the vegetables with a 3,000-gallon rainwater tank.

Nonpotable Need

To install a system just for nonpotable uses (toilets and washing machine), they estimated 32 gallons/day in the toilets and 11 gpd in the washer; 43 gallons/day total. Their storage needs are:

120 days × 43 gallons/day = 5,160 gallons.

Cost Overview

Costs for a complete rainwater system depend on the size, complexity, type of tank, who installs the system, and permitting requirements. If you're converting salvaged barrels to rain barrels yourself, you might spend a few hundred dollars for a few thousand gallons of storage capacity. Home-built systems for irrigation typically cost less than a dollar per gallon of storage capacity; for example, a 1,000-gallon system costs less than $1,000. Professional installation costs two or three dollars per gallon of storage capacity. Whole-house systems for potable indoor water range from $10,000 to $20,000 with 10,000

Average Indoor Water Use in the U.S.

Low-flow toilet: 1.6 gallons/flush; 6 flushes/person/day

Showerhead: 2.2 gallons per minute (gpm); 5 minutes/person/day

Bath: 50 gallons for each bath

Faucets: 2.2 gpm; 5 minutes/person/day

Clothes washer (front-loading): 18 to 25 gallons/load; 2.6 loads/person/week

Source: American Water Works Association

to 15,000 gallons of storage. Though pricey, compared to other water supplies (such as drilling a well), rainwater harvesting can be cheaper and provide better-quality water.

Financial Incentives

Financial incentives to promote rainwater harvesting are found across the country. Arizona offers a tax credit for water conserving systems (residential greywater and rainwater). Texas doesn't require sales tax on water harvesting systems. Dozens of water companies incentivize systems with rebates and free components. And a few places in the U.S. even require systems, such as Santa Fe County in New Mexico. See Resources for a website that lists rainwater incentives for the United States, Canada, Australia, and beyond.

Codes and Regulations

U.S. STATE AND NATIONAL REGULATIONS for rainwater are lacking in many places. However, rainwater systems are typically allowed, particularly for outdoor irrigation (and often without a permit). Indoor, potable use of rainwater is the most challenging system to get a permit for. Rainwater tanks may require a building permit if the tank is over a certain size, often 5,000 gallons. Other relevant local agencies to consider include the zoning authority, the fire department, the building department, and the health department (although health departments typically are involved in permitting indoor systems, not irrigation).

The American Rainwater Catchment Systems Association (ARCSA), in partnership with the American Society of Plumbing Engineers, developed *ARCSA/ASPE 63: Rainwater Catchment Systems*, a guidance document on proper design, installation, and maintenance for irrigation and potable rainwater harvesting systems. The International Association of Plumbing and Mechanical Officials (IAPMO), an organization that writes codes used by many states, created a rainwater code; find it in chapter 17 of their plumbing code.

Many states and local governments, such as San Juan County in Washington state, offer guidelines and other helpful information to encourage rainwater collection. And some states, including Oregon, Texas, Ohio, Virginia, and Arizona, promote rainwater harvesting through incentives and education. In Hawaii, entire subdivisions have been built without a water supply — each house has its own rainwater tank to supply all household water needs. In British Columbia, Canada, the Regional District of Nanaimo offers a $750 rebate to install a rain tank, and many rebates are provided in Australia, including $200 for a tank from the South Australia government and $1500 from the Victoria government (at the time of writing). Tucson, Arizona, passed the first municipal rainwater harvesting ordinance for commercial projects in the U.S. It requires that 50 percent of landscaping must be irrigated with rainwater, increasing to 75 percent after three years. The U.S. Virgin Islands require cisterns (or a well) for every new home built.

Health and Safety Guidelines

Harvesting the rain is a safe and healthy practice, for people and the planet. As with any construction project, there are important guidelines to follow to avoid unintended problems.

As previously discussed, a rainwater tank poses similar dangers as any body of water (drowning, mosquitoes); the use of screens, lids, and internal ladders help reduce many common risks. Other potential hazards include leaching of toxins into the water from unsuitable materials, flooding your house if the tank breaks, or liability concerns if you flood a neighbor's property. If your site is challenging, with steep slopes, hurricanes, etc., get advice from a structural engineer.

Rainwater systems for indoor use that are installed in houses and connected to a municipal supply are subject to additional requirements to prevent a potential "cross-connection" (when non-potable water contaminates the municipal supply). The health department wants to be sure your rainwater system isn't going to get people sick (or be the cause of a lawsuit). Their worst-case scenario: your roof is covered in raccoon poop, a rat has drowned in the tank, and your improperly designed system pumps raccoon-poopy, dead-ratty water into the city supply. The water sickens the neighbors, who then sue the city and the water district. Regulations from the health department prevent this potential disaster.

If your rainwater is not potable, make sure to label pipes and spigots: "UNTREATED RAINWATER, DO NOT DRINK."

Whole-House Rainwater Systems: RainBank

KEN BLAIR IS THE FOUNDER and principal of RainBank (see Resources), a design-build, accredited rainwater harvesting company in Washington state. Over the past decade, Ken has installed over a hundred rainwater systems, the majority of them for whole-household use.

Ken also works in developing countries to promote affordable rainwater catchment systems for safe drinking water with the nonprofit Bank On Rain (see Resources) he helped establish. I spoke with Ken about his work.

What advice do you have for people considering installing a rainwater catchment system?

First of all, do your research. Talk to designers, installers, and suppliers; and ask lots of questions. There are several ways to go with rainwater systems, and you need to determine the best one for you. Check references, check out actual functioning systems if possible, installed by the person you are considering hiring. There are gimmicky products available, and you can spend a lot of money needlessly. Secondly, plan as much rainwater storage as you can. The most common complaint I hear is that people wish they had installed more storage.

Do you have clients who rely entirely on rainwater? How do they feel about their systems?

I have many clients who use rainwater for all of their household use, including myself. Many homes on Lopez and the other San Juan Islands are 100 percent reliant on rainwater. Some clients have both rainwater harvesting systems and well water, but once they have a rainwater system they rarely switch back to the well unless necessity dictates.

Can you describe a "typical" system for a home that is supplied by rainwater?

A basic system consists of three elements:

Storage. In our area I usually design the storage to hold a 90-day supply of water; the size depends on the home's usage (usually 30 to 50 gallons/person/day). I try to keep tanks away from the house and out of sight.

Filtration. There are basically two areas of filtration. The first is when the rain exits the roof and usually consists of screening the gutters from roof debris and filtering the downspouts (vortex filter) to ensure the cleanest possible water arrives in the storage tank. The second area of filtration (usually for household potable water) is when the water is pumped from the tank to the house. A typical potable water filtration setup may be: 5-micron sediment filter, 10-micron carbon filter, 1-micron absolute sediment filter (for cyst removal), then UV with a solenoid sensor, which shuts off the system if the UV isn't working.

Infrastructure. This consists of the gutters, pipes, and pumps. Where gravity feed is not an option, we use a sump tank to pump the rainwater into the storage tank via connecting pipes. Water is delivered to the house by a booster pump delivering water when required.

Approximately how much is a professionally installed rainwater catchment system?

Storage is the biggest cost. The south end of Lopez Island where I live gets 16 inches of rainfall per year. Tanks are usually around 15,000 gallons for 90 days of storage. I am currently installing a system on the coast, where they get 12 feet of rain per year (that's 144 inches!), so the storage for them can be much smaller as the tank is constantly being replenished.

Our cost estimates typically range from $1.50 to $3 gallon, with 10,000 gallons a usual minimum size. Complete residential systems run between $13,000 and $20,000, but that is dependent on so many variables, it's nearly impossible to provide a blanket cost estimate. For cost-conscious consumers, aboveground plastic tanks are the least expensive and buried rainwater storage tanks and steel tanks cost the most.

Can you talk a bit about your design service for do-it-yourself installers?

I work with the budget-minded do-it-yourselfer to help install their rainwater harvesting system. I discuss their needs and lay out a detailed instruction plan they can follow, including supplying them with parts. My design costs vary, but can be $750 for a simple system or $1,500 for a system with added functionality and complexity.

Building Rainwater Harvesting Systems

IN CHAPTER 6 you calculated your rainwater potential — how many gallons you can collect off your roof each year — considered your goals, assessed your site, and determined the best system for you. In this chapter you'll learn how to construct several types of rainwater harvesting systems, including a rain garden and roofwater catchment using barrels and cisterns. I'll also discuss methods for using the stored rainwater, including how to install a gravity-fed drip irrigation system.

Before you build a rain garden or install a tank, make sure you've located all the utility lines so you don't place any tanks or basins above them, or break them during construction. Call 811 several days before you dig, and a utility locator will come to your site to mark utility lines (see Call Before You Dig on page 84).

IN THIS CHAPTER:

Planning and Designing a Rain Garden

DOES RAINWATER RUN OFF YOUR ROOF or driveway into the street? Where will the overflow from your tank go? Design a rain garden to collect this runoff. In addition, incorporate other strategies covered in chapter 6 to increase the infiltration capacity of your site, such as removing hardscape, adding mulch, and directing runoff to parts of your yard that can handle the extra water.

The key components of the rain garden include the inlet, the outlet, and the sunken planting area, or basin. You may also build a berm, a mound of soil, around the planted rain garden to visually define the area and provide extra capacity inside the basin. Depending on how water soaks into the native soils of your landscape, you may need to remove soil and add in a well-draining rain garden soil mix to the basin, or at least add compost. You'll also choose plants well suited to your climate to soak up the rain.

If your gutter is currently flowing into your yard, all you'll need to do is direct the water to the rain garden. Some cities direct roofwater into the sewer system, called a "combined sewer system." See Does Your City Have a Combined Sewer System? (page 182) for advice on how to safely disconnect your downspout.

The rain garden building project on page 172 is designed for a fairly flat site. If your site is sloped or very large, or if you need to move water away from buildings, research other methods to infiltrate water safely; see Resources for designs for rain gardens on sloped sites. Building a rain garden is a straightforward process, with a few important considerations. The main challenge is all the digging.

A Rain Garden App

Have a smart phone? Download the new rain garden app, created by the University of Connecticut (see Resources); it contains basic information about rain gardens, design guidelines, and plant selection advice. Currently focused on southern New England, the authors are creating a national version at the time of writing.

Locating Your Rain Garden(s)

Determine the best location for the rain garden before considering its size and shape. You can build multiple small rain gardens for each downspout, or combine downspouts and send all the roofwater to one larger rain garden. There are several factors that influence rain garden placement.

Natural flows. Where does rainwater flow on and off your property? Look at the roofs, driveways, patios, and tank overflows. Observe the yard during a rainstorm, or use a garden hose to mimic rainfall onto your hardscape. Observe where the water flows naturally due to ground contours and changes in elevation. Locate the rain garden(s) so it captures as much runoff as possible.

Infiltration. How well does water infiltrate on your site? Locate the rain garden in a place where water readily soaks into the ground, but **not** anywhere the ground is often soggy or stays wetter than other parts of the yard. Test the infiltration rate of the soil (see Conduct an Infiltration Test on page 61). Whenever possible, do this test during the rainy season when the soil is saturated. Or, fill the hole with water

ANATOMY OF A RAIN GARDEN

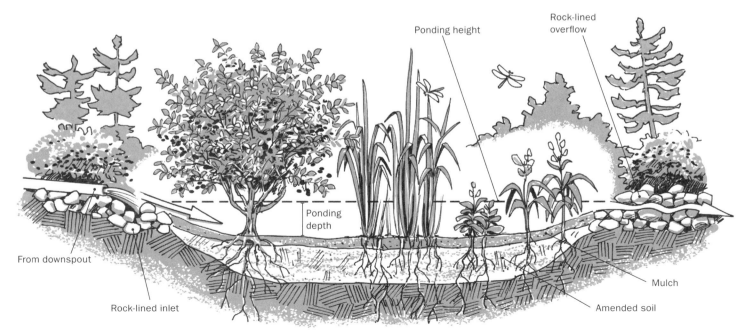

Ponding height

Rock-lined overflow

From downspout

Ponding depth

Rock-lined inlet

Mulch

Amended soil

and let it drain three times to saturate the surrounding soil before conducting the test. Your test result should give you an infiltration rate in inches per hour. For example, if the water level dropped 8 inches in 10 hours, the infiltration rate would be 8 ÷ 10 = 0.8 inch per hour. You can also determine your soil type following the directions on page 60.

An infiltration rate greater than 0.25 inch per hour means the location is good for a rain garden. If it's between 0.25 and 0.1 inch per hour, it's still okay, but there may be extended times of pooling due to the slow drainage. If it's less than 0.1 inch per hour, the site is not suitable for a rain garden. Look for another location, or consult with a local rainwater harvesting expert or soils engineer for other options.

If your first test found slow-draining soils, try other locations within the desired rain garden area, as they may infiltrate quicker. Also, dig about a foot deeper than the planned depths of the rain gardens to observe the soil characteristics. You may find a shallow layer of clay above faster-infiltrating soils; if so, break it up or remove it to increase infiltration.

Aesthetics. A rain garden can provide a beautiful visual separation between your yard and a neighboring property or the street. Make sure the overflow can be directed to a safe location, not toward your house or a neighbor's yard.

Slope. Find a flat or gently sloping (10 percent slope or less; see Calculating Slope on page 166) place for the rain garden. If your yard has greater than 10 percent slope you can install other water harvesting features, though more info may be needed to avoid potential problems, such as landslide

▼ **Observe where rain runs off, and locate rain gardens to capture that water. (Arrows show runoff.) Note: Rain gardens should be at least 10 feet from buildings.**

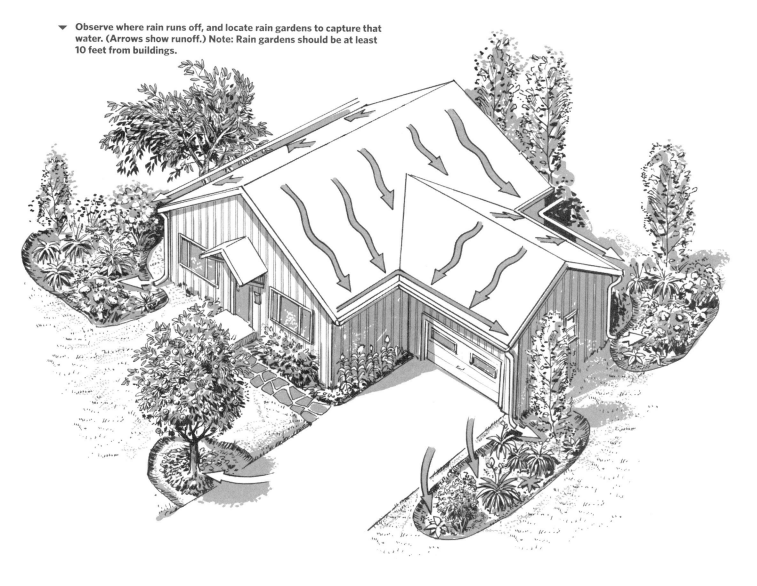

hazards. Consult with a local rain garden installer, your city, and other expert sources (see Resources).

Once you've chosen the rain garden location(s), double-check that rainwater can flow there by pipes or diversion swales before you build. For example, the location cannot be uphill of the downspout outlet. Pipes and swales must slope by 2 percent (or ¼ inch per foot) from the downspout end to the rain garden.

In established landscapes, be sure to locate the rain garden outside of the drip line (where the branches end) of any established bushes and trees. Typically only smaller roots will be encountered outside of the drip line, and trimming them won't harm the tree.

Where Not to Put a Rain Garden

Here are some locations to avoid:

- Within 10 feet of a building foundation

- Near a septic drain field or tank

- Over buried utility lines

- Near the edge of a steep slope, as the extra water could erode the slope or cause landslides (consult with a rainwater expert if you're working near slopes greater than 15 percent)

- In low spots of your yard that do not drain well

- Anywhere healthy and established plants are growing; they are already filtering and absorbing rainwater.

- Where groundwater is within 1 foot of the bottom of your basin

- Near a drinking-water well

Determining Size and Shape

The rain garden size depends on how much rainwater will drain into the basin and how quickly water soaks into the soil, as well as how much space is available:

1. Measure the areas draining into your rain garden. Measure roof area following the steps on page 144, then determine what fraction of the roof will drain into your garden. For example, if your roof is 1,200 square feet and half of the roof will be draining into the rain garden, plan to infiltrate runoff water from 1,200 ÷ 2 = 600 square feet of contributing area in the rain garden. For hardscape, like a driveway, multiply the length by the width, then determine what fraction drains to the garden (e.g., one-half). The contributing area you calculate in this step is *not* the size of the rain garden; that calculation is coming up shortly.

Calculating Slope

If your yard has a noticeable slope, you'll need to determine how steep it is in order to plan the rain garden placement. To find the percent slope, divide the rise of the slope by the length of the slope, then multiply by 100:

Percent slope = Rise of slope ÷ length of slope × 100

Example:
Rise of slope = 2 feet; length of slope = 20 feet:
$$2 ÷ 20 = 0.10 × 100 = 10\%$$

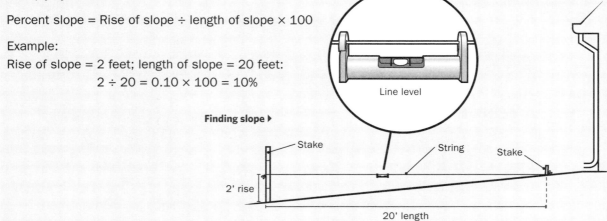

Finding slope ▶

Line level

Stake

String

Stake

2' rise

20' length

2. Measure the available space. Consider having multiple smaller rain gardens from individual gutters, if convenient.

3. Decide how large and deep to make the rain garden, based on the infiltration rate, the drainage area, and the rainfall data. There are several methods to do this, as well as regional variations. The quantity of rain during a typical rainstorm and the amount of water you want to hold affect sizing. The chart Sizing a Rain Garden (below) offers general guidelines. Alternatively, if there is a rainwater manual for your region, use its sizing method, as it will incorporate local rainfall patterns. Sizing is important so you infiltrate as much rainwater as possible in the area available for the rain garden. You may find that a small yard with slow-draining soils doesn't have enough space to infiltrate 100 percent of the runoff.

If you are unable to find sizing recommendations based on your specific rainfall patterns, don't worry. So long as excess water can safely overflow out of the basin, sizing errors won't cause problems: over-sized rain gardens may never overflow, and under-sized ones may overflow frequently.

Sizing guidelines typically relate to the bottom area of the basin and don't include the extra space required to slope the sides. For example: a typical rain garden with a 3:1 slope and a 6-inch ponding depth requires 18 inches of sloped sides for the 6-inch depth (3 × 6 = 18); this means the outer footprint of the rain garden is 18 inches larger than the bottom of the rain garden in each direction, totaling 3 feet wider and 3 feet longer.

4. Confirm that you have sufficient space available, using your size estimates. If there's not enough room in one area, consider multiple rain gardens in different areas, or build the rain garden as large as fits and know you'll still be infiltrating and treating a lot more water than you would if you had not built a rain garden at all! Another option is to incorporate a tank under the downspout to provide surge capacity and slowly drain the water into the rain garden. This **detention cistern** catches and slowly releases rainfall into the rain garden, allowing a smaller rain garden to infiltrate the same amount of rainwater as a larger garden. Some jurisdictions provide reduced sizing guidelines for rain gardens that incorporate detention cisterns (see Options for Slow-Draining Soils on page 168).

Size Calculations

The size of a rain garden is based on the area draining into it (in square feet) multiplied by the corresponding size factor percent (based on infiltration rate). For example, using the roof size and soil from the previous examples, 600 square feet and a soil infiltration rate of 0.8 inch per hour corresponds to 20 percent according to the chart:

600 square feet × 0.2 (20%) = 120 square feet

SIZING A RAIN GARDEN

Soil type*	Infiltration rate	Required size of rain garden	Excavation depth	Soil amendment
Sandy loam or sand	1" to 8"/hour	10% of catchment area	Shallow (6" to 12")	Spread 3" compost and dig into soil.
Silty loam	0.25" to 1"/hour	20% of catchment area	Shallow to moderate (12" to 18")	Spread compost and dig into soil.
Clay loam	0.10" to 0.25"/hour	30% of catchment area	Moderate to deep, depending on whether you amend or replace soil (18" to 24")	Consider replacing some soil (6" to 12") with a rain garden mix (60% sand, 40% compost) or employ other strategies to improve infiltration.
Clay	0.02" to .10"/hour	As large as possible; make sure to have overflow in case all the water won't infiltrate. Plant with more wetland plants.	Moderate to deep, depending on whether you amend or replace soil (18" to 24") Consider installing a dry well or detention cistern to increase the capacity.	Consider replacing soil with a rain garden mix to increase infiltration and employ other strategies for poorly draining soils.

*Soil type is given here to provide a general range of typical infiltration rates, but always use your measured infiltration rate, which is much more accurate for each specific site.

That means the rain garden would measure about 10 × 12 feet at its bottom. Adding area for 3:1 sloping sides and a 6-inch ponding depth, the sides would extend 18 inches in each direction. The total rain garden footprint would be 13 × 15 feet.

Rain Garden Depth

The faster water soaks into your soil, the less you need to dig. Sites with slower-draining soils will have longer periods of pooling water. They key is to allow rainwater to pond *and* ensure it drains before mosquitoes breed (about two days). In general, after you've added any compost and mulch to the basin the depth should be around 6 to 12 inches, and water should empty within two days. Remember, the ponding depth is the height difference between the bottom of the rain garden and the overflow. The Sizing a Rain Garden chart (page 167) offers general guidelines. If you find your rain garden isn't draining quickly enough, lower the outlet so less water stays in the basin. For example, if you choose a 6-inch ponding depth and the soil drains at 0.2 inch per hour, it would take 6 inches ÷ 0.2 inch/hour = 30 hours to drain.

Here are two examples of excavation depths:

- A rain garden with a 6" ponding depth in well-draining soils would require: 6" ponding depth +

2" mulch + 3" compost mixed into the bottom = 11" of excavation depth.

- A rain garden with a 6" ponding depth in slower-draining soils (with a foot of rain garden mix to replace native soil) would require: 6" ponding + 2" mulch + 12" rain garden mix = 20" excavation depth.

Note that a 6-inch berm should be added around the outside of the basin to provide additional capacity in heavy rains if the overflow clogs.

If you have well-draining soils and are growing native plants, adding lots of compost may not be necessary. Rainwater harvesting expert Brad Lancaster notes that in the Southwest he's found that native plants don't need the compost. He plants directly into the native soils and adds a thick layer of mulch to prevent evaporation and increase the organic matter in the system, which increases infiltration.

OPTIONS FOR SLOW-DRAINING SOILS

There are several techniques to address potential issues with slowly draining soils, including:

- Install a dry well before the rain garden inlet. A **dry well** is a hole, for example a 3-foot cube filled with 2 to 2½ inches of clean drain rock (commonly used in septic systems). The dry

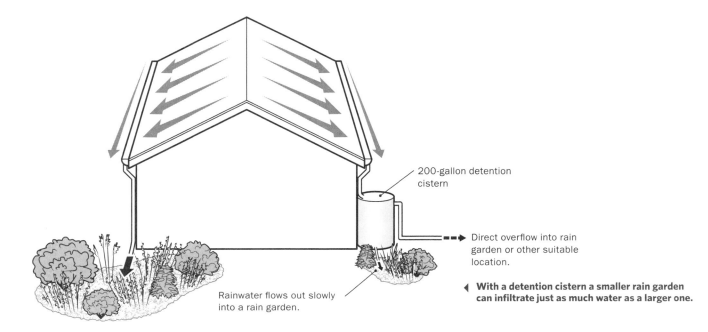

200-gallon detention cistern

Direct overflow into rain garden or other suitable location.

Rainwater flows out slowly into a rain garden.

◀ **With a detention cistern a smaller rain garden can infiltrate just as much water as a larger one.**

well provides additional capacity to hold rainwater during a rainstorm so water can soak into the ground slowly.

- Install a **detention cistern** before the inlet. A detention cistern collects rainwater from the gutter and slowly releases it into the rain garden. Typically 200 gallons, a detention cistern can reduce the area needed in the rain garden. Some areas, like the City of Seattle, have reduced sizing guidelines for rain gardens that incorporate a detention cistern.

- Remove soil and replace it with a rain garden mix.

- Plant thickly with deep-rooting plants; their roots will open the soil and improve infiltration.

Rain Garden Shape

Shape your rain garden how you like. Curve the edges so it looks interesting and fits well with your landscape. The shape is often determined by the need to work around existing landscape features, such as driveways, trees, utilities, and structures. You may be limited in length or width due to your site configuration. Common shapes include amoeba-shape, circular, and oval. Looking at images of existing rain gardens is an easy way to get ideas for what might look good in your own landscape. If you are constructing near a gentle downward slope, a long narrow rain garden works well. Keep the long side running parallel to the slope, as this simplifies leveling the bottom.

COMMON RAIN GARDEN SHAPES

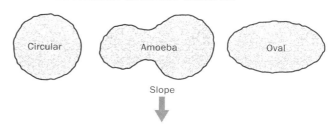

Circular   Amoeba   Oval

Slope

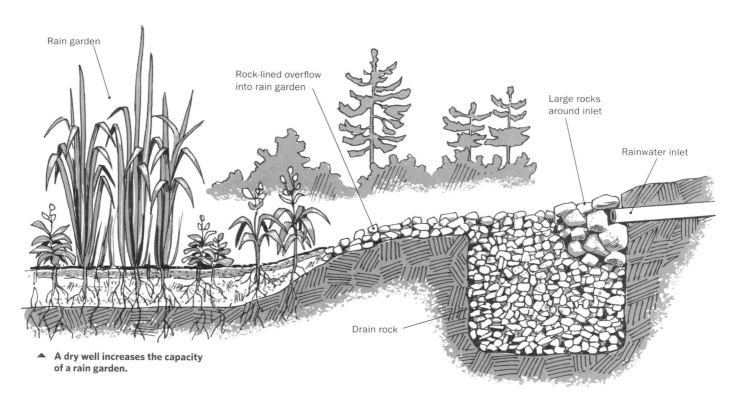

Rain garden

Rock-lined overflow into rain garden

Large rocks around inlet

Rainwater inlet

Drain rock

▲ **A dry well increases the capacity of a rain garden.**

Moving Water to the Rain Garden

The next piece of the rain garden system is the means of conveyance from the water source — the roof, overflow of a rainwater tank, or surface runoff from a driveway or street — to the rain garden basin. There are two main options: a buried pipe and a diversion swale. A third (and simpler) method is to rely on natural ground contours that slope toward the rain garden, allowing water to flow across land (or lawn) to reach the basin.

If you'd like to see rainwater flowing to the rain garden, install a **diversion swale** — a shallow trench lined with gravel and rock — sloping to the rain garden. Note that some water will drain into the soil in a diversion swale so less rainwater reaches the rain garden. If you'd prefer to keep the conveyance system out of sight, bury a large, **rigid pipe** (ABS or Schedule 40 PVC) sloping downward to the rain garden. Both systems require a gentle slope of at least 2 percent. Rigid pipes can slope as steeply as needed, but swales shouldn't slope more than 8 percent to prevent problems with erosion.

Choosing Plants for Your Rain Garden

Plants create the living ecosystem of your rain garden and must be adapted to both wet and dry conditions. Every rain garden has three different planting areas, each with plants suited for the specific conditions:

1. Bottom of the rain garden, the wettest portion. Plants must tolerate both standing water and extended dry times between rains.

2. Sloped sides, occasional flooding, less wet than the bottom. Plants must tolerate occasional soggy roots and mostly dry times between rains.

3. Top or berm, the driest area. In a desert climate, these plants may be cactus.

▼ **Two ways to move water to rain garden (pipe and diversion swale)**

Buried pipe

Rock-lined diversion swale

Rain garden

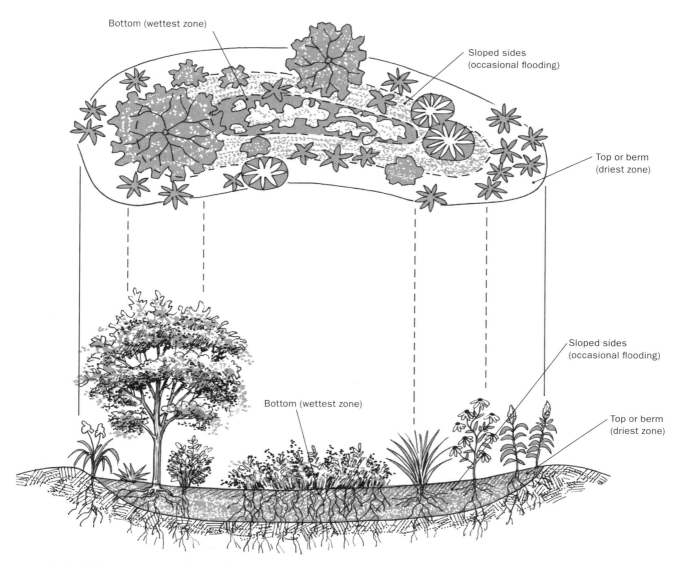

Bottom (wettest zone)

Sloped sides
(occasional flooding)

Top or berm
(driest zone)

Sloped sides
(occasional flooding)

Bottom (wettest zone)

Top or berm
(driest zone)

▲ **Aerial view and cross-section of a rain garden (planted area)**

You may want a theme for your rain garden, such as a bird and butterfly garden, or a special focus on certain colors or fragrances of the plants and flowers. There are countless options. Make sure you match the sun requirements of plants with your site. Trusted nurseries specializing in native plants, native plant organizations, or landscape professionals can assist in choosing plants. There is a wealth of free resources online, including planting templates for various sizes of rain gardens in different geographic areas.

When choosing plants, consider their mature size and space them with adequate room to grow. This prevents endless (and easily avoidable) pruning maintenance for the rest of the plants' lives. If you expect

extended times of pooling in your rain garden due to slow infiltration rates, plant more wetland and bog plants that can handle having soggy roots. A nice way to choose plants is to walk around natural areas nearby. Look for plants growing in seasonal creek beds, plants thriving on dry hillsides, and plants in-between. Make sure you don't choose invasive ones, though!

If you plant the rain garden in the cooler, rainier season, plants will need less frequent irrigation to become established. It's also fine to construct the rain garden during the dry summer and wait until fall to plant. If you do this, cover any bare soil with mulch or burlap so weeds don't grow.

Constructing a Rain Garden

To construct the rain garden you will excavate the basin, amend the soil, and create an entry for the water to flow into the basin and an overflow for water to exit when the rain garden fills. After you connect the water source to the garden (with a pipe or swale, most likely), you'll give it all a test run before adding plants and mulch. Wood chips make the best mulch. You can often get them for free from a local tree trimmer, delivered to the site.

A few tips about digging the garden: Enlist the help of friends, or perhaps a mini-excavator. Don't dig after heavy rains, which can compact the soil. Spring is the best time to install a rain garden (moist soil, but not too wet). If you use an excavator, make sure it doesn't enter the basin, as it will compact the soil.

The proper method for laying out and digging the garden depends on your site. If the site is level (flat ground), follow step 1. If your site is gently or moderately sloped (5 to 10 percent), follow step 2; you will dig soil from the uphill side of the rain garden and place the soil in a berm on the downhill side to create a flat bottom in the basin.

Note: Most buried utilities are within striking distance of the rain garden bottom, and often they are buried more shallowly than they should be. Call 811 and have all utility lines marked before you start digging (see Call Before You Dig! on page 84).

MATERIALS

3" or 4" ABS or Schedule 40 PVC pipe, fittings, and pipe cement/glue (if using pipe to move water; see step 5)

Small rocks or gravel (if using a diversion swale to move water; see step 5)

Large, flat rocks (for inlet splash guard)

Round, washed river rock or cobble, about 2" or larger (to stabilize inlet and outlet)

Plants and soil amendment (as needed)

Wood chips/mulch (see step 8)

TOOLS

Garden hose or rope

Flour or stakes (for marking on level site; see step 1)

Stakes, string, and line level (for sloped sites)

Excavation tools (shovel, mattock, digging bar, etc.)

Straight 2×4

4-foot level

Rake

Pitchfork

Plumbing tools (if using pipe to move water; see step 5)

1. Dig the basin — for level sites.

Outline the shape of the rain garden with a garden hose or rope, keeping in mind how far the sloped walls will extend beyond the bottom of the basin. Once you're satisfied with the shape, sprinkle flour or use stakes to mark the shape, and remove the hose or rope. This shape represents the bottom of the basin.

Next, mark a second line outside the first for the edge of the sloped sides. A 3:1 (3 feet horizontal to 1 foot vertical) slope is recommended; 2:1 is the maximum (the slope helps prevent the walls from caving in; use 2:1 only if space is limited). Use the ponding depth to determine the distance for sloping the walls; for example, a 6" ponding depth with 3:1 slope would require an 18" (6 × 3) extension on all sides of the basin.

Excavate the garden, by hand or with an excavator. Slope the edges from the bottom of the basin to the outer line you marked. Mound the excavated soil around the edges of the basin to create a berm, or use it to create an elevated path. The berm should be around 6" higher than the overflow to provide extra ponding capacity if the overflow should clog in a rainstorm.

Mark the overflow of the rain garden. Form a 3"- to 4"-deep channel at the top of the berm to create the overflow outlet and plan to direct the water to an appropriate location (a second basin, a vegetated area, or the storm drain). The difference in height from the bottom of the mulched basin to the overflow will set the ponding depth, typically 6". Plan to reinforce the overflow to prevent erosion (see step 5 on page 174).

2. Dig the basin — for sloped sites.

Place stakes or flags at the uphill and downhill sides of the excavation area, about 5 feet apart from each other along the length of garden. Tie a string at ground level from the first stake on the uphill side to the first stake on downhill side, then level the string with a line level, as shown on next page. Remove soil from the upper side of the basin and place it along the lower side to begin building a berm that's the same height as the uphill side. Repeat for each stake so the berm curves around the lower side of

the rain garden. Continue moving soil from the upper side of the basin to the lower side until the bottom of the basin is flat and you have created a berm the same height as the uphill side. To ensure the berm is well-compacted, stomp on it (with your feet or a hand tamper) after adding every few inches of soil. Check the level of the berm (use a second string level line) parallel to the length of the berm. Level the top of the berm as needed so it is at the same elevation along its length.

The berm should be at least 2 feet wide at the bottom, with gently sloping sides, and at least 1 foot wide at the top.

Mark the overflow of the rain garden. Form a 3"- to 4"-inch deep channel at the top of the berm to create the overflow outlet and plan to direct the water to an appropriate location (a second basin, a vegetated area, or the storm drain). The top of the berm should be at least 6" higher than the overflow, providing extra holding capacity in the event the overflow is blocked (so water doesn't spill over the berm). The difference in height from the bottom of the mulched basin to the overflow will set the ponding depth, typically 6". Plan to reinforce the overflow to prevent erosion (see step 5).

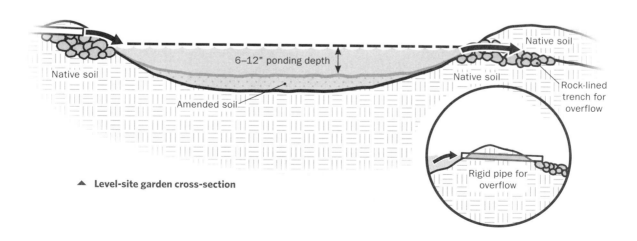

6–12" ponding depth

Native soil

Amended soil

Native soil

Native soil

Rock-lined trench for overflow

Rigid pipe for overflow

▲ **Level-site garden cross-section**

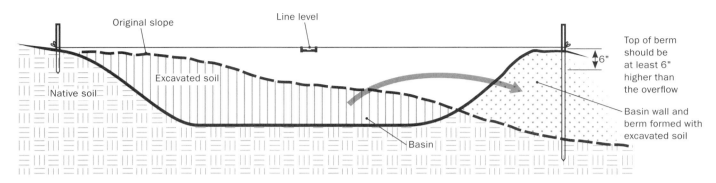

Original slope | Line level | Top of berm should be at least 6" higher than the overflow

Excavated soil

Native soil

Basin

Basin wall and berm formed with excavated soil

▲ **Sloped-site garden cross-section**

3. Level and prepare the basin bottom.

Cut a straight 2×4 so it fits easily inside the rain garden excavation (or use a laser level). Place a 4-foot level on the board and move it around the bottom of the basin, leveling the area by digging out shallow places and filling in deeper spots. After you've flattened the bottom, roughen it up (scarify it) with a pitchfork or shovel to promote root growth and increase drainage.

4. Amend the soil.

Add compost or a rain garden mix as needed, or employ another method to improve water infiltration (see Amending Your Soil on facing page and Options for Slow-Draining Soils on page 168).

5. Install a pipe or diversion swale.

Now you'll prepare the conveyance system to send rainwater to the rain garden (see Moving Water to the Rain Garden on page 170).

Pipe from downspout or tank overflow: Use a downspout adapter at the base of the house to transition from the downspout into a 3" or 4" pipe. Schedule 40 PVC and ABS are more durable pipe options and will last longer than flexible black plastic drainpipe. Purchase an adapter appropriate for your downspout and pipe (there are multiple downspout shapes and sizes, requiring different adapters.)

When piping from a tank overflow, remember to size your tank overflow to be as large as the inlet

pipe. Use the same size of pipe, often 3" or 4", to plumb to the rain garden.

Run the pipe on the surface of the ground to determine where the trench will go. Then, move the pipe to the side and dig the trench. If you're trenching through a lawn, try to remove sections of turf with a flat shovel so they can be replaced after burial. Dig the trench so the pipe slopes at 2 percent or greater, following standard drainage plumbing techniques. Dry-fit, test for flow, and glue all the joints before burying the pipe. See Plumbing Basics for Greywater Installation on page 135 for more information on plumbing materials and techniques.

Diversion swale from downspout or tank overflow: Start the diversion swale underneath the downspout, or near the edge of the rainwater tank. First determine the location and shape of the swale. It must slope downward to the rain garden but can meander on the way if desirable (to create a dry-creek look).

Excavate a shallow trench, about 2 feet wide and 1 foot deep, sloping gently down toward the rain garden. Keep the slope at least 2 percent but not more than 8 percent (to avoid erosion problems). Line the swale with rocks to prevent erosion as rainwater flows through it on its path to the rain garden; or, in wetter climates, plant with a groundcover and mulch it. Use large, flat rock or cobble where the downspout or overflow pipe enters the swale to slow the flow of rainwater and prevent erosion.

Amending Your Soil

Depending on the native soil, you may want to add compost to promote infiltration and provide nutrients for the new plants. In well-draining soils (infiltration rate of at least 1" per hour) add a few inches of compost to the basin and mix it in with a shovel or digging fork, loosening the bottom of the basin as you mix it in. With slower-draining soils, consider some of these options to infiltrate more water into your site:

- Dig out extra soil and replace it with well-draining soil, such as a rain garden mix of 60 percent screened sand and 40 percent compost, by volume. Mix it in with a few inches of native soil and then refill the basin (but still leave room for pooling). Gently compact it with your feet by walking over it. Do not add sand to heavy clay soils, as this can create a concrete-like substance.

- Include a "catch-and-release" cistern or rain barrels to provide surge capacity to the rain garden (see Options for Slow-Draining Soils on page 168 for more details).

- Dig a dry well before the inlet or after the overflow to collect more water (see Options for Slow-Draining Soils on page 168 for details).

- Dig a larger basin and have an overflow plan.

- Once the basin is planted, roots will open the soil and increase infiltration. If you have poorly draining soils, you may be able to remedy this with plants.

- Enlarge the basin or reduce the amount of rainwater entering it.

- If your basin isn't infiltrating as quickly as you'd like, lower the overflow to drain the water elsewhere.

A five-year study by the U.S. Geological Survey (USGS) found that rain gardens worked well in all soil types, even thick clay, if planted with deep-rooting plants. In clay soils native prairie grasses increased the infiltration rate each year as their roots penetrated the clay soil layer, while regular turf grass didn't.

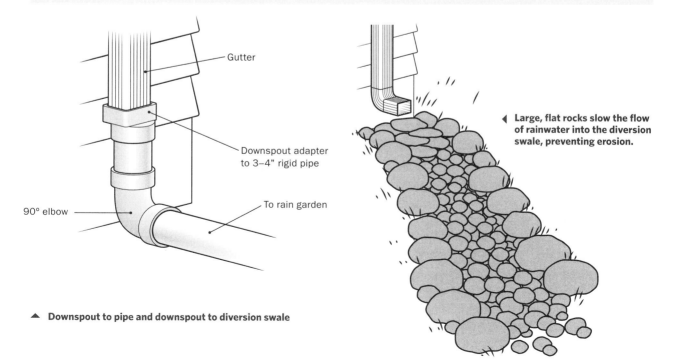

Gutter

Downspout adapter to 3–4" rigid pipe

90° elbow

To rain garden

▲ **Downspout to pipe and downspout to diversion swale**

◀ **Large, flat rocks slow the flow of rainwater into the diversion swale, preventing erosion.**

6. Reinforce the inlet and outlet.

Flowing water causes erosion. As rainwater flows in and out of the rain garden, it can erode the inlet and outlet areas. Prevent erosion with a splash guard under the inlet, and rock reinforcements around the outlet. Create a pad with large, flat stones under the inlet and extending a few feet, to dissipate the water's energy as it flows into the rain garden. Fill in cracks with smaller rocks.

The overflow outlet should be about 4" to 6" lower than the berm around the basin. The overflow location determines the ponding depth and will vary according to the desired depth and the height of the berm you build. The berm rising above the overflow provides extra ponding capacity during a large rainstorm in case the overflow gets clogged.

Reinforce the outlet by lining the area with rocks or bricks, or use a short length of drainpipe, a few feet long. The pipe can be covered with soil and concealed with rocks. Extend a rock overflow about 4 feet outside the rain garden to slow exiting water.

7. Perform a flow test.

Watch the system during a rain (with the first rain you may run outside excitedly, like many new rain garden owners do!) or turn a hose on at the base of the gutter downspout (or rainwater tank overflow) and watch where the water goes. Look for places where water is washing away soil. Check to make sure it overflows properly out of the rain garden basin. You may need to add stones where water is eroding soil, and adjust the height of the outflow.

8. Plant and mulch the rain garden.

Plant your rain garden according to your plan (see Choosing Plants for Your Rain Garden on page 170). Add a 2" to 3" layer of woody mulch over the soil (1 cubic yard will cover about 100 square feet with 3" of mulch). Keep mulch away from the trunks of plants to avoid trapping moisture at the trunk and reduce the risk of diseases, such as crown rot. Heavier mulches won't float as much as lighter mulches when the basin pools.

Rain Garden Maintenance

Like any part of the landscape, a rain garden requires some ongoing maintenance:

- Weed, especially when the plants are small.

- Water for one or two years (rain garden plants shouldn't require any water after a year or two).

- Check the inlet and outlet seasonally. Remove debris and large leaves that may block the inlet or outlet. Reinforce any eroding areas with rock.

- Check the berm annually. If any parts of the berm are lower than before or show signs of eroding, add soil to restore berm to its original shape, retamping as needed.

- Check mulch annually. Reposition mulch as needed so it covers the soil. As plants mature they will shade the soil, so adding mulch won't be necessary. (Adding too much mulch over time can fill in the basin, reducing its infiltration capacity.)

- Prune plants, cut back, and thin as needed.

Roofwater Collection Systems

THE BENEFITS OF A RAIN GARDEN are many, but once the rain is in the garden soil it's not coming back out in its watery form. To save liquid rainwater for longer dry spells, store it in a tank or barrel.

A single rain barrel system is simple to install and can be a satisfying first step into rainwater collection. It's great for watering potted plants and starting seeds, but if you live somewhere with more than a few weeks between rains, the water will quickly run out. Connecting multiple barrels together provides a lot more storage for just a little extra work. This system can be low-cost (particularly when local, food-grade, repurposable barrels are available) and can increase your irrigation water supply considerably. However, most landscapes require thousands of gallons of irrigation each season, so one larger tank often is a more practical option. Larger tanks store water for both irrigation and indoor reuse (potable or nonpotable). If your storage capacity is larger, typically a few thousand gallons, consider a gravity-fed drip irrigation system to water your landscape automatically.

This section contains step-by-step instructions for converting 55-gallon barrels into rain barrels and installing a cistern (and a first-flush diverter).

Gutters and Downspouts

Well-functioning gutters and downspouts are important components of your rainwater collection system. To divert rainwater into a tank or barrel, tap into a gutter or downspout. If your house has damaged or missing gutters, you may need to install or repair them. While there are general guidelines for gutter design, regional rainfall patterns influence sizing. Areas with more intense rainstorms require a larger capacity than do places with less intense rains. Because of this, it's a good idea to consult with local installers or building officials if you'll be installing or significantly altering your gutter system.

Note: Rainwater systems supplying drinking water should not use gutters made from zinc, copper, or wood.

A pipe collecting water from the downspout should match the downspout; for example, if you tap into a 3-inch-round downspout you will use a 3-inch round pipe. This pipe is called a "trunkline" as it travels to the rainwater tank. Trunklines are rarely smaller than 3 inches in diameter.

The following are conservative, general guidelines for sizing of gutters and downspouts. See the Resources for more information and how to include the intensity of local rainfall patterns for proper sizing. Consult local resources for geographically specific considerations, such as snow loads.

Basic Gutter Guidelines

- Use gutters at least 5 inches wide and support them every 3 feet.

- Slope gutters $\frac{1}{16}$ inch per 1 linear foot of gutter (or more; increasing slope increases gutter capacity).

- Keep the front of gutter $\frac{1}{2}$ inch lower than the back.

- Don't exceed 45-degree bends when traveling horizontally.

Basic Downspout Guidelines

- Downspouts are typically 20 to 50 feet apart.

- Provide 1 square inch of downspout area for each 100 square feet of roof surface.

- Round downspouts. 3-inch: up to 700 square feet of roof surface; 4-inch: up to 1,255 square feet

- Square downspouts. 2 × 3-inch = 600 square feet; 3 × 4-inch = 1,200 square feet

Example Calculation

Consider a house with a 2,000-square-foot roof and four downspouts, each draining 500 square feet of roof surface. The rainwater system will collect water from half of the roof and combine two downspouts to carry rainwater from 1,000 square feet of the roof area. This would require a 3-inch downspout for each and a 4-inch pipe (the trunkline) after they combine (4 inches will accommodate up to 1,255 square feet of roof). **Note:** This example doesn't include rainfall intensity, which affects sizing.

Converting a Single 55-Gallon Rain Barrel

With a few tools and supplies, you can convert any food-grade plastic barrel into a rain barrel. There are two common types of barrels: open-top and closed-top. *Open-top* barrels have a large lid that either unscrews or lifts off. These barrels can be easier to convert because you can access the inside of the barrel. *Closed-top* barrels have two holes on top, called *bung holes*, that are covered with threaded caps. If you have a closed-top barrel (or barrels), read through this project, as well as Connecting Rain Barrels Together: A Daisy Chain (page 184), and Working with Closed-Top Barrels (page 186), and decide which of the conversion methods you prefer.

The parts for converting barrels (barbed fittings, PVC parts, and bulkhead fittings) are sold by online irrigation stores and through some rain barrel installers (see Resources). Many local irrigation or large hardware stores also carry the necessary parts, though bulkhead fittings, which are used to create the outlet, may be more expensive here. Bulkhead fittings can also be found at specialty aquarium stores. An alternative is to use electrical conduit adapters in place of a bulkhead, and you can get these parts at any hardware store. Note that the term *bulkhead fittings* and *tank adapters* are used interchangeably. Make sure the one you use is threaded (not *slip*). For general information on plumbing parts, terminology, and techniques, see Plumbing Basics for Greywater Installation on page 135.

To find used barrels, check with breweries, bakeries, food import stores, and bottling companies. Also look online at classified ads (such as Craigslist) or search for "repurposed or used 55-gallon drums or barrels." Because 55-gallon barrels are used in many industries, use only **food-grade** barrels that never contained toxic liquids or other harmful materials. You can use steel barrels, but they corrode over time and are more difficult to work with than plastic versions. They're also closed-top barrels; see Working with Closed-Top Barrels (page 186).

The barrel design in this project makes it easy for you to add more barrels onto the system in the future. If you're absolutely sure you only want one barrel and will never add capacity, see Alternate Outlet for a Single Barrel (page 181) for a simplified method of adding a single outlet.

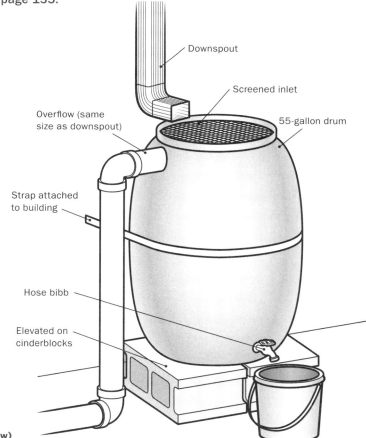

Downspout

Screened inlet

55-gallon drum

Overflow (same size as downspout)

Strap attached to building

Hose bibb

Elevated on cinderblocks

▶ **Rain barrel system (overview)**

MATERIALS

One 55-gallon plastic barrel

Mosquito screen (nylon or aluminum netting, 40 mesh or smaller)

Silicone caulk

Pipe thread tape

One ¾" bulkhead fitting or tank adapter

One ¾" MPT hose bibb or full port ball valve hose bibb (or one ¾" MPT to garden hose thread adapter and hose shutoff valve; see step 4)

One 2" male adapter (PVC electrical conduit fitting)

One 2" female adapter (PVC electrical conduit fitting)

Pipe or other supplies to send overflow to rain garden (see step 5)

Supplies for supporting and anchoring barrel (see step 6)

Downspout diverter and fasteners (see step 7)

TOOLS

Drill and ½" bit

Jigsaw or thin-bladed handsaw

Staple gun

Permanent marker

Hole saw (sized for bulkhead and overflow fittings)

Tongue-and-groove pliers or large wrench

Hacksaw

1. Determine the barrel location.

Locate the barrel next to a downspout and near an area where you need water. Keep in mind that downspouts can be rerouted to a more desirable location, if convenient.

2. Create a rainwater inlet.

Cut a 10"–12"-diameter circle in the barrel lid or top: Drill a starter hole with a ½" drill bit, then insert a jigsaw blade (or thin-bladed handsaw) into the hole and complete the circular cutout with the saw. Alternatively, you can use a large hole saw to drill multiple holes, then cut or snip the connecting strips of plastic.

Cut the mosquito screen a few inches larger than the hole, then staple it over the hole. If you have an open-top barrel, staple the screen from beneath the lid so it looks cleaner. Seal all edges of the screen with silicone caulk to close all potential mosquito entrances. Alternatively, if you have larger screen, remove the barrel lid, cover the whole opening with screen, then replace the lid over the screen.

Common Rain Barrel Errors

A quick online search for "rain barrel images" shows the most common errors, over and over again. Here are some things to avoid:

- Overflow undersized. If the overflow is smaller than the inlet, water will back up in the barrel during a rainstorm and pour out the top. Don't use a ¾-inch or 1-inch hose for the overflow unless you have a small hose bringing rainwater into the system.

- Outlet too high. Locate the outlet as low as possible. Any water below the outlet is inaccessible.

- Setting up an irrigation system, a pump, expensive parts, etc. for a small system (a few barrels). The quantity of water in a small rain barrel system doesn't warrant spending the money or resources for additional accessories. A garden hose or watering can should suffice.

You may start out thinking a few rain barrels will capture enough water to meet your irrigation needs. If they do, great! Your yard consumes very little water compared to most. Rain barrels are a fabulous way to get your feet wet and experience the rewarding practice of catching water from the sky, but typically don't reduce irrigation need by much. Plan for more future storage and rain gardens for the extra water.

3. Install the rainwater outlet (bulkhead fitting).

Use a permanent marker to mark the outlet hole location, about 2" to 4" above the bottom of the barrel, where the bulkhead fitting can sit flush against the tank wall. Drill a hole with a hole saw that's very slightly larger than the male threads of the ¾" bulkhead fitting but smaller than the washer; typically 1½" or 1⅝". If the hole is too large, the fitting will leak.

Unscrew the bulkhead fitting (it will separate into two parts). Reach inside the barrel and push the male-threaded side of the fitting, with the washer attached, through the hole. Connect the other side of the fitting from the outside of the barrel and hand-tighten; bulkhead fittings are reverse-threaded, so tighten to the *left*. Tighten the fitting more with tongue-and-groove pliers or a wrench.

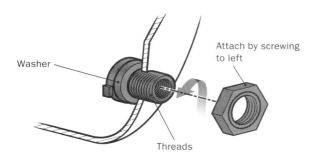

Washer — Attach by screwing to left

Threads

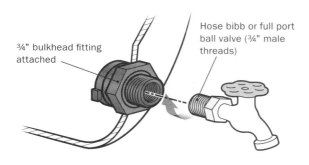

¾" bulkhead fitting attached

Hose bibb or full port ball valve (¾" male threads)

▲ **Bulkhead fitting with garden hose bibb**

4. Attach the garden hose bibb to the bulkhead.

◆ **Using a hose bibb:** Wrap the bibb's threads with pipe thread tape and thread it directly into the bulkhead fitting.

◆ **Using a garden-hose shutoff (cheaper option):** Wrap pipe thread tape on the threads of an MPT × MHT garden hose adapter (MPT = male pipe thread, MHT = male hose thread), then thread the male pipe thread side (the side of the fitting with the threads closer together) into the bulkhead fitting. Next, attach the garden hose shutoff valve. A garden hose can be attached to the shutoff, or the valve can be opened to fill a watering can.

Note: For a faster flow from the outlet use a "full port ball valve hose bibb" instead of a regular hose bibb. Full port valves don't reduce the diameter inside the valve, which restricts flow.

Bulkhead Alternatives

Bulkhead fittings (and tank adapters) work great: they're easy to install, durable, and don't leak. But they're not cheap — about $8 each. If you're on a shoestring budget and are installing lots of barrels, you may want to try one of these lower-cost alternatives.

Less than $3: Use a ¾" male adapter threaded into a ¾" female-threaded coupling, with a rubber washer in between. (You must use plastic electrical conduit fittings because they will screw together all the way, while plumbing fittings are tapered.) Place the female-threaded coupling on the outside of the barrel. If they're installed properly they won't leak.

Less than $4: Use ¾" uniseal flexible tank adapter. These are made for watertight holes on curved surfaces. Proper installation is key; if the hole is rough or the wrong size, they may leak. Order uniseals online.

Alternate Outlet for a Single Barrel

If you never plan to add more capacity to your system, consider this lower-cost method for the outlet: Directly connect the ¾" hose bibb or full port ball valve hose bibb with male threads to the barrel. First drill a hole at the bottom, just large enough to thread the ¾" hose bibb into the barrel. Wrap pipe thread tape on the threads of the hose bibb, put an O-ring and a ¾" metal washer over the threads, then firmly thread the hose bibb into the barrel (the metal threads on the hose bibb will cut into the plastic). From the inside of the barrel, place another O-ring and washer onto the male threads and connect a ¾" female-threaded coupling to it, tightening with tongue-and-groove pliers. Put a bead of silicone caulk around the outside and inside to prevent leaks.

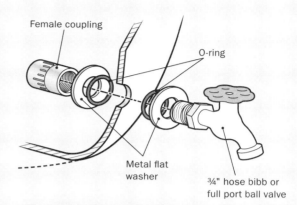

Female coupling

O-ring

Metal flat washer

¾" hose bibb or full port ball valve

▲ **Single outlet — hose bibb to barrel**

5. Install the overflow assembly.

A rain barrel fills up quickly in a rainstorm, and excess water needs somewhere to go. A properly designed overflow directs excess rainwater to a rain garden, planted area, or, as a last resort, to the storm drain. If the overflow is undersized or absent, overflowing rainwater will pour out the top of the barrel and splash against the house.

Before installing the overflow, set the barrel where it will be located to see which side of the barrel is more convenient for the overflow. Drill a hole slightly larger than the male threads on the 2" adapter, as high as possible on the side of the barrel. Insert the male adapter through the hole. From the inside of the barrel, screw the female coupling to the male. If you want a watertight seal (optional), use a large rubber washer between the fittings (or use silicone caulk) where they touch the barrel.

Alternatively, you can use a 90-degree elbow for the outside portion of the overflow, so the pipe is pointing down. To do this, start from inside the barrel and push the threaded side of the male adapter out of the hole. From the outside, screw a threaded 90-degree elbow to the male adapter so the 90 points toward the ground.

Direct overflow to the rain garden area via a rigid pipe, a downspout extender, or a gravel trench (diversion swale); see page 174 for details.

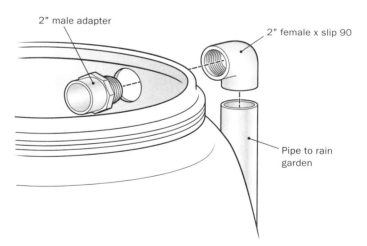

2" male adapter

2" female x slip 90

Pipe to rain garden

▲ **Overflow connection: Pipe diameter should be the same size as the downspout/inlet to the barrel.**

6. Install the rain barrel.

Level and compact the ground where the rain barrel will stand. Create a cinder-block base (or other sturdy platform) on the ground to support the barrel. Set the rain barrel on the base and secure the barrel to the house or other structure with strapping, such as metal plumbers tape or (a stronger option) water heater strapping if barrels will be near children. For stucco homes use an anchor kit, which includes anchors, screws, and a stucco bit. Caulk over any fasteners driven into the house to prevent water intrusion.

▲ **Two platform options**

7. Divert the downspout to the barrel.

If your downspout is connected to a combined city sewer, take necessary steps to cap off the connection; see Does Your City Have a Combined Sewer System?, below. There are several easy ways to get rainwater from your downspout into the barrel, including:

- ◆ Downspout bend to fit on your existing downspout. (Check the bottom of the downspout for a bend to use.)

- ◆ Flexible tube that fits over the downspout and bends into the barrel. (Called a flexible downspout connector or adapter; available from hardware stores)

- ◆ Downspout diverter that inserts into your existing downspout and allows you to manually switch rainwater flow between the barrel and the downspout, important in freezing climates where you aren't able to use the system all year long. Some brands, like Fiskars, have a method to automatically send the water into the downspout when the barrel is full, obviating the need for an overflow on the barrel. (I wouldn't recommend this type of diverter with a large tank system, however, because if it leaks or plugs up it can lose a lot of rainwater.)

- ◆ Trough (such as a small piece of gutter) to direct rainwater into the barrel

- ◆ 3" or 4" plastic (ABS or PVC) 45-degree elbow

Does Your City Have a Combined Sewer System?

Does your downspout direct rainwater into your yard? If so, great! You just have to cut it in the appropriate location and direct it to the rain barrel instead. In some cities, like San Francisco or Portland, the sewer system is combined with the stormwater system (called a **combined sewer system**). This means that the rainwater downspout may be connected with the city sewer system; after you disconnect the downspout, it is critical to cap off the connection to the sewer system to avoid sewer gas from escaping into your yard, or worse, sewage if the sewer main backs up. Cities with a combined sewer system may require permits to disconnect the downspout.

Hold the connector up to the barrel to see where you should cut the downspout. Use a hacksaw to cut the downspout. Attach the connector using small screws appropriate for your downspout (e.g., sheet metal screws for a metal downspout). Crimp the edges of the downspout as needed to insert it into the connector. Make sure the connector is secure so it doesn't come out of the barrel when rainwater runs through.

Maintaining a Rain Barrel System

Rain barrels require maintenance about once a year, but you should check on them before it rains if they have sat empty for many months. Typical maintenance tasks include:

- Checking screens. Remove leaves and debris as needed. Replace any damaged screens.

- Keeping your roof and gutters clean.

- Checking outlet for leaks. If leaking, tighten connections or seal with silicone caulk as needed.

- Clearing clogs. If water isn't flowing well out the outlet, remove the hose and check for debris. Clean as necessary (a small twig or toothpick is good for scraping out gunk). To prevent clogging, use a full port ball valve hose bibb (instead of a regular hose bibb); it has a larger opening inside the valve.

- Observing overflow. Ensure water flows to an appropriate area. If the overflow is undersized, make it larger. Water should flow out without backing up and spilling out the inlet.

- Cleaning. If your barrel gets stinky or very dirty, empty and rinse. Always use plant-friendly soap.

- Weatherizing the rain barrel for the winter. Water left inside the rain barrel, hose, or fittings could crack the plastic if it freezes. Some types of rain barrels won't split; others will. To err on the side of caution, drain the rain barrels and all tubing before winter if you live in a freezing climate. Divert the downspout back to its original placement or to a rain garden.

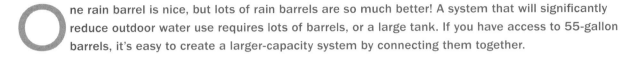

Connecting Rain Barrels Together: A Daisy Chain

One rain barrel is nice, but lots of rain barrels are so much better! A system that will significantly reduce outdoor water use requires lots of barrels, or a large tank. If you have access to 55-gallon barrels, it's easy to create a larger-capacity system by connecting them together.

Barrels can be connected together from the top or the bottom. When they're connected at the bottom they fill and empty in unison, functioning like one large tank, and require only one outlet. When they're connected at the top, one barrel overflows into the next, so each barrel requires a separate outlet. This setup costs more, but since each barrel functions like a mini-system you know exactly how much water is left.

This project shows you how to connect multiple barrels together from the bottom, in what's called a **daisy chain**. Every barrel requires a bulkhead fitting at the bottom. The first barrel needs an inlet and overflow as described in the single 55-gallon project (page 178). The remaining barrels need a connecting piece at the bottom, plus a vent. The outlet can be located anywhere along the tubing that connects barrels together, though it's often at the first or last barrel, since they tend to be in the most convenient location to access the water. To ensure good flow out of your barrels use a "full port ball valve hose bibb" instead of a regular hose bibb for the outlet. Full port valves don't reduce the diameter inside the valve, which restricts flow. For small systems of just a few barrels, the slower flow may not be a problem and either type may be suitable.

MATERIALS

Plastic barrels (if you want to use steel barrels, which may rust, see Working with Closed-Top Barrels on page 186)

Mosquito screen (nylon or aluminum, 40 mesh or smaller)

Pipe thread tape

¾" bulkhead fittings or tank adapters (one for each barrel; to make a watertight outlet, make sure it's threaded, not a slip connection)

One 2" male adapter (plastic electrical conduit fitting; for overflow)

One 2" female adapter (plastic electrical conduit fitting; for overflow)

Pipe or other supplies to send overflow to rain garden (see step 3)

One ¾" threaded PVC nipple (to connect threaded tee to bulkhead)

One ¾" threaded PVC tee (for barrel with outlet)

One ¾" MPT full port ball valve hose bibb

One ¾" MPT barbed adapter (to connect first barrel to middle barrels)

¾" MPT barbed tee (one for each middle barrel) or ¾" FPT barbed tee with a ¾" nipple

One ¾" MPT × barbed 90 (for last barrel)

Supplies for supporting and anchoring barrels (see step 6)

¾" poly tubing

¾" hose clamps (optional)

TOOLS

Same as for single-barrel project (page 179)

1. Create an inlet on the first barrel.

Follow steps 1 and 2 on page 179 to determine the location for the barrel system and create an inlet for rainwater on the first barrel.

Note: The inlet can be anywhere along the line of barrels, but most commonly is on the first barrel.

2. Add the rainwater outlets.

Follow step 3 on page 180 to install a bulkhead fitting on each barrel in the system.

3. Install an overflow assembly.

Follow step 5 on page 181 to install an overflow assembly onto the first barrel in the system (the barrel with the inlet) to send the overflow water to your rain garden. The overflow should be the same size as the downspout pipe supplying the inlet to prevent water overflowing out the inlet during a large rainstorm.

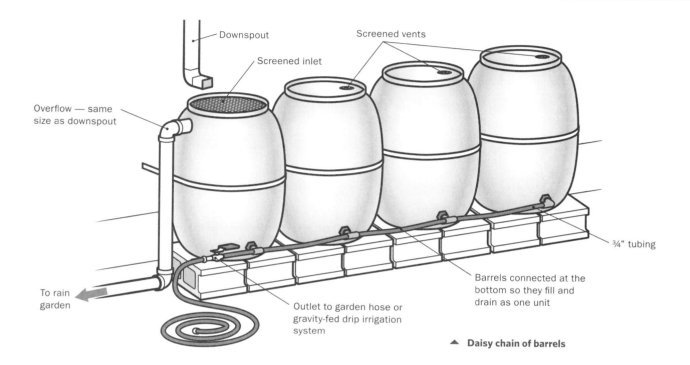

Downspout

Screened vents

Screened inlet

Overflow — same size as downspout

¾" tubing

Barrels connected at the bottom so they fill and drain as one unit

To rain garden

Outlet to garden hose or gravity-fed drip irrigation system

▲ **Daisy chain of barrels**

4. Vent the barrels.

Each barrel needs an opening for air to exit as rainwater enters. The inlet on the first barrel functions as a vent, but all other barrels need to have a vent installed. The vent is a simple hole in the top of the barrel, screened to prevent mosquitoes from entering. If your barrel lid has a cap, remove it and cover the hole with a screen. If the barrel has no cap, drill a 1" or larger hole in the top of the barrel and cover it with mosquito screen (staple it in place, then seal the edges with silicone caulk). For a sturdier option use a 1"-diameter *hose aerator filter screen*, a half-dome stainless steel screen with a rubber edge (available from hardware stores); silicone it into the hole.

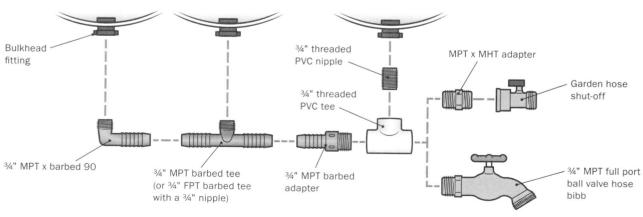

Bulkhead fitting

¾" threaded PVC nipple

MPT x MHT adapter

¾" threaded PVC tee

Garden hose shut-off

¾" MPT x barbed 90

¾" MPT barbed tee (or ¾" FPT barbed tee with a ¾" nipple)

¾" MPT barbed adapter

¾" MPT full port ball valve hose bibb

▲ **Close-up of fittings**

Working with Closed-Top Barrels

Closed-top barrels are manufactured with two threaded holes on top (called *bung holes*). It's more challenging to use closed-top barrels and follow the open-top barrel instructions for connecting them together, because you can't reach inside the barrel to install the bulkhead fitting. The solutions are to cut a large hole in the top (so you can reach inside) or drop half of the bulkhead fitting into the barrel through the bung hole and carefully fish it out the hole you drilled in the bottom (this requires nimble fingers and persistence). An easier way to use closed-top barrels is to connect directly to the threaded holes. This method is cheaper and simpler than trying to access the inside of the barrel. After all the fittings are installed, you'll flip the barrels upside down and connect them together via the threaded holes.

Unfortunately, closed-top barrels are not all the same; the prefabricated holes range in size and thread type. Barrels commonly have two threaded holes (with caps): One is a 2" NPT (national pipe thread; see page 135), and you can remove the cap and easily connect a threaded fitting to it, such as a 2" × ¾" threaded reducing bushing. The other hole has thicker threads (called *coarse* or *buttress* threads) that will not connect to NTP pipe thread fittings. Buttress thread adapters do exist but are special-order parts. Luckily, many of the caps on these holes come with a ¾" *knockout*, a small, threaded plug in the cap that you can remove (typically by carefully drilling it out) and then connect a ¾" fitting to.

Follow these general instructions when connecting closed-top barrels:

- Remove caps. Hold a flathead screwdriver at an angle against a ridge in the cap and tap on it with a hammer to unscrew the cap. If one cap has a ¾" knockout, use this to connect the fitting. Wrap pipe thread tape on the threads of the caps and screw them back in. Add silicone sealant around the edge of the cap if there's a concern or chance of leaking. Since the barrels will be flipped upside down, the caps must create a watertight seal.

- Once you have one hole sealed with a cap and one ¾" threaded hole (either from a knockout or adapting a larger hole using a threaded bushing), you are ready to add the fittings. Follow step 5 on page 188 for which fittings to use.

- The barrels require a platform so the fittings and connecting tubing will be elevated. Use cinder blocks, or build a sturdy wooden frame. Set the barrels in place, then connect them with ¾" tubing. The platform may be slightly different than for open-top barrels to avoid interfering with the tubing: in this system the tubing must run directly underneath the barrels, from one bung hole to the next.

- Create a vent in the top of each barrel to let air out (follow step 4 on page 185).

- Make an overflow. If you cut a large hole for the inlet, you can reach inside to install the overflow; see step 5 on page 181.

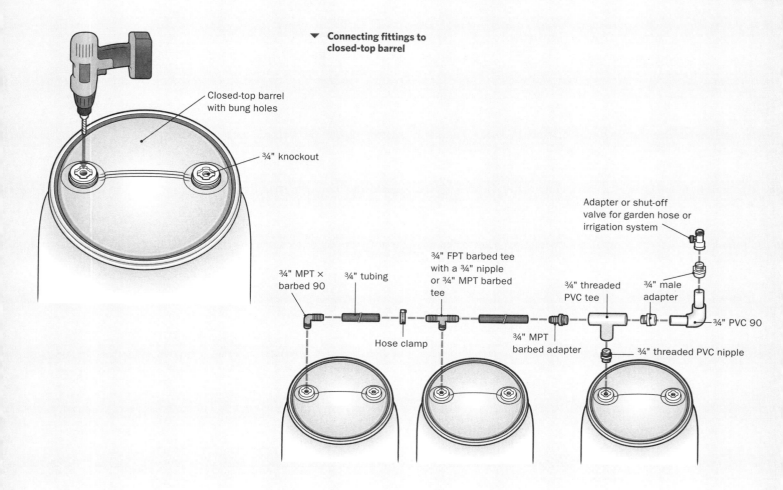

▼ **Connecting fittings to closed-top barrel**

Closed-top barrel with bung holes

¾" knockout

Adapter or shut-off valve for garden hose or irrigation system

¾" MPT × barbed 90

¾" tubing

¾" FPT barbed tee with a ¾" nipple or ¾" MPT barbed tee

¾" threaded PVC tee

¾" male adapter

¾" PVC 90

Hose clamp

¾" MPT barbed adapter

¾" threaded PVC nipple

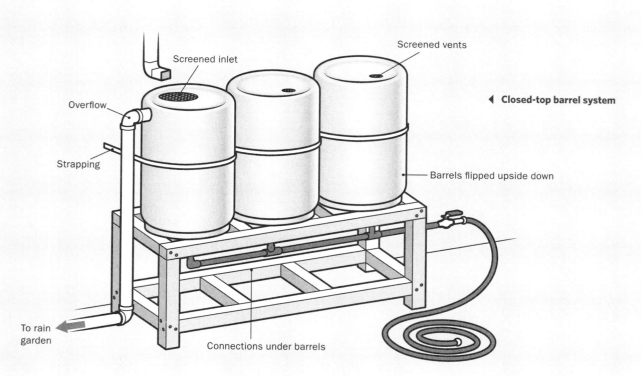

Screened vents

Screened inlet

◀ **Closed-top barrel system**

Overflow

Strapping

Barrels flipped upside down

To rain garden

Connections under barrels

5. Add the remaining fittings.

Different barrels will get different fittings, depending on your configuration. Be sure to wrap pipe thread tape onto all threaded fittings.

Outlet (to a garden hose or irrigation system). It's often convenient to put the inlet, outlet, and over-flow on the first barrel, but they can go anywhere in the line. Choose the most convenient configuration for your situation, and locate the outlet closest to the plants you'll irrigate. In this example the outlet is the first barrel in the line: Thread the nipple into the bulkhead. Attach the middle port of the threaded female PVC tee to the nipple. Attach the ¾" full port ball valve hose bibb to the other side of the threaded tee. Attach the MPT x barb to the side of the threaded tee facing the remaining barrels.

Middle barrels. Screw the threaded branch of the MPT barbed tees into each bulkhead fitting. (If you can't find MPT barbed tees, use FPT barbed tees; first screw the ¾" nipple to the FPT barbed tee.)

End barrel. Thread the ¾" MPT x barb 90 into the bulkhead fitting.

6. Arrange the barrels.

Barrels are commonly placed in a single line, but they can also wrap around the house, be doubled up, or installed in any other arrangement that fits your site. To install the barrels, level and compact the ground in the installation area. Place cinder blocks or a sturdy platform on the ground, and set the rain barrel on the platform (see step 6 on page 182). Make sure all barrels are level with one another. If you use different-sized barrels, consider how to arrange them so you don't lose capacity: for exam-ple, different platform heights could level taller and shorter barrels.

7. Connect the barrels.

Use ¾" poly tubing to connect the barrels together. Push the tubing ends onto the barbed fittings, cover-ing all barbs. If it's difficult to push the tubing over the barbs, heat the tubing ends by inserting them into a cup of hot water, or use a hair dryer.

The tubing shouldn't leak if it's undisturbed. If your barrels are located where the tubing may be stepped on, tugged, etc., use hose clamps to secure each connection. Make sure the tubing isn't tweaked or angled off the fitting, as this will create leaks. If you need to turn a corner, use a barbed 90 elbow.

8. Divert the downspout to the inlet barrel.

Follow step 7 on page 182 to modify the downspout to direct the rainwater into the first barrel (with the inlet).

9. Anchor and test the barrels.

Secure the barrels to the house or other structure with strapping (see step 6 on page 182). Partially fill the barrels with a hose and check all connections for leaks. Tighten any leaking fittings, and add silicone caulk if necessary.

You can now use rainwater by manually open-ing the outlet valve to fill a watering can or supply water for an attached garden hose. To install gravity-fed drip irrigation for your rain barrel system, see page 199.

Installing an Aboveground Plastic Rainwater Tank

An aboveground plastic tank is the most economical option for a large supply of rainwater. Most homes need thousands of gallons of water to significantly offset their consumption: a big tank supplies this. In general, once the rainwater tank is located, the installation is straightforward, requires no special tools, and can take just a few hours. Gutters and the tank foundation are the complicating factors. Homes without gutters require the additional work of installing them (or existing gutters in bad shape need repairs). Flat sites don't require a special foundation for the tank, while sloped or rocky land will.

Tanks can be located adjacent to the house, or not. Try to shade your tank with trees to keep the stored rainwater cooler. If you prefer that your tank is not clearly visible, install a "wet" delivery system to move rainwater from the gutters to a relatively distant location. For example, hide the tank discreetly behind some hedges. This method works so long as the tank's inlet is a foot or so lower than the gutters (see illustration on page 193). Any "wet" delivery system requires a drain at the lowest part of the pipe run so you can drain and clean out the pipe.

Depending on where you live, you can buy a tank locally or order it online and have it shipped to your home. Though plastic tanks are lightweight compared to other types of tanks, they are still big and bulky and may be hard to situate. A tank can be rolled across flat ground by two people, but if you need to lift it up, for example over a fence, you'll want many hands to help, or mechanical assistance (such as a tractor with a scoop, a forklift, a crane, etc.).

These instructions are specific to installing a readily available and lower-cost polyethylene (poly) plastic tank, from a few hundred gallons to many thousand. These tanks can be tall and narrow, or short and squat. Tanks installed on the ground with a height-to-width ratio of 2:1 often are exempt from permit requirements. Taller, narrower tanks and/or those holding 5,000 gallons or more often require permits (check with your local regulator for details). In most cases you'll place the tank directly onto the ground, though small tanks may be elevated on a strong platform. Medium-sized tanks may be elevated on a concrete or cinder-block foundation to get a little extra height.

Irrigation-only systems are the easiest to install and often don't require permits. Indoor reuse systems, either for potable or nonpotable uses, save more water overall than irrigation-only systems, since the tank water can be used during the rainy season. There is the additional cost and complication of pumps and filters, as well as permitting, to include in your budget. If you ever plan to drink the stored rainwater, make sure you use materials rated for potable water whenever possible.

Your system can collect rainwater from just one downspout or from multiple downspouts. Use the calculations from page 144 to determine how much of the roof area to divert into your tank to fill it up. For example, if you discover your tank will fill up with the first inch of rain, you probably don't need to tap into more than one downspout. If you decide to combine downspouts, make sure the pipe with combined flows is sized large enough. Or, if you run multiple downspouts separately into the tank, remember to size the overflow to account for the total flow. See page 177 for sizing the downspout.

MATERIALS

Plastic rainwater tank

Downspout screen with a circular 3" outlet (to fit into a pipe)

2-hole straps and fasteners (to secure downspout)

3" plastic pipe (ABS or Schedule 40 PVC) and fittings (for pipe run from gutter or first-flush diverter to tank)

3" first-flush kit with adapters and downspout pipe (if applicable; size varies; see page 197).

Adapter for overflow to 3" pipe (size of overflow varies)

Threaded ball valve sized for the tank outlet with a nipple (typically 2")

Threaded bushing to reduce to ¾" (if outlet is 2", use a 2" × ¾" threaded bushing)

¾" MPT full port ball valve hose bibb

Irrigation parts (see page 199)

Pipe thread tape

Glue or cement (appropriate for your pipe material)

One 3" tee with reducing bushing, ball valve, and valve box (for "wet" systems; see step 5)

Latex exterior house paint

TOOLS

Tubing cutters with plastic wheel or hacksaw

Screwdriver

Tongue-and-groove pliers or large wrench

Marker

Level

Cordless drill

Shovel

Tamper

1. Determine the tank location.

Find a location that works with gravity: the tank should be at the highest place possible that is still lower than the gutters so it can still be filled by gravity. For irrigation-only systems, choose a spot where stored rainwater can flow by gravity to the landscape. The surface should be flat, stable, and free of protruding roots or rocks, and should include plenty of room for you to walk around the tank. If possible, choose a spot that's shaded and protected from anything that may damage the piping (e.g., children, cows, etc.).

Observe the downspouts during a rain, noting how water flows out of them. Older homes may not have properly sloping gutters, resulting in uneven distribution of water. Locate the tank near functioning downspouts (or rehang the problem gutters). Once you've settled on a spot, remove any tree branches hanging over the roof to reduce leaf litter and debris and to eliminate roof access for squirrels, rats, raccoons, lizards, and other critters.

If the best location for your tank is not near an existing downspout, you can either move the downspout closer to the tank, or pipe from an existing downspout to the tank. (Any alterations in the downspout location may require repositioning the gutters for the proper slope.)

If rainwater is your only water source, place the tank where a water truck could bring more water to it in the event of an extended drought. If you're converting from a well system to a rainwater system, place the tank close to the well pump to tap into the existing plumbing with ease. If you plan to add more tanks in the future, find a place that can accommodate them nearby.

Warning: Do not place the tank on top of utility lines; see Call Before You Dig! on page 84.

2. Prepare the ground or build a foundation.

Small tanks of a few hundred gallons can be elevated with strong wooden platforms. You can calculate the weight of a full tank by multiplying the tank capacity by 8.34 (the weight of a gallon of water). For example, a 1,000-gallon tank weighs roughly 8,340 pounds — that's over 4 tons. Make sure any supports or platform can easily hold the tank's weight; it's a good idea to get help from a qualified building expert. Securely strap or otherwise anchor any elevated tank.

Plastic Pipes and pH

Plastic isn't eco, especially during the manufacturing process. Yet plastic pipe is the most practical option for rainwater systems. It's easy to work with and readily available, and it resists the corrosive nature of rainwater. PVC is the most common type of plastic pipe used in rainwater collection system, but unfortunately it's also the most toxic (during its manufacturing). There are two alternatives for irrigation-only systems: ABS (for the larger-dimension pipes to deliver rainwater into the tank and out the overflow) and HDPE (for pressurized lines). ABS costs more than PVC, is more prone to sun damage (paint it with latex paint to protect it), and is not rated for potable water. In pressurized lines for indoor systems, use HDPE (high-density polyethylene) or perhaps PEX (cross-linked polyethylene) tubing. In potable systems, always use materials rated for drinking water and keep plastic pipes out of the sun.

Be aware that rainwater is acidic and soft, which makes it "hungry" for metals, like copper pipes, and can corrode them. (This may not be a problem; it depends on the pH of the rainwater and the type of pipes.) The pH of rainwater varies from place to place. If you'll be connecting rainwater to a household system, or installing copper pipe, test the pH to find out whether you may experience future plumbing problems or will need to use a pH-neutralizing filter. Never use thin-walled, type M, copper pipe with rainwater, because this material is susceptible to developing pinhole leaks.

Larger tanks need to be on flat, firm ground, or a gravel bed or other type of built foundation. If your site is flat and free of tree roots, rocks, and other protrusions, you may not need a foundation. Most plastic tanks can be set directly on firm, flat ground, but always check the manufacturer's recommendations for your specific tank and ensure you meet the warranty requirements.

If your ground is not suitable, build a foundation. This could be as simple as using a galvanized steel band bolted to itself to create a circular frame. Stake the band firmly to the ground and fill inside the ring with pea gravel. Sites with high winds require anchors on the tank so it can't blow over when empty. A foundation also serves to elevate a tank slightly, which may provide enough rise for a gravity drip irrigation system (see page 199).

If your site is on or near a slope, your tank is much higher than it is wide, or you have other factors requiring extra safety precautions, consult with a rainwater harvesting specialist or an engineer.

Finally, make sure the overflow, drip from a first-flush system, or any other source of water does not erode the ground under the tank.

3. Divert the downspout and install leaf screens.

Smaller systems may not require screens if the water will be used quickly, the roof surface is relatively clean, and there is no irrigation system to clog. Otherwise, install a leaf screen and possibly a first-flush diverter to keep organic matter and debris out of the system. Organic matter in the tank rots (and causes odors); debris clogs irrigation equipment, and filters will require more frequent cleaning. Install the downspout screen at a convenient location, high enough so you can pipe into the tank (it must be higher than the tank inlet) and as low as possible so it's easier to clean the screen.

In general, if you're diverting the gutter from a one-story house, install the downspout screen directly under the point where the gutter meets the downspout. On a two- or three-story house, install the screen after the downspout has traveled lower down, where it's easy to reach on a ladder.

If you'll be installing a first-flush diverter, calculate the height requirements of your diverter standpipe before deciding where to cut the downspouts (see page 197). Make sure the diverter is visible and accessible for cleaning. If you'll be installing a "wet" system, measure how high you need the connection to be so that it's at least a foot higher than the inlet of your tank.

Set up a ladder on firm ground (with someone to hold it for you) to detach the downspout. Depending on how the downspout is connected, detach the clips or screws that are holding the downspout to the house. You may cut the downspout with a hacksaw if the best location for the screen is not at a

joint. Remove the entire downspout, and set it aside.

Secure the downspout screen to the house, a few inches below the stub of the downspout. Attach the screen following the manufacturer's instructions (there is some variation among brands), either using provided screw-slots or 2-hole straps; use screws appropriate for your siding material (e.g., wood, stucco, etc.).

Connect the pipe that travels to the tank to the bottom of the downspout screen. Or, if your system includes a first-flush diverter, connect the tee from the first-flush to the bottom of the screen.

4. Install a first-flush diverter (optional).

See Installing a First-Flush Diverter (page 197) for information on sizing a diverter and tips on installing a diverter kit.

5. Pipe to the tank.

Now you've installed a screen under the gutter and are ready to move rainwater into the tank. Remember, if you plan to combine downspouts, you may need to increase the pipe diameter to accommodate the increased flow; see Gutters and Downspouts on page 177.

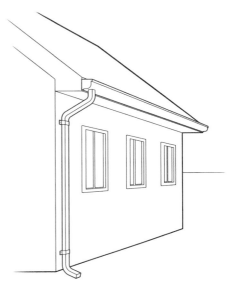

▲ **House with gutter and downspouts**

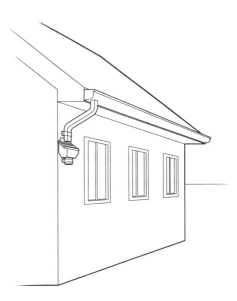

▲ **Remove downspout and attach leaf screen.**

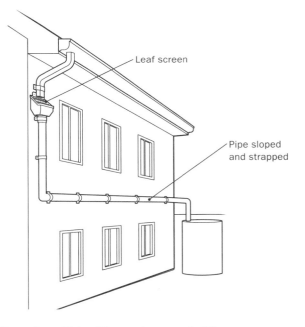

Leaf screen

Pipe sloped and strapped

▲ **Dry system with trunkline running across building**

LOCATIONS FOR FIRST-FLUSH DIVERTERS

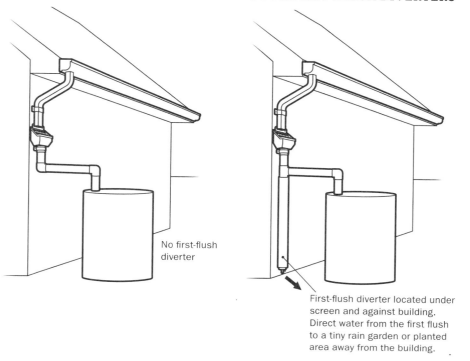
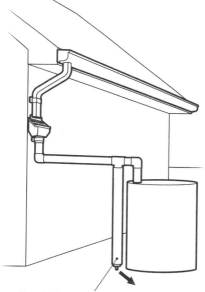

No first-flush diverter

First-flush diverter located under screen and against building. Direct water from the first flush to a tiny rain garden or planted area away from the building.

First-flush diverter located next to tank. Direct water from the first flush to a tiny rain garden or planted area away from the building.

WET SYSTEM WITH CLEAN-OUT DRAIN INSTALLED (AT THE LOWEST POINT IN THE PIPE RUN)

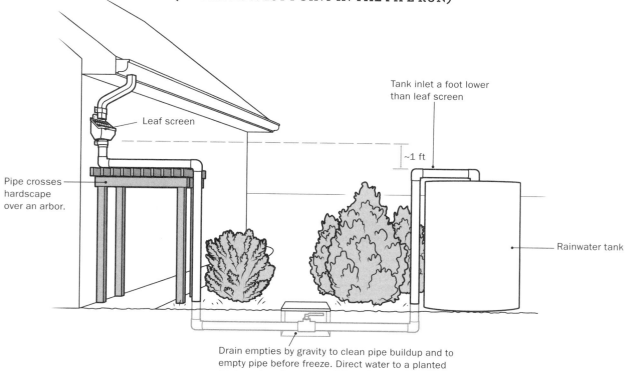

Tank inlet a foot lower than leaf screen

Leaf screen

~1 ft

Pipe crosses hardscape over an arbor.

Rainwater tank

Drain empties by gravity to clean pipe buildup and to empty pipe before freeze. Direct water to a planted basin or gravel seepage pit (not shown).

If your system uses a first-flush diverter, connect the other branch of the diverter's tee to the trunk-line and run it to the inlet of the tank. In a "dry" system, run the pipe in the air directly to the inlet; it can run in the air for a few feet so long as you've secured it to the house as well as to the tank inlet. Using drainage plumbing fittings, dry-fit the pipe and strap it loosely. After the pipe is in place, go back to glue the pipe and fittings and securely strap the pipe. (See pages 137 and 138 for tips on working with plastic pipe.)

In a "wet" system, run the pipe down the side of the house, as shown, then bury it or run it against a fence to the tank. Run it back up into the tank, supporting it as needed (it will be heavy when filled with water). Install a drain at the low point of the line to flush it, drain it for repairs, or empty it before a freeze. Consider creating a drip in the drain: this will empty the line a day or two after a rain.

Install the drain by placing a 3" tee at the low point in the line. Glue a 3" × 1½" reducing bushing into the tee, then glue a small section of 1½" pipe into the tee, and glue a 1½" ball valve to the other end of the pipe. Depending on your site, this valve may be subsurface; if so, you'll need to cover it with a valve box and create a basin to infiltrate the water. Keep the valve shut or allow a slow drip so you don't lose rainwater accidentally.

Note: Confirm your "wet" system has about a foot of height difference between the inlet of the tank and the gutter or downspout connection, to account for friction loss in the pipe.

6. Calm the inlet.

Many tanks come with a basket screen under the inlet: the screen diffuses the energy of the water falling into the tank and prevents the sludge layer at the bottom from getting stirred up. Make sure the overflow is lower than the screen; otherwise when the tank is full the organic matter caught in the screen can steep as if in a tea strainer. Another option is to calm the incoming water with a J-shaped inlet pipe. Run the inlet pipe down to the bottom of the tank and then curve it back up by attaching two long-sweep 90-degree elbows.

7. Glue and strap pipe and fittings.

Go back through the system and glue all pipe and fittings. Check that all piping is strapped and secured.

8. Install the overflow.

The overflow should be the same size or larger than the inlet pipe (if you have multiple inlets, it must be as large as the inlets combined). This prevents water from backing up and overflowing, potentially destabilizing the tank foundation or damaging the gutters, depending on where backed-up water would overflow.

The pre-installed overflow outlet size varies greatly among tank manufacturers. If the overflow is larger than you need, reduce its size. Some companies offer adapters with their tanks, so ask before you purchase. You may find the tank overflow is smaller than you'd like. For example, the tank comes with a 1½" overflow when the inlet is 3"; in this situation you can either use a fitting to bump up the size to 3"

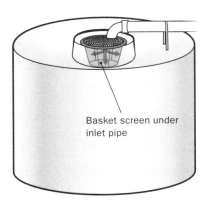

Basket screen under inlet pipe

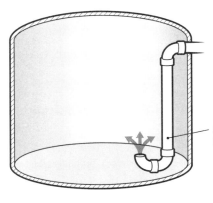

◀ **Two methods to "calm" inflow of water to prevent bottom sludge layer from getting stirred up. Keep the overflow lower than the basket screen to prevent the screen from steeping leaves and debris in the rainwater.**

Inlet pipe ends in a J-shape

(there will be a small reduction in pipe size, but this should be okay) or drill your own overflow and install a 3" bulkhead fitting. Plug up the undersized opening.

Assuming you have a 3" bulkhead overflow, screw in a 3" male coupling to the bulkhead fitting. Then, using 90 and 45 elbows, pipe down the side of the tank to a rain garden or other suitable location. Glue all connections and strap the pipe as needed.

See page 170 for information on moving water to a rain garden. Insect-proof the outlet of the overflow with a backwater valve in the horizontal position, or purchase an overflow with stainless steel screen installed (from suppliers of rainwater components).

Note that in most situations the overflow, as well as the inlet pipe, allow airflow out of the tank, so a separate vent is not needed.

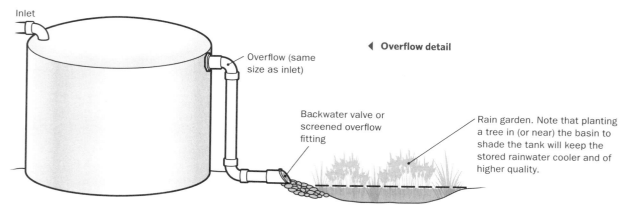

Inlet

◀ **Overflow detail**

Overflow (same size as inlet)

Backwater valve or screened overflow fitting

Rain garden. Note that planting a tree in (or near) the basin to shade the tank will keep the stored rainwater cooler and of higher quality.

Connecting Tanks Together

Multiple tanks can be connected at the top or bottom, similar to the way multiple barrels are connected. When tanks are connected at the tops, one tank fills up, then flows over into the next tank. Advantages to this method are that the water level is more obvious and the piping is less likely to be damaged because it's higher up. When tanks are connected at the bottoms they drain and fill as one unit, so only one overflow and one outlet are needed. Also, there is no need to switch the system over to another tank when one empties.

There are several design details to keep in mind when connecting tanks together:

- Connecting pipes between tanks must be large enough to accommodate the influx of water during a large storm, and may need to be larger than the inlet to account for friction loss in the pipe. If the pipe is undersized, the first tank could back up and overflow through the inlet. An easy way to prevent potential overflows is to place the overflow assembly for the system on the first tank, where water can exit harmlessly if the system backs up. Then, the connecting pipe size is less critical (though the system could lose water during large storms).

- Consider using flexible pipes between tanks to prevent leaks if tanks shift position.

- Install shutoff valves on each side of every tank to allow for isolating the tanks for repairs (and prevent the need to drain all the tanks).

- If the tanks are different heights, align them to avoid losing capacity in the taller tank. For example, a tall tank can overflow into the inlet of a shorter tank with no capacity loss, but if they were connected at the bottom the shorter tank would need to be elevated to the height of the tall tank to prevent capacity loss.

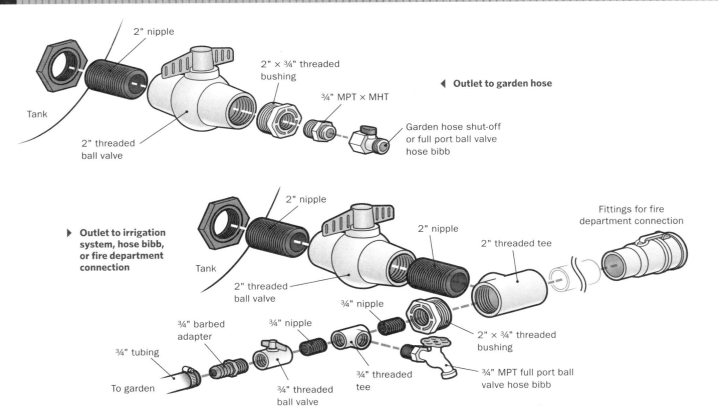

2" nipple

2" × ¾" threaded bushing

¾" MPT × MHT

◀ **Outlet to garden hose**

Tank

2" threaded ball valve

Garden hose shut-off or full port ball valve hose bibb

Fittings for fire department connection

▶ **Outlet to irrigation system, hose bibb, or fire department connection**

2" nipple

2" nipple

2" threaded tee

Tank

2" threaded ball valve

¾" nipple

2" × ¾" threaded bushing

¾" barbed adapter

¾" nipple

¾" tubing

¾" threaded ball valve

¾" threaded tee

¾" MPT full port ball valve hose bibb

To garden

9. Install a shutoff valve on the outlet.

Install a shutoff valve to the tank's outlet. Use a ball valve (so you can easily see if the valve is open by the position of its handle; don't use a globe valve), the same size as your tank outlet. The valve allows you to quickly shut off the flow if the irrigation system springs a leak. For example, if you have a 2" FPT outlet, thread a 2" nipple into the outlet, then thread a 2" threaded ball valve to the nipple. Thread a 2" × ¾" threaded reducing bushing into the ball valve. Now you can add a hose bibb to use with a garden hose by threading a ¾" MPT full port ball valve hose bibb to the bushing, or connect an irrigation system.

10. Check and test the system.

Go through the system and make sure everything is properly sloped, glued, and strapped. Then paint any exposed plastic pipe with latex exterior house paint (the same color as your house if you want the pipe to blend in). Place a hose in the gutter and run a flow test to make sure the system is working properly (if it happens to rain at the right time, you can let the rainwater help you run the test).

Maintenance for a Rainwater Tank System

Regular maintenance is critical to ensure a long-lasting, high-functioning system. Unless you get a maintenance contract with a local installer (which is a great option), you are responsible for changing filters, checking gutters, and promptly fixing leaks. Here is a basic list for maintenance:

- Clean gutters and screens annually or as needed, depending on level of debris in gutters.

- Drain pipe in a wet system.

- Inspect tank and foundation annually.

- Weatherize the system for the winter (depending on climate). See page 154, Cold Climate Considerations.

Installing a First-Flush Diverter

Consider a first-flush diverter in places with long, dry periods between rains, since more debris builds up on the roof. (If you live somewhere with frequent, light rainfall, a first-flush diverter system may divert too much water from your tank, as it empties between rains and must fill again before any water enters the tank. See First-Flush or Roof-Washing System on page 148 for more information on how these systems function.)

First-flush diverters are commonly installed immediately after the downspout screen, or adjacent to the tank. Small amounts of water will drain from the tube at the bottom of the diverter as it empties. Direct this water to an appropriate location — away from your tank's foundation and ideally to a planted area. All first-flush diverters, even self-cleaning types, will eventually clog and require maintenance. Locate your diverter where you will notice it and clean it out as needed.

SIZING THE DIVERTER

The capacity of your diverter depends on how large and how dirty the catchment surface is. Larger, dirtier roofs have more dirty water flowing off them in the first rain than smaller, cleaner roofs have. You'll need the following info to size the diverter:

- Potential height of the diverter pipe (measure from below the first leaf screen to 6" above the ground)

- The roof area that the diverter will be collecting from. It may be from the entire roof, or a portion if you're not collecting from all downspouts.

- There is debate among rainwater experts about how much water, if any, should be diverted. As a general guide, plan on diverting 10 gallons per 1,000 square feet of roof (0.01 gallons per square foot).

Steep roofs tend to get cleaned more quickly than flat ones, and roofs exposed to prevailing winds tend to be dirtier. If your roof is very dirty and you don't have much height for the diverter pipe, use a larger-diameter pipe, such as 6" or 12", to increase the capacity of the diverter, or install first-flush diverters at multiple downspouts.

Example: A 2,000-square-foot roof with four downspouts; one downspout is directed to the tank (2,000/4 = 500 square feet). If the roof is not too dirty, the diverter should hold 0.01 gallon per square foot: 0.01 × 500 square feet = 5 gallons.

Using the chart below, a 10-foot section of 4" pipe would hold 6.7 gallons; this is large enough. To be more precise, you could calculate the total length of pipe needed using the value for 1 foot of 4" pipe: 5 gallons ÷ 0.7 = 7 feet. If you're using 3" pipe, you would need: 5 gallons ÷ 0.4 = 12.5 feet of pipe.

CAPACITIES OF SCHEDULE 40 PVC STANDPIPE DIVERTERS				
Length of pipe (in feet)	3" pipe capacity (in gallons)	4" pipe capacity (in gallons)	6" pipe capacity (in gallons)	12" pipe capacity (in gallons)
1	0.4	0.7	1.5	5.8
3	1.2	2.0	4.5	17.4
5	1.9	3.3	7.5	29
10	3.8	6.7	15	58
15	5.8	10.5	22.5	87

DIVERTER KIT INSTALLATION

I've used kits from the company Rain Harvesting Supplies (see Resources) and from my local irrigation store. Diverter kits usually come in 3" or 4" sizes. In addition to the kit (sized for your installation), you'll need ABS or schedule 40 PVC pipe (sized to fit the kit), 2-hole straps for the pipe, glue for the pipe connections, and exterior latex house paint to protect the pipe from sunlight.

If you use a larger-diameter pipe, such as 6", use adapters to connect to the diverter kit. For example, to connect 6" pipe to a 4" diverter, use a 6" × 4" reducing coupling (plus a short piece of 4" pipe to connect the 4" side of the coupling to the 4" tee of the diverter kit, as well as another for the bottom portion).

The diverter relies on a small-diameter hole to drain the water between rains. If your system has clogging issues, consider installing a ball valve at the bottom to manually open and flush the line.

Here are the basic steps for installing a kit:

1. Connect the tee from the first-flush kit to the leaf screen.

2. Measure and cut the appropriate length of pipe. Keep a 6" space between the diverter and the ground for removing the cap.

3. Insert the reducing bushing into the tee, then insert the pipe into the tee (the reducing bushing prevents the ball from floating out of the diverter pipe).

4. Insert the ball into the pipe. Make sure it cannot pass through the tee.

5. Connect the bottom portion from the diverter kit to the end of the pipe; confirm that the ball is inside.

6. After all the pieces are in place, go back and glue them together using the appropriate glue for your pipes (either PVC cement, or transition glue if you are gluing dissimilar plastics).

7. Strap the pipe securely in place using 2-hole straps.

Note that commercial diverter kits use different types of plastic; some use schedule 40 PVC and others use triple-walled HDPE drainage pipe. Use the same pipe as the fittings in your kit are made from, otherwise they won't fit together. ABS, PVC, and triple-walled HDPE drainage pipe have slightly different dimensions, even if they are all labeled the same (i.e., 3"). Use the appropriate glue for the materials you are working with.

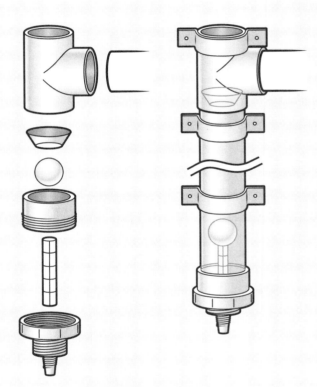

▲ **First-flush kit parts, separated and together**

Irrigation Systems

SHOULD YOU INSTALL a drip irrigation system from your rain tank, or should you simply water with a hose? An irrigation system can be a good investment to maximize use of the water in your tank. However, depending on your climate and landscape, you may find that your tank supplies only a tiny fraction of the irrigation required for the season. If your rainwater system is small and will empty after a few weeks of irrigation, consider hand-watering instead of installing an irrigation system. If you're not sure how large an area your rainwater tank will cover, review how to calculate plant water requirements in your climate on page 65.

Consider these options if you don't have enough rainwater to irrigate the whole landscape:

- Size the drip irrigation system so it will supply the entire water needs for a portion of the yard. For example, if a typical dry spell in your area is two months and you have 2,000 gallons of storage, you have 2,000 ÷ 8 weeks = 250 gallons per week available. If your climate requires 0.5 gallon per square foot, you could irrigate 250 ÷ 0.5 = 500 square feet of landscape with the tank. In the remaining landscape, plant native plants and use rain gardens to irrigate passively with the rain.

- Install a drip irrigation system for the entire landscape. After the rainwater runs out, disconnect the system and reconnect it to an alternative supply (the existing outdoor hose bibb).

- Design the system to automatically switch over to the municipal supply if you run out of rainwater. This is slightly more complicated to do and will require considerations for backflow prevention. Consult with a professional and your local jurisdiction for regulatory requirements.

Gravity-Fed or Pumped System?

The size and contour of your landscape will determine whether you can install a gravity-fed (no pump) drip irrigation system or whether you'll need a pump to deliver the water to the plants through a standard drip irrigation system. A gravity drip irrigation system can be connected to a rain tank (or large multiple-barrel system) so long as the tank is higher than the area you'll be irrigating. A gravity drip irrigation system requires no electricity and is easy to install. This system may not irrigate quite as uniformly as a pressurized system (for example, the emitters at the beginning of the line may receive a little more water than those at the end), but the difference shouldn't bother the plants. If your landscape is uphill (or very far away) from your tank, your system will need a pump. Pumped irrigation systems can use any standard drip irrigation parts, while gravity-fed systems are limited to low-pressure components.

Next I'll discuss elements of an irrigation system, for both gravity-fed and pumped systems. In most situations water from a backyard rain tank won't cover a very large landscape, so the discussion here is geared toward a small or medium-sized drip system that irrigates vegetables or small annuals. For more information on irrigating native plants with a rain garden and greywater for trees and large perennials see Planning and Designing a Rain Garden (page 163) and Choosing Plants for Greywater Irrigation (page 63). If you are installing an irrigation system for your entire landscape, or you're irrigating a lawn, consult additional sources (see Resources) to determine what controller, irrigation zones, and types of emitters are best suited to your landscape.

Elements of a Drip Irrigation System

Both gravity-fed and pumped drip irrigation systems have the same basic components. They can both use the same filters and the same main-line tubing, but the specific timer and emitters in the system may be different. Standard drip irrigation equipment requires at least 10 psi (pounds per square inch) of pressure to operate properly. Water gains about half a pound per foot (0.433 psi) of elevation. If your tank is 6 feet tall, the water in the upper levels will be around 3 psi, and the lower levels will be 0.5 to 0 psi. In a gravity drip system be sure to choose materials compatible with zero or very low pressure.

A number of online retailers offer supplies and kits to create drip irrigation systems, both for standard pressure and for gravity-fed (see Resources). You can also create your own system using irrigation components available from an irrigation store. The following sections discuss basic drip irrigation system components and how to choose parts that are compatible with a gravity-fed system. The basic components of a drip system include a filter, a timer, main-line tubing, and emitters.

Filters

All drip irrigation systems require filtered water — this prevents sediment from clogging the small holes in the emitters. If you pre-filter the rainwater, with downspout screens or a first-flush system, a simple irrigation Y-filter (150 mesh) should be sufficient for filtering the drip system. The filter is installed between the shutoff valve on the rain tank and the main irrigation line, and after a timer (if you use one). Many filters are not rated to be under constant pressure, so if you install one before a pump or timer you'll need one that withstands constant pressure. You can purchase a filter with either pipe or hose threads. If you find there is sediment or algae in the water, use a filter that's designed to remove whatever is in your tank; for example, disc filters remove algae. (Or improve the tank water quality by pre-screening, cleaning the gutters, preventing light from entering, etc.) Consult with experts at irrigation stores for advice on specific filter capabilities.

Note: These filters must be cleaned manually; check them after the first week, then every few months to gauge the necessary frequency, which could be once a year or less.

Mesh vs. Micron

Filter terminology can be confusing at times. Essentially, there are two different ways to describe the size of a filter: *mesh* and *micron*. Mesh describes screen filters and refers to the number of squares per inch on a screen: the *larger* the number, the finer the filter. Micron refers to the size of the particle that is being filtered out: the *smaller* the number, the finer the filter. Standard drip irrigation typically requires 100-micron filtration, or 150-mesh filter. Beach sand is around 28 mesh and 700 microns. Plant pollen is around 400 mesh and 37 microns.

Timers and Controllers

With a pumped system, you can use a conventional irrigation controller or any of the methods described below. Conventional controllers won't operate with the low pressure of a gravity system. To control the flow of water in a gravity system, the easiest and cheapest method is to turn the system on and off manually. This works great if you don't forget about it and run your tank dry! If you've ever left a garden hose running overnight, a manual method is *not* for you. A simple alternative is to use a wind-up manual timer, such as a Gilmour Single Dial ($20; see Resources); it's inexpensive and doesn't require any batteries, electricity, or programming. Just turn the dial to the amount of time you want the system to run and walk away. Another option is a programmable battery timer, which will turn the system on and off at designated times. A zero-pressure timer, such as the Toro Battery-Operated Hose-End Zero Pressure Timer ($40), can be programmed to run every day, every second day, or up to once a week, for a specified length of time.

Main-Line Tubing

Both pumped and gravity-fed drip irrigation systems use solid tubing (nonperforated; no water comes out) to deliver water from the tank to the landscape. Depending on how far away the plants are, this could be just a few feet, or much farther. Main-line tubing is typically poly tubing, either ½ or ¾ inch in diameter. Typically ½ inch is used for a flow range of 0 to 3 gpm (gallons per minute) and ¾ inch for a flow range of 3 to 6 gpm. Increasing the size to ¾ inch in a gravity system reduces friction in the tube. Emitters and drip tubing are connected to the main line.

Emitters

Many standard emitters require pressure from a municipal water supply or a pump to operate. There are several types of emitters that do work with low-pressure gravity-fed systems. The emitters slowly release water to specific plants, or they wet an area where multiple plants grow. Emitters are rated by how much water they release per hour (gph). Plants growing in sandy soils require more water released at a time, while plants growing in clay soils require less since the water spreads out more through capillary action in the soil. General recommendations are to use 0.5 gph emitters in clay soils, 0.5 to 1 gph in medium soils, and 1 to 2 gph in sandy soils. Your drip system may use two basic types of emitters: individual emitters that connect to the main line, or tubing with built-in emitters in the line.

There are three common low-pressure drip tubing methods to deliver the water to the plants:

To irrigate specific plants: Connect ¼-inch flow-control valves or "take-apart flag emitters" (the emitter has a flag-shaped component on top) to the main line and irrigate plants next to the main line directly with the valves, or add ¼-inch tubing to reach more distant plants. These emitters can be pulled apart for cleaning if they become clogged. Smaller plants get one outlet; larger ones get two or more depending on their water needs. These come in several flow rates (1, 2, 4 gph), although they won't flow at this rate at low pressures. Manufacturers often provide a graph of flow rates under different pressures for your reference; however, checking the actual flow rate (by putting a cup under the emitter) is important for determining how much water your plants will actually be receiving. Use the actual flow rate to determine how long to run the system to deliver the desired amount of water to the plants. For example, if you find the emitters flow at 1 gph, and you want to deliver 2 gallons to each plant, you'll need to run the system for 2 hours.

For closely planted landscapes: Connect ¼-inch soaker dripline (has emitters every 6, 9, or 12 inches) to the main ½-inch line. Water will drip out the length of the soaker dripline at the specified intervals. Check soil moisture with your finger to determine how long to run the irrigation system.

For the most even distribution at the furthest distance: Use non-pressure-compensating tubing with inline emitters designed for "dirty water." These are less susceptible to clogging and work well with low pressure. Some tubing, such as Irrig-GRAY, requires only 40 mesh (400 micron) filtration and spreads the water out more evenly over a larger area than do the previously mentioned methods, with 0.4 gallon per hour (gph) flow per emitter with just 1 foot of elevation (½ inch psi). This is also the most expensive method.

Designing a Drip Irrigation System

The first step to designing your drip irrigation system is to determine what plants you will water. Look for suitable plants closest to the tank — vegetables, annuals, newly planted perennials or trees that require irrigation to become established, etc. Drip irrigation is not suitable for lawns.

Determine how much irrigation water you have available on a weekly basis during the irrigation season, and how much your plants require. This can help you choose an appropriate area to send the rainwater to (review the overview of drip irrigation on page 36, and see page 65 for how to calculate plant water requirements.

You can create multiple zones by installing ball valves to control different sections of the system; the zones would be controlled manually. A more complex system with automatic irrigation zones requires further research (see Resources) and/or consultation with an irrigation specialist.

Make a sketch of your landscape, including the tank, where to run the main irrigation line, and where the emitters will go. (For ideas, see drawing on page 203.) A few tips:

- Try to make the sketch as accurate as possible, with lengths of irrigation tubing, as a base for creating a materials list.

- Use tees to run the main line in two directions, and use 90s to make sharp turns, such as going up into a raised bed.

- Run the main line as close to the plants as possible and keep the drip tubing lines as short as possible, no longer than 20 feet if you're using ¼-inch soaker dripline.

- A grid layout can help minimize the length of drip tubing, as can running the main line to the middle of the run of drip tubing, so the dripline tees out from the main line.

After you've chosen what area you'll irrigate, decide what emitter method will best irrigate the plants (see Emitters on page 200). You can order materials online (see Resources) or purchase them from a local irrigation store.

Now you're ready to install the system. For a gravity-fed system, it's a good idea to install a portion of the system and check it with the gravity flow to observe the distribution uniformity. For example, if you plan to irrigate five garden beds, set up two beds first, check them, then add more beds to the system if the water is flowing well. This will save you time and headaches if you find that water isn't traveling as far as you wanted. It's better to start with a small system and add on than to have to remove portions of a larger system.

Installing a Drip Irrigation System

You can install a drip system with basic hand tools in a few hours. Cut poly tubing with hand pruners and tap stakes into the ground with a hammer. Use a punch tool to make a hole in the ½-inch main-line tubing to insert the ¼-inch emitters or soaker dripline.

On a gravity system, you will install the irrigation system after the shutoff valve on your tank. You may wish to add a hose Y-ball valve so you can connect the irrigation system on one side and a garden hose on the other. On a pumped system, you'll first install the pump (see Using a Pump for Irrigation on page 204) and then the irrigation system. Depending on your pump type you may need a pressure regulator as well. Remember to wrap any threaded fittings with pipe thread tape and tighten with a wrench to prevent leaks.

Here is an overview of installing the main elements:

1. Timer (if used). Connect the timer after the tank shutoff valve. Wind-up and battery timers are typically connected with hose threads. Use an MPT-to-hose-thread adapter from your tank to connect the timer.

2. Filter. Many filters are not made to be under constant pressure; connect them after the shutoff valve or timer so they are under pressure only when water runs through the system. Connect a garden hose thread Y-filter (150 mesh) directly to the timer. If you are not using a timer, connect this directly to the tank, after the shutoff valve.

3. Main-line tubing. Use a ½-inch female hose start to connect the tubing to the filter (screw one side onto the filter and insert the other into the ½-inch tubing). Note that not all ½-inch irrigation tubing is exactly the same size — be sure to purchase fittings compatible with your tubing (and if your fittings will just not quite fit in . . . it's probably because you have incompatible parts).

Unroll the ½-inch poly tubing from the tank to the landscape. Trench and bury the tubing if you need to keep it out of the way; otherwise, leave it on the surface of the ground and stake it down as needed. Use compression fittings to make 90-degree turns; add a tee for branching off with another main line, or

FILTER AND TIMER SETUP

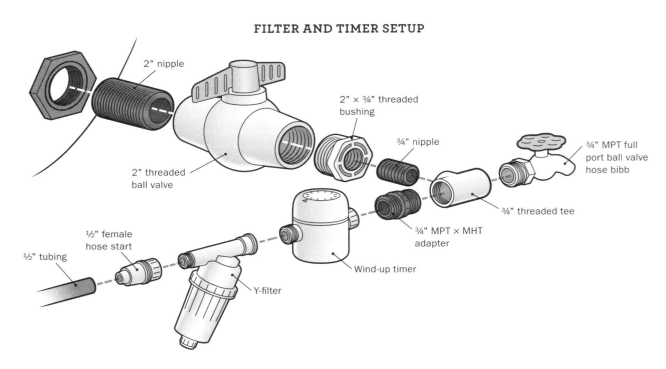

2" nipple

2" × ¾" threaded bushing

¾" nipple

¾" MPT full port ball valve hose bibb

2" threaded ball valve

¾" threaded tee

½" female hose start

½" tubing

¾" MPT × MHT adapter

Wind-up timer

Y-filter

a coupling to connect pieces together. Flush the tubing before connecting any drip emitters or capping the end to remove any debris in the line and prevent clogging of emitters. (A gravity-fed system will need to be temporarily connected to a pressurized garden hose to flush the line.) Close the end of each main line with a *figure 8 hose end* (this simple part kinks the end of the line to close it).

4. Add emitters. To insert a take-apart emitter, use the punch to create a small hole in the main line and insert the emitter. Place an emitter at the drip line of the plants you wish to irrigate. For ¼-inch soaker dripline, punch a hole and insert a ¼-inch barbed coupling, then attach the ¼-inch dripline to the coupling. Run the line next the plants to be irrigated, cutting the tubing to length. Close the end of

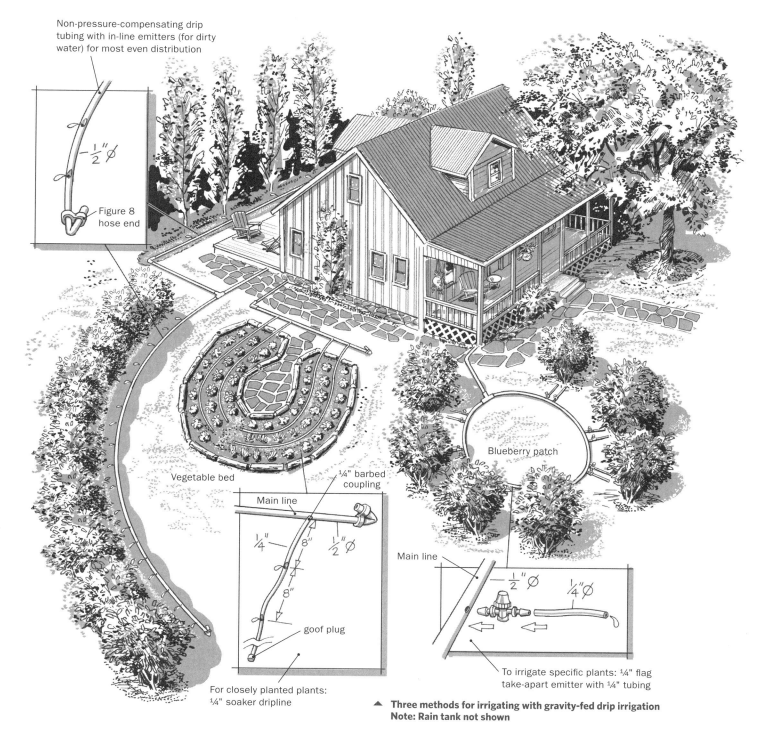

Non-pressure-compensating drip tubing with in-line emitters (for dirty water) for most even distribution

$\frac{1}{2}"\varnothing$

Figure 8 hose end

Vegetable bed

Blueberry patch

Main line

¼" barbed coupling

¼" 8" $\frac{1}{2}"\varnothing$

8"

goof plug

For closely planted plants: ¼" soaker dripline

Main line

$\frac{1}{2}"\varnothing$ ¼"$\varnothing$

To irrigate specific plants: ¼" flag take-apart emitter with ¼" tubing

▲ **Three methods for irrigating with gravity-fed drip irrigation**
Note: Rain tank not shown

the ¼-inch lines by pushing a *goof plug* firmly into the open end of the tubing. These small plugs are also used to seal up any undesired holes in the main line. Stake the dripline as needed.

5. Test the system. Send water through the system. Check for leaks and for even distribution of water. Use goof plugs to stop any small leaks from holes, and push tubing deeper into pressure fittings if they're leaking. If you have any barbed connections (where the tubing is pushed over a barbed fitting), add a hose clamp to prevent drips.

6. Mulch the landscape. Cover the tubing and emitters with mulch to protect them from sun and prevent evaporation losses in the soil. Don't bury any emitters with soil unless they are made for "subsurface" application; otherwise roots could clog them. Main-line tubing may be buried as needed.

Maintaining and Repairing Your System

A drip irrigation system typically requires maintenance about once a year. Gravity-fed systems require flushing of the lines, while a pressurized system probably won't. Remember to check your filter frequently after you install the system to get a sense of how much debris enters the system. Ideally the filter won't require cleaning more than once a year, but it may be more frequent if the water is dirty. Systems installed in freezing climates must be weatherized each season to avoid damage to equipment. Here's a standard maintenance checklist:

- Flush the system annually. In a gravity-fed irrigation system, debris in the lines settles and may cause clogs over time if not cleaned out. First check and clean the filter. Then, connect a pressurized garden hose to the beginning of the system. Open the ends of the lines and flush with water until the ends run clear. Recap the ends of the lines.

- Reconnect to the rainwater system and turn on the system, then check for leaks. Repair small holes with goof plugs. For larger breaks in the line, cut out the damaged portion and reconnect it with a repair coupling.

- With the system running, walk along the line and check the driplines. If they aren't flowing,

check for clogs and unclog or replace sections as needed. If a section isn't working, check for a kink in the main line. Cut out any kinks and reconnect the tubing with a coupling.

- Winterize the drip system: Plastic valves, filters, pipes, and fittings can be easily damaged if water freezes inside them. Before the first freeze, detach the irrigation system from the rain tank and drain water out of the filter and tubing. Bring the filter and timer inside. If your yard is sloped, make sure to drain the pipe thoroughly; you can install a drain-down valve at the low point or simply lift the tubing up to drain it. Depending on the severity of your winters, you may simply disconnect the system, or may need to bring parts inside for the winter; contact a local irrigation expert for recommendations. See page 154 for more on rainwater systems in freezing climates.

Using a Pump for Irrigation

Rainwater systems typically use an on-demand pump that responds to a drop in pressure in the supply pipe, either when you open a hose bibb or when an irrigation controller turns on an irrigation valve. These pumps are always ready, but only pump when water is needed. This is different from greywater pumps, which typically operate with a float switch and turn on based on how much greywater is in the tank.

Pump options include a submersible pump installed inside the tank or an aboveground pressure pump installed outside of the tank. Aboveground pumps are easier to monitor and service but are not an option for belowground tanks. A good-quality pump costs several hundred dollars but is a more economical option than replacing cheap pumps that break. More powerful pumps are not necessarily better: for highest efficiency a pump should be operating as designed and not be over- or underworked. Overly powerful pumps can heat up and become damaged, while pumps that aren't powerful enough won't supply sufficient flow and pressure for your system. Choosing a proper-sized pump reduces energy costs, maximizes the life of the pump, and reduces maintenance. Aqua Press (available from Rain Harvesting Supplies; see Resources) is one pump designed for residential-size drip irrigation systems.

How to Choose a Pump

Finding a pump for a small irrigation system from your rain tank requires thoughtful planning. Most irrigation systems include sprinklers that use many more gallons per minute (gpm) of water than a drip system will. Many standard pump experts aren't familiar with pumps suitable for a residential drip irrigation system supplied by an aboveground tank — they're accustomed to working with more powerful pumps. I've gotten the best recommendations from a company selling rainwater-specific parts.

Remember, you have to design the irrigation system before you can select the pump. There are multiple factors to consider when selecting a pump: after collecting site-specific info, you'll need to consult friction loss charts and pump efficiency curves. Or, collect information specific to your site and talk to a pump expert like Rain Harvesting Supplies (see Resources), an online store for rainwater parts, or a local rainwater installer and find out what pumps they recommend. They will use their spreadsheets and product specifications to find a pump suitable for your system. Before calling for advice, have on hand details of your irrigation system, including the size, material, and length of each type of tubing you'll be using, the total vertical elevation gain, and the flow and pressure requirements of your emitters (this will be provided by the manufacturer).

If you want to size a pump yourself, you'll need to collect the following information, keeping in mind that you can always get assistance for this part if it feels confusing:

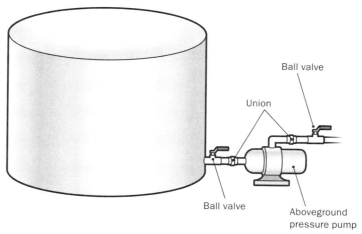

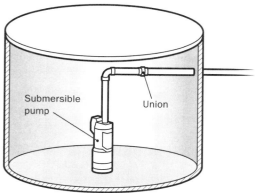

▲ **Rainwater pumps can supply pressure for irrigation systems or indoor use.**

1. Flow and pressure requirements of your largest irrigation zone (in gpm at × psi). What is the output requirement of the irrigation system? (The system will need to be designed to determine this info.) If you have multiple irrigation zones, choose the zone with the highest gpm and pressure requirements.

   Calculate both the pressure required to operate the emitters and the gpm required. Emitter manufacturers specify gpm under different pressures. For example, 100 feet of ¼-inch soaker dripline tubing puts out 80 gallons per hour (1.3 gpm) at 30 psi, but at 10 psi the same tubing would put out 42 gallons per hour. If the largest zone uses 200 feet of this dripline, the total requirements are 2.6 gpm at 30 psi.

2. Pipe friction loss pressure (in psi). How far will the main-line tubing travel (and what size of tubing)? For example: 100 feet of ¾-inch poly tubing. Consult a pipe friction loss chart to determine what the pressure loss (in psi) is of the design flow rate moving through the length of pipe from the pump to the farthest outlet. For example, 3 gallons per minute (gpm) (we'll round 2.6 to 3) moving through 100 feet of ¾-inch poly pipe will experience a pressure loss of 0.83 psi.

3. Vertical head loss pressure (in psi). How many vertical feet will the water travel from the pump to the highest outlet in the system? For example, 20 feet can be converted to psi:

2.3 feet = 1 psi, so 20 feet ÷ 2.3 = 8.7 psi.

Once these three variables are determined, perform some simple calculations to find the pump requirements:

Pump size (gpm) = flow of largest irrigation zone + 10 percent safety factor:

2.6 gpm + 0.2 gpm = 2.8 gpm

Pump size (psi) = pressure of largest zone + pipe friction loss + vertical head loss + 10 percent safety factor:

30 psi + 0.83 psi + 8.7 psi + 3.9 psi = 43.43 psi

Therefore, your system requires a pump that can supply a minimum of 2.8 gpm at 43.43 psi. (For larger, more complex irrigation systems, consult an irrigation designer for help with sizing the pump.)

Pay attention to details from the manufacturer when installing your pump; your situation may require a check valve, which prevents water from draining from your irrigation system back into the tank, or a pre-filter installed before the pump. Install ball valves and unions on each side of the pump to make it easy to shut off the water and remove the pump for servicing.

Convert a Swimming Pool to a Rainwater Tank

AN UNWANTED SWIMMING POOL can be a great receptacle for collecting rainwater. Mike Garcia, founder of Enviroscape LA, an ecological landscaping company in Los Angeles, California, converted a swimming pool to a 6,000-gallon rainwater harvesting cistern. See page 157 for a diagram of this type of system.

Here's how he did it: The pool was a typical backyard pool, measuring 12 × 28 feet. Mike and his crew started by adding a foot of sand to the bottom, then covered it with geotextile fabric. They used EcoRain boxes on top to fill the pool, then covered it with another foot of sand. A large pipe was inserted to house a submersible pump. The pump sucks up rainwater, stored in the air spaces in the EcoRain boxes, to irrigate the property's landscaping though a drip irrigation system. They built an attractive patio on top of the system. He used ProEco Products for the pipes, pumps, and rain boxes.

This was no small job — two weeks with a crew of eight. Labor was the main cost ($40,000 total, including $15,000 for the patio), and materials were around $10,000. Not cheap, but neither is removing a swimming pool or having a patio and landscape installed. Cost of pool removal alone ranges from $6,000 to $15,0000 depending on the size of the pool and the local permitting requirements.

Mike recommends getting professional help if you're considering a pool conversion. "Too many things can go wrong!" he says.

Waterless and Composting Toilets

COMPOSTING TOILETS ARE NOTHING NEW. From Africa to Asia, Europe to the Americas, our ancestors recycled nutrients without polluting the water. Multistory earthen buildings in Yemen, some of which still stand today, were constructed with built-in dry toilets. Europeans used an "earthen closet" before the "water closet" we are so familiar with today. China collected its "night soil" to fertilize the fields. Not all these practices were problem-free; without understanding how diseases spread, reusing unprocessed human feces transmitted illness, though the scale was much smaller than when water transports feces.

Nowadays, we understand how diseases are transmitted and can create safe and effective waterless toilets. In fact, they are safer than the municipal sewer system. When you compost your poop at home it's really hard for someone else to contact it, which is how diseases are spread. Toilets connected to the sewer treatment plant, prone to overflows, often flush untreated sewage into waterways where people swim, surf, and fish. This direct "recreational" contact with feces causes millions of cases of illness each year in the U.S. alone. Canada, Australia, and Western Europe face a similar situation, and even more sewage is discharged, with more illnesses, in poorer nations.

A waterless toilet is the single largest water-saving device you can install, though it is more than a device: it's a living, breathing ecosystem. Billions of microbes transform human excreta into nutrient-rich compost. As described by the composting toilet manufacturer Clivus Multrum, "the composter is . . . a forest floor in a polyethylene tank."

This chapter begins with a discussion of the composting process, then covers basic types of toilets, health and safety considerations, and how to determine what type of toilet is best for you. You'll then learn how to build a simple sawdust bucket toilet, a urine-diverting toilet, and a few types of composting systems.

IN THIS CHAPTER:

- Composting Is Composting
- Toilet Types
- Composting Toilets and the Law
- Using Urine as Fertilizer
- Choosing a Composting Toilet
- Building a Sawdust Bucket Toilet
- Building a Urine-Diverting Toilet
- Compost Piles and Bins
- Building a Barrel Composting Chamber with Netting

Composting Is Composting

A COMPOSTING TOILET uses the same composting process as a backyard food-scrap compost pile. Microbes and fungi break down organic material, be it food scraps or poop, into soil-like **humus**. The resulting compost is a valuable, nutrient-rich soil amendment and can be used to grow food or ornamental plants. The key difference between composting last week's dinner leftovers and the contents of this morning's trip to the bathroom is safety. Though the end result is healthy to handle, uncomposted feces may not be.

Isn't This a Health Hazard?

Some people believe human excreta is inherently disease causing, when it's actually not. You can't infect yourself or others with a disease you don't have. Though possibly stinky, the feces from a healthy person do not contain parasites, cholera, or dysentery. Regardless of the health of the people in your house, all composting toilets should be designed so they are safe for everyone and no one contacts uncomposted poop. Extra precautions are taken with public toilets and in places where many people suffer from fecally transmitted diseases and parasites.

There are several potential ways for diseases to be spread from a composting toilet (assuming someone infected with a fecally transmitted disease uses it): by direct contact with uncomposted feces (and then ingestion of feces by humans from unwashed hands, etc.); indirectly through **vectors** such as flies that contact feces and then food; and by ingesting water contaminated by the feces. Every type of toilet should prevent these possibilities. Always keep uncomposted humanure isolated and never allow leachate, liquid that has drained from a composting toilet or compost pile, to contaminate water sources.

A Safe Toilet

It's easy to make your toilet safe for everybody (except the pathogens). Follow these guidelines:

Keep out. Prevent people, animals, and flies from contacting the composting humanure. Outdoor compost piles should be enclosed, screened, or covered. Manufactured toilets have enclosed chambers built in.

Could Poop Be Good for You?

Even uncomposted poop has its benefits. Daniel Pomp, PhD, professor at University of North Carolina's School of Global Public Health, was asked, "Can you eat your own poop?" in an interview for the popular blog "Hey Science" on Gawker.com (February 21, 2013). He replied:

> "A big difference between urine and poop is that urine is sterile while poop is, well, you know, smelly and full of bacteria.
>
> "That said, those are the same bacteria that live in your gut and play many healthy roles in your body, so coprophagy [this means "eating poop"] is not necessarily unhealthy unless the poop originates from an unhealthy individual.
>
> "In fact, a recent article published in the prestigious *New England Journal of Medicine* showed that fecal transplants, where poop from one individual is infused into another individual's intestines, have performed better than regular antibiotics in treating certain bacterial infections that cause severe diarrhea."

Kill all pathogens. The composting process is unforgiving to human pathogens. They'll die from being outside of their human host, from the heat generated by the microbes, or from predation by other microbes (it's very competitive in a compost pile). Three months in even a low-temperature composting system is enough to kill all pathogens, except possibly worm eggs. Parasitic worm eggs, especially roundworms (*Ascaris lumbricoides*), die at a relatively high temperature; one day at 122°F (50°C) or one week at 115°F (46°C) will kill all pathogens including worm eggs.

Keep the microbes happy. The composting process needs:

- Oxygen for the aerobic bacteria. To prevent compost with a rotten-egg smell, provide the microbes with lots of oxygen; otherwise, their anaerobic counterparts will flourish, producing stinky sulfide and ammonia. Add a **bulking agent**, such as wood shavings, to keep the material loose and ventilated.

Word of the Day: Humanure

Human manure, aka *humanure,* contains valuable nutrients that if returned to the land reconnect nutrient cycles. The composting process renders any disease organisms in the material harmless, and creates a nutrient-rich soil amendment: high-quality compost.

- Moisture. Too much liquid will drown the aerobic microbes; too little will dry them out. The pile should be moist, not soggy or puddly. Add sufficient sawdust to absorb urine or drain it out of the composter to an appropriate location. Compost piles in arid climates may require additional water to succeed.

- Warmth. Different bacteria live at different temperatures and offer different levels of effectiveness. If the compost is too cold (below 41°F), little to no active composting takes place.

Bacteria Basics

Bacteria turn fresh humanure (and kitchen scraps) into safe and usable compost. Different types of bacteria dominate at different stages of the compost process. As they break down organic matter they release heat, which raises the temperature and enables other types of bacteria to thrive.

Psychrophilic bacteria typically kick off the composting process and live at temperatures between 42°F and 67°F. Their heat warms up the compost so the **mesophilic** bacteria, which live between 68°F and 112°F, take over. As the mesophilic bacteria decompose and release heat, the hot, **thermophilic** bacteria dominate. These live at temperatures of 113°F to 160°F. The high temperatures generated by the thermophilic bacteria kill pathogens as well as weed seeds. After these bacteria exhaust their food supply the pile cools, and the mesophilic bacteria finish the composting process.

Cooler compost piles don't get hot enough to render some types of parasitic worm eggs inactive, though other types of potential pathogens die in the compost process. If there is any doubt about the safety of compost from a cooler composting process, the finished product should be buried around ornamental plants or trees — not used in the vegetable garden. Or, it can be added to a hot compost pile.

Some manufactured composting toilets use heaters to raise the temperature and speed up the process. Other systems utilize a large outdoor compost bin to support thermophilic bacteria. The microbes generate enough heat to keep temperatures up, even in cold climates.

LIKE MAGIC: POOP TO COMPOST

First-time humanure composters can hardly believe their eyes at the first harvest. How is it possible that a composter filled with poop, toilet paper, and sawdust can turn into crumbly, earthy, pleasant-smelling compost? The magic makers are the microorganisms, bacteria, fungi, and actinomycetes. These chemical decomposers use enzymes to break down (and eat) organic matter, chemically altering the material. They release carbon dioxide, water, and heat to create **humus**, the stable end product.

A "Dry" Alternative

Bulking agents — wood shavings and other organic material for helping to oxygenate a composting toilet — are not readily available in some areas. Another method to safely process human excreta is with a "dry," or dehydrating, toilet. This waterless method does not compost; it dehydrates. In a dry toilet urine is always removed and is either evaporated, diverted into a container, or drained away to a planted mulch basin or constructed wetland. A mix of soil and ash or lime is added (not sawdust) to create a dry, alkaline environment inhospitable to human pathogens. Toilet paper, which will not break down, must be separated. Consider a dry toilet if you live in an arid climate and don't have access to wood shavings or enough moisture for composting (see Resources for more information).

Managing Leachate and Urine

Most composting toilets must manage liquid, either urine diverted before it enters the compost chamber or leachate that drains out the bottom of the compost chamber. Urine that is diverted from a toilet can be collected for reuse or directed to an evapotranspiration bed, a small constructed wetland. In places far enough from rivers, creeks, and drinking water wells, urine can also be directed to a small mulch basin with salt-tolerant plants growing around it to benefit from the nutrients. Because some nutrients may soak below the biologically active layer of the soil, it's important to consider nutrient contamination of the groundwater; not every location is suitable for this use of urine (see Prevent Urine from Polluting the Water on page 222).

Some types of composting toilets require a drain at the bottom of the compost chamber to drain leachate, as too much liquid can create anaerobic conditions resulting in bad odors and poor composting. This nutrient-rich leachate has an increased potential to contain pathogens because it has been in contact with feces and requires careful management. Some larger composting systems collect it, while most others drain it to an evapotranspiration bed where the nutrients fertilize plants (see Building a Urine-Diverting Toilet on page 233).

An Ultra-Low-Flow Option

If a composting toilet isn't for you, a low-consumption alternative is to combine an ultra-low-flow toilet with urine diversion. Install a 0.8- or 1.3-gallon/flush toilet (such as Niagara's *Stealth* toilet; see Resources) along with a simple dry urinal, which can be added to a bathroom with minimal effort. New products, such as *Why Flush*, a toilet water neutralizer, minimize odors when you practice "if it's yellow, let it mellow." Or, install a urine-diverting flush toilet, such as the EcoFlush Porcelain Urine-Diverting Toilet (see Resources). With this setup, solids flush to the sewer, while urine can flow to the sewer, a mulch basin, or evaporation bed, or it can be collected for fertilizer (see step 4 on page 235).

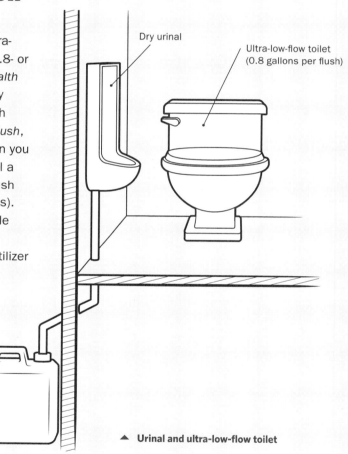

Dry urinal

Ultra-low-flow toilet
(0.8 gallons per flush)

▲ **Urinal and ultra-low-flow toilet**

Toilet Types

UNDERSTANDING THAT THE JOB of a composting toilet is to facilitate the natural decomposition process helps you assess the different types available. Keep in mind that all composting toilets interact with billions of living microorganisms, and there is no "flush and forget" option. **Note:** Costs and product models mentioned in this section are accurate at the time of writing and may vary.

A composting toilet system consists of four basic parts:

- Toilet, what you sit on; also called a commode, or a "toilet stool" or "toilet pedestal" by some manufacturers

- Collection chamber or receptacle, where the poop goes

- Compost location (pile, bin, or chamber), where the poop composts. In some toilets, the composting occurs in the collection chamber; in others, the two parts are separate.

- A management plan. Someone must be responsible for the system and understand what maintenance it requires. Usually one person in the household maintains the system, although some composting toilet manufacturers and installers offer a maintenance contract and perform the required maintenance.

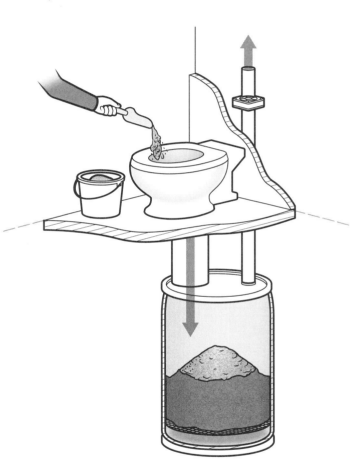

▲ **Simple composting toilet system**

Should I Turn or Inoculate My Compost?

If you've ever felt guilty for not turning the compost pile, you'll be happy to hear there's no need to. Turning a compost pile is a common method to provide oxygen, but there is an easier way. Just layer the pile with straw or other coarse material to allow air in and provide oxygen for the microbes. This is particularly important in a humanure compost pile so the process happens without the need to shovel uncomposted poop.

You'll also be glad to hear that inoculation is unnecessary. As Raymond Regan notes in the article "Approaching 50 Years of Compost Research," "No data in the literature indicate that the addition of inoculates, microbes, or enzymes accelerates the compost process." It would be rather unfortunate if we had to inoculate every fallen leaf and dead animal out in nature so they'd decay. The microbes that compost our poop are ubiquitous: they're always here waiting for their chance.

Composting Systems

Different composting toilet systems come with different usability and maintenance factors. For example, a person using a foam-flush toilet that is connected to a large composting chamber below may not even know they're using a composting toilet, whereas anyone using a self-contained toilet can look under the toilet seat and see the compost pile.

Micro-flush or foam-flush toilet. Resembling a standard flush toilet, this type uses a few ounces of water to "flush" material down a gently sloping pipe, enabling the compost chamber to be offset from the toilet (not directly below it). A vacuum-flush toilet is an option for sites that don't have space below the bathroom for the chamber. The toilet can flush the contents up to a compost chamber on the same level. These use more water and are more finicky than the micro- or foam-flush toilets, so they should only be considered if there aren't other options.

Self-contained systems. These toilets have all components in one unit. The toilet seat is directly above the collection chamber, which is where the composting process occurs.

Continuous composting system. The toilet sits on the floor of the bathroom and a collection chamber is located below the floor, often in a basement, where the material collects and composts. Finished compost is removed from the bottom of the chamber while fresh material is added to the top.

Batch system. The toilet is located above a collection receptacle, usually a bin or barrel. After it fills, the bin is replaced with an empty one, and the full bin is left to compost.

Urine diversion. A urine-diverting toilet seat separates urine from feces. A funnel-like portion in the front of the toilet directs urine through a tube to a separate receptacle or planted area.

Home-Built (Site-Built) Composting Toilets

Home-built composting toilets cost less and often function better than their manufactured counterparts. Unfortunately, if you need a permit, this may not be an option; most regulations currently require a toilet to be NSF-certified. However, some states are beginning to change this policy; for example, the state of Oregon now includes site-built composting toilets as a legal option. Oregon's "Reach Code" composting toilet section includes site-built toilets.

For a home-built system you need the toilet and a compost chamber or collection receptacle that is emptied into an outdoor compost bin or barrels. You can either build your own toilet or purchase one. A homemade toilet consists of a wooden box with a hole cut into the top for a toilet seat. Below lies the compost chamber or collection receptacle. Some toilet manufacturers make dry toilet stools, such as the SunMar Dry Toilet ($325; see Resources) that can

Eco-Toilets: An Alternative to Sewers in Falmouth, Massachusetts

Residents of Falmouth, Massachusetts, decided eco-toilets may be a better solution for their water woes than a new sewer system. Their primary problem is nitrogen: 97 percent of Falmouth homes and businesses rely on septic systems that discharge nitrogen, a nutrient pollutant, into sensitive coastal ponds and estuaries of Falmouth and Cape Cod. Falling out of compliance with the state's Clean Water Act, the town had to take action.

One proposal was a $600 million sewer system, far too costly for the small town. Instead, they are pursuing eco-toilets, both composting and urine-diverting (among several other strategies), and voted to fund a $500,000 pilot program to replace residential flush toilets with an eco-model. They're studying the rates of nitrogen reduction, as well as costs and regulatory barriers to wide-scale implementation of the eco-toilet systems. Many different types of toilets are permitted in this program (not just NSF-certified models) and approved by the Massachusetts Plumbing Board as an "alternative system." Homeowners and businesses who participate in the program receive a $5,000 subsidy for installing their toilet.

work well with home-built systems. Common home-built toilets include the sawdust bucket toilet and a batch toilet using 30- to 55-gallon receptacles (see below and page 217).

The Sawdust Bucket Toilet

Before spending thousands of dollars on a manufactured toilet, consider a sawdust bucket toilet. You'll save money (and possibly headaches) and can benefit from an active online support community (see Resources). This simple system consists of a toilet seat on top of a bucket to collect the material, and a large compost pile outside to process it. A sawdust bucket toilet is technically a collection toilet because the actual composting process happens outside.

After each toilet use, a scoop of sawdust is added to cover the poop and absorb moisture (urine). This prevents odors from escaping and flies from contacting the material. When the bucket is full, it gets emptied into the outdoor pile (typically once a week). The pile is then covered with straw to prevent odors and flies from creating a nuisance. The beauty of this toilet is that not much can go wrong. Any fly or odor problems in the bathroom can be solved in a minute, by removing the bucket and starting fresh. Problems with the composting system outside won't directly impact your life like problems in bathroom can. The solution to outside problems is to simply add more straw. See page 230 for instructions on building a sawdust bucket toilet.

I had used sawdust bucket toilets many times over the years — at cabins, outdoor parties, and workshops — but never in my own home, until recently. When we moved to Los Angeles I decided

Want an Instant Toilet?

For about 20 dollars, you can buy a "hunting bucket toilet" or "luggable loo" toilet seat that snaps onto a 5-gallon bucket. Or, place a free-standing "handicap toilet seat" over a 5-gallon bucket. Put a container of sawdust next to it, and you have a composting toilet. This is a great option for outdoor parties; just set up a privacy tent around it and make signs. Include a sawdust urinal option: a full bucket of sawdust with a toilet seat above it, and a "pee only" sign. It will hold several gallons of urine, around 20 to 30 uses, with no odor.

to install one in our apartment instead of replicating our former urine-diverting toilet. We don't need much urine to fertilize our garden plot here, and I was attracted to the simplicity of this toilet. It's been great so far: easy to use and maintain, with no problems.

Sawdust bucket toilets are used all over the country (and the world), in both urban and rural areas. They're used for seasonal cabins, permanent homes, and large gatherings. If you don't want to build your own, you can purchase a professionally made version for $225 (see Resources).

Pros: Sawdust Bucket Toilet

■ Low cost

■ Easy to build

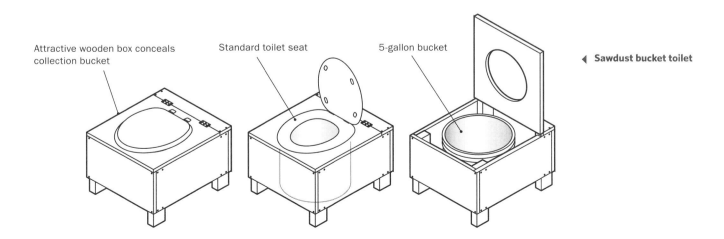

Attractive wooden box conceals collection bucket

Standard toilet seat

5-gallon bucket

◀ **Sawdust bucket toilet**

- Made from readily available materials

- Works in a large range of situations, from very urban to rural

- No breakable parts

Cons: Sawdust Bucket Toilet

- Requires someone to maintain toilet (empty buckets into compost pile)

- Requires source of sawdust and straw

- Requires space for a compost pile outside

- As bucket fills, the poop pile gets close to the toilet seat.

Ecological Sanitation

Ecological sanitation, or **ecosan**, refers to sanitation practices that protect the environment and human health and are affordable, socially acceptable, and regionally appropriate. Ecosan projects cover the globe and include thousands of urine-diverting dry toilets in Afghanistan, urine-separating toilets in German office buildings, use of urine in aquaculture in India, and wetlands for blackwater treatment in the Philippines. This movement is strong and growing, improving sanitation, protecting water, and recycling nutrients for millions of people around the world. See Resources for places to learn more.

Self-Contained Manufactured Toilets

Self-contained models are the smallest of the manufactured toilets. Common brands include SunMar, Envirolet, and Biolet. The toilet seat is directly on top of the composting chamber. A small amount of a sawdust-like bulking agent is added after each use. The humanure composts in the chamber and is removed once it has fully composted. The small chamber size limits the capacity, and these toilets can't accommodate increases in use (accurately estimating toilet usage is important in choosing a proper-sized toilet). Some versions use heaters to evaporate urine, while others are nonelectric and designed without heaters (and do not work as well).

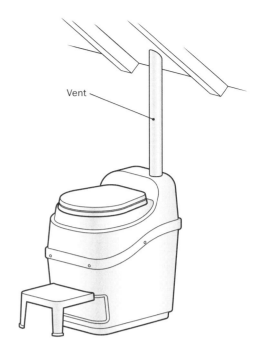

Vent

▲ **Small manufactured self-contained toilet**

Having a leachate drain is important for proper functioning of the toilet in case of a power outage or short-term increase in use.

In operating and maintenance manuals, even for toilets rated for full-time use, you find text directing users to remove compost more frequently when the self-contained unit is the primary residential toilet, implying you'll remove unfinished compost if it's your everyday toilet. If this toilet is used regularly, it may function as an expensive bucket.

Self-contained toilets are recommended for seasonal use only, such as in cabins. Do not attempt to employ them for year-round, regular household use unless you can remove partially composted material if the toilet fills up too quickly; in this case you'll need a place for the material to finish composting, like an outdoor pile. The cost for these toilets ranges from $1,200 to $3,300.

Pros: Self-Contained Toilets

- Small enough to fit in most bathrooms

- Easier to install than larger toilets

- NSF-certified models available, which are allowed by some states to replace a flush toilet

The First Commercial Composting Toilet: The Dry Earth Closet

The cholera outbreaks of 1854 converted the Reverend Henry Moule of Fordington, England, to dry toilets. After burying many people from his congregation, he linked the appalling sanitation conditions to the deadly disease. Sanitation of the time consisted of overflowing cesspools, and streams and rivers used as open sewers. Moule filled in his own cesspool and instructed his wife and eight children to use buckets instead; he buried the contents in the yard. After a few weeks he dug up the ground and was amazed to see the contents had transformed back into earth (and was an excellent fertilizer). This discovery led him to develop a commercial version, first patented as the "Moule Patented Earth Closet" in 1860. A funnel-shaped hopper full of sifted soil or ash released a small amount to cover each deposit. When the collecting bucket was full, the contents were buried outside.

Moule believed widespread use of his dry toilet would prevent the spread of disease. Others agreed. Moule educated and advocated for his toilet around the world. It was adopted by schools, hospitals, and army camps (used by 2,000 men every day). Even Queen Victoria used an earth closet at Windsor Castle. Moule's dry toilet competed successfully with the water closet (WC) until the end of the nineteenth century.

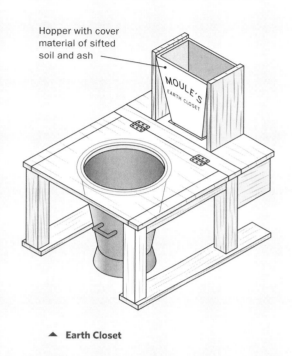

Hopper with cover material of sifted soil and ash

MOULE'S EARTH CLOSET

▲ **Earth Closet**

Cons: Self-Contained Toilets

- Small capacity

- May have odor issues if too much urine enters the toilet, if the vent isn't working properly, or if leachate builds up and the drain clogs

- Most require a drain for excess liquids.

- Most require maintenance every other day, such as turning cranks.

- Most companies want you to use their own products, such as a special bulking agent, compost inoculates, etc., for the toilet to function as designed ($25/bag is a typical price for proprietary mulch).

- Typically a low-heat composting process

Larger Manufactured Composting Toilets

Large-capacity toilet systems are designed to replace the flush toilet in a home. These systems have a large chamber below the bathroom to collect and compost the pee and poop. Vents and fans move odors away from the bathroom; heaters and leachate drains reduce the volume and speed the composting process. Some regular maintenance is required, but the chambers aren't emptied for months or years depending on the capacity. Larger systems can accommodate multiple toilets on different floors, either dry or micro-flush commodes.

With a dry toilet stool, the composting chamber is located directly below the toilet. With a foam- or micro-flush toilet, the chamber and toilet can be slightly offset because the small amount of liquid (a few ounces) moves the material down a sloped pipe.

The compost chamber is not visible to the toilet user. Foam- and micro-flush toilets look like standard flush toilets and don't require the user to do anything differently — they even flush.

Midrange toilets, like the SunMar Centrex ($2,000), are designed for regular use and require material to be moved from the main chamber to a "finishing chamber" every few months. These systems may require a leachate drain if there is too much urine entering the toilet, with the leachate draining to a safe location. Some people add a urine diverter to this toilet and drain excess liquid to a disposal or collection area.

A few companies design large toilet systems with sufficient capacity to serve homes, offices, and public bathrooms. These systems are an accepted technology in many Northeastern states and, in combination with a greywater system, can replace a septic system. Instead of a leachate drain to the outside, the system collects liquid in a separate container for annual removal. In terms of cost, the company Clivus Multrum has a complete system (including toilet) for $4,000 to $6,000; systems with foam-flush toilets range from $6,000 to $8,000. Another complete system is the Phoenix Composting toilet from Advanced Composting Systems, for $5,500 to $6,500.

Pros: Large Manufactured Systems

- Sufficient capacity to replace a flush toilet in a house

- Compatible with foam-flush toilets — feels to users like a normal flush toilet

- Often allowed with a permit in new home construction to replace a septic system (in combination with a greywater system)

- Installers may offer a maintenance contract.

Cons: Large Manufactured Systems

- Requires space for the compost chamber

- More expensive

- Some require electricity

Poop at the Zoo

If you visit the Bronx Zoo in New York City, make sure to go to the bathroom. Their sewerless public bathroom is equipped with Clivus Multrum composting toilets and a greywater system for the sink water. More than a half million visitors per year use the foam-flush toilets (6 ounces of water per use) and save over a million gallons of water each year. This bathroom was named New York Construction's 2007 Eco Project of the Year.

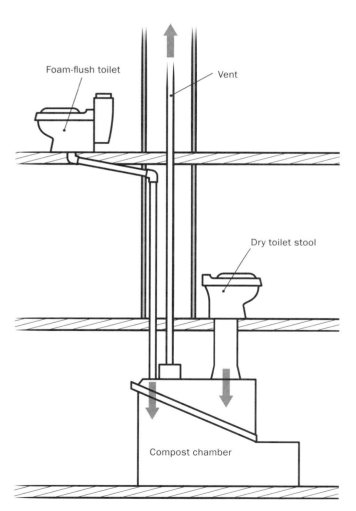

Foam-flush toilet

Vent

Dry toilet stool

Compost chamber

▲ **Large manufactured toilet**

Large-Batch Systems

A batch composting toilet system is another option for replacing the flush toilet of a home: it has unlimited capacity. In a batch system, the toilet sits above a collection container, usually a bin or barrel. Once the container fills up, it's removed and replaced with an empty one. The full container sits undisturbed until the material has fully composted, usually after one year. Batch composting systems can be home-built or purchased. Manufactured systems include a toilet with multiple compost chambers. Home-built systems often use 50-gallon wheelie bins or barrels for the receptacle. This method is low-cost and allows for endless capacity: all you need is more bins. Urine is often diverted or drained from these toilets to reduce the volume of composting material. Batch toilet systems are used in both residential and commercial applications. Home-built systems cost from $100 to $600 (using a manufactured toilet stool increases the cost). One manufactured system, the EcoTech Carousel, costs $3,000 to $5,000, not including the toilet.

Composting Toilets at Music Festivals

Large music festivals across Australia and the U.K. have bid farewell to the noxious portable chemical toilets. The Australian company Natural Event (see Resources) provides waterless, nutrient-recycling toilets that festival users love. (It is a batch system, using large wheelie bins for the collection.) Natural Event has operated at more than 240 festivals across six countries in the last 10 years. And, importantly, they have exposed hundreds of thousands of people to pleasant, clean, fully functional waterless toilets.

One U.K. music festival user reflects on Latitude music festival's forum, "'Twas a weekend of toilet extremes. I had one of the most pleasant poo's in ages at the compost dunnies [toilets] and then the scariest-ever poo by the main stage [in the chemical toilet]."

Pros: Batch Toilets

- Large capacity with multiple bins
- Easily able to accommodate more users
- Infrequent maintenance
- No management of unprocessed material
- Can be zero-discharge if there is no drain — container is watertight

Cons: Batch Toilets

- Require space below toilet for a container
- Require monitoring and occasional movement of a large container
- Typically a low-heat compost process

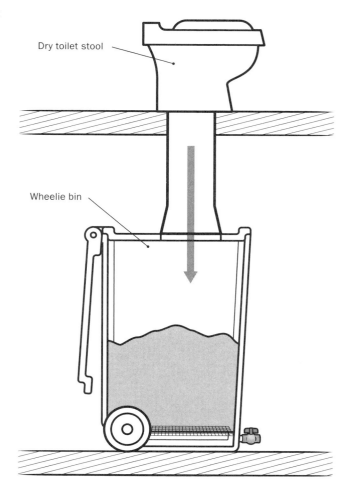

Dry toilet stool

Wheelie bin

▲ **Batch system**

Double-Vault System

Double-vault systems are very common internationally in places without sewers and include residential, commercial, and school applications. A double-vault toilet consists of two vaults, or chambers, located directly below the toilet. One chamber is used at a time: when the active chamber is filled, the toilet is physically moved over a few feet to sit above the second chamber. While this second chamber fills, the first chamber composts. Chambers are sized so they take a year to fill, each measuring about 3 × 3 × 4 feet. This low-maintenance system isolates the material until it's fully composted. The only regular maintenance is to rake down the "mountain" that forms in the center of the chamber. These toilets are often constructed as a separate structure, like an outhouse, but can be incorporated into new home construction or during a remodel. Urine is commonly diverted to reduce the volume inside the chamber.

Looking at cost, there are few examples of double-vault toilets in the U.S. If you build one yourself, the cost is for materials to build a small structure, roughly $400 to $600; professional installation might add $800 to $3,000 to the cost.

Pros: Double-Vault Toilets

- Simple design; no moving parts to break
- Low risk for contacting uncomposted feces
- Can be constructed with local materials, such as concrete blocks for the chambers, and with any type of bathroom above

Cons: Double-Vault Toilets

- Require a large space; not easily incorporated into an existing home
- Inflexible once constructed
- Typically a low-heat composting process

Urine Diversion

Urine-diverting toilets separate pee and poop. A funnel in the front of the toilet directs urine down a tube to a separate container; everyone has to sit down to pee (or use a urinal). Poop drops into a compost chamber or container below. You can purchase a urine-diverting composting toilet or make your own. Many of the composting toilet systems previously mentioned could incorporate urine diversion.

Urine is typically drained into a collection container, such as a 5-gallon jug, where it can be used for fertilizer or be added to a dry compost pile full of straw or leaves. Alternatively, it's drained directly to a mulch basin where it soaks into wood chips and is absorbed by nearby plants. It could also be diverted to a constructed wetland or evapotranspiration bed, a watertight planted area designed to soak up all the urine with no discharge.

Manufactured toilet options include Nature's Head or the Separett Villa, small toilets designed for boats, RVs, or cabins (see Resources). Pee and poo containers must be emptied regularly. The poop container in these toilets fills more slowly than in a toilet that combines urine, and it requires less sawdust, but it operates similarly to a sawdust bucket system in that it's a collection toilet — the composting happens elsewhere.

Alternatively, you can build your own toilet for a fraction of the cost of a prefab system. This is what

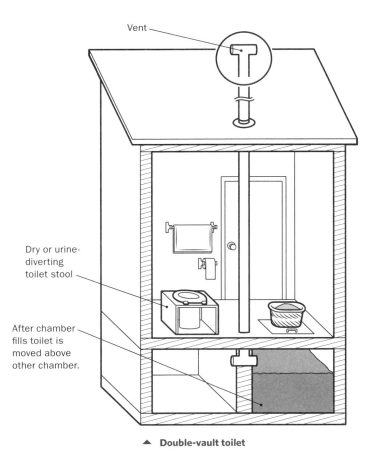

Vent

Dry or urine-diverting toilet stool

After chamber fills toilet is moved above other chamber.

▲ **Double-vault toilet**

▲ **Urine diverter**

I've done: I bought a urine-diverting insert, used a regular toilet seat above it, and built a small box under the seat to conceal the collection containers. These could be as large as 55-gallon barrels, but I prefer 5-gallon buckets. See Building a Urine-Diverting Toilet (page 233) for instructions on building a similar system.

Here are some options for materials and products you can use:

Make your own urine diverter, using a large funnel (such as a FloTool giant funnel, sold at automotive stores). Or cut the top off a plastic jug if you're on a tight budget.

Urine-diverting inserts, such as those from Ecovita or Separett. The Separett Privy Kit 500 ($100) is the standard diverter. It comes with a foam lid, but I put a regular toilet seat on top instead. The Privy Kit 501 ($160) comes with a more typical white seat and lid so you don't need to add your own toilet seat.

Dry urinal. A plastic urinal costs about $50 and is simply mounted to the wall. Direct the urine tube to a collection or absorption area.

Manufactured toilets, such as those from Separett Villa ($1,200) or Nature's Head ($1,000). Most elegant is the EcoDry porcelain urine-diverting toilet seat, made by Wostman Ecology ($600). This toilet

seat does not include the collection chamber, so you will need to purchase or build that yourself. The Eco-Flush porcelain urine-diverting flush toilet (Wostman Ecology; $700 plus shipping) uses 0.05 gallon for a urine flush and 0.66 gallon per solids flush.

Pros: Urine-Diverting Toilets

■ Urine is a valuable nitrogen fertilizer that can be used immediately without composting.

■ The poop composting requires less cover material (e.g., sawdust) because there is less liquid to soak up.

■ Separating pee from poo means there is less volume to compost and the chambers don't have to be as large.

■ Less chance of odor in poop-only compost chambers

Cons: Urine-Diverting Toilets

■ Quality of compost is lower in nutrients than when urine is also composted.

■ If you can't soak away urine into a mulch basin or evapotranspiration bed, the system will require two containers to manage.

■ Requires a small amount of education for new people to use the toilet

■ Can have odor issues with drips or urine spills if there is urine collection in the bathroom

Composting Toilets and the Law

THINK YOU'LL BE BREAKIN' THE LAW if you compost your poop at home? Not if you still have a flush toilet. The legality of composting toilets is typically only relevant for people building a new home and requesting an alternative wastewater system permit (the home will not have a septic system or be connected to the sewer). Some states allow composting toilets, usually NSF-certified manufactured types. (NSF International is an organization that tests products and materials to provide third-party certification. Unfortunately, NSF certification is expensive and cost-prohibitive for small companies.)

If you're building a new home and want an alternative wastewater system, be aware that most jurisdictions still require a septic or sewer option (in other words, the land needs to meet percolation requirements so a septic system could be installed in the future). Check with your local environmental health department for composting toilet regulations. You can always request an experimental permit, or volunteer your home to be a pilot project so the local agencies can study and learn about these systems.

In most cases, a composting toilet doesn't break the law (even when it's not explicitly allowed) if the following conditions are met:

1. You keep your poop at home. You can't transport human waste across property lines unless you are licensed to do so (like a portable toilet company). If you compost the material in your own yard, you are not breaking this law.

2. There are no restrictions in your area prohibiting backyard compost piles. (As a courtesy to neighbors, be sure not to create a nuisance with any outdoor compost pile, such as bad odors or attracting rodents.)

3. You have one flush toilet. U.S. regulations require every legally habitable dwelling to have at least one flush toilet connected to an approved wastewater system. If you have another bathroom, you meet this requirement.

The Wonders of Pee

If you're reading this chapter thinking, "I can't install a composting toilet where I live right now," consider a pee-only system. It is easy to do, urine contains most of the nutrients we excrete, and you can collect urine in almost any situation. Even with a full composting toilet, separating pee and poo may be right for you (see Urine Diversion on page 218). A urine-only system can be as simple as peeing in a yogurt container and walking outside to fertilize plants, or as formal as installing a porcelain urine-diverting toilet in the bathroom.

Urine is often separated in situations where:

- A full composting toilet is infeasible/unpractical.

- Urine is needed for fertilizer.

- An existing composting toilet suffers from odor or liquid issues.

- A waterway is being polluted by nitrogen/nutrients from poorly functioning septic systems.

Using Urine as Fertilizer

Urine fertilizer works wonders. Diluted urine has proven to be as effective as any commercially produced nitrogen fertilizer in backyards and commercial agriculture sites around the world. To start fertilizing, all you need is a watertight container, freshwater, and plants. Here are some basic tips and considerations:

Collection. Collect urine in a jug, urinal, or urine-diverting toilet. For best results, use urine soon after it's collected, or keep it in an airtight container. When it's exposed to oxygen, the nitrogen turns into ammonia and gets stinky.

Applying as fertilizer. First dilute the urine with a minimum of 3 parts water to 1 part urine before applying as plant fertilizer (8:1 is another commonly used ratio). Alternatively, apply undiluted urine before a rain or before irrigating. Apply to well-mulched (carbon-rich) soil to ensure your plants can access the nitrogen in the urine. Apply only to the root zone; never touch the plant with urine, especially the leaves.

When to apply. Apply urine according to the nutrient needs of plants. In general, plants require more nutrients during the growing season for leafing and fruiting. Once fruits have formed, plants generally take up few nutrients. Urine is particularly beneficial to nitrogen-loving crops, such as corn.

Some group households and small communities that fertilize with urine choose to follow World Health Organization (WHO) guidelines. (These guidelines were created for urine collected from the public to protect public health.) WHO recommends that the last application of urine fertilizer occur 30 days before crops are harvested when urine touches the edible portion of the crop (i.e., root crops or salad greens.)

How much to apply? Use fertilizing guidelines for your specific plants, if available. Otherwise, a rough generalization is that each quart of urine contains enough fertilizer for 6 square feet of crops for the season, or an adult's daily urine (1.6 quarts) fertilizes around 10 square feet of crops a season. Adding more urine is fine, but not too much more (up

Compost Toilet Pioneers Legalize Site-Built Toilets: David Omick and ReCode

DAVID OMICK (TUCSON, ARIZONA) and Matthew Lippincott, of the organization ReCode (Portland, Oregon), work to legalize site-built composting toilets.

David Omick has designed and constructed composting toilets since 1989. In 2005 he worked on rewriting Arizona's composting toilet regulations (with the state's Department of Environmental Quality, or DEQ). Currently, he's working on a pilot project studying site-built composting toilets in Tucson with the University of Arizona, Arizona DEQ, and local nonprofit the Watershed Management Group (see Resources for more information on the project).

What is your advice on changing state regulations regarding site-built composting toilets?

Changing composting toilet regulations is usually a long-term project, so don't be discouraged if you don't get quick results. Keep in mind that regulators are typically engineers, so approach them with facts, not feelings. Be friendly, not confrontational. Make clear that this is an effort you believe in, not something you expect to make money from.

The real regulatory action is usually at the state level, not the county or city level, so begin by focusing your efforts there. Before approaching regulators, do your homework. Read and understand the regulations in your state regarding composting toilets. Understand the public health and environmental concerns of regulators. Since regulators are more comfortable making changes based on precedents, find out what is being done in other states, such as Washington, Oregon, New Mexico, and Arizona [see Resources].

ReCode, a grassroots organization based in Portland, Oregon, works to legalize sustainable building practices with a focus on sanitation. ReCode successfully legalized site-built composting toilets, as well as non-NSF-certified manufactured toilets, in the state's 2011 Reach Code (a statewide code of optional construction standards for energy efficiency). Matthew Lippincott is a ReCode member.

What is your advice for changing composting toilet codes?

Regulators and officials expect you to complain. Their interactions with citizens are usually around complaints, whether reasonable or unreasonable. They do not expect friendly people who understand the topic, the jobs of officials and professionals in the field, or the complexity of change on a social, technical, and bureaucratic level.

Show up and be both a sympathetic voice for the problems of the current system and an honest and well-informed advocate for change. If you can offer real solutions to current problems facing your city/county/state, you'll find allies. We were able to put in the Reach Code because we found those allies in the Building Codes department, and made our case: the state only allowed a handful of composting toilets, and there were better designs out there. We were aiming for letting site-built toilets in, but also focused on how a site-built category would enable manufactured toilets that were from other countries.

The one-liner was "The King of Norway has a composting toilet in his vacation home, and that model is illegal to install in Oregon." This was the truth — the King of Norway's "throne" is an Ecotech Carousel, and someone had tried to install one in their home and been told it was against code because it lacked an NSF certification.

to four times, or so). Full-time, stay-at-home users will produce around 120 gallons/adult/year, which requires around 430 to 540 square feet of garden per person (assuming a three-to-six-month growing season). Like most fertilizers, urine contains salts, and too much may harm the plants. Areas with sandy soils or heavy rainfall are less prone to salt buildup in the soil than arid areas with clay soils.

Nitrogen content. The precise amount of nitrogen in urine depends on our diet; roughly 3 to 7 grams of nitrogen are in each quart of urine. Urine has an NPK (nitrogen–phosphorus–potassium) ratio of 10–1–4.

Prevent Urine from Polluting the Water

Nutrient-rich urine must be kept out of rivers, lakes, oceans, and groundwater. If your site is near a creek or river, use urine (and any fertilizer) sparingly if you fertilize plants. Or compost the urine (don't separate it) or direct it to an evapotranspiration bed (see Urine-diverting toilet on page 235).

Septic effluent, another nutrient-rich water, is linked to groundwater contamination across the U.S. and Canada. In La Pine, Oregon, elevated levels of nitrates found in drinking water wells originated from residential septic systems in the area. Since nitrogen contamination is both an environmental and drinking-water-quality issue, and aquifers are facing contamination from septic systems, it's important to make sure your situation is suitable for sending urine directly to the landscape.

Though urine is an amazing fertilizer, collecting and using it may get tiresome, which is why many users of urine-diverting toilet systems opt to send the urine directly outside. In many places this is a safe practice and involves directing urine to a mulch basin planted with salt-tolerant plants. The plants uptake nitrogen, while the wood chips used for absorbing urine remove excess nitrogen. Wood chips (a source of carbon) are employed in other applications to prevent nitrogen pollution, and have shown good potential to reduce nitrogen levels from contaminated rainwater runoff from dairy farms. However, specific removal rates vary depending on the site conditions (such as soil type or temperature), so more research is needed to determine whether this is a safe practice in an area prone to groundwater contamination. If you live in such a place, use an evapotranspiration bed to be safe.

Pharmaceuticals and Hormones in Urine

More than half of the active ingredients of medicines and hormones we ingest are excreted in our urine. Is this a problem for using urine to fertilize? Urine researchers wondered the same thing. Currently, wastewater treatment plants discharge these chemicals into waterways — a big problem for fish and amphibians that absorb them through their skin. But when these micro-pollutants are discharged into biologically active soil, they can break down. Oxygen levels in soil are around 50,000 times higher than in water, and widely biodiverse soil organisms are well equipped to break down various types of organic compounds. According to the report *Practical Guidance on the Use of Urine in Crop Production*, by the Stockholm Environmental Institute, "it is likely to be safer to discharge urine to soil, rather than to let it pass [through] the conventional [water] system."

Don't Need the Urine?

If you are diverting urine and don't need it for the fertilizer value, you can compost it or ecologically dispose of it. To compost the nitrogen-rich urine, add it to a high-carbon material, such as dry leaves, straw, sawdust, or cardboard, and it will compost the dry material. A lower-maintenance alternative is to run the urine pipe directly outside to an evapotranspiration bed or a mulch basin planted with salt-tolerant plants.

It's Not Rocket Science, But . . .

The first time someone uses a urine diverter they may get pee, poo, or sawdust in the wrong place (or feel anxious about it). Because of this, urine-diverting toilets aren't the best fit for high-traffic bathrooms or for use during house parties. When someone poops or dumps toilet paper or sawdust in the diverter and clogs it, the toilet quickly becomes disgusting, requiring immediate cleaning. My household learned the hard way about shutting off our urine-diverting toilet to party guests. It's no fun to leave your own party to

Urine Fertilizes the World

Research on using urine as a fertilizer for food crops is being carried out around the world, both in the lab and in the field.

- Sweden and Germany tested urine fertilizer on large-scale production of barley, finding it performed on par with mineral fertilizers.

- In India, field experiments found corn grew healthily with urine.

- In South Africa, small plots of cabbage, spinach, corn, and tomato were fertilized with urine. Plots with adequate urine fertilizer showed increased growth, but plots with excessive amounts of urine did not thrive, due to the increased salt content in the soil. Overuse of urine can salinify soil, as can overuse of mineral fertilizers.

- In Finland, urine was used to fertilize cabbage that was made into sauerkraut. Researchers evaluated plant growth, pest-resistance, chemical quality of the crop, and the flavor of the sauerkraut. They found urine performed on par with chemical fertilizers and crops were less likely to be damaged by insects. The quality of cabbages was similar between plots, and the sauerkraut tasted equally good!

The first authorized, public, community-scale urine recycling project in the United States is under way in Brattleboro, Vermont. The Rich Earth Institute has been collecting urine since 2012 and uses it to fertilize farmland growing hay. They are studying the effects of urine on the hay and soil.

OPTIONS FOR USING URINE

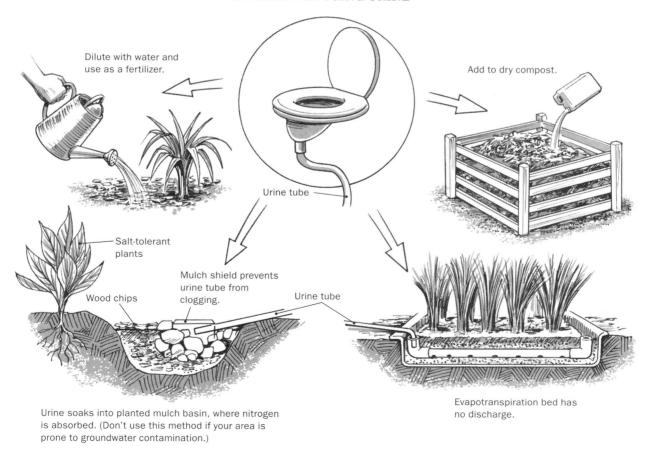

Dilute with water and use as a fertilizer.

Add to dry compost.

Urine tube

Salt-tolerant plants

Wood chips

Mulch shield prevents urine tube from clogging.

Urine tube

Urine soaks into planted mulch basin, where nitrogen is absorbed. (Don't use this method if your area is prone to groundwater contamination.)

Evapotranspiration bed has no discharge.

clean a clogged urine diverter. And importantly, everyone's first experience with a composting toilet should be positive.

Health and Safety Precautions for Using Urine

Urine from you and your family is safe to reuse immediately, as urine typically is sterile. Only a few pathogens are found in urine, including ones that cause tropical schistosomaisis (bilharzia) and typhoid (*Salmonella typhi* and *paratyphi*), which die outside of the body. The more likely health risk is from fecal contamination of the urine, which could introduce other pathogens. If you ever collect urine from a more public situation (house party, etc.) don't consider it sterile; make sure to "purify it" before reuse. This is very easy to do (especially for procrastinators); all you have to do is wait. Urine is inhospitable to pathogens; left alone, they all die. This takes six months (at 68°F) to a year in cooler climates. Always store urine in an airtight container to prevent nitrogen loss to the air.

Choosing a Composting Toilet

AS YOU RESEARCH COMPOSTING TOILETS you'll find many people happy and satisfied with their toilets, while others are unhappy and frustrated. The difference? Since a composting toilet is merely a place for microbes to do their work, all toilets will "work" under the right conditions. The unhappy people chose a toilet that's incompatible with their expectations and/or their situation. For example, if a manufactured toilet requiring a 65°F room with a leachate drain is installed without a drain in a freezing basement, it won't compost the poop and will produce a disgusting slurry. Or, if a bucket collection toilet fills up and no one empties the bucket, the toilet will be unusable.

If you're new to composting humanure, consider starting out with a simple system, such as a sawdust bucket toilet, to get accustomed to the process and how much work is involved. Your expectations may shift to the point where it's frustrating to find yourself pooping in clean drinking water when you're not at home.

Questions to Guide Your Toilet Selection

The best toilet for you depends on your situation. How many people will use it? What are the space limitations? What's your budget? Answers to these types of questions will guide you to an appropriate toilet.

Sizing

How often will the toilet be used? Daily? Weekends only? One week out of the year? Daily-use toilets have more liquid to manage. Infrequently used toilets, such as in a cabin, can be smaller and self-contained; the material can compost when the toilet isn't being used.

How many people will use it? Will this number be roughly consistent? Or do you host dinner parties? Systems that can handle fluctuations in users include batch toilets, sawdust bucket toilets, or larger manufactured toilets. Small, self-contained toilets installed where they're used year-round don't handle out-of-town guests or parties very well.

Logistics

What space constraints are there? Does the toilet have to fit inside the bathroom, or can the composting chamber be below the floor? Locate chambers in basements, laundry rooms, or utility rooms.

Is there a power supply? If not, you'll need non-electric models and may have leachate issues. Install a drain, divert urine, or install a sawdust-type toilet.

Is there somewhere to drain leachate safely? If not, consider diverting urine, using a larger system (that pumps leachate), or a sawdust-type toilet.

What materials do you have access to? Sawdust? Straw? Lots of dry leaves? Wood shops and mills give away sawdust. In much of North America you can buy or order it. In remote or international settings it may be more difficult to find; consider diverting urine or install a "dry" toilet (see A "Dry" Alternative on page 209).

Can the composting chamber be in a heated room? When the temperature drops, microbial activity slows. Can you install a vent from the chamber? The vent should run above the roof and will require drilling holes in the ceiling or wall to exit the house (see Ventilation on page 228). Sawdust bucket-type toilets don't require a vent, since the composting happens outside.

Aesthetics

Who will use the toilet? Just people you know well? Or does your home get a lot of visitors? Toilets used by people you know don't have to be "foolproof." For the others, it should operate just like a flush toilet minus the flush (no urine diversion), and could even flush, if it's a foam or micro-flush toilet.

Does the toilet have to look like a regular flush toilet? Or can it have the home-built aesthetic? If you require a small conventional-looking toilet, consider a Separett Villa (see Resources); it also requires outdoor composting, as for a sawdust toilet. Foam- or micro-flush toilets look "normal" in the bathroom and require a large composter in a chamber below.

Composting toilets that sit directly above a chamber may have an off-putting view into the pile. One solution is to light the room from below (lights low on the wall, pointing toward the upper walls) instead of the typical ceiling light, to minimize the view down the toilet; this changes the look dramatically.

Maintenance

Who will maintain the system? If no one on-site will maintain it, choose a system requiring infrequent maintenance. Large manufactured toilets with a maintenance contract are one option, as are batch systems with the toilet emptying into a wheelie bin.

If you're installing a toilet for your home, think deeply about regular maintenance and whether you'll tire of it over time. Small, self-contained toilets were designed for cabin use — not continuous use — and require a lot of maintenance to keep them working well in a home. Larger systems designed for home use cost more initially but have fewer maintenance needs. Maintenance for simple home-built systems is straightforward: you'll be emptying containers, switching containers, and monitoring the compost, but you'll never be picking dried toilet paper out of a crank arm, or vacuuming out dried feces that won't fit through a grate, like you might with a self-contained manufactured toilet.

After identifying a potential toilet, ask yourself, "What can go wrong?" Are there grates to clog? Drains to clog? Heaters to break? Cranks to break? And how will you deal with the potential problems?

Cost and Permits

The whole cost: In addition to the sticker price, systems have energy costs, replacement part costs, and maintenance costs. The more mechanized the system, the more parts you'll be repairing or replacing. The more electricity required for operation, the higher the energy costs. Systems with no moving parts, such as the sawdust bucket toilet or a batch system, have fewer surprise costs, as do larger whole-house systems that were built for daily use.

Do you need a permit? If you are building a new home, or doing a major remodel and want to completely remove the flush toilet, you may have trouble getting a permit for a site-built system. Often, only NSF-certified models meet permit requirements. (Oregon now permits site-built systems, due to strong community involvement; see Compost Toilet Pioneers Legalize Site-Built Toilets: David Omick and ReCode, on page 221, for tips on legalizing site-built toilets in your state.)

Special Considerations for Manufactured Toilets

If you are considering purchasing a manufactured composting toilet, be sure to do your homework. Companies use different methods for sizing toilets, and operation and maintenance requirements vary greatly.

Sizing. Find out how the company sizes their toilets. Most rate toilets based on the number of users, but there is variation in how many uses per day they use in their estimates. Some size the toilet based on three uses per person per day, while others allow for five uses per person per day (one poop, four pees). Most water companies estimate six uses per person per day. If you purchase a toilet rated for three uses per person per day and you use the toilet six times a day, you've exceeded its rated capacity by 100 percent!

Removing unfinished material. Ideally you'll never have to remove unfinished compost, but if your system is improperly sized or has technical problems, you may find yourself with the gloves on. Find out before choosing a toilet how easy this will be, especially for smaller toilets.

Check the specs. Critical information about manufactured toilets is in the fine print. Find out what temperature the room housing the compost chamber should be, whether a leachate drain is required, and what situations the system is designed for (cabin or household use). It's a good idea to request a copy of the operation and maintenance manual for any system you're considering (that is, before you purchase) and read all the fine print! General info on a website can be extremely misleading.

Get referrals. Seek out personal reviews from others who have owned the same toilet for at least a few years. If you don't know anyone personally, Internet forums and reviews can help. Users of composting and low-water-use toilets discuss their experience on forums for boats, RVs, rural living, and permaculture. In an online forum on Northern Arizona Wind & Sun, discussing the differences between heated and nonelectric small, self-contained toilets, one user wrote: "The issue with the nonheated units is that for more than one person, they can't evaporate liquid nearly fast enough. You then go to empty them, and instead of nice fluffy compost as advertised, you are left with a slurry of turd tea that is truly disgusting! (Sorry to be so graphic but the truth hurts!)"

You won't find that kind of info on a company website. A good way to learn about potential issues with a toilet is to search online with key phrases such as "problems with ____ (insert the name of the toilet you're considering)" or "nightmare ____"). Keep in mind that problems often arise from improper sizing, installation, or maintenance of the system, not necessarily from the toilet itself. And, of course, problems and nightmares are ubiquitous within our existing sewer system.

Best Options for Home Use

If you want to replace your home's flush toilet with a composting one, I recommend the following choices:

- Build or buy a small toilet and empty the contents into a large outdoor compost receptacle.

- Get a large-capacity manufactured toilet.

- Build or buy a batch system toilet that provides large capacity without the large chamber a manufactured toilet requires.

Compost Poop on Your Deck

Until the birth of her daughter, Steph Lind lived in a tiny studio with no bathroom, so she built a urine-diverting composting toilet using a Separett urine diverter, a 5-gallon bucket, and a wooden box (with a fan and vent in the box). Her poop bucket filled up about once a month when she was the only user, but the small pee container had to be emptied every day or two.

Steph composted directly into the 5-gallon buckets on her small deck. When the bucket was almost full she topped it off with soil, added a handful of worms, then planted into the soil on top. She grew peas, herbs, flowers, and beans, and only watered occasionally in the summer (there was no drain in the bucket).

After 10 to 12 months she emptied the bucket. "The soil was beautiful, black, delicious-looking, and earthy-smelling. This was always an exciting day, digging into the bucket and seeing how transformed it was. It was teeming with worms, even though I started each bucket with just a handful," Steph reflects.

Overall, Steph "loved" her toilet. The only problem was an annual fly attack. "Otherwise it was very easy, didn't smell, and made me happy knowing that I wasn't using any water. The worms were the best part, and the fan really helped since it was inside, making it easier for guests and relatives to use it without weird smells."

The main inconvenience of the toilet was having to empty the urine container so frequently. She wishes she could have piped it directly outside into the garden or a hay bale, but since the bathroom was lower than the yard, that wasn't possible.

And how did the poop-peas taste? "They were delicious!"

SYSTEM SELECTION SUMMARY

Type of system	Small self-contained	Sawdust bucket	Urine-diverting sawdust bucket or small urine-diverting manufactured toilet	Batch (site-built)	Large manufactured (for dry toilet or micro-flush toilet stools)	Foam-flush with large manufactured
Recommended for seasonal use	Yes	Yes	Yes	Yes	Yes	Yes
Recommended for year-round use	No	Yes	Yes	Yes	Yes	Yes
Accommodates fluctuations in use (i.e., lots of visitors)	Not well	Yes	Yes	Yes	Yes	Yes
Works well without leachate drain option	No	Yes	Yes	Maybe (requires the right design and mixing of the materials with a compost crank)	Yes, with liquid removal system	Yes, with liquid removal system
Looks "normal"	No	No	No (Separett Villa almost does)	Yes (if purchased with toilet stool)	Yes	Yes, even flushes
Cost range (excluding shipping and installation costs)	$1,200–$3,300	$25–$225	$150–$1,200	$100–$600	$2,000–$6,000	$6,500–$8,000
Likely to be permitted	Yes (NSF models)	No/maybe (may be allowed in places that permit site-built toilets)	No/maybe (may be allowed in states that don't require NSF-certified toilets)	No/maybe (may be allowed in states that don't require NSF certified toilets)	Yes (NSF models)	Yes (NSF models)
Visible poop pile	Yes	Yes	Yes	Maybe (strategic room lighting can minimize view of pile)	Maybe (strategic room lighting can minimize view of the pile; micro-flush toilets don't have a view)	No
Requires outdoor compost pile	Maybe (it depends on sizing and usage)	Yes	Yes	No	No	No
Requires more or less maintenance (than other types of composting toilets)	More	More	More	Less	Less (could be very little maintenance with a maintenance contract)	Less (could be very little maintenance with a maintenance contract)

As you review toilets, keep in mind that simpler often is better. Systems that rely on moving parts, built-in heaters, and other gizmos will be more likely to break down. It may be hard to believe, but a bucket, some sawdust, and a compost pile outside (with someone to empty the bucket) will perform better than all the heaters, cranks, fans, and engineered plastic you can buy.

Ventilation

Systems that compost in a chamber (not in a compost pile outside) require ventilation. The compost chamber is vented, either using a fan or a passive vent, to prevent odors from entering the bathroom and to bring in fresh air for the compost microbes. Small electric fans (12 volts is standard) pull air up a vent pipe, creating a negative pressure that sucks odors out of the chamber. Fans can be powered by a battery or a solar panel or can be adapted to plug into a standard outlet. Another option is a passive vent, typically a large black pipe running up to above the roof with a tee, or a wind turbine ventilator, on top. Air is pulled out of the chamber as wind blows past the tee. Passive vents don't work as consistently as active vents, and may not be sufficient for odor control, though this depends on the site.

Passive vents usually are 4- to 6-inch plastic pipes and are installed vertically without any bends. Vents with fans typically include 2- or 3-inch piping and are installed as vertically as possible, with no horizontal sections; it's best to use 45-degree elbows (instead of 90s) and run above the peak of the roof to prevent downdrafts (wind blowing odors down to ground level). Any exposed vent pipe requires insulation in cold climates.

Be aware that standard bathroom ventilation fans, which are designed to suck moisture and odors out of the bathroom, could potentially suck air and odors from the composting chamber into the bathroom — clearly not a desirable situation. If you ever experience odor issues, consider how other fans or airflows (e.g., from a chimney) in the home may be contributing to the problem. Potential solutions might include keeping the bathroom door open or closed, sealing the toilet seat with foam tape (to prevent airflow from exiting the chamber into the bathroom), or altering the vent itself (raise it, add a fan, etc.). To test for proper ventilation, place a stick of burning incense in the toilet and watch where the smoke goes; it should go out the vent, not into the bathroom. Most manufactured toilets require a fan to run 24 hours a day and come with detailed instructions for vent installation.

Shoo, Fly!

Flies in the toilet? If you have a batch system, empty the current receptacle and replace it with a clean, empty one. If you can't empty the receptacle, apply neem oil (found at nursery or garden stores) to the compost chamber; it's an effective and nontoxic way to deal with a fly infestation. Spray diluted oil into the receptacle daily. Install a fly trap to prevent future insect infestations (see page 237).

Composting Toilet Pioneers:

Carol Steinfeld and Joe Jenkins

CAROL STEINFELD is the author of *Liquid Gold: The Lore and Logic of Using Urine to Grow Plants* and *The Composting Toilet Systems Book*.

What is your favorite composting toilet?

Composting toilets are so context-driven that I don't have an all-time favorite. Of the high-end toilets, my favorite was designed by David del Porto and installed in a resort in Fiji. It consists of micro-flush toilets connected to a net-barrel composting system. The leachate and greywater drain together. The EcoWaters net barrel system could be installed anywhere, it's very adaptable, easy to maintain, and low cost ($400 for materials). And since it includes a "flush" toilet, it's easy for people using it to feel comfortable.

What advice do you have for people considering a composting toilet?

Be clear on your intent. If you're interested in living out ecological ideals, start by diverting urine. It's easy to do, very low in public health risk, and presents very few opportunities to "get it wrong." Urine has most of the nutrients we excrete, it's beneficial to keep them out of the wastewater stream, and it reduces the amount of flushing needed.

For composting solids, make sure you set up a good system that is easy to maintain. Keep it airtight to prevent odors, and make sure you like composting! Remember, a composting toilet is like a little wastewater treatment system; it will require some maintenance, which is very different than what we're used to with the "flush and forget" toilet.

If you're a contractor or work internationally and plan to recommend a composting toilet on a project, make sure you live, in your own home, with exactly what you are proposing other people have. You need to know exactly what is entailed in using and maintaining a toilet before you recommend it to others.

AUTHOR OF THE AWARD-WINNING *Humanure Handbook* (see Resources), Joseph Jenkins is a world-renowned expert on composting humanure. Joe is committed to providing quality information to the public; his entire book is downloadable from the Internet, he maintains an active forum for composters, and he travels around the world lecturing and consulting. He's currently working on a project to compost the humanure from 1 million people in Mozambique.

What advice do you have for people considering a composting toilet?

Realize that all organic material is recyclable and has value, including what typically goes into the toilet. It can be recycled pretty easily and be used to grow food. If someone feels apprehensive about managing a toilet, just do it! It's not hard or unpleasant to maintain these systems.

It seems to me the Humanure Handbook *method (the sawdust bucket toilet) is the most versatile and accessible of all the systems. Do you agree? Are there situations it may not be a good fit?*

I think the humanure system is the most likely to be sustainable and can be applied over the widest possible variety of situations, in the widest range of socioeconomic situations. Rich or poor can still use the same system. It may not be a good fit where there is no organic material to compost with, or if the culture does not have an agrarian lifestyle, for example in the desert or in the tundra. Other than that, there's no reason why it can't be used anywhere else in the world.

I think the future of composting toilets will look like our current system for trash and recycling. The user will fill the container, then set it outside where a trained team will collect and compost it off-site. We're doing this right now with communities of one to two thousand people in Haiti. The U.S. is way behind the rest of the world because of being out on a limb with the flush toilet. Other countries without flush toilets don't have to unlearn that mentality.

Building a Sawdust Bucket Toilet

E asy to build, easy to use, this sawdust bucket toilet can be constructed in a few hours using off-the-shelf materials. The design shown here is a classic home-built toilet: a wooden box with a toilet seat over the collection bucket, adapted with kind permission from Joe Jenkins (see Composting Toilet Pioneer: Joe Jenkins on page 229). Joe calls his version "The Loveable Loo" and sells it pre-made. There are many possible variations on this design, such as building the toilet into a bench, with a different size of container, or reusing an old toilet tank for the sawdust receptacle. You can find more design options in Joe's book, *Humanure Handbook* (see Resources). The classic toilet shown here measures 18" wide × 21" long, but you can modify the dimensions of the box as desired.

MATERIALS

Two ¾" × 10" × 18" boards (see step 1)

Two ¾" × 10" × 19½" boards

One ¾" × 3" × 18"

One 18" × 18" piece of ¾" plywood

2" screws

Four identical 5-gallon buckets with lids

Two 2" × 2" hinges with ½" or ⅝" screws

Four ¾" × 3" × 12" boards (or 12"-long 2×4s)

1¼" screws

One standard toilet seat

Wood finish materials (see step 6)

TOOLS

Circular saw, table saw, or handsaw

Drill with ½" bit and piloting bits (sized for screws)

Jigsaw

Flathead screwdriver or small pry bar

1. Cut the box materials.

Cut the sides, front, back, and lid support for the box as shown. You can use ¾" plywood or solid lumber for the box boards. Furniture-grade hardwood plywood looks nicer and is stronger than standard plywood, but it's more expensive. Cut the lid to size at 18" × 18" from ¾" plywood.

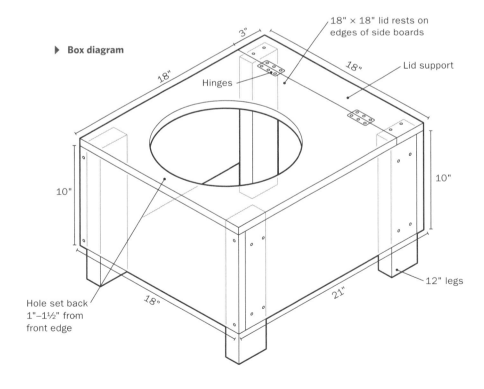

▶ **Box diagram**

18" × 18" lid rests on edges of side boards

3"

18"

18"

Hinges

Lid support

10"

10"

12" legs

Hole set back 1"–1½" from front edge

18"

21"

2. Assemble the box.

Fasten the box front and rear pieces to the ends of the side pieces with 2" screws, forming a box that's 18" wide × 21" long. Pre-drill the wood (with a bit slightly smaller than your screws) before screwing to prevent splitting the wood. Fasten the lid support to the top rear of the box, using 2" screws. Attach the lid to the lid support with two hinges and ½" or ⅝" screws (so the screws don't protrude through the bottom surfaces of the plywood). The lid will lift up on the hinges so you'll be able to remove the bucket easily.

3. Cut a hole for the toilet seat.

Cut a hole in the lid to fit the top of your 5-gallon bucket. Locate the hole 1" to 1½" from the front edge of the lid and centered side to side. If you set it too far back, the toilet seat may interfere with lifting the lid for bucket removal. Flip the bucket upside down and trace its top onto the plywood. Drill a ½" starter hole just the inside the marked circle, then use a jigsaw to cut out the circle, staying along the *outside* edge of the pencil line so the hole is slightly larger than the bucket. (The bucket will extend through the hole about ¼" to ½" when toilet is complete.)

4. Add the legs.

Cut the four legs to length at 12". You can use ¾" lumber or plywood or 2×4s for the legs. Mark the leg positions so that the bucket will protrude through the top of the box by ¼" to ½", depending on the height of your toilet seat bumpers (located on the bottom face of the toilet seat), so the toilet seat will sit flush atop the bucket. Screw the legs to the inside of the box, using 1¼" screws (or 2" screws for 2×4 legs), predrilling to prevent splitting the wood.

5. Prepare the toilet seat.

The preinstalled bumpers on the toilet seat must be rotated so they don't contact the bucket; the toilet seat will rest on top of the bucket, forming a snug fit. Pop one side of each bumper out of its hole (removing a screw, if necessary), rotate the bumper, and mark the location for a new hole. Drill the new hole, then set the bumper into its new position.

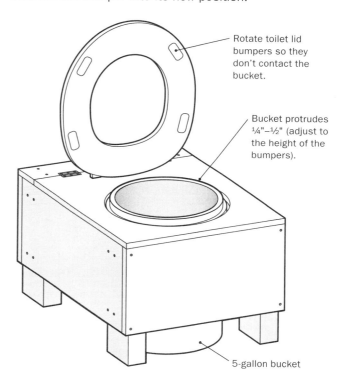

Rotate toilet lid bumpers so they don't contact the bucket.

Bucket protrudes ¼"–½" (adjust to the height of the bumpers).

5-gallon bucket

▲ **Toilet seat with adjusted bumpers**

6. Finish the box and install the seat.

Finish all surfaces of the box with a wood sealer, such as linseed oil, polyurethane (or other varnish), or primer and paint, and let the finish dry completely. Mark holes on the lid for the toilet seat bolts, drill holes, and attach the toilet seat with the provided bolts.

Using Your Sawdust Toilet

Before using the toilet, cover the bottom of the bucket with a few inches of sawdust. After peeing or pooing, place toilet paper into the toilet and cover with a scoop of sawdust, about one or two cups. If there are ever odors or unsightliness, add more sawdust. The layer of sawdust keeps odors out of the bathroom and keeps flies from getting to the poop. When the bucket is full, firmly attach the lid and either empty it or set it aside and replace it with an empty bucket. (We store our buckets, both full and empty, in the hall closet.) You may prefer to empty two buckets at a time, or have a "big dump" day with four or five buckets. In general, each person using the toilet will fill up one bucket a week.

Cover material. Use untreated wood sawdust. Joe Jenkins recommends moist, rotted sawdust from mill yards where trees are cut into boards. I can't get this in cities, so I use "kiln-dried" sawdust, available from woodworking shops (specifically from shops working with untreated wood, not painted or pressure-treated wood; call around to find one in your area). Dried sawdust is less effective as a biofilter for odor. Improve it by partially rehydrating it with water. (I've never had a problem using dry sawdust in my system, however.) Some people buy peat moss and mix it with fine organic mulch. Other options include rice hulls, grass clippings, and dried coffee grounds. If sawdust decomposes too slowly in your system, try leaf duff (shredded leaves) instead.

The compost pile. You will need a compost bin outside to empty the contents of the bucket into (see Compost Piles and Bins on page 239). Purchase a compost thermometer (see Resources) to monitor temperatures of the pile. Make sure to add all your kitchen and yard (weeds) scraps to the same pile.

Maintenance and troubleshooting.

Maintenance typically consists of a weekly emptying of the container(s), similar to taking out the trash and recycling. You may switch out containers more frequently depending on how many users there are, but with extra buckets you don't need to go outside more than once a week. Annually, you'll switch between compost piles and empty the decomposed one.

Cleaning the buckets. Wash buckets with water, lightly scrubbing with a long-handled toilet brush. Use biodegradable soaps and never use bleach. Dump the wash and rinse water on top of the compost pile — never anywhere people could contact it. Before using the bucket again, put a few inches of sawdust into the bottom. Don't want to wash out the bucket? Get biodegradable bags that can be tossed into the pile and decompose with everything else.

Dealing with odor. Anytime the bucket or the pile smells, add more cover material. Inside, add enough sawdust to absorb and cover urine so it doesn't smell. Some people mix essential oils into the sawdust for fragrance. See Resources for an active online forum with more than 700 composting toilet users and thousands of messages.

Variations on the sawdust bucket toilet. The concept of the sawdust bucket toilet can be scaled up to accommodate tens, hundreds, or thousands of people. More people means more buckets or larger containers. Have more than four people and don't want to switch out buckets so often? Use 10-gallon buckets, 30-gallon barrels, or 60-gallon wheelie bins. Build your toilet to fit over whatever receptacle size works for you. These larger containers will be heavy, so have a plan for moving them around.

Large containers can serve as the compost chambers and don't need to be emptied into a pile. Material can compost in place through a **moldering** or **warm composting** process (see Bacteria Basics on page 209). Simply set the barrel aside and come back a year later. It should be fully composted, provided you used enough sawdust. See page 239 for how to turn a barrel or bin into a compost chamber. With larger containers, consider diverting or draining urine, otherwise the material may need to be aerated with a compost crank or the bottom of the bin won't compost well.

If your receptacle is in use for more than two weeks, flies may become an issue. (It takes a week or two before flies pupate into adults.) Ideally your compost container is fly-proof, but realistically they will occasionally get in. See Shoo, Fly! (page 228) and step 6 on page 237 for information on fly traps.

Building a Urine-Diverting Toilet

Y ou can build your own urine-diverting toilet using a purchased urine-diverting insert (see Resources) or make one yourself with a large funnel. The optimum design depends on your bathroom, whether you have room for the collection chamber below the floor, how many people will be using the system, and how often you want to empty or change containers. Small poop containers, such as a 5-gallon bucket, must be emptied into a larger bin/barrel compost or hot compost pile for processing. Larger (30- to 55-gallon) containers can collect and compost the material as in a batch system, with no need to empty the containers. You can either collect urine to use as a fertilizer, or direct it to an appropriate area of the landscape. This section covers the general installation considerations and steps that you can adapt for your specific situation.

1. Assess Your Site.

Determine what size of collection containers you want and where they can be located. You'll need a poop container, and either a urine container or a system to drain the urine outside. Smaller poop containers, like 5-gallon buckets, are easy to empty and fit inside the bathroom, but they require more frequent effort. It typically takes two to three weeks for one person to fill a bucket. A 5-gallon urine container will take about two weeks to fill with one user. Any urine container larger than 5 gallons will be very heavy and hard to manage. Whenever possible, place the urine container outside of the bathroom to avoid messes inside the bathroom from an overflow.

Larger poop containers can be located below the bathroom and function as a batch system (see page 217 for more details on batch systems).

2. Choose a Toilet Configuration.

There are a few common toilet configurations:

- A 5-gallon poop bucket inside the bathroom with urine collection outside (to either a planted mulch basin, an evapotranspiration bed, or a 5-gallon jug). Construction for this toilet can be identical to a sawdust bucket toilet (see page 230), except the hole cut in the lid will be shaped to accommodate the urine diverter, as shown on page 234.

- Both 5-gallon (pee and poo) containers inside the bathroom. Modify the sawdust bucket toilet design to accommodate the extra space required for the urine jug. Locate the jug next to or in front of the bucket. Depending on where you locate the jug, the height of the toilet may need to be slightly higher than that of the sawdust toilet design to enable the urine tube to enter the top of the urine jug, as shown on page 234.

- Collection containers below the floor of the bathroom. Build or buy a toilet, and create a drop through the floor into the container. Larger containers get very heavy and must be easy to move; consider a wheelie garbage bin or similar container. If there is a drop between the toilet seat and the poop container, use a large tube (8" to 12" in diameter) to direct the poop and toilet paper into the container and prevent spills over the edge. A tube may not be necessary if the opening of the poop container is wide and the drop is short (see Batch System, page 217). You can either directly vent the larger container or build a box around the container and vent the box.

Building a Urine-Diverting Toilet *(continued)*

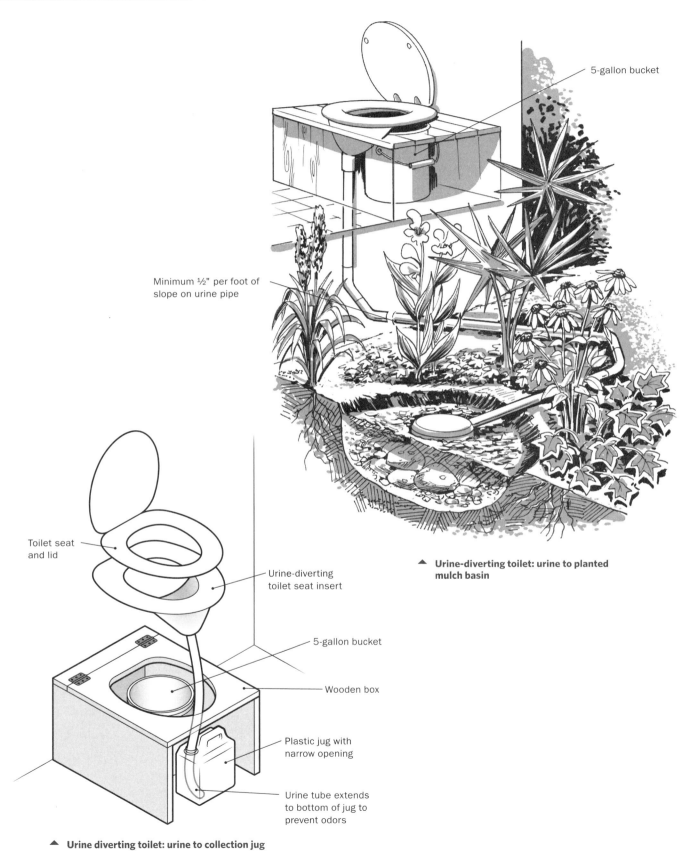

5-gallon bucket

Minimum ½" per foot of slope on urine pipe

▲ **Urine-diverting toilet: urine to planted mulch basin**

Toilet seat and lid

Urine-diverting toilet seat insert

5-gallon bucket

Wooden box

Plastic jug with narrow opening

Urine tube extends to bottom of jug to prevent odors

▲ **Urine diverting toilet: urine to collection jug**

Salt-tolerant water-loving plants

▼ **Urine-diverting toilet: urine to evapotranspiration bed**

Urine (or leachate) tube

4" perforated pipe with 90° elbows

Waterproof planter

Open pipe for ventilation

Gravel layer

3. Build (or Buy) a Toilet Commode.

Construct a wooden box to support your toilet seat. If the pee and poop receptacles are inside the bathroom, the box will conceal them (as with a sawdust bucket toilet). If they aren't, the box just supports the toilet seat. If your poop container will take longer than two weeks to fill, fly-proof the area to avoid an infestation. (The sawdust bucket system doesn't require fly-proofing because the containers are filled quickly enough.) Fly-proof the system by sealing cracks with silicone caulk, screening the vents, and adding foam insulating tape around the toilet seat lid.

Make sure it's easy both to remove the containers and to observe how full they are.

If the containers are below the bathroom, build a box to sit on at a comfortable height. Cut a hole in the floor below. Use a large tube or adapted bucket to direct poop from the toilet seat to the receptacle below the floor. Buy a wide (8"- to 12"-diameter) section of pipe, or use another bucket for a short drop

(cut off the bottom of the bucket) and paint it a dark color to help hide unsightly skid marks.

To cut a hole for the urine-diverting toilet seat, place the urine diverter on the top of the box and determine where the hole should be cut. Try to keep the toilet seat as close to the front of your box as possible so it's more comfortable to sit on. Trace a circle large enough for your diverter (manufactured diverters will have a template for you to follow). If you're not using a template, cut a circular hole under the toilet seat, leaving enough edge for the seat to sit firmly onto.

4. Attach the Urine-Diverting Insert.

Screw down the urine-diverting insert above the hole and attach a toilet seat on top. Attach the urine tube or pipe from the diverter to the container, evapotranspiration bed, or planted mulch basin. Diverter kits come with a 1" flexible tube that's long enough to send urine to a nearby location. If you'll be sending urine farther than the tube can reach, replace it with rigid plastic pipe, sized to prevent future clogging (scale tends to build up on the inside of the pipe). In most homes a 1" pipe is an appropriate size; however, if the pipe will be installed somewhere that is very difficult to access for future maintenance, such as running inside a wall or buried in a concrete foundation, use a 2" pipe.

To maximize flow of urine and prevent clogs, keep the pipe sloping down at least 1" per foot and use 45-degree elbows instead of 90s. Always use plastic pipe; urine is caustic and will corrode metal.

If you're sending urine to a planted mulch basin or evapotranspiration bed, make sure urine can drain freely and the tube won't clog. Use large rocks around the tube exit, or create a small enclosure (similar to a mulch shield; see page 98). Plant with salt-tolerant plants, as urine is high in salts. If you live somewhere where there's potential for nitrogen contamination of the aquifer or local waterways, use an evapotranspiration bed instead of a mulch basin (see Prevent Urine from Polluting the Water on page 222).

If you will collect urine in a container, use one with a narrow opening that has a removable, tight-fitting lid for transporting the full jug. Fit the tube snugly into the container, but don't make it completely airtight (or you'll need to vent the container). Direct the tube to the bottom of the container to create a seal of the freshest urine in the tube and prevent odor from rising up from the collection container. Or, create a "pee" trap in the tube by dipping down and then up, forming a U-bend before entering the container. This works much like a conventional P-trap in a fixture drain. The trap is self-cleaning, in that fresh urine flushes old urine out of the trap. The urine seals the bottom of the trap to prevent (much stronger) odor from rising up from the collection container.

5. Vent the Compost Chamber.

In most home-scale systems, you'll ventilate the airtight chamber that encloses the buckets or bins. If you're using large containers, such as 55-gallon barrels, you can either vent the container itself (for this to work, the toilet–container connection must be airtight) or build a box around the barrel and vent the box (this makes it easy to switch barrels as you won't need to disconnect and reconnect a vent pipe). You can ventilate *passively* (without a fan) by using a large pipe, typically 4" to 6" in diameter. A tee on top of the vent keeps rain out, and a screen at the bottom keeps flies out (screening the bottom rather than the top of the vent makes it easier to monitor or repair the screen). Alternatively, provide *active* ventilation with a 12-volt fan in a 2" to 4" vent pipe.

Customizing a Separett Privy Kit

If you're using a Separett Privy Kit (see Resources), you may want to use a regular toilet seat instead of the foam seat from the kit. Here's how to adapt the diverter so the toilet seat sits flush:

1. Remove the bumpers under the toilet seat.

2. Set the toilet seat flush onto the urine diverter; either cut off the plastic knobs sticking up from the diverter or drill holes on the toilet seat so the knobs insert into the seat.

3. Adhere (and seal) the toilet seat to the top of the diverter with silicone caulk.

4. Seal the crack between the toilet lid and toilet seat with foam insulating tape. Alternatively, you can remove the toilet lid from the seat and flip the lid upside down so it sits flush on the seat. Add foam for an airtight seal.

6. Fly-proof the Receptacle.

No matter how meticulously you seal off the area, an occasional flying insect will still get into the poop container. A simple insect trap can help prevent a single insect from starting an infestation. Use sticky fly tape, or make an insect trap as shown. The trap (designed by David Omick) consists of a transparent funnel inside a clear container. Insects are attracted to the light from outside and can easily enter the container through the wide portion of the funnel, but they can't easily find their way back out.

To create this simple trap, cut the top of a clear plastic bottle so it fits partially inside a wide-mouth glass canning jar. Screw the lid on the jar and insert the jar into a hole you've created near the top of the composting chamber. To be effective, the insect trap must reach a light source — flying insects will be attracted to the light and get stuck inside. Attach it to the composter (or the compost chamber enclosing smaller containers).

7. Add the Finishing Touches.

Finish the toilet box with paint, stain, or tile. If your collection containers are inside the bathroom, make sure it is easy to clean the floor in case of an accidental urine spill when you remove the container (or if it overflows). A large drain pan under the urine container works well. If the container is below the bathroom or outside, this is less important.

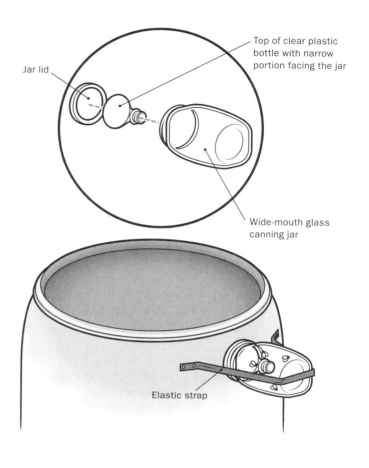

▲ **Insect trap**

Maintenance and Troubleshooting

Typical maintenance for a urine-diverting composting toilet entails emptying, cleaning, and replacing collection containers and cleaning the urine diverter. You'll also maintain a compost bin or pile, unless you collect poop directly into larger (30-gallon or larger) bins where it composts.

EMPTYING CONTAINERS

How often you empty the containers depends on their size and how many people use the toilet. Two adults using a 5-gallon container each for both the poop and urine need to empty them about once a week. Before emptying the urine container, make sure all urine is drained from the tube, then remove the tube from the container (placing the end on a rag to catch drips). Urine can be used to fertilize plants (see page 220) or poured onto an outdoor compost pile. Clean containers with biodegradable soap and a long-handled brush. Dump the wash water in an appropriate location (into compost barrel or a well-mulched area not accessible by people, etc.).

CLEANING THE TOILET

Clean the toilet with a sponge and biodegradable soap. Scrub the urine diverter regularly to avoid buildup of **struvite**, or urine crystals, which will harden on the diverter and discolor it (baking soda works well for this). Rinse the urine pipe with water weekly during cleaning (pour water down the diverter) to help prevent mineral buildup. If your urine pipe is long, has bends, or would be difficult to replace, clean it with citric acid and hot water every two months to prevent minerals from clogging the pipe over time. Dissolve three tablespoons of citric acid (available from grocery stores) in a quart of hot water. Plug the bottom of the urine tube, pour the mixture down the urine diverter, let sit for a few hours, then flush with a quart of hot water.

Maintain compost bins or barrels as discussed in Using the Bins (page 240) and Using Your Barrel Composter (page 243). Note that when urine is diverted the quality of the compost is lower, and it may be harder to maintain a hot compost pile than when urine is combined; this is due to the lower moisture content and reduced nitrogen levels.

DEALING WITH ODOR

Odor from a urine-diverting toilet often comes from the urine: a drip over the edge of the diverter, a leaky connection where the tube connects to the urine diverter, or an overflow from the container itself (when someone forgets to empty it). The easiest way to solve this is by keeping urine collection outside the bathroom, or, if you smell pee, investigate the source and stop the drip, either by caulking a leaking connection or by placing a sawdust-filled tray under the urine jug to absorb any small drip. If there is odor from the poop collection, add more sawdust or remove the container and replace it with an empty one.

Compost Piles and Bins

SAWDUST BUCKET TOILETS, or any of the small composting toilets, need a safe place to compost the material. One good option is building compost bins for a hot compost system — the most effective type for killing pathogens and creating good compost (from your toilet, kitchen scraps, and yard trimmings). Another option is to create a moldering, or *warm*, compost system using a prefabricated container or adapting a plastic barrel, solely to compost the humanure.

Hot Compost Bins

Build compost bins to enclose your hot compost pile. The discussion here involves wooden compost bins, but other materials can also be used, such as a large piece of wire mesh or corrugated plastic attached to itself to create a large circle. In arid climates, design the bins to conserve moisture. Locate the bins so they're convenient to get to, as you'll be emptying buckets there on a weekly basis.

The compost pile should not smell bad, although any hot compost, poop or no poop, may release some odor, particularly on warm days. A thick cover layer of straw absorbs these odors. The practice of layering the pile with weeds, grass clippings, and straw creates air gaps so the pile stays aerobic (anaerobic piles smell bad). Building a simple bin requires basic woodworking skills and can be completed in a day or two.

Gathering Materials

To create a hot compost pile, you will need two or more compost bins. The multi-bin system allows for the contents of the full bin to compost and cure while the active bin is being filled. Each bin should measure approximately 5 × 5 × 4 feet, with the smallest dimension at least 3 feet; this ensures the volume is great enough to get the thermophilic process going. If you live in an urban area or have concerns that rodents will enter the bins, use ½-inch galvanized hardware cloth to keep them out.

Basic materials you will need:

- Wood, such as wooden pallets, or 4×4 posts with 1×4 connecting boards

- Fasteners (screws or nails)

- ½-inch galvanized hardware cloth and staples (optional)

- Cover material for the pile: straw, grass clippings, etc.

Building the Bins

Wooden pallets are a cheap and easy material to build the bins with, but the lower-quality wood won't hold up for decades like a rot-resistant lumber, such as locust or redwood, will. Build the bins directly on top of the soil. Start by clearing and flattening the area underneath the bins. Use posts around the outer perimeter for attaching and supporting the board to form the walls. Or, if using pallets, connect the pallets directly to each other to form the walls.

To rodent-proof the bins, staple the hardware cloth to cover the inside of each bin, being careful to overlap the seams.

To create a lid, either construct a hinged lid or set a piece of chicken wire or hardware cloth wire on top of the pile (this is not rodent-proof). Cover the front of the bin with slats of wood. These should be removable so you can empty out the finished compost.

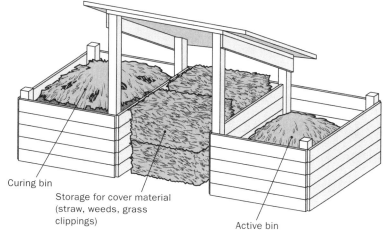

Curing bin

Storage for cover material (straw, weeds, grass clippings)

Active bin

▲ **Three-bin compost system made from wood**

Using the Bins

Dig a slight depression in the middle of the bin, placing the soil around the walls of the bin so that the soil level is highest around the edges and dips down in the center. This will direct any excess liquid into the center and prevent runoff. Next, put a thick "sponge layer" of straw, grass, weeds, etc. to soak up liquids in the pile, at least 18" deep. Now the pile is ready.

Note: If you construct the bins over a nonpermeable area, place a waterproof membrane, such as a pond liner, at the bottom and slightly up the sides of the bins to prevent leachate runoff. Ensure the sponge layer is very thick, and cover the pile in rain.

Empty buckets of fresh humanure into the center of the pile, then cover with a 6" to 12" layer of straw. If you ever see or smell urine or poop, add more straw on top.

Also add all your kitchen and yard compost to the pile, including bread, cheese, meat, weeds, etc. The heat of the pile will kill weed seeds and compost everything from your kitchen. Layer the pile with straw and weeds as you use it to maintain airflow throughout. You won't need to turn or mix the pile if it's layered with straw.

For subsequent bucket emptying, rake away the cover material, dig an indentation into the center of the pile where the compost is the hottest, and dump the bucket. Add more cover material. Always add fresh humanure into the hottest center of the pile. When you dig the depression in the center to empty full buckets, you'll be slowly pushing material toward the sides of the bin.

After one pile fills up, move to the second. Let the first pile finish composting untouched. Do not turn or stir the pile. Cover the pile in heavy rains if water could drain out of the pile. Let it sit for one year undisturbed, then use the compost. In places without freezing winters, this time can be reduced since microorganisms are active year-round. If the pile doesn't heat up or you know there are pathogens in the pile (for example, someone with parasites used the toilet), wait longer (two years) or bury the material near ornamental plants to be safe.

Cold-Climate Considerations

Compost all winter long, even in freezing climates. If the pile freezes, it will heat up again in the spring, and many hot composts keep cooking throughout a cold winter. Humanure composters from freezing climates, like Alaska, share that even after weeks of below-zero weather their active compost bin stays toasty warm (over 110°F). Other cold-climate composters report

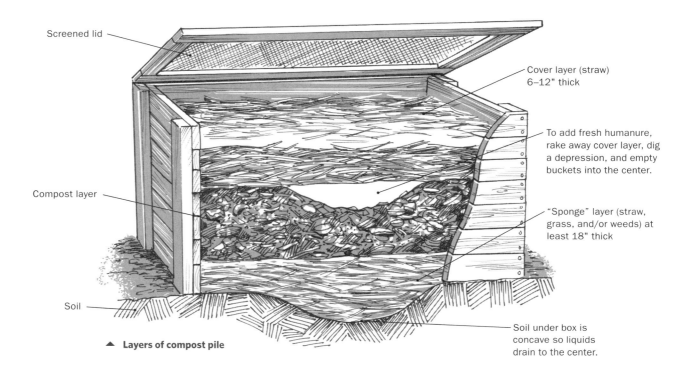

Screened lid

Cover layer (straw) 6–12" thick

To add fresh humanure, rake away cover layer, dig a depression, and empty buckets into the center.

Compost layer

"Sponge" layer (straw, grass, and/or weeds) at least 18" thick

Soil

Soil under box is concave so liquids drain to the center.

▲ **Layers of compost pile**

their piles do freeze in the winter, but it's not a problem. They add material all winter long, and in spring the pile quickly thaws and heats up again.

Warm Composting (Moldering)

Batch composting systems often use a large barrel or wheelie bin for the compost receptacle. Smaller-scale systems, such as a sawdust bucket toilet, also can employ barrels for composting instead of a hot pile; you empty the buckets into the barrel (55-gallon barrels are easy to convert and use). The process inside the bin will be a warm compost, with less heat than in a larger pile. In this environment, most pathogens die within three months, although worm eggs may not (see Bacteria Basics on page 209). Batch compost containers typically require one year to fully process the material.

Pros: Bin/Barrel Composting

- Easy to construct

- Easy to create more capacity as needed

- Smaller than a compost bin; fits in more locations, such against a house or in the garage

- In a batch system, barrel can directly collect feces, eliminating the need to empty a smaller container into it.

Cons: Bin/Barrel Composting

- Process may not kill ascaris eggs (roundworm). If users are infected or you are uncertain, use the compost for ornamental plants or around fruit trees (not in the veggie garden).

- Unless urine is separated, receptacle may fill quickly.

- Flies can be a problem — when you don't use fly traps; see Shoo, Fly! (page 228) and step 6 on page 237.

- Heavy when full, not easy to move

- May need to mix contents, or use a net, to prevent anaerobic conditions in the bottom of the barrel

- If urine isn't diverted, the barrel may require a leachate drain (or more frequent mixing) to prevent anaerobic conditions.

Sizing a Barrel System

If you will divert or drain urine, you'll need about:

- 2 barrels for 1 adult

- 3 barrels for 2 adults

- 4 barrels for 3 adults

- 5 barrels for 5 adults

If you don't divert urine or drain leachate, you'll need approximately twice as many barrels (and frequent mixing of the contents). The beauty of this system is that if the barrels fill up too quickly, you just get another.

Mixing and Netting

Composting in a plastic barrel typically requires you to regularly mix the contents or to hang a net in the barrel to increase airflow around the contents. Without a net or mixing, the lower layers of the contents will become anaerobic and not compost properly. The project on the next page shows how to hang a net in your barrel. Alternatively, you can purchase a "compost crank" for about $50 (see Resources) to mix the contents every few weeks. A compost crank is like a long corkscrew that you screw down and lift up, with minimal effort and no direct contact with the material. Note that the volume available for composting is reduced with a net, but using one means you don't need to mix the material.

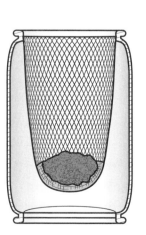 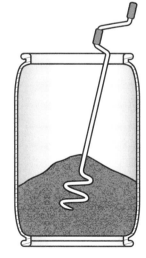

▲ **Two methods to keep barrel contents aerobic: net or compost crank**

Building a Barrel Composting Chamber with Netting

Large plastic barrels are easy to convert for composting humanure. These barrels can be located next to the house, behind the garage, or even inside a shed or garage. Find repurposable barrels at local breweries, bakeries, or online classified ad sites, or buy them new at home improvement stores. Hanging netting inside the barrel helps prevent anaerobic conditions at the bottom, which means you don't need to aerate using a compost crank.

Note that you can either locate the barrel outside and empty buckets of fresh humanure into it from a bucket system, or place it below the toilet, as in a batch system, to directly collect poop for composting.

A drain at the bottom of the barrel is optional, but is recommended if you will not be diverting urine or if there is any chance rain could enter accidentally. It's helpful to have an easy way to remove excess liquid. If you add a drain, you'll need to protect the outlet so it doesn't clog. Remember to treat leachate draining from a barrel with care and handle it responsibly. Either compost it with sawdust or drain it to an evapotranspiration bed (see Prevent Urine from Polluting the Water on page 222).

MATERIALS
One plastic barrel (30 to 55 gallons)
Supplies for optional drain:
1" bulkhead fitting
1" threaded plastic nipple
1" threaded ball valve
Pipe thread tape
Nylon net
Nylon rope
Screen (20 mesh or finer)
Elastic cord (for closed-top barrel; see step 3)
Silicone caulk
Corrugated fiberglass roofing and a few bricks (see step 3)
Burlap or cardboard

TOOLS
Drill and bits
Hole saw (for optional drain; sized for 1" bulkhead fitting)
Jigsaw
Staple gun
Adjustable wrench
Snips (for cutting screen)

1. Install a drain (optional).

Follow the instructions on page 180 for installing a bulkhead fitting (a watertight outlet), but use a 1" fitting instead of the ¾" used for the rain barrel (the hole saw size will be larger, too). After installing the bulkhead fitting, wrap pipe thread tape around the threads of the 1" nipple. Screw the nipple into the bulkhead fitting. Then, screw a 1" threaded ball valve to the nipple. Test for watertightness by filling the barrel with water; if the drain assembly leaks, tighten the fitting and seal the connections with silicone caulk.

Option: Connect a pipe to the drain and direct leachate to an evapotranspiration bed if liquid builds up. (Use a union so you can easily disconnect the pipe and access the drain in case of clogging.)

2. Hang the net.

Using a drill bit that's slightly larger than your nylon rope, drill holes around the lip of the barrel, spaced about 2" apart. Fit the net into the barrel, then weave the rope through the barrel holes and the net so the net hangs inside the barrel, stopping about 12" above the bottom; it will sink when filled. Seal the holes around the rope with silicone caulk to prevent insects from entering the barrel.

If you use a closed-top barrel, cut a large hole in the top (as large as possible without compromising the strength of the barrel).

3. Add a screened lid.

Cover the barrel with a screen. Secure it with elastic cord so it is firmly attached with no loose portions, as shown.

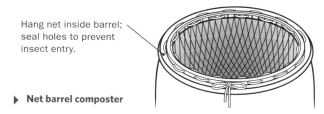

Hang net inside barrel; seal holes to prevent insect entry.

▶ **Net barrel composter**

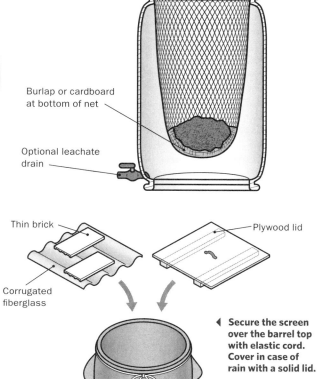

Burlap or cardboard at bottom of net

Optional leachate drain

Thin brick

Plywood lid

Corrugated fiberglass

◀ **Secure the screen over the barrel top with elastic cord. Cover in case of rain with a solid lid.**

Any barrels outside and unsheltered need a lid to prevent rainwater from entering the barrel while allowing air to flow, as shown. Use a piece of corrugated fiberglass roofing, weighted down with thin bricks. Or, get a piece of plywood large enough to cover the barrel and attach two strips of 1"-thick wood along it, elevating the plywood above the barrel so air can flow around it.

4. Prepare for compost.

Line the bottom of the net with burlap, cardboard, or other biodegradable material to prepare it for receiving compost. As an option, you can add some moist leaves, worms, and healthy garden soil to jump-start the system.

Using Your Barrel Composter

Keep the screen on the barrel at all times so flies and rodents can't get inside. Locate the barrel in a sheltered place so rain won't enter the screen on top. If the barrel will be exposed to rain, make sure to keep the solid lid (of roofing or plywood) on it.

After the barrel is filled (which will take several months), allow the contents to cure, or compost. Decomposition occurs faster in warmer temperatures, so in cold climates consider locating barrels inside a garage, shed, or basement.

It typically takes between four months (in warmer climates) to one year (in cooler places) for the material to fully compost. The decomposition process stops in freezing weather, so you may have to wait more than a year if you experience long periods of cold weather.

If anaerobic conditions arise in the lower levels of the compost bin, use a compost crank to mix the compost and add more sawdust as needed to soak up excess liquid (though in dry climates you may need to add liquid to get good compost, especially if you're using kiln-dried sawdust as a cover material).

My favorite part of the decomposition process in my barrels was the "mushroom" stage, when a bloom of mushrooms grew from the top of the pile. Then the decomposing worms took over. If you add a little garden soil to the barrels, worm eggs will find their way in to help process the humanure.

Resources

Chapter 1: Why Conserve Water?

Global Water Program
The Nature Conservancy
www.nature.org
Learn where your drinking water comes from.

Surf Your Watershed
U.S. Environmental Protection Agency
http://cfpub.epa.gov/surf/locate
Find your watershed and connect with local watershed groups.

Additional Reading

Allen, Laura, Bryan, S., and Woelfle-Erskine, C. "Residential Greywater Irrigation Systems in California: An Evaluation of Soil and Water Quality, User Satisfaction, and System Costs." Greywater Action, 2012.
Results of study of 83 residential greywater systems including water-saving data

Chapter 2: What's Wrong with Our Water Systems?

American Rivers
www.americanrivers.org
Nonprofit organization working on river restoration, dam removal, and stopping water pollution

International Living Future Institute
http://living-future.org
Organization administers the Living Building Challenge and offers workshops on sustainability.

International Rivers
www.internationalrivers.org
Nonprofit organization working on dam issues globally

Tracking Down the Roots of Our Sanitary Sewers
www.sewerhistory.org

Winnemem Wintu
www.winnememwintu.us

Chapter 3: Saving Water in the Home and Landscape

H2ouse.org
California Urban Water Conservation Council
www.h2ouse.org
Resources for repairing all parts of the toilet, as well as many water-saving tips

Plumbing
DoItYourself.com
www.doityourself.com/scat/plumbing
Diagrams and instructions for how to stop leaks

WaterSense Program
U.S. Environmental Protection Agency
www.epa.gov/watersense
Find native and low-water-use plants for your region and connect with local native plant organizations.

Additional Reading

Dell, Owen E. *Sustainable Landscaping for Dummies*. Wiley Publishing, 2009

Hemenway, Toby. *Gaia's Garden: A Guide to Home-Scale Permaculture*, 2nd ed. Chelsea Green Publishing, 2009

Jenkins, Joseph C. *The Humanure Handbook*, 3rd ed. Joseph Jenkins, Inc., 2005

Patton, Bruce, Douglas Stone, and Sheila Heen. *Difficult Conversations: How to Discuss What Matters Most*, 10th ed. Penguin, 2011

Chapter 4: Greywater Reuse: Planning Your Home System

A&L Western Laboratories, Inc.
www.al-labs-west.com
Soil laboratory offering low-cost soil-texture testing (for soil type)

Greywater Action
www.greywateraction.org
List of greywater-compatible soaps and detergents

"A Guide to Estimating Irrigation Water Needs of Landscape Plantings in California"
www.water.ca.gov/wateruseefficiency/docs/wucols00.pdf
University of California Cooperative Extension and California Department of Water Resources, 2000.
Document containing the species factor of many landscape plants and a reference for low-water-use plants

Plant Finder
Sunset Magazine
http://plantfinder.sunset.com
Find water and soil pH requirements for specific plants in your region.

San Francisco Water Power Sewer
http://sfwater.org/graywater
Greywater reuse information

SinkPositive
sinkpositive.com
Retrofit device for toilet lid that turns it into a sink

Skin Deep Cosmetics Database
Environmental Working Group
www.ewg.org/skindeep
Ingredients for personal care products

Water Rebate and Incentive Programs
City of Tucson
www.tucsonaz.gov/water/rebate

WaterSense Program
U.S. Environmental Protection Agency
www.epa.gov/watersense
Find native and low-water-use plants for your region and connect with local native plant organizations, as well as an online tool for ET rates and average rainfall for peak irrigation month

Additional Reading

Friedler, Eran and Roni Penn. "Study of the Effects of On-Site Greywater Reuse on Municipal Sewer Systems." The Grand Water Research Institute and the Technion Research and Development Foundation, 2011

Kuru, Bill and Mike Luettgen. "Investigation of Residential Water Reuse Technologies." Presentation at the WaterSmart Innovations Conference and Exposition, 2012
Study on 4 different toilet-flushing greywater systems.

Ludwig, Art. *Create an Oasis with Greywater*, 5th ed. Oasis Design, 2009

———. *Water Storage: Tanks, Cisterns, Aquifers, and Ponds for Domestic Supply, Fire, and Emergency Use.* Oasis Design, 2005
Information on how to build a rainwater pond

Toensmeier, Eric. *Perennial Vegetables: From Artichoke to 'Zuiki' Taro, a Gardener's Guide to Over 100 Delicious, Easy-to-Grow Edibles.* Chelsea Green, 2007

Chapter 5: Installing Your Greywater System

Aqua2Use Division
Matala Water Technology Co.
info@aqua2use.com
www.aqua2use.com
Manufactured greywater systems

Banjo Corporation
765-362-7367
www.banjocorp.com

Full port 3-way valve

Best Home Water Savers
800-513-6414
www.besthomewatersavers.com
Manufactured greywater systems

Dripworks
800-522-3747
www.dripworks.com
Fittings for L2L systems

Evergreen Lodge
Yosemite National Park
www.evergreenlodge.com
Simple and complex greywater systems

Fimco Manufacturing, Inc.
www.fimcomfg.com
Indexing valve for zoned irrigation; Wastewater Hydro Indexing Valve (10 psi)

Gray2Green
www.gray-2-green.com
Kits for building L2L systems

Greywater Action
www.greywateraction.org
Greywater reuse projects

Hydro-Rain
888-493-7672
www.hydrorain.com
Blu-Lock 1-inch irrigation tubing and fittings

Infiltrator Systems Inc.
800-221-4436
www.infiltratorsystems.com
Subsoil infiltrators

Legend Valve
800-752-2082
www.legendvalve.com
Full port 3-way valve

Morrow Water Systems
morrowwatersavers.com
Automated greywater systems

NSF International
www.nsf.org
Standard 50 certification for 3-way diverter valves

NutriCycle Systems
John Hanson
301-371-9172
http://nutricyclesystems.com

Installs subsoil infiltrators for greywater systems

Orenco Systems, Inc.
www.orenco.com
Indexing valve for zoned irrigation; mechanical distribution valve

Pentair Ltd.
www.pentairpool.com
Pentair 3-way diverter valve

PlumbingSupply.com
www.plumbingsupply.com
AAV and auto-vents

San Isidro Permaculture
Jeremiah Kidd
505-983-3841
http://sipermaculture.com

Sierra Watershed Progressive
www.sierrawatershedprogressive.com

SludgeHammer
800-426-3349
www.sludgehammer.net
Blackwater recycling system: septic system effluent to irrigation

WaterSprout
510-541-7278
www.watersprout.org
Designs and installs high-end greywater and rainwater systems

Zodiac International
www.zodiacpoolsystems.com
Jandy Space Saver diverter valve

Flow Splitters

HD Supply Maintenance Solutions
800-431-3000
http://hdsupplysolutions.com
Flow splitters (double ¼ bend)

Oasis Design
http://oasisdesign.net
Flow splitters with pre-installed threaded plug

Additional Reading

Creative Publishing International. *Black & Decker: The Complete Guide to Home Plumbing*, 5th ed. Cool Springs Press, 2012

————. *Black & Decker: The Complete Guide to Wiring*, 6th ed. Cool Springs Press, 2014

Chapter 6: Rainwater Harvesting: Planning Your System

American Rainwater Catchment System Association
512-617-6528
www.arcsa.org
Lists accredited installers

Bank On Rain
http://bankonrain.com
Organization creating low-tech international rainwater systems (with Ken Blair)

Compare Average Rainfall for US Cities
FindTheBest
http://average-rainfall.findthebest.com
Easy-to-navigate website to find average rainfall using NOAA data

Desert Harvesters
www.desertharvesters.org

Earthship Biotecture
575-751-0462
http://earthship.com

HarvestH20
www.harvesth20.com
Lists of financial incentives for rainwater harvesting

Harvesting Rainwater for Drylands and Beyond
www.harvestingrainwater.com
Website of Brad Lancaster's 2013 book by that name

Laboratory Certification Program
United States Environmental Protection Agency
Safe Drinking Water Hotline 800-426-4791
http://water.epa.gov/scitech/drinkingwater/labcert

National Climatic Data Center
National Oceanic and Atmospheric Administration
www.ncdc.noaa.gov
Annual precipitation data

NSF International
734-769-8010
www.nsf.org/Certified/DWTU
List of certified drinking water treatment units

RainBank
Ken Blair
http://rainbank.info
Washington-based rainwater installer and designer/consultant for clients in other states

Rain Dog Designs
David Hymel
www.raindogdesigns.com
Designs and installs rain gardens near Puget Sound

WATER Institute
Occidental Arts and Ecology Center
707-874-1557
www.oaecwater.org
Designs for gravity-fed rainwater systems

Watershed Management Group
520-396-3266
www.watershedmg.org

Additional Reading

Banks, Suzy, and Richard Heinichen. *Rainwater Collection for the Mechanically Challenged*, 2nd ed. Tank Town Publishing, 2004

Lancaster, Brad. *Rainwater Harvesting for Drylands and Beyond,* Volumes 1 and 2 (2nd and 3rd reprints). Rainsource Press, 2013

Ludwig, Art. *Water Storage: Tanks, Cisterns, Aquifers, and Ponds for Domestic Supply, Fire, and Emergency Use.* Oasis Design, 2005

Mechell, Justin. *Rainwater Harvesting: System Planning.* Texas AgriLife Extension Service, 2010
Technical information on designing and building a rainwater catchment system

Mendez, Carolina, B., Brigit R. Afshar, Kerry Kinney, Michael E. Barrett, and Mary Jo Kirisits. *Effect of Roof Material on Water Quality for Rainwater Harvesting Systems*. Texas Water Development Board, 2010
http://nsf.kavi.com/apps/group_public/download.php/18168/Effect-of-Roof-Material-on-Water-Quality-for-Rainwater-Harvesting-Systems[1].pdf

Reynolds, Michael. *Water from the Sky.* Earthship Biotecture, 2005.
Book about Earthships, with details on their greywater and rainwater harvesting systems

Cold Climate Resources

Alberta Municipal Affairs. "Alberta Guidelines for Residential Rainwater Harvesting Systems." 2010

Canada Mortgage and Housing Corporation. *Guidelines for Residential Rainwater Harvesting Systems Handbook*. Canada Mortgage and Housing Corporation, 2012

Nash, Art. "Water Cistern Construction for Small Houses." Alaska Building Research Series HCM-01557. University of Alaska Fairbanks Cooperative Extension Service, 2011

Chapter 7: Building Rainwater Harvesting Systems

Rain Garden App
College of Agriculture and Natural Resources, University of Connecticut
http://nemo.uconn.edu/tools/app/raingarden.htm
Rain garden app

Dripworks
800-522-3747
www.dripworks.com
Supplies for rainbarrel conversions

Uniform Plumbing Code, 2000 Edition, Chapter 11: "Storm Drainage"
Sizing charts for downspouts and rainwater piping based on rainfall intensity

The Uniseal Warehouse
321-527-2558
www.aussieglobe.com
Bulkhead fittings and Uniseal fittings

Rain Barrel Conversion Kits

Aquabarrel
301-253-8855
www.aquabarrel.com
Kits for closed- and open-top barrels, and IBC totes

BlueBarrel Systems
707-394-5009
www.bluebarrelsystems.com
Kits for converting closed-top barrels

RainHarvest Systems
www.rainharvest.com
First-flush diverter kit, Leaf Eater downspout screen, and rainwater tanks

Rainwater Tanks

Loomis Tanks
800-549-5514
www.loomistank.com
Also sells fire-hookup accessories

Plastic-Mart
866-310-2556
www.plastic-mart.com

The Tank Depot
866-926-5603
www.tank-depot.com

Irrigation System Information

IrrigationTutorials.com
www.irrigationtutorials.com

Sprinkler Warehouse
281-500-9800
www.sprinklerwarehouse.com

WaterSense Labeled Irrigation Controllers
United States Environmental Protection Agency
www.epa.gov/watersense/products/controltech.html
Watersense labeled irrigation controllers

Gravity-Drip Irrigation Kits and Parts

Best Home Water Savers
800-513-6414
www.besthomewatersavers.com
IrriGRAY Kit Rainwater by Gravity Includes 150 feet drip line; irrigates most uniformly of all the methods

Drip Depot
866-246-7707
www.dripdepot.com
Dirty-water kits for gravity-fed irrigation using ¼-inch drip-line to direct water to plants

The Drip Store
877-597-1669
www.dripirrigation.com
Gravity-fed kits using ¼-inch dripline

Dripworks
800-522-3747
www.dripworks.com
Online plans (and parts list) for gardens of various sizes using ¼-inch dripline with 12-inch spacing between emitters

Gilmour
Robert Bosch Tool Corporation
800-458-0107
www.gilmour.com
Single Dial Timer

Irrigation Direct
925-449-1300
www.irrigationdirect.com
Gravity-fed, "dirty water" kits using ¼-inch dripline or ¼-inch micro tubing with adjustable flow-control valves

The Toro Company
www.toro.com
Battery Operated Hose End Zero Pressure Timer

Pumps for Irrigation Systems

Rain Bird Corporation
www.rainbird.com
Example pipe friction loss chart

Rain Harvesting Supplies
877-331-7008
www.rainharvestingsupplies.com

Additional Reading

Kourik, Robert. *Drip Irrigation: for Every Landscape and All Climates 2nd. ed.* Metamorphic Press, 2009. Good overview of simple drip irrigation systems and how to install them

Lancaster, Brad. *Rainwater Harvesting for Drylands and Beyond,* Volume 2 (3rd reprint). Rainsource Press, 2013

Mechell, Justin. *Rainwater Harvesting: System Planning.* Texas AgriLife Extension Service, 2010. Manual for rainwater installers

Selbig, William R., and Nicholas Balster. "Evaluation of Turf-Grass and Prairie-Vegetated Rain Gardens in a Clay and Sand Soil, Madison, Wisconsin, Water Years, 2004–08." University of Wisconsin, Scientific Investigations Report, 2010–5077. USGS study on rain gardens in clay soils

Texas Water Development Board. *The Texas Manual on Rainwater Harvesting,* 3rd ed. Texas Water Development Board. 2005

Woelfle-Erksine, Cleo, and Apryl Uncapher. *Creating Rain Gardens: Capturing the Rain for Your Own Water-Efficient Garden.* Timber Press, 2012

Chapter 8: Waterless and Composting Toilets

Ecovita
978-318-7033
www.ecovita.net
Eco-Flush urine-diverting toilet and urine-diverting inserts

Humanure Headquarters
Joseph Jenkins, Inc.
814-786-9085
www.humanurehandbook.com
Manufactured sawdust toilets, compost toilet information, and compost thermometers

Nature's Head
natureshead.net

Natural Event
www.naturalevent.com.au

Niagara Conservation
888-750-4104
www.niagaraconservation.com
Niagara Stealth toilet

Sun-Mar
888-341-0782
www.sun-mar.com
SunMar Dry Toilet

Why Flush?
855-593-5874
www.whyflush.com
Why Flush? toilet water neutralizer

Ecological Sanitation

EcoSanRes
Stockholm Environment Institute
www.ecosanres.org

Ecovita
978-318-7033
www.ecovita.net

Humanure Handbook
Joseph Jenkins, Inc.

The International Compost Sanitation Forum and Message Board
Joseph Jenkins, Inc.
www.jenkinspublishing.com/messages
Online forum for using sawdust toilets

Living Outside the Box
David Omick
www.omick.net
Information on composting toilets

Lotech Products
www.lotechproducts.com
Compost crank

ReCode
www.recodeoregon.org

Separett
800-682-8619
www.separett-usa.com
Urine-diverting inserts

Sustainable Sanitation Alliance
www.susana.org

Watershed Management Group
http://watershedmg.org
Pilot project for legalizing site-built toilets

Additional Reading

Conant, Jeff and Pam Fadem. *A Community Guide to Environmental Health*, 2nd ed. Hesperian Foundation, 2012. Reference book for development workers around the world; includes details and diagrams on ecological toilets and protecting community water supplies

Jenkins, Joseph C. *The Humanure Handbook*, 3rd ed. Joseph Jenkins, Inc., 2005

Lechner, Markus. "Dry Toilets." EcoSan Club Manual, Volume 2. EcoSan Club, 2007

Porto, David Del, and Carol Steinfeld. *The Composting Toilet System Book*. The Center for Pollution Prevention, 2000. Focus on manufactured toilets

Regan, Raymond W. "Approaching 50 Years of Compost Research." *BioCycle* 39, issue 10 (October 1998): 82

Acknowledgments

MY DEEPEST THANKS to all the pioneers, individuals, and organizations committed to a sustainable water future. These people's work and technical expertise supported the content in this book — thank you for what you do! Art Ludwig (Oasis Design), Brad Lancaster *(Rainwater Harvesting for Drylands and Beyond)*, David Hymel (RainDog Design), John Russel (WaterSprout), Regina Hirsch (Sierra Watershed Progressive), Sherry Bryan (Ecology Action and the Central Coast Greywater Alliance), Erin Axelrod, Trathen Heckman (Daily Acts), Bill Wilson, Joe Jenkins, Carol Steinfeld, Leigh Jerrard (Greywater Corps), Neeraja Havaligi, Brock Dolman (WATER Institute), Cleo Woelfle-Erskine, Apryl Uncapher, Jeremiah Kidd (San Isidro Permaculture), Ken Blair (Rain Banks), Steve Bilson (ReWater), Brad Crowley (Harvest the Sky), Jesse Froelich (BlueBarrel Systems), Melina Winterton, Carl Warren, John Hanson (Nutricycle Systems), Daniel Ginting, Paul James (Just Water Savers), Mike Garcia (Enviroscape LA); Paula Kehoe, Rosey Jencks, Rachel Kraii and John Scarpulla (SFPUC), Tom Bressan and Jeff Parker (Urban Farmer Store), David Omick, Mathew Lippincott (ReCode), and Catlow Shipek (Watershed Management Group).

I am so grateful for your support with my technical questions: David Hymel, Brad Lancaster, John Russel, Bill Wilson, Art Ludwig, Ken Blair, and Christina Bertea.

Thank you to the Bay Area water community, for all the collaborations: The Greywater Alliance, Hyphea Design Laboratory, DIG Coop, Wholly H$_2$O, EBMUD, and The Ecology Center.

Thank you to my first plumbing teacher and favorite inspector, Jeff Hutcher; I have learned so much from working with you.

Thank you to Brad Banner and Rob Kostlivy for your pioneering work in Environmental Health Departments for sustainable water systems. Thank you to Doug Hensel and all the staff at the Department of Housing and Community Development who worked on California's much-improved greywater code of 2009. Thank you to all the inspectors and regulators who work to improve the permitting process in your jurisdictions; in particular Jeff Hutcher (City of Oakland), Roger Rushing (City of Berkeley), and Osama Younan (City of Los Angeles).

Enormous thanks to Peter Ralph and Christina Bertea for reading all of the early drafts. Thank you Kathy Lee, Al Decker, Tom Allen, Dan Erhseman, Kirstie Stramler, and Sarah Shourd for your invaluable comments and editing support; this book is so much better because of you. Thank you to the LA EcoVillage for your reviews and support with this project (Carol, Yuki, Thiago, Susie). Aurisha and Bethany, Carol and CJ, thank you for the play-dates with Arlo and the extra hours on the computer.

Huge thanks to my parents, for your steady support for the idea, and especially for all the fun-filled childcare with Arlo while I worked.

So much of the content in this book was developed and refined though years of Greywater Action workshops. Big thanks to all members past and present. Thank you to Cleo Woelfle-Erskine for founding the group with me, Christina Bertea for elevating all our plumbing skills with your expertise, Andrea Lara for making every installation seem possible and fun, Tara Hui for starting us on rainwater workshops at your house, and Gemma Bulos for your inspiring international work and support with our group structure. And big thanks to all the homeowners who opened up your homes for workshops and to everyone who came to help and learn.

Thank you, Lisa Gonzalves, for the years of collaboration with our home water systems and your support for all my projects.

Huge thanks to Deb Burns and Storey Publishing for bringing this book to life. And enormous thanks to Philip Schmidt; your expert and thoughtful editing made this book so much better.

And Peter, thank you for everything. I could never have done this without you.

Index

Page numbers in *italic* indicate pictures and illustrations; page numbers in **bold** indicate charts and tables.

Psychrophilic bacteria, 209
P-traps, 49
Puget Sound, Washington, 23
Pump filters, 85, 96
Pumps
  installing, 120
  for irrigation, 204–206, *205*
  rainwater harvesting and, 149, 199
  selecting, 118
Puyallup, Washington, 143
PVC pipes, 191

R

Rain, 15, *16*, 17–18. *See also*
  Precipitation
Rainbank, 150, 162
Rain barrels
  common errors of, 179
  connecting several together, 177,
    184–188, *185*, *187*
  creating, 178–183, *178*
  maintaining, 183
  overview of, 41, 152–153, *153*
Rain cubes, 157, *157*
Rain Dog Designs, 143
Rain gardens
  anatomy of, *164*
  constructing, 172–176
  landscape design and, 33
  maintenance of, 176
  overview of, 41
  planning and designing, 163–171,
    169
  rainwater harvesting and, 142–143,
    142
  sizing, 167–168, **167**
Rain Harvesting, 198
Rainharvesting Supplies, 205
Rainwater, conventional water system
  and, 15
Rainwater Catchment Systems
  (ARCSA/ASPE), 161
Rainwater harvesting
  Brad Lancaster and, 146
  catchment systems for, 147–149,
    147
  codes and regulations and, 160–161
  for emergency water, 152
  filtration and, 150–152, *150*, **151**
  indoor uses and, 150–151, *150*
  overview of, 40–42, *40*, 140
  permeable hardscape, rain gardens
    and, 141–143, *141*
  RainBank and, 162
  rain barrels for, 152–153, *153*
  roofwater collection and, 144–146,
    144, 177
  tanks and cisterns for, 153–160,
    153
  uses of water from, 140–141
*Rainwater Harvesting for Drylands and
  Beyond* (Lancaster), 146
Rainwater pillows, 157
Rainwater ponds, 159
RainWise program, 143

Raised garden beds, 100, *100*, *101*
Rajasthan, India, 21
Rapid sand filters, 130
Reach Code, 212, 221
Reagan, Raymond, 211
Rebates, 75, 161
ReCode, 71, 221
Regulations. *See* Codes and
  regulations
Renters, tips for, 80
Reservoirs, conventional water system
  and, 15
Retention time, 129
ReWater, 130
Reynolds, Michael, 41, 145
Ribbon test, 59–60, *60*
Rich Earth Institute, 223
Rivers, 15, 16–17, *16*
Roofs
  area of, 144, 166
  overview of, 147, *147*
Roof washers. *See* First-flush diverters
Roofwater catchments, 144, *144*, 177
Roundworms, 208
Rudolph, Linda, 71
Rule-of-thumb estimate of irrigation
  need, 65–66, *65*, 85
Runoff, *16*, 24–26, *25*. *See also*
  Stormwater
Russell, John, 131

S

Sacramento River, 13
Safe Drinking Water Act of 1974, 15
Safety. *See* Health and safety
Salmon
  dams and, 17
  Mattole River, Sanctuary Forest and,
    13
  PCBs, orca whales and, 23
  Yuba River, Bullards Bar Dam and, 17
Salts, 68, 69
San Antonio, Texas, 11
Sanctuary Forest, 13
Sand filter systems, 130
Sandy River, 17
San Francisco Bay Delta watershed,
  13
San Francisco Public Utilities
  Commission (SFPUC), 24, 74
San Isidro Permaculture, 132
San Joaquin River, 13
Santa Rosa, City of, 24
Sawdust, 232, 238, 242–243
Sawdust bucket toilets
  building, 230–232, *230*, *231*
  compost piles and bins and, 239
  overview of, 42–43, 213–214, *213*,
    227
Scarcity, 19–21
Screens
  rain tanks and, 158, 194, *194*
  rainwater harvesting and, 148, **151**,
    191

Seattle, Washington, 24
Seawater, 20–21
Second standpipe systems, 101, *101*
Self-contained composting systems,
  212
Self-contained manufactured toilets,
  214–215, *214*
Separett, 218, 226, 236
Separett Privy Kit, 236
Septic systems
  diverting 100% of greywater and, 58
  effluent reuse for irrigation, 131,
    132, *133*
  nitrogen and, 212
  rain gardens and, 166
Service accesses, 158, *158*
Setbacks, 67–68, **67**
Sewage treatment, 21–22
Sewerless homes, 126
SFPUC. *See* San Francisco Public
  Utilities Commission
Shasta Dam, 19
Showers
  calculating flow from, 55, 57
  energy use of, 10
  fixing leaks in, 30, *30*
  as greywater source, 39, 47, 53
  outdoor, 124, *124*
  soaps for, 69
  tips for, **30**
  treatment of rainwater for use in,
    151
  water consumption of, 30
Shutoff valves, 196, *196*
Sierra Watershed Progressive, 76
Sink Positive systems, 47
Sinks
  calculating flow from, 55, 57
  as greywater source, 47–48, *48*, 53
  outdoor, 124, *124*
  soaps for, 69
  tips for, **30**
  treatment of rainwater for use in,
    151
Siphons, 80
Site assessments, 103
Site-built composting toilets. *See*
  Home-built composting toilets
Sizing a rain garden, 167–168, **167**
Skin Deep Cosmetic Database, 69
Slope
  calculating, 166
  feasibility of greywater use and, 69
  laundry-to-landscape systems and,
    82–83, *82*
  rain gardens and, 165–166, *165*,
    169
Sludgehammer Aerobic Bacteria
  Generator, 131
Soaps, 54, 68–69